THE IMPERIAL GERMAN EAGLES
IN WORLD WAR I

THE IMPERIAL GERMAN EAGLES
IN WORLD WAR I

THEIR POSTCARDS AND PICTURES

Lance J. Bronnenkant, PhD.

Schiffer Military History
Atglen, PA

Acknowledgements
I would like to thank Ken Greenfield and the late Neal O'Connor for rekindling and encouraging my interest in the field of World War I aviation; Peter Kilduff for his help and expertise in reviewing this manuscript; Helge Dittman, Peter Grosz, Rainer Haufschild, Peter Kilduff, Walter Musciano, Jeffrey Sands, Marton Szigeti, and Greg VanWyngarden for their photographic contributions; Thorsten Pietsch for his private manuscript on Hans Hintsch; the following organizations, whose personnel were exceedingly helpful and patient during my research: Kriegsarchiv Bavaria in Munich (Claus Mannsbárt & staff), McDermott Library History of Aviation Collection at the University of Texas at Dallas (Paul Oelkrug & staff, and volunteer Ken Rice), Staatsbibliothek Berlin, Stadtarchiv Konstanz (Norbert Fromm & staff), Stadtarchiv Krefeld (Michael van Uem & staff), Stadtarchiv Memmingen (Christoph Engelhard & staff), Stadtarchiv Nürnberg (Marina Weber & staff), Stadtarchiv Solingen (Andrea Wendenburg & staff); and especially all of the World War I aviation historians before me whose dedication, hard work, and generosity to the field made this effort possible.

Dedication
To those who took me under their wing:

Paul H. Bronnenkant
Albert B. Lord
Ray I. Page
George L. Mugler
Paul Creager

Printed in China.
ISBN: 0-7643-2440-3

We are always looking for people to write books on new and related subjects. If you have an idea for a book, please contact us at the address below.

Published by Schiffer Publishing Ltd.
4880 Lower Valley Road
Atglen, PA 19310
Phone: (610) 593-1777
FAX: (610) 593-2002
E-mail: Info@schifferbooks.com.
Visit our web site at: www.schifferbooks.com
Please write for a free catalog.
This book may be purchased from the publisher.
Please include $3.95 postage.
Try your bookstore first.

In Europe, Schiffer books are distributed by:
Bushwood Books
6 Marksbury Ave.
Kew Gardens, Surrey TW9 4JF
England
Phone: 44 (0)20 8392-8585
FAX: 44 (0)20 8392-9876
E-mail: info@bushwoodbooks.co.uk
www.bushwoodbooks.co.uk
Free postage in the UK. Europe: air mail at cost.
Try your bookstore first.

CONTENTS

Hptm. Martin Zander, one of Germany's first *Staffelführers* when *Jasta 1* was created on 22 August 1916, sits in the cockpit of his Albatros fighter. Willi Sanke featured Zander on postcard No 407.

INTRODUCTION

German World War I picture postcards were prolific and covered all aspects of the conflict, ranging from humorous depictions of life in the trenches to gruesome views of rotting corpses. Certain themes provided a particular focus, such as the war in the air. Postcard publishing firms like W. Sanke, G. Liersch & Co., and NPG (Neue Photographische Gesellschaft) were run by shrewd businessmen who appreciated that airplanes and the men who flew them were capturing the imagination of the general public. The once-compelling façade of war – its individual heroes, colorful uniforms, bugle calls, dashing charges, noble victory, and honorable surrender ceremonies – had been shredded by the brutal realities of the current conflict's mud, blood, and pointless human sacrifice amid stagnation. Massive, faceless armies were struggling on the ground for vast expanses of land without resolution. In contrast, air combat, despite having literally added a whole new dimension to warfare, offered a simpler picture that resonated familiar overtones. It involved recognizable individuals that the public could relate to, rather than antlike, anonymous armies. Here were men of action who charged swiftly into battle mounted on powerful, motorized steeds. Their panoply of colors and markings shone brightly in the sun while their personal skills resolved the fight in black and white terms: swift victory or defeat. In the end, both victor and vanquished were often accorded respect and the recognition and honor of military ceremony. To the general public who usually had no direct exposure to it, the war in the air represented the last vestiges of noble combat in a world turned upside down. Thanks to newspaper and other published accounts, people could vicariously experience the daring exploits of the combat aviator who rode at the forefront of a young, exciting, and rapidly evolving technology. And thanks to the postcard publishers, people could add faces to the names they read about.

Of course, we now know that this romantic perception was often different than the reality. Combat pilots were taught to achieve the best "kill" through stealth, with an opponent ideally never being able to fire a shot. Many skillful and brave airmen did not die in "glorious battle;" rather, they fell victim to random chance, accidents, fatigue, illness, and the brittleness of their own aircraft. In the final analysis, the victory totals of all the aces combined figured little in the final outcome of the war. Nevertheless, the airmen themselves contributed to their romantic, gallant image by sometimes performing true acts of chivalry. Lives were risked by flying over enemy lines and dropping off news of a captured pilot or a personal tribute to one who had been lost. Lives were also spared by men who faced a helpless opponent and refused to deliver the *coup de grâce*. The vanquished were sometimes honored by their victors with a full military funeral. Salutes and cocky waves were indeed occasionally exchanged among combatants in the midst of deadly duels; and a downed foe was periodically entertained at his victor's airfield to delay his internment as a prisoner of war. Such acts were not the norm and occurred less frequently as the war progressed, but they happened nonetheless and had a noticeable impact. Though it is true that similar incidents took place among the ground troops, air combat, by its very nature, placed the airman and his exploits in a more conspicuous position that was less apt to be obscured by the fog of war. Airmen – and especially combat pilots – supplied the public with identities and achievements that could be followed week by week and that fulfilled the public's desperate desire for heroic and romantic imagery during distinctly unromantic times. The German High Command and the press understood this, as did the publishers of postcards featuring *Unser erfolgreicher Kampfflieger* (our successful combat flier).

Today, ninety years later, there remains a strong interest and brisk trade in the Sanke, Liersch, and NPG postcards that featured German airmen of the Great War. For some collectors, the romantic and chivalrous appeal the pictures originally conveyed still beckons. For others, it is an appreciation of the surprisingly high quality of many of the photographs: the crisp detail, elegance, and at times sheer artistry. Some peruse them for their mute testimony on medals, uniforms, aircraft, and other period militaria, while others prize them most for the very human faces they place on the terrible price of war – the tragic extinction of so many young, promising lives.

The focus of this study is to attempt to determine when, where, why, and by whom various photographs of German World War I aviators were taken, and when and why they were issued as postcards by the Sanke, Liersch, and NPG publishing companies. Hopefully, it will demonstrate the relatively untapped potential that photographic artifacts from World War I still have to offer when combined with the factual and narrative data available to us. The ultimate goal, however, is to try to place the photographs and their publication in context with the lives of these remarkable young men. What was going on when the images were captured, and what happened to inspire their publication? The Sanke, Liersch, and NPG postcards are momentary yet timeless portraits of a particular group of young men who, despite their many differences, were united by the risks and sacrifices they made in the service of their country. In this capacity they truly are representatives of all the men and women in history who have been placed "in harm's way." As such, their stories deserve to be recorded, presented, and preserved. It is hoped that this work, dependent upon the contribution of so many others before it, will offer new knowledge and insight to supplement our understanding and appreciation of the Imperial German Eagles of World War I.

Methodology

The photographs themselves usually provide the most useful and reliable clues to their origin. For example, an airman's outfit sometimes displays a particularly noteworthy item that may have been worn only during a certain period in his career, such as regimental insignia or a flying unit's identification patch. The presence or lack of certain medals and other decorations and even their arrangement on a tunic or *Grossordenschnalle* (full dress medals bar) can be significant – so too the evidence of rank that the airman bears. Uniform style, creases, and folds, and even the bends and kinks of shoulder boards can provide important clues, particularly when they can be related to other dateable photographs. The same is true for an airman's physical appearance: the length, style, and part of his hair, the presence of scars or other signs of injury, and even the trim of his moustache. The inclusion of aircraft, personnel, landscapes, structures, and other potentially identifiable elements in the background can also be helpful in establishing the picture's location and timeframe. In a few instances, the postcard actually names its photographic source.

The photographs also should be examined in context with a broad survey of the many different kinds of extant written sources. For example, several of the same or similar pictures appear in contemporaneous newspapers, pictorial magazines, and books that provide firm dates and occasionally informative captions. The diaries, letters, and biographies of the airmen at times allude to events that can be related to the pictures. Official records inform us when the decorations an airman is wearing were awarded and when he was promoted to a certain rank. They also sometimes help us pinpoint where he was physically located during his career – with what unit, at which airfield, and with whom. Sifting through these different records and information sources can yield valuable clues that can help trace a picture's origin.

The same written sources are also essential in trying to determine when and why a photograph was published as a postcard. For example, several cards were issued soon after their subject was awarded Prussia's highest bravery award for officers, the *Orden Pour le Mérite*; so the record of when that occurred is of paramount importance. But it should also be noted that dates listed in many records are sometimes imprecise for our purposes. For example, though they normally relate when an award was officially granted or approved, it often took several days or weeks longer for the decoration to arrive or be pinned on during a ceremony.[1] So when we see a photograph of the recipient wearing a particular decoration, it almost certainly was taken sometime later than the official award date reflected in the records. The same is true for transfer, posting, and home leave dates. There are several instances where a pilot's record stated that he had been transferred to another unit only to have a diary or letter indicate that he had actually arrived at his new post sometime earlier or later. All in all, the inaccuracies usually amount to only a few days or a week; so in the absence of hard evidence to the contrary, the official date is referred to in this work without attempting to second-guess what it otherwise might have been.

The most convincing evidence by far of when a postcard was first published comes in the form of a postmark or dated message on its back. Several years have been spent identifying the earliest such examples of each Sanke, Liersch, and NPG postcard examined herein. This effort, both difficult and time-consuming, will continue. Enough of a pattern has emerged at this time, however, to be presented as the cornerstone of this work.

What follows then is essentially a detective story that assembles and investigates evidence from a wide variety of sources in an effort to answer questions regarding the "who, what, why, where, and when" of World War I German aviator postcards. All the witnesses are long gone, and both the ravages of a second world war and the passage of time have conspired to destroy much of their testimony. Nevertheless, they left behind tantalizing clues that this writer has pieced together to reach several conclusions. The reader will ultimately judge how well each case is made.

Though this first volume initially discusses all the Sanke, Liersch, and NPG postcards of the most famous pilots (i.e., Boelcke, Immelmann, and Richthofen), it is mostly devoted to a card-by-card examination of Sanke's S340 (Max Immelmann) through S543 (Carl Allmenröder) publications. Depending on the response, a second volume addressing the remainder of Sanke's cards up to Karl Bolle's S685, as well as a third featuring the Liersch and NPG cards, will follow.

W. Sanke & Co.

We actually know very little about Willi Sanke – he spelled his first name with an "i," not a "y" – or the business he once owned and operated from 185 Schönhauser Allee in Berlin. Sanke's advertisements and later postcards referred to *"Postkartenvertrieb"* or "postcard sales." Several of his earliest cards carried the slightly different phrase *"Alleinvertrieb"* (exclusive marketing or distribution rights) instead. Indeed, G. Liersch & Co., who duplicated several of Sanke's cards, placed his name on each one. Yet various contemporaneous newspapers and books that routinely revealed their sources and used the very same photos rarely mentioned Sanke. The implication is that Sanke's rights to the photographs he published were generally limited to providing them in postcard form. We also have *Lt.* Erwin Böhme's letter of 21 November 1917 that refers to Sanke's shop as a *"Kunsthandlung"* ("art store"). An entry in the *Berliner Adressbuch* of 1899 for Johann Friedrich Stiehm of nearby 171 Schönhauser Allee identified his business as *"Landschaftsphotograph, Stereoskopfabrik, Kunsthandlung"* ("landscape photographer, stereoscope manufacturer, art store"). Stiehm was a noted photographer who published pictures and stereoscopic views of exotic, foreign locales, and it seems clear that "art store" in his case referred to the sale of photographs and prints. The same may have been true for Sanke who, apart from postcards, may also have traded in lithographs, *Kabinett* photos (i.e., portraits), and the like.

It has been speculated that Sanke employed a battery of his own photographers. It is now clear, however, that he actually obtained most, if not all, of his photographs from independent, outside sources. Many of his earliest cards depicted scenes from *Flugplatz Johannisthal* – the airfield adjacent to Berlin that served as Germany's center of aviation – and they often listed Franz Fischer of Johannisthal as copyright owner.[2] This indicates that if Fischer himself did not take the photographs, he at least maintained control over their distribution to Sanke. The two men apparently parted company sometime after S274 because from that point on the label *"Flugplatz Johannisthal"* and Fischer's name appear separately on only a few more cards (S282, S285, and S386). After S274, Sanke only occasionally divulged his sources. But when he did, they were usually well-known studios like those of Nicola Perscheid, C. J. von Dühren, and Hugo Erfurth, who either had the power to ensure their recognition or the prestige to make it attractive for Sanke to do so. His remaining sources, as will become evident during the course of this study, were smaller studios, independent photographers, companies like the Berliner Illustrations Gesellschaft (Berlin Illustration Company, often abbreviated as "B.I.G." or "Berl. Ill. Ges.") that frequently supplied pictures to newspapers and other publications, and the airmen or their families. There is no actual evidence that Sanke had his own staff of photographers or took any of the pictures himself. This is consistent with the fact that Sanke did not print most of his cards either. That job was almost always performed by Rotophot AG of Berlin, represented on Sanke's cards by an encircled R-P-H symbol. This name, identified in full on other period postcards, may have been derived from the technology known as *Rotationsphotographie* that was introduced in the 1880s, where bromine silver and chlorine silver gel papers were exposed and processed in roll form to mass produce *Kabinett* photos. This process vastly improved their quality and was eventually employed in postcard manufacture as well.[3] Essentially then, Sanke was a marketer who solicited photographs from a wide variety of sources, secured exclusive rights to them in postcard form, had them printed by another firm, and then distributed them through his *Kunsthandlung*.[4] His was not a large, self-contained business like G. Liersch & Co. or NPG, but that did not prevent his products from establishing an enduring popularity.

Sanke's postcards were almost unfailingly devoted to aviation matters. Even S403's Christmas wishes were dropped from an airplane. Some have viewed S632-33's portraits of naval hero *Fregattenkapitän* Nerger as an exception, yet he too was connected to aviation by virtue of his effective use of a seaplane manned by the celebrated *Oberflugmeister* Paul Fabeck (S635) and *Lt.z.See* Alexander Stein (S637) during his daring sea raids. Sanke's series started with prewar publications that featured Zeppelins (S2) and early aircraft including the Rumpler Taube (S73), Dr. Huth's all-metal monoplane (S127), and even the Wright Flyer (S90). Pioneers of flight were also presented, including Prince Friedrich Sigismund of Prussia, one of the first members of the German royal family to go up in an airplane (S16), Melli Beese, one of the first females to pilot a plane (S70), Alfred Friedrich, a German record holder (S106), and Pégoud, the daring French stunt-pilot (S220). Most of the prewar cards originated from events taking place at *Flugplatz* Johannisthal, Germany's aviation center, and many of those numbered from S70 to S274 were labeled as such.[5] The military made its initial appearance in S237's *Militär-Luftschiff Z 5* (military airship Z.5) and S238's *Rumpler-Militär-Eindecker 1914* (Rumpler military monoplane 1914). The first display of the maltese cross against a white rectangle came in S268, and was soon followed by a series on captured enemy aircraft running from S277's French Deperdussin to S284's English BE.2. The aerial bomb, held by Sanke's first recognizable but unidentified combat pilot, was introduced in S311. Two cards later,

seven *Militär-Flieger* (military fliers) who had won the Iron Cross were presented and named. Anthony Fokker and his "new" single-wing fighter appeared on S338, no doubt because of his *Eindecker*'s deadly achievements during the early part of what is now known as the "Fokker Scourge." It was *Lt.* Max Immelmann's S340, however, that marked the advent of the *Kampfflieger*, literally translated as "battle-flyer." Though Sanke still featured the occasional aircraft, it was the *Kampfflieger* that dominated his work from that point forward. He maintained the *Kampfflieger* series until the closing days of the war, when *Lt.* Karl Bolle's S685 was offered as its final contribution. Sanke's postcard business apparently ceased then along with the conflict, for unlike Liersch and NPG, we find no examples of a postwar card bearing his label.

What happened to Sanke? Did he simply discontinue making postcards and go back to selling lithographs and photos at his *Kunsthandlung*? Did the dire economic times or even the violent uprisings in postwar Germany destroy his business? Did his enterprise end because he sold it, went out of business, or even died? Future research may yet uncover the answer.

Sanke's postcards provide their own mysteries too. Many were assigned a number, but not all. Some were presented in two forms – with and without a number (e.g., "*Das neueste Ago-Wasserflugzeug*," S319 and unnumbered), or with different labels (e.g., S208's "*Pfeil-Taube*" and "*Harlan-Pfeil-Taube*") – while others with different subjects shared the same number (S242's "*Gotha-Taube*" and "*Fliegerschule Rumpler Luftfahrzeugbau*"). In other instances, one scene was represented by two different numbers ("*Jeannin Stahltaube*" as both S104 and S133). Sometimes they were not published in the order that their numerical sequence implied (e.g., S316, a compilation of six postcards numbered S903, S1008-11, and S1014). To further complicate matters, representatives of many numbers, particularly those from earlier parts of the series, cannot be found. For example, where copies of S2 and S99 are extant, only 20 of the cards between them are known to us. Though much of this may be attributable to the ravages of time, some gaps are not so easily explained. The most puzzling occurs after *Lt.* Hermann Pfeifer's S451 in the airmen's series. *Lt.* Erwin Böhme's S502 is the next card to follow, and not a single example numbered S452 to S501 has so far come to light. Again, there is always a glimmer of hope that future research will uncover important clues pertaining to why these things occurred.

Notes

[1] For example, *Lt.* Oswald Boelcke and *Lt.* Max Immelmann were officially granted their *Pour le Mérite* awards on 12 January 1916 though they actually received them at the hands of the Crown Prince of Bavaria on 17 January. A more extreme example is a series of photographs of *Lt.* Max *Ritter* von Mulzer's Military Max Joseph Order ceremony held on 6 September, 1916. The award's official date was 21 August.

[2] Many, but not all, of Sanke's cards that included a "*Flugplatz Johannisthal*" label also listed Fischer's copyright. Conversely, many of the cards that did not bear a "*Flugplatz Johannisthal*" label did not name Fischer. Fischer's name was preceded by the English phrase "Copyright by," which the Germans adopted because of its recognized legal significance.

[3] The difference can be seen among Sanke's cards themselves. Several high-quality cards from the S1000 series also appear in cruder, less detailed, unnumbered versions (e.g., S1006, S1009, S1010, S1013, S1019, S1034, and S1053) that never carry Rotophot's R-P-H symbol.

[4] Many Sanke cards bear postmarks from major city centers other than Berlin. Though one possible explanation is that individuals who purchased the cards in Berlin mailed them from another location, their sheer volume suggests that they were actually distributed in other places – either through a direct relationship with Sanke, through shop-owners buying them for eventual resale elsewhere, or a combination of both.

[5] True to Sanke's pattern of inconsistency, several of these cards also exist minus their "*Flugplatz Johannisthal*" label.

CHAPTER ONE

IMMELMANN & BOELCKE

The foundation for determining the "who, where, when and why" of World War I German aviator postcards rests on the most solid body of evidence we have today: the wealth of biographical materials and photographs that exist for their most famous subjects, Max Immelmann, Oswald Boelcke, and Manfred von Richthofen. Together, these three men were featured in almost eighty distinct Sanke, Liersch, and NPG photo postcards. The existing details of their careers not only give us a reliable indication of how their postcard photos originated, but provide us with valuable insight into the evolution of their compatriots' cards as well. Fittingly, we begin with Max Immelmann and Oswald Boelcke, the first recipients of Prussia's highest bravery award for officers, the *Pour le Mérite*, and the first combat aviators to be presented in the Sanke and Liersch series.

The Tapestry Photos

One key observation has nothing to do with the pilot subjects themselves. Rather, it concerns their backgrounds – literally. The wall tapestry that hangs behind Immelmann in S360, S361, and S610 is also behind Boelcke in S363 and S369. A thorough review of other photographs reveals this tapestry again in two pre-*Pour le Mérite* photos of Boelcke (BOELCKE1, BOELCKE2), a picture of Immelmann that served as the basis for S340 (see S340: IMMEL1), *Oblt.* Maximilian von Cossel's L7783 postcard, and a private photograph given to Boelcke by his former observer, *Lt.* Willy Aschenborn (BOELCKE3). An identically patterned chair is also present in Immelmann's S340, IMMEL1, and BOELCKE1-3, further securing the link. The tapestry is not draped in the same fashion in all these photos, indicating that most of them were taken at different times. It is clear, however, that they were taken at the same place, so an exploration of the histories of these pilots and where their paths crossed may help us uncover the photo site.

We know that Immelmann, Boelcke, Cossel, and Aschenborn all served at various times with *Feldflieger-Abteilung 62* at Douai, south of Lille. Boelcke and Immelmann were posted to *Feldflieger-Abteilung 62* on 25 and 26 April 1915, respectively. The unit moved from Döberitz to Douai on 19 May 1915, where the two future aces settled in and eventually began their scoring careers.[1] Though Immelmann remained at Douai until his death on 18 June 1916, Boelcke left and returned several times.[2] With three victories to his credit, he was transferred to Metz on 21 September 1915 as part of a special Fokker *Eindecker* unit assigned to escort heavy bombers operating from that area. He was brought back to Douai on 15 December after achieving his sixth victory. He stayed there long enough to add three more to his tally and receive the *Pour le Mérite* order, but left again for the last time on 20 January 1916. Cossel was an observer with the unit and became famous after he and *Vzfw.* Rudolf Windisch executed a daring raid on the Eastern Front behind enemy lines in October 1916. Not much is known about Aschenborn's tenure with *Feldflieger-Abteilung 62* other than his having served as Boelcke's observer until mid-June 1915.[3] The back of BOELCKE1 is dedicated "in memory of *FA 62*" and BOELCKE3 specifically refers to "Douai, June 1915." There can be little doubt then that the "tapestry photos" were taken somewhere in the vicinity of Douai.

A closer look at S360-63, S369, and the events surrounding them sheds further light on their source. These were the first Sanke photos that depicted Boelcke and Immelmann wearing their *Pour le Mérite* orders. Though the decorations were officially awarded on 12 January 1916, Immelmann and Boelcke traveled to headquarters at Lille several days later to receive them:

> "Immelmann and I were summoned to lunch again with the Crown Prince of Bavaria on the 17th. Before the meal he gave us our orders with some very nice words and helped us to pin them on properly with his own hands. I sat on the prince's right hand at table; he is very nice to talk to. Yesterday we were invited to H.Q.; the general nearly killed himself with affability and expressed the wish that we might soon return to his corps. I enclose a couple of the new photos. If the 'Woche' is absolutely determined to have one, send it along as far as I am concerned – as a knight of the 'Pour le Mérite' I can no longer keep myself out of the press." (Werner, *Knight of Germany*, p.148)[4]

The letter above, dated 20 January 1916, implies that the "new photos" were taken earlier in Lille. The original source of S363 (see S363: BOELCKE4) still exists today; and S363's and S369's pictures seem to have been taken at the same location at the same time.[5] It is possible then, that S363 and S369 came from the "new photos" enclosed with Boelcke's letter. This finds further support in the chronology of events surrounding Boelcke's *Pour le Mérite* investiture. He received the order in Lille on 17 January, was at headquarters at Lille again on 19 January, had possession of and mailed two "new photos" on 20 January, and made his final departure from *Feldflieger-Abteilung 62* the next day.[6] According to this schedule, S363 and S369 were most likely taken sometime during 17-19 January before Boelcke's departure – either at Douai or, perhaps more likely, at one

Flieger-Oberleutnant Boelcke,
der in Luftkämpfen bisher 13 feindliche Flugzeuge vernichtete.

Above: An early photograph of *Lt.* Oswald Boelcke taken near Douai/Lille while he was serving with *FFA 62.* It is possible that this picture and BOELCKE2 were taken to commemorate his first victory on 4 July 1915. This picture shows the makeshift arrangement of the tapestry cloth that was used to provide a more elegant background in many of his and Immelmann's portraits.

Top right: A companion to BOELCKE1. Note that Boelcke sports a cleanly shaved head in both.

of the two official functions at Lille honoring the new knights of the Order *Pour le Mérite*.[7] By association, it seems likely that Immelmann's S360 and S361 were taken around the same time for the same reason.[8] Both Boelcke and Immelmann appear to be appropriately dressed for such a ceremony in their best uniforms.[9]

Another card in the series, S362, has Immelmann standing outdoors with his pet dog, Tyras. A careful examination of Immelmann's uniform in S362 shows that its appearance is identical to the one worn in S360 and S361. We know that Tyras stayed with Immelmann at Douai, and that he also occasionally accompanied his master to other locations including Lille:

> "I was ordered to go out there and give a demonstration of flying. I had gone from Douai to Lille by air, and my batman went by train with the necessary luggage and the little dog." (Immelmann, *Eagle of Lille*, p.153)[10]

Therefore, Tyras could have been with his master at the time of one or both *Pour le Mérite* functions held near Lille in mid-January 1916.

S610 also points to Lille as the site of the "tapestry photos." It portrays Immelmann wearing the Commander's Cross of the Military

An enlarged section of BOELCKE2 that shows *Telegraphen-Bataillon Nr.3*'s insignia on Boelcke's shoulder board.

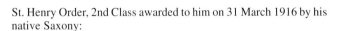

BOELCKE3

The G. Liersch Company used an early portrait of *Lt.* Maximilian von Cossel, taken at Douai/Lille while he was an observer with *FFA 62*, to produce postcard No.7783. Cossel can be seen in the company of other *FFA 62* personnel in S373.

A photograph of *Lt.* Willy Aschenborn that was included in an auction of Boelcke family memorabilia. Aschenborn met Boelcke when *FFA 62* was formed in mid-May 1915. He accompanied Boelcke on Boelcke's final test flight to qualify for his pilot's badge and served as his observer until mid-June.

St. Henry Order, 2nd Class awarded to him on 31 March 1916 by his native Saxony:

> "Finally I received instructions to report to the Crown Prince of Saxony, who gave me the King's 'surprise', which turned out to be the Commanders' Cross of the Order of St. Heinrich…Then he asked me to lunch in the mess, where His Excellency von Laffert spoke some words of appreciation and called upon those present to give three cheers for the new Commander of the Order of St. Heinrich. After the inevitable photographs had been taken, I went off back to Douai, feeling pleased and happy." (Immelmann, *Eagle of Lille*, p.189)[11]

Was S610 a direct descendant of one of those "inevitable photos"? The frontispiece to Immelmann's biography, which displays a similar, nearly identical picture to S610, may be another.[12] We know that both were taken around the time of the award, because Immelmann was promoted to *Oberleutnant* a few weeks later on 18 April 1916

and the single "pip" insignia that would have indicated his new rank is not present on his shoulder boards.

Immelmann's account above stated, and Boelcke's implied, that posing for photographs at important award ceremonies was to be expected. There is little doubt then that Boelcke's S363 and S369 photos were taken sometime during 17-19 January at either Douai or Lille, and that the same was probably true for Immelmann's S360-62. Though either location is possible, the evidence weighs slightly in favor of Lille, close to the time when Immelmann and Boelcke received their *Pour le Mérite* decorations. No other photos that may have been taken of these two airmen at their investiture ceremonies have come to light, so it is reasonable to deduce that S360, S361, S363, and S369 originated from the pictures that both airmen stated were taken at that time. It therefore appears that these particular Sanke cards may have originated from portraits taken at noteworthy award ceremonies by one or more attending photographers. Having dealt with these key images, we can move on to a review of Immelmann's and Boelcke's remaining Sanke, Liersch, and NPG postcards.

The Sanke Series

Max Immelmann was the first combat aviator to be featured in the Sanke series when his picture was published in S340. It captures him in a relaxed pose, sitting in the same patterned chair seen in BOELCKE1-3, but standing out against a black background. Fortunately, we can trace its derivation from two predecessors, IMMEL1 and IMMEL2 (see S340). They both display the now familiar tapestry as the original backdrop and therefore confirm Lille/Douai as the location. IMMEL1 is an early, untouched version of S340's image. IMMEL2 matches S340 but offers two important clues to its origin. First, the facsimile signature is accompanied by the date "1915." Second, it is markd with an "E-R-O" symbol that we now know stood for Emil Richter of Oschatz (Saxony). Immelmann's only decoration is the Iron Cross 1st Class, which figures prominently in the photo. Immelmann was awarded the Iron Cross 1st Class on 2 August 1915, the day after his first victory. Dr. Ernst Sieverts, who served with Immelmann in *Feldflieger-Abteilung 62*, recalled: "He loved to have himself photographed each time he got a new medal." (O'Connor, *Aviation Awards VI*, p.376) Immelmann certainly was quite pleased with his Iron Cross:

> "Yesterday I received the First Class of the Iron Cross as a mark of distinction. So now I have the nicest decoration any young officer can get." (Immelmann, *Eagle of Lille*, p.120)

The picture was taken sometime between 2 August, the date of his Iron Cross award, and 10 September 1915, the date of his next award, the Saxon Albert Order Knight 2nd Class with Swords, which he is not wearing. In fact, it is likely that it was taken soon after 2 August in celebration of "the nicest decoration any young officer can get."

Right after discussing his Iron Cross, Immelmann wrote:

> "I have nothing against you letting it be known in the ordinary way that I have got the I.C.I, but you must in no case give anyone a photograph of me which might get into the papers. Also, the description of the fight is for you alone, and not for the press." (Immelmann, *Eagle of Lille*, p.120)

Boelcke echoed the same sentiment regarding this kind of publicity:

> "Father asks whether my report may be published in the papers. You know that I do not think much of publicity in the press. Moreover I consider that my victory does not afford the proper style and scope for a paper. The good readers want a more poetic and awesome description, with psychical tension of fear-tortured nerves torn to shreds, followed by exultant glee, clouds that tower like Alps or the blue sky of heaven full of whispering zephyrs, etc. If, however, it would give you great pleasure to see it published, I shall not object. But naturally no names must appear." (Werner, *Knight of Germany*, pp.114-15)
>
> "The Berlin Illustration Company will manage quite well without my photo – I beg you not to send them one. I don't like all this publicity – I find quite enough articles in the papers about myself to be sick of it all." (Werner, *Knight of Germany*, p.131)[13]

On the other hand, Immelmann seemed to enjoy the personal convenience that picture postcards could offer, because he wrote on 17 November 1915:

> "My mail has risen to something enormous. Everyone wants a detailed report from me. It is quite impossible for me to answer even a portion of the letters. But you mustn't think that writing letters to other people will stop me writing to you. I never write the others more than a card, with my photo on it." (Immelmann, *Eagle of Lille*, p.155)

This may in fact explain the origin of IMMEL2. We know from its markings that it was produced by Emil Richter of Oschatz, Saxony, in 1915. Oschatz lies on the main road between Dresden, Immelmann's birthplace, and Leipzig, where his mother lived during the war. We can speculate that Immelmann (or his family) directly supported the postcard's publication because it bore a facsimile of Immelmann's signature. It is also possible, however, that Richter made an entrepreneurial decision to honor the neighborhood hero without official permission. At any rate, we know that Immelmann was not above using such a product when it became available in 1915.

Boelcke, on the other hand, frowned on such a device. On the back of one example of the very same IMMEL2 postcard, he wrote: "*Findet Ihr das schön? Ich nicht!* " ("Do you find this nice? I don't!").[14] Another brief note from Boelcke to his parents on 31 January 1916 further attests to his displeasure with postcard publicity:

> "*Mutters Brief vom 27. erhalten. Postkarten von mir möchte ich nicht im Handel sehen. Also nicht mit der Photo-Gesellschaft. Ich meinte nur mein Bild ein für Woche zur Verfügung stellen...Brief folgt.*"
> "I received mother's letter from the 27th. I wouldn't like to see postcards of myself in commerce, nor with the photo company. I only meant to make one picture of myself available to the 'Woche'…A letter follows." (trans. by this writer)[15]

Boelcke's mother had answered his letter of 20 January, where he had sent the "new photos" home and grudgingly given permission to give one to the "Woche" (see p.10). There he had definitely referred to *Die Woche,* an illustrated weekly periodical published by the Berlin firm, Verlag August Scherl, because his very next sentence stated "But Herr Scherl had no luck when he made his offer for a book." Presumably, "Woche" meant the same thing in his note. Though a copy of his mother's letter is not available, it seems clear that it raised the subject of the commercial publication of Boelcke's picture. This compelled him to respond as quickly as possible in a brief note rather than in his usual letter.[16] Clearly, Boelcke disapproved of this kind of publicity.

Willi Sanke did not though, for he used Immelmann's IMMEL2 picture and even the same autograph (minus the date) for his first fighter pilot postcard, S340. Furthermore, he may have borrowed from IMMEL2's heading, "*der erfolgreiche Kampf-Flieger*" ("the successful combat flier"), when he later printed a similar phrase at the top of many of his cards: "*Unser erfolgreicher Kampf-Flieger*" ("our successful combat flier").[17] IMMEL2 unquestionably preceded S340, and it is perhaps just possible that it was the very card that inspired Sanke to begin his series on combat aviators.

Before leaving IMMEL2, we should return to BOELCKE1. The following dedication appears on the back in Boelcke's handwriting: "*S. l. Fokkerschüler, z. E. an Flieg 62, O.Boelcke*" ("To the dear Fokker-student, in remembrance of *FA 62*, O. Boelcke"). The meaning behind this inscription is possibly found in Immelmann's letter home, dated 3 August 1915:

> "I have already written to you about the visit paid to us by Fokker, the director of the Fokker Works, which supply so many one-seater fighters to the army. At that time I had a great desire to learn to fly one of those fast, light monoplanes, but I should have had to be posted to his flying school at Schwerin, and I did not want that." (Immelmann, *Eagle of Lille*, p.116)

Anthony Fokker visited *Feldflieger-Abteilung 62* in late June 1915. After a day of exhibition flying, Fokker and *Lt.* Otto Parschau left two *Eindeckers* behind to be flown by only the most experienced pilots (one being Boelcke). Those with less experience were evidently required to undergo flight training at Fokker's factory in Schwerin, which may explain Boelcke's inscription. He may have given a picture of himself to a departing and now unknown "Fokker-student" to commemorate their time together in *Feldflieger-Abteilung 62*. If so, the photograph would have been taken sometime before July or August 1915 when such training was taking place. The various adornments to Boelcke's uniform support such an early date.[18] In particular, a close inspection of his shoulder boards shows that he is not wearing the winged propeller insignia later commonly employed by the *Fliegertruppe*.[19] The "T-3" cipher of his former *Telegraphen-Bataillon Nr.3* unit rests there instead (see also BOELCKE2a). BOELCKE1 and BOELCKE2 were taken at the same sitting – a possible indication of some special event.[20] Like IMMEL1 and IMMEL2, that event could have been Boelcke's first victory on 4 July 1915. Immelmann states:

> "…several days ago Lieutenants Boelcke (pilot) and von Wühlisch (observer) brought down a French Parasol machine…There was great rejoicing in the section! Von Wühlisch got the First Class of the Iron Cross; Boelcke has it already." (Immelmann, *Eagle of Lille*, p.107)

The victory was one of the German Air Service's earliest and generated a great deal of interest and recognition. Nevertheless, we can only state with confidence that BOELCKE1 and BOELCKE2 were taken at some point between Boelcke's arrival at *Feldflieger-Abteilung 62* on 19 May 1915 and his departure from the unit on 21 September 1915.

S342 is a picture of Immelmann standing alongside his seventh victim, brought down on 15 December 1915. Immelmann's letters and a similar photo give us the background story:

> "I asked our section-leader for permission to proceed to Valenciennes at once, which he granted. When I arrived there, I learnt that the wreckage had been cleared away and the bodies (Lieutenants Hobbs and Johnston) already buried…The machine crashed on to the wall of a house and was smashed to bits. No gun was found in the machine. But I induced the men to make a further search, because I had heard the enemy's shots. Finally they discovered the machine gun a long way to one side; it had fallen out." (Immelmann, *Eagle of Lille*, pp.163-64)

S342 shows Immelmann, still in his flying clothes, posing next to a destroyed English airplane. A different view of the same scene, showing Immelmann holding a machine gun upright, completes the link (see S342: IMMEL4). S342 was taken on 15 December 1915 soon after Immelmann's arrival to inspect the wreckage of his seventh victim after it had been moved to another location, presumably in or around Valenciennes.

We can similarly pinpoint the date and location of S347's photo after referring to Immelmann's words and other pictures concerning the particular event:

> "The King intended to inspect Flying Section 24, a Saxon section led by Captain Rosenmüller, on the following morning. I was ordered to go out there and give a demonstration of flying. I had gone from Douai to Lille by air, and my batman went by train with the necessary luggage and the little dog. I arrived at No.24's aerodrome at 10 a.m. Two photographers promptly rushed at me and begged for the honour of taking my photo. I was very gracious to them. I was snapped about twenty or thirty times and then filmed…All the machines of Flying Section 24 were drawn up in parade order. First came the English machine, then my monoplane and finally the ten machines of No.24. The King arrived at 10:30 a.m. He went straight up to me, inspected and expressed surprise at Englishman No. 4, and then took a

photo of myself standing in front of this machine – just imagine, the King snapped me himself. Several generals and excellencies did the same, but it no longer made such a great impression on me. The film camera then put in some violent work when the King approached my machine. I explained everything as accurately as possible in order to give some idea of my machine to those who were complete laymen in such matters. His Majesty showed visible interest in it." (Immelmann, *Eagle of Lille*, pp.153-54)

Photos of *Feldflieger-Abteilung 24*'s lineup that day, Immelmann in front of the "English machine," and the ace standing beside the King of Saxony have survived. IMMEL11 (see S347), unquestionably taken the same time as S347, was exhibited during an auction of Immelmann memorabilia in 2000. Unlike S347, it shows the airman looking to his left in front of his unretouched Fokker *Eindecker*.[21] Immelmann is dressed identically in all these images, so it is certain that S347's photo was originally taken during the King of Saxony's inspection of *Feldflieger-Abteilung 24* near Lille on 15 November 1915.

We have already discussed S360-63. Boelcke and Immelmann appear together in the next card, S364. At first glance, S364 is nothing more than a compilation of the two photos used in S361 and S363. It is distinctive, however, in that its earliest version ranks Boelcke as an *Oberleutnant* as opposed to S363's *Leutnant*.[22] Though the exact date of Boelcke's promotion is unknown, his biographer alludes to its having occurred before 2 February 1916 (see Werner, *Knight of Germany*, p.148). Immelmann wrote: "Boelcke has been a full lieutenant since February 18th, which was about the time when he shot down his 9th." (Immelmann, *Eagle of Lille*, p.183) Boelcke's ninth victory occurred on 14 January 1916 and he did not score again until March, so Immelmann may have meant 18 January. We have a letter, however, from *Leutnant* Boelcke to his parents dated 21 January 1916, and another from *Oberleutnant* Boelcke dated 12 February. We therefore know that his promotion came between these dates, and probably sometime in late January to early February 1916 as his biographer – who was granted direct access to Boelcke's records by his family – indicated.

Boelcke and Immelmann appear together again in S373. Immelmann's biography identifies S373's picture as having been taken on 20 January 1916 (see Immelmann, *Adler von Lille*, opposite p.141), and other photos confirm its location as Douai. This was the day that Boelcke sent the "new photos" home, and the day before he left *Feldflieger-Abteilung 62* for another assignment.[23] S373 is particularly noteworthy for several reasons. First, it is a group photo of *Feldflieger-Abteilung 62* personnel that was almost certainly taken in commemoration of Boelcke's last day with the unit; and posing among them are three men who would later become Sanke card subjects in their own right: Max Mulzer, Maximilian von Cossel, and Ernst Hess. Second, it identifies Immelmann as *Oberleutnant* and Boelcke as *Hauptmann*, the significance of which will become apparent when we discuss probable Sanke card publication dates later on. Third, the fact that Boelcke and Immelmann are less formally attired than they are in S360-63 and S369 adds further support to the conclusion that S360-63 and S369 were taken at an earlier, more formal function.[24]

S377, a black postcard displaying an elegiac poem printed beneath a reduced version of Immelmann's S360 photo, was obviously published sometime after his death on 18 June 1916. Conversely, a poem honoring a still-living Boelcke appears on S393 below a reproduction of his S363 photo. Immelmann's S361 and Boelcke's S363 pictures are reprinted once more on S408, a card celebrating 12 famous airmen (the first 10 *Pour le Mérite* recipients and the celebrated duo, Cossel and Windisch) who had already been featured on individual Sanke postcards. This was immediately succeeded by Boelcke's S409, a death card that combined a poetic eulogy with S363's portrait bordered in black. Immelmann's S610 followed much later and was labeled as his *"letzte Aufnahme"* ("last picture"). Though not true in the strictest sense, it was accurate with respect to Immelmann's and Boelcke's appearance in the Sanke series.[25]

The Liersch Series

For the most part, photos of Immelmann published on Liersch postcards are repeats of the Sanke series.[26] L7713 (see S347) is the sole exception.[27] It shows Immelmann holding a circular object, standing in a lineup of various German officers and the King of Saxony. Like S347, this was taken at the time of the King's inspection of *Feldflieger-Abteilung 24* near Lille on 15 November 1915. Immelmann identifies the round object for us:

> "When the machine came to a standstill, the King snapped me again. Then he came up to me and expressed his appreciation of what he had seen. Suddenly he grew plainly embarrassed and said: 'It's really fine what you did, hm, hm, hm, hm. I've brought you something as well. Hm, hm, hm. There's a monoplane on it, haha, a monoplane.' And with that he handed me a plate of Meissen porcelain, on which there was a charming picture of a fight between a German 'Taube' and an enemy biplane. It is really quite nicely done…His Excellency von Wilsdorf then told me that the plate was a special mark of distinction, because the King went into the Royal Porcelain Factory at Dresden himself and chose it. It is really very nice of him. Such a present is certainly a far more personal thing than an order." (Immelmann, *Eagle of Lille*, p.155)

Two things are curious about this postcard. First, though Immelmann is depicted with a *Pour le Mérite* at his neck, he did not in fact receive it until the following January. Clearly, someone touched up the original photo to include the decoration. Second, it calls Immelmann an *Oberleutnant* when he was not promoted to that rank until 18 April 1916. In fact, all the Liersch cards refer to him as *Oberleutnant*, and someone even went to the trouble of adding the rank's single pip to his shoulder board in L7705, L7716, and L7717. As we shall see in a later volume, this was because the Liersch series came out after Immelmann's death on 18 June 1916 and his photos were sometimes altered to bring them more up to date.

Similar to Immelmann, Liersch's Boelcke postcards repeat several Sanke photos. They too were issued after his final promotion (Boelcke became a *Hauptmann* on 21 May 1916) and for the most part, posthumously.[28] L7761 is the only one to display a unique photo that is labeled as Boelcke's *"letzte Aufnahme"* or "last picture." Though it offers few clues as to when and where it was taken, several features suggest that it originated relatively early in his career. The ribbon on Boelcke's chest could be for his Royal Hohenzollern House Order, Knight's Cross with Swords, but more probably represents his Iron Cross 2nd Class since it does not bear the Hohenzollern order's usual sword device. Magnification of his shoulder board reveals some kind of object that does not appear to be the *Fliegertruppe*'s winged propeller insignia. There are hints that it is the "T-3" cipher of his former unit, *Telegraphen-Bataillon Nr.3*, that is also observable in BOELCKE1 and BOELCKE2, but the image is too faint and indistinct for an absolutely positive identification. Boelcke appears younger than he does in many other photos, and the *Pour le Mérite* at his neck was very crudely drawn in – two more signs that the picture itself was taken before he received the award.[29] All things considered, L7761 could not really have been Boelcke's "last picture."

L7785 is a drawing, rather than a photo, that requires no further attention at this point except to note that it is an interesting memorial card that includes several patriotic images and symbols of the day.

The NPG Series

Unlike Liersch, NPG normally published unique photos of its subjects.[30] N5613 shows Immelmann in full dress uniform displaying all his decorations. Close examination reveals that his *Pour le Mérite* was drawn in later, so the picture was snapped sometime before the award ceremony on 17 January 1916. His decorations include the Royal Hohenzollern House Order, Knight's Cross with Swords awarded 9-11 November 1915, but not the Bavarian Military Merit Order 4th Class with Swords that he received next on 9 December 1915. Finally, the card credits "Pieperhoff, Leipzig" as the photographer – a person almost certainly alluded to by Immelmann's 20 December 1915 letter home:

> "Yesterday I sent you two large photos, taken by P. They will have to be our Christmas surprise." (Immelmann, *Eagle of Lille*, p.164)

This was Immelmann's first letter after his 28 November to 6 December 1915 leave back to his Saxon homeland (the only one he took after joining *FFA 62*). He had been granted time off to attend a flying exhibition at Leipzig's Mockau aerodrome that had been organized to raise funds to buy Christmas presents for airmen. Anthony Fokker also participated, and after Immelmann at the last minute had been asked not to fly (presumably to spare him the risk) Fokker himself demonstrated his *Eindecker* fighter. Immelmann was photographed at the event with his mother, and he can be seen wearing the same uniform and decorations, minus the drawn-in *Pour le Mérite* depicted in N5613.[31] Another photo ascribed to Pieperhoff survives in A393, a postcard issued by "E.P. & Co." ("P." for Pieperhoff?). Once again, Immelmann is shown in the same outfit, sans *Pour le Mérite*. Lastly, a lovingly preserved photo identical to N5613's but autographed "Max, Dez. 1915" (*"Dez."* stands for *"Dezember,"* "December") was among the Immelmann family memorabilia auctioned in 2000. This final piece of evidence all but confirms that N5613's and A393's photos were taken during Immelmann's leave in Leipzig and that they probably were the "two large photos, taken by P." that Immelmann sent home.

N5614 is a memorial card that has a symbolic representation of Immelmann's grave beneath an inset, cropped version of N5613's picture. N5632 follows next and is a montage of three Immelmann photos against a patriotic backdrop. The first is the now familiar N5613 picture, labeled with the date "1916." The second, marked "1914," shows Immelmann with the insignia of *Eisenbahn-Regiment Nr.2* on his shoulder strap. The third is also dated "1914" and depicts Immelmann and his dog Tyras. An original of the third one later reappeared as the frontispiece for Hermann Kohl's 1939 biography of Immelmann, whose caption assigned it to Berlin 1914 as well.

Cropped versions of N5613's photo appear again in N5690, a collection of airmen featured in prior NPG postcards, and N6004, a memorial card to Immelmann and Boelcke.

Boelcke first appears in the NPG series in two striking photographs published as N5579 and N5580. The first has him facing and inclined toward the camera while the second presents him in profile. Boelcke is called a *Hauptmann*, and a careful examination of his shoulder boards in N5579 reveals the two pips that signified that rank (one above and the other below his *Fliegertruppe* device). Both were taken at one sitting by Julius Müller in Boelcke's hometown, Dessau, situated in the Duchy of Anhalt. Müller was the court photographer there who was responsible for many pictures of the duchy's royal couple, Duke Joachim (also Prince of Prussia) and Duchess Marie Auguste.[32] A fuller version of Müller's N5580 photo appears on the cover of the 9 July 1916 edition of Frankfurt's *Das Illustrierte Blatt* (BOELCKE5), so the pictures must have been taken sometime before then but after Boelcke's promotion to *Hauptmann* on 21 May 1916. Boelcke was in Dessau twice within this timeframe. Shortly after 4 July he passed through his hometown on his way to

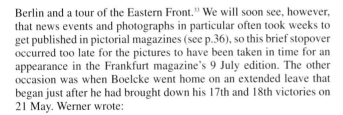

N5613 is based on a portrait of *Lt.* Max Immelmann taken in Leipzig during his 28 November to 6 December 1915 leave there. The postcard itself was published much later after his receipt of the *Pour le Mérite* (drawn in) and promotion to *Oberleutnant*.

A393's picture was taken the same time as N5613's, but this postcard was published earlier when Immelmann was still a *Leutnant*.

Berlin and a tour of the Eastern Front.[33] We will soon see, however, that news events and photographs in particular often took weeks to get published in pictorial magazines (see p.36), so this brief stopover occurred too late for the pictures to have been taken in time for an appearance in the Frankfurt magazine's 9 July edition. The other occasion was when Boelcke went home on an extended leave that began just after he had brought down his 17th and 18th victories on 21 May. Werner wrote:

"On the night of that victorious day and evening Boelcke started for home on a leave that had been granted some time previously. It began with a most joyful surprise. When he reached Köthen on the following afternoon, he had to wait for a connection to Dessau, and went for a stroll in the street. He read the latest communiqué in a shop window: 'Lieutenant Boelcke shot down his 17th and 18th opponents south of Avocourt and the Mort Homme respectively. His Majesty the Emperor has shown his appreciation of this superb flying officer's services by promoting him to captain.'…Those days in Dessau formed a zenith which gave him ample experience of

the joys and drawbacks of being a famous national hero. The news: 'Boelcke is here!' spread through the town with the speed of the wind. Deputations made their appearance; his old headmaster came, accompanied by the 1st form, the band of the 93rd reserve battalion serenaded him in the morning, he was invited to lunch with the duke and tea with the duchess, the 'young guard' marched with flags flying and music playing to his home, which became the goal of a daily pilgrimage of persons anxious for a sight of their distinguished fellow-citizen." (*Knight of Germany*, pp.171-72)

Perhaps it was during one of Boelcke's visits with the royal couple that they mentioned their personal photographer to him or even arranged for a sitting to honor his triumphant return home. There is no doubt that they visited the same studio, because two postcards of the Duchess (L7649 and L7651) show her sitting in the same chair that Boelcke occupies in N5579. On the other hand, Boelcke simply may have visited Müller's studio on his own, or by Müller's invitation.

Though it is virtually certain that N5579 and N5580 were taken at the same time, N5579's chair is different than the one seen in N5580 (see BOELCKE5). A third picture in the series shows up later in N6005, with Boelcke in a slightly different pose than that found in N5580. It too is credited to "J. Müller, Dessau." The frontispiece (BOELCKE6) of *Hauptmann Boelckes Feldberichte*, a 1916 compilation of his letters, may offer yet a fourth print from the session, for Boelcke's uniform and medal details appear to be identical to those depicted in N5579, N5580, and N6005.[34] This photograph was also reproduced on the cover of *Die Wochenschau*'s 8 July 1916 edition (the same time that N5580's image appeared in Frankfurt's *Das Illustrirte Blatt*), where it was described as Boelcke's "*neueste Aufnahme*" ("latest picture") and credited to NPG. In this instance, Boelcke is turned toward the camera with head resting lightly on his upraised right hand – and he is sitting in a third type of chair! Evidently, Müller wanted to be sure to capture Boelcke in just the right way and had him try several poses (and chairs) during the photo shoot. Though BOELCKE6 and its *Die Wochenschau* version do not specifically name Müller (unlike N5579, N5580, and BOELCKE5), they both list NPG as their photo's source.

Boelcke's N5579 portrait is placed at the top of N5601 against a backdrop reportedly showing the wreckage of his 40th and final

victim. Boelcke's 40th fell on 26 October 1916, two days before his death in a collision with squadron mate *Lt.* Erwin Böhme. Boelcke encountered a BE.2c of RFC Squadron No.5 and reported:

"About 4:45 p.m. I attacked several English biplanes with seven machines of my Staffel in the area west of Puisieux-au-mont. The observer of the machine I attacked did not return my fire after my first attack; the machine began to smoke heavily the second time I attacked it. Both inmates seemed to me to be dead. The machine sideslipped, fell into the second English line and remained burning on the ground. As I was attacked by a Vickers scout at about two to three hundred metres, I could not watch it any longer. According to the evening report from Group A. of H.Q.1 a B.E. attacked by a scout at 4:45 fell into trench section 34. Testimony of Lieut. König: I saw an enemy biplane attacked by Captain Boelcke catch fire at about six hundred metres up and fall to earth." (Werner, *Knight of Germany*, pp.225-26)

Though the downed plane on N5601 does appear to be a BE.2, it bears no sign of fire, and the surrounding landscape and casual manner of the German soldiers inspecting the wreck rule out a

N5579 and N5580 displayed images from a photo session at Julius Müller's studio in Dessau during *Hptm.* Oswald Boelcke's leave there in late May and early June 1916.

BOELCKE5

BOELCKE6

This more complete version of N5580's portrait of Oswald Boelcke was presented on the cover of a German newspaper dated 9 July 1916. It demonstrates that Boelcke posed in at least two different chairs during his N5579 and N5580 photo session.

Another portrait of Oswald Boelcke probably taken the same time as those seen in N5579 and N5580.

location in the English trenches; so this cannot be a photo of Boelcke's final victim. One source has identified it as BE.2c 4092, shot down by *Lt.* Ernst von Althaus on 5 December 1915.[35] The later N6255 (featuring Manfred von Richthofen) carries the same crash scene and the two planes flying overhead appear again in N5690 (six pilots). Evidently, NPG allowed a certain amount of artistic license in the creation of its postcards.

N5619 is a group photo of Boelcke, *Lt.* Kurt Rackow, Crown Prince Wilhelm of Prussia, and *Oblt.* Cordt von Brandis – all holders of the *Pour le Mérite*.[36] Boelcke, posted to Sivry on 11 March 1916, had befriended the Crown Prince whose headquarters were located at nearby Stenay. Boelcke visited Douai to attend Immelmann's funeral services on 22 June and stayed there a few days to fly over his old hunting grounds. When he returned to Sivry the afternoon of 26 June 1916 following a summons from the Crown Prince, Boelcke learned firsthand that concern for his safety was growing among powerful circles as a result of Immelmann's demise:

"These doubts were strengthened when I heard shortly afterwards that after Immelmann's death the Crown Prince said he would not let me fly again under any circumstances. The next day I reported to the chief [of Field Aviation, *Oberstleutnant* Hermann Thomsen] in Charleville and lo! my anticipations were

exceeded in every respect. The chief made a long speech, the purport of which was that I was to sit in a glass case in Charleville; I was not to fly at all for the present, because my 'nerves' must be rested, but I could organise a Fokker Staffel in Charleville. Well, you can just imagine my rage! I was to sit in a cold water sanatorium in Charleville, stare up at the sky and take over the job of leading a crowd of weak-nerved pilots in need of rest! The chief tried to make me say that I would be willing to take over the post 'provisionally' on the strength of the reasons he had adduced. But I could only protest vigorously and then, knowing no better counsel, took my leave. When I got outside I cursed the adjutant and other pen-pushers in a most offensive fashion, which only, however, provoked mirth from all concerned. One of the fellows gave me a wise lecture to the effect that I was no longer a private individual who could play with his life at will but the property of the German nation, which still expected much from me. Finally, Captain Förster told me that for the present I was not to fly any more – there was nothing doing there because it was a direct order from the Emperor, who had continually kept himself informed about me through the air chief. But if I had any other wish, I had only to express it; for example, I could go to Turkey and have a look at the other fronts." (Werner, *Knight of Germany*, pp.180-81)

Boelcke figured that a tour of Turkey and the Balkans was better than sitting in Charleville, so he took the man up on his offer. He immediately went back to Sivry to pack his belongings, then returned to Charleville two days later to make final preparations before going to Berlin to begin his tour.[37] Werner states that N5619's photo "was taken at Stenay in June" (*Knight of Germany,* p.155). One of the photo's subjects, *Lt.* Rackow, was officially awarded the *Pour le Mérite* he is seen wearing on 7 June 1916. Thus the photo was taken either sometime between Rackow's 7 June award and Boelcke's departure to Immelmann's funeral (22 June) or during 27-29 June when Boelcke was back in Sivry. Publication of the same picture in the 2 July 1916 edition of *Berliner Illustrirte Zeitung* favors the earlier period because photographs often took several weeks to make their way into publications.

N5690 is a collection of images of six airmen who had already been featured in previous NPG postcards: Seydler (N5566), Boelcke (N5579), Immelmann (N5613), Mulzer (N5630), Banfield (N5678), and Höhndorf (N5679). A *Pour le Mérite* with oakleaves is placed beneath them, yet only four earned the award and none with oakleaves. Two airplanes seen earlier in Boelcke's N5601 appear again above the men's heads. The top of the wreath encircling Immelmann's photo is marked with the initial "I," while Seydler's wreath is capped with a black bow. These devices did not denote deceased pilots though, because Mulzer and Boelcke – their images free of such marks – had also died before the card was published.[38] All in all, it is a curious card that was apparently created to engender a certain sentimental appeal.

N6004 posthumously honors Boelcke and Immelmann in a fabricated joint portrait. Someone took Boelcke's N5579 image, redrew his right arm to place it closer to his body, then superimposed the result immediately next to Immelmann's N5613 picture to give the impression that they were standing side-by-side. N6005 is another post-mortem memorial, and as discussed above, includes one of the poses from the Müller series taken in Dessau possibly in late May or early June 1916.

N6225 is the last of NPG's Boelcke portraits. This time he is shown in flying clothes sitting in the cockpit of a Fokker D.III, a plane that he flew in combat for only a brief time. Boelcke began assembling his new *Jagdstaffel 2* fighter unit after returning from his tour of the Eastern Front in August 1916. He personally picked up one of the unit's first machines, Fokker D.III 352/16, from a nearby aircraft park on 1 September. He flew it in combat the next day and thereafter until he and his men exchanged the type for new, superior Albatros fighters on 16 September. It is usually assumed that N6225 shows Boelcke in Fokker D.III 352/16. The card is labeled *"die letzte Aufnahme in seinem Kampfflugzeug"* ("the final photograph in his fighter-plane"). It would have been, too, had he actually flown the aircraft in combat, because it has no machine guns. Several independent photos of D.III 352/16 show a pair of machine guns protruding into the cockpit where only a windscreen is present in N6225; so N6225 must depict another Fokker D.III.[39] Fokker historians tell us that the D.III prototype was officially accepted on 26 June 1916 and subsequently sent to Adlershof (the military extension of Johannisthal airfield) for further flight evaluation on 20 July. The first seven D.III fighters were delivered by 1 September, with one of them, D.III 352/16, going to *Jasta 2* to be flown by Oswald Boelcke. They also note that the prototype machine was later redesignated as D.III 350/16.[40] BOELCKE7 and BOELCKE8 are photos of D.III 350/16, which shares three distinct features with the plane shown in N6255. Both aircraft are marked with identical circular patches that have some kind of short metal tube or attachment

at their center. Though similar patches can sometimes be seen on other Fokker D models, they are located farther forward, with longer metal protrusions and a different stained appearance. The match cannot be called exact, however, because BOELCKE7-8 and N6255 display opposite sides of the fuselage. Production Fokker D.IIIs carried upper wings that were connected to the fuselage with N-shaped struts forward of the cockpit. BOELCKE7-8 show that the prototype employed parallel vertical struts – a unique characteristic shared by the Fokker in N6225.[41] Production D.IIIs also had a slight hump behind the cockpit where a curved metal fairing joined the flat, upper fuselage surface. BOELCKE7-8 and N6225 are unique in that they share a smoothly curved upper fuselage surface with no metal fairing behind the cockpit. Boelcke's D.III 352/16, seen in BOELCKE9, has only the usual N-shaped struts and exhibits no fuselage patch. If BOELCKE7-8 and N6225 are indeed the same aircraft, then N6225 is a picture of Boelcke sitting in the prototype before it had been fitted with machine guns for active service. This implies that the photo was taken during an inspection or test flight of Fokker's new model somewhere away from the Front and most likely during its development period in Germany. The fact that N6225's image is credited to Julius Müller of Dessau, the same photographer named on N5579 and N5580, lends further support to this because it is difficult to imagine Müller (Anhalt's court photographer) or his representative traveling all the way to the Front to snap a picture of Boelcke in a non-combat airplane. Fokker's factory in Schwerin is an obvious candidate for the picture's location, yet we have no record of a trip there by Boelcke any time in 1916. The next possibility is Adlershof, just outside of Berlin and only 60 miles north of Dessau. We know that the D.III's prototype was tested there on 20 July, but by that time Boelcke was already well into his tour of the Eastern Front. Nevertheless, there may have been two other opportunities to fly the D.III prototype before then. As we have seen, Boelcke was home in Dessau in late May and early June 1916. Was Fokker's prototype in Berlin around this time as part of the formal acceptance process that ended on the 26th? Alternatively, Boelcke wrote on 4 July during a train stop on his way home: "The only thing I did in Charleville was to make brief preparations for the journey, get my passport, etc., and now I am on my way to Dessau and Berlin." (Werner, *Knight of Germany*, p.182) Boelcke did not depart from Berlin until 8 July. Would this have left him enough time to inspect Fokker's recently-approved prototype if it were still in the vicinity or had returned in preparation for the tests conducted on 20 July? Yet another possibility comes later after Boelcke's return to Germany. His diary stated:

"18.8.16: Travelled with Martin to Kovno, then on to Berlin.
19.8.16: Various business at inspectorate and Johannisthal.
16.16.16: Travelled to Dessau." (Werner, *Knight of Germany*, p.202)

Did a portion of his "business" at the Inspectorate of Military Aviation and Johannisthal airfield involve the Fokker D.III that was going to be supplied to his new *Jasta* on 1 September? Someone from Müller's studio could easily have made the trip from Dessau to Berlin on any of these occasions, or could have already been in Berlin on other business. Our desire for an answer notwithstanding, we cannot escape the fact that all these possibilities are purely speculative. Without more concrete information, we can only surmise that N6225's photo of Boelcke in Fokker's unarmed D.III prototype was taken sometime during the prototype's development while Boelcke was still in Germany, i.e. late May to early July or in late August of 1916.

Hauptmann Bölcke,
die letzte Aufnahme in seinem Kampfflugzeug.

6225

Phot. J. Müller, Dessau

N6225 showing Oswald Boelcke in the cockpit of an unarmed Fokker D.III. (photo courtesy of Jeffrey Sands)

Fokker D.III 352/16, flown by Oswald Boelcke.

BOELCKE9

Two views of Fokker's D.III prototype after it was assigned the number 350/16. It is the same plane seen in N6255.

Notes

[1] *Feldflieger-Abteilung 62* started for the Front on 13 May 1915 and arrived at their initial destination, Pontfaverger, on 16 May. The unit had just begun to settle in when it received new orders on 18 May to relocate to Douai. After an 18-hour train trip, *Feldflieger-Abteilung 62* arrived there on 19 May.

[2] Immelmann and *Feldflieger-Abteilung 62* parted company, however, when the unit left Douai on 13 June 1916. He remained behind to welcome its replacement, *Feldflieger-Abteilung 5b*, but was killed in action five days later, 13 months to the day after *Feldflieger-Abteilung 62* had been assigned to Douai. Ironically, Immelmann once related the positive significance that the number 13 had in his career:

> "What events happened on 13ths? I was transferred to aviation on Friday, November 13th (two crashed to their deaths on that day), and Flying Section 62 went off to the front on May 13th. I was first mentioned in the communiqué on October 13th. I scored my first victories on the Fokker E.13. I shot down my first brace on March 13th. I received His Majesty's letter on the occasion of my 13th victory." (Immelmann, *Eagle of Lille*, p.191)

[3] See Werner, *Knight of Germany*, pp.105-6. Boelcke began flying with *Lt.* Heinz-Hellmuth von Wühlisch in mid-June, and it was with him that Boelcke achieved his first confirmed victory on 4 July 1915. Evidently, Boelcke and Aschenborn remained good friends, for he mentions visiting Aschenborn in Berlin on 7 July 1916 just before departing on his tour of Turkey and the Balkans (Werner, *Knight of Germany*, p.187). After the war, Aschenborn wrote an article about his time as Boelcke's observer for Walter von Eberhardt's *Unsere Luftstreitkräfte 1914-18*, pp.215-18.

[4] Boelcke's and Immelmann's *Pour le Mérites* were of two different styles despite having been awarded at the same ceremony. Immelmann's possessed the more traditional "pie-slice" suspension, while Boelcke's had the baroque loop attachment that grew to be the norm among wartime issues (see O'Connor, *Aviation Awards II*, p.58). This design difference is consistently seen among all their photographs, including those of their awards on their *Ordenskissen* (a pillow that displayed the deceased's decorations at funeral services). Because it is also seen in pictures apparently taken soon after the award ceremony, it is improbable that either of them had substituted a private purchase *Pour le Mérite* for their original as was sometimes done in later years. The most likely explanation is that the decoration, rare and made of solid gold at that time, was difficult to come by and that two jewelers (who used different templates) had to be contacted to supply them.

[5] The tapestry drape pattern, the nearby chair (different from the patterned chair seen in S340, IMMEL1, and BOELCKE1-3), the position and hang of his decorations and even the curve and bend of his shoulder boards are identical in S363 and S369.

[6] The trip from Douai to Lille was short: "I flew back to Douai about 5 p.m. My batman went back by train. The railway journey lasts an hour and a quarter, while I fly it in 12-15 minutes." (Immelmann, *Eagle of Lille*, p.155)

[7] It is unlikely that the photos Boelcke sent home were snapped and developed the same day of his letter, so they were probably taken 17-19 January 1916.

[8] S360's image certainly was not taken beyond February because it can be found in the 27 February 1916 edition of the *Berliner Illustrirte Zeitung*. It should also be noted that the tapestry does not hang precisely the same in S363 and S369 as it does in S360 and S361. There are slight differences in the folds, particularly in the upper left corner (when facing the picture). Yet enough similarities exist that it is plausible that the tapestry was slightly adjusted or disturbed as the different subjects and photos were posed.

[9] Note Immelmann's *Grossordenschnalle* (full dress medals bar), leather gloves and belt, and Boelcke's crisply creased trousers. Compare this to their more casual appearance in S373, a photo taken at Douai on 20 January 1916.

[10] See also:

> "The following morning I was in Cologne at 8:30 a.m., and my next train did not leave till noon. I strolled through the town; later I travelled on in the direction of Herbesthal, reaching Liège in the afternoon (Wednesday), and left again (on Thursday) for Namur, Mauberge and St. Quentin, reaching Tergnier finally at about 11 a.m. I then went on to Charleville, via Laon, where I had a wait from 1 a.m. to 6 a.m., after which came the final stage to Rethel, which I reached about 10 a.m. So I arrived on Friday, the 12th. My good Tyras made the whole journey with me." (Immelmann, *Eagle of Lille*, p.58)

> "I took off at 2 p.m., in order to reach my destination by air. My batman took dog and luggage on a lorry." (Immelmann, *Eagle of Lille*, p.71)

[11] The precise location of this meeting is not given, though we know that Immelmann had met with the King of Saxony, the Prince of Saxony, and Laffert near Lille on 14-15 November 1915 (see Immelmann, *Eagle of Lille*, pp.153-55). After his description of the Commander's Cross award lunch, Immelmann states: "On my way through Lille I met Claus, and went with him to a café…" (Immelmann, *Eagle of Lille*, p.189) – another indication that the lunch meeting took place somewhere close to Lille.

[12] The differences, though slight, are definite. For example, the cleft in Immelmann's chin lines up with the edge of his collar *Litzen* in the biography's frontispiece photo, but is farther to his left in S610. The bottom of the Commander's Cross of the Military St. Henry Order (suspended from his collar) completely overlaps the medals bar in the frontispiece, but partially projects outside the medals bar in S610. The Knight's Cross of the Military St. Henry Order overlaps his tunic button in the frontispiece, but does not in S610. Yet another photo from this series has been rediscovered recently in the obscure work, *Unsere Luftwaffe*, written by *Hauptmann a. D.* Funk and published in Leipzig by Kunstverlag Bild und Karte in late 1916.

[13] Evidently, his wishes were circumvented because BOELCKE2 appeared in the 22 January 1916 edition of Berlin's *Die Woche* and was credited to "B.I.G.," an abbreviation for Berliner Illustrations Gesellschaft (Berlin Illustration Company).

[14] An auction of Boelcke family memorabilia was held in Germany in 2001. This card and its note were pictured in the catalog, Thies, *Auktion Boelcke*, p.211.

[15] A photograph of this note appears in Thies, *Auktion Boelcke*, p.202. A close inspection of the handwriting shows that the catalog mistakenly printed "*haben*" for "*sehen*." It is tempting to interpret Boelcke's statement as referring directly to the NPG (Neue Photographische Gesellschaft) postcard publishing firm. "*Photo-Gesellschaft*", however, could have been used in a more generic sense.

[16] An examination of all of *Die Woche*'s issues for the first half of 1916 yields only one picture of Boelcke. BOELCKE2, a pre-*Pour le Mérite* portrait probably taken in July-September 1915 (see p.14), appeared in *Die Woche*'s 22 January 1916 edition, as it had previously in the 16 January 1916 edition of *Berliner Illustrirte Zeitung*. Obviously, this was not one of the photos sent home by Boelcke in his 20 January letter.

[17] This phrase, however, did not appear on any of Sanke's cards until Wintgen's S378 – photographed and published after Immelmann's death in mid-June 1916.

[18] Boelcke is wearing his Pilot's Badge and Iron Cross 1st Class, as well as ribbons for the Iron Cross 2nd Class and Anhalt's Friedrich Cross 2nd Class. His Iron Cross 1st Class was awarded on 27 January 1915 and the Friedrich Cross a few days later on 31 January. His next award, the Prussian Royal Hohenzollern House Order, Knight's Cross with Swords, came on 1 November 1915. It does not appear in the photo.

[19] The use of a winged propeller insignia on the shoulder boards of *Fliegertruppe* members was ordered by Prussia on 18 September 1913 and by Bavaria on 8 May 1914 (see OTF 17:3, p.271). Nevertheless, photographic evidence indicates that many officers, and particularly those transferred from other service branches, did not begin employing the insignia routinely until late 1915.

[20] We can be sure that BOELCKE1 and BOELCKE2 were taken in 1915, because BOELCKE2 appeared in the 16 January 1916 edition of the *Berliner Illustrirte Zeitung*, and as we shall soon see, it usually took several weeks for photographs to make their way into newspaper publications.

[21] The editors of S347's photo brushed out the *Eindecker*'s machine gun and engine details in an apparent effort to keep them secret.

[22] Another version of S364 identifies both Boelcke and Immelmann as *Oberleutnante*, while yet another lists Boelcke as a *Hauptmann*. We see a similar progression where Immelmann's rank is printed on S360-62 as either *Leutnant* or *Oberleutnant*, and where Boelcke's rank in various S363 versions goes from *Leutnant* to *Oberleutnant* to *Hauptmann*. Obviously, the postcards were reprinted each time the airmen were promoted.

[23] Though it is just possible that there was enough time to take the picture, develop it, and mail it with his letter, it is improbable that S373's photo was one of those he sent home that day. In any event, Boelcke specifically refers to new photos in his letter, so S363's and S369's pictures, as offered on p.10, still seem to qualify as the most plausible candidates.

[24] Boelcke's trousers do not exhibit the crisply pressed crease seen in S363. Immelmann is minus his medals bar, gloves, and belt; and unlike S360-62, he wears the Royal Hohenzollern House Order ribbon in his buttonhole.

[25] Better candidates for Immelmann's "last photo" will be presented in the next volume's discussion of S610.

[26] Most of the Liersch postcards and associated photographs discussed in this section will be reproduced in a future volume. The Liersch card numbers cited herein are included to allow readers who have independent access to them to make their own comparisons until that time.

[27] L7705 = S360, L7716 = S360, L7717 = S361, L7718 = S362, L7719 = S340, L7720 = S373, L7793 = S408. Note that the Liersch series does not follow the chronological sequence that Sanke's generally did.

[28] L7720 = S373, L7721 = S363, L7776 = S363, L7793 = S408.

[29] The picture is credited to "R. Sennecke," who is named only once more among the World War I German pilot cards as the photographer of N6196's portrait of Friedrich Manschott. Sennecke's studio, advertised as an *Internationaler Illustrations-Verlag* (international illustrations company), was located at Hallesches Ufer 9, Berlin, S.W. 11.

[30] Most of the NPG postcards and associated photographs discussed in this section will be reproduced in a future volume. The NPG card numbers cited herein are included to allow readers who have independent access to them to make their own comparisons until that time.

[31] See the photo in Immelmann, *Adler von Lille*, opposite p.140 or Immelmann, *Eagle of Lille*, opposite p.160. Immelmann's bemedaled appearance was impressive and attracted much attention. During his trip back to the Front, he stopped at Brunswick to visit his niece: "I had to promise Ilsa that same evening before she went to bed that I would call for her at the school the following day without an overcoat (because of the decorations)." (Immelmann, *Eagle of Lille*, p.159)

[32] For example, see L7508-11, L7605-6, L7649-54 (not reproduced in this work).

[33] See Werner, *Knight of Germany*, p.182.

[34] For example, compare the drape of his collar and its position vis-à-vis his *Pour le Mérite* – one of the collar tips rests behind the left cross arm (i.e. facing the award) whereas the other tip slightly overlaps the right cross arm in all the photos. The white shirt collar is barely discernible under the tunic collar to the same degree. The buttonholed ribbons are identically positioned and the lower of the two (for his Prussian Life Saving Medal) is exposed and covers one button in exactly the same way. The swords on the higher ribbon (denoting his Royal Hohenzollern House Order) are attached at precisely the same angle. The shoulder boards are bent in the same manner, and the length and style of his hair are identical. Other photos of Boelcke show many differences among all these factors.

[35] See Ferko, *Richthofen*, p.36.

[36] As noted previously, Boelcke was awarded his *Pour le Mérite* on 12 January 1916. Rackow was granted his on 7 June 1916 in recognition of his assault on Fort Vaux at Verdun. He, two other officers, and 30 men were the first to enter the fortress on 2 June, leading to its eventual surrender. Crown Prince Wilhelm was awarded his *Pour le Mérite* by his father, *Kaiser* Wilhelm, on 22 August 1915 in recognition of his distinguished military planning and successful operations during several battles on the Western Front. Brandis was granted his award on 14 March 1916 because of his role in the capture (without a shot being fired) of Verdun's Fort Douamont on 25 February 1916.

[37] Though Boelcke himself states that we was told not to fly, he apparently had some amount of leeway because he wrote that he returned quickly to Sivry to "thoroughly exploit the two days flying left to me." He shot down a plane on his second flight of the evening, but "did not report this combat to the staff officer in case he might positively forbid me to fly during my remaining day and a half." (Werner, *Knight of Germany*, p.181) He was then ordered to Charleville to confer with Thomsen about the basic principles of single-seat combat before going to Berlin to begin his tour. It was at this time that his famous "Dicta Boelcke" – rules of engagement essentially followed by decades of fighter pilots until the advent of airborne radar and air-to-air missiles – was recorded.

[38] We have no information on Frank Seydler's status at this point in the war.

[39] It is neither a Fokker D.I nor a D.II. The D.I had a distinctly different appearance where the engine fairing met the fuselage. The D.II had a noticeable metal hump behind the cockpit where it joined the flat, upper fuselage surface.

[40] For example, see Leaman, *Fokker Aircraft*, p.70

[41] Again, neither the Fokker D.I nor the D.II used this kind of strut. They employed struts shaped like either a closed or a slightly open "N."

CHAPTER TWO

RICHTHOFEN

The Sanke Series

Karl Bodenschatz, adjutant of Manfred von Richthofen's *Jagdgeschwader Nr.1* combat wing, revealed that his commander's picture postcards had a value all their own:

> "The adjutant prepares to undertake some little trips in order to procure provisions and maybe even nab something special somewhere. There is, of course, scarcely anything to be had in a wide radius, not for love nor money. Until one day he hits upon a miraculous remedy. And from then on, whenever he runs into someone with all sorts of good things to give away, but who shrugs his shoulders and spreads his hands with regret, the adjutant simply reaches into his tunic pocket and pulls out a postcard. On this postcard is pictured Rittmeister von Richthofen, in his finest uniform with all of his medals and his most winsome face, and what is more, under the photograph is Richthofen's autograph, written in his own hand. That works wonders and proves more precious, more valuable, and more effective than love or money. The adjutant never comes back from his little travels empty-handed any more." (Bodenschatz, *Hunting with Richthofen*, p.52)

Presumably, Bodenschatz was referring to a picture taken by Berlin photographer C.J. von Dühren that Sanke presented as S450: Richthofen in his dark blue Uhlan dress uniform wearing his *Pour le Mérite* and five other decorations. Although it technically does not depict "all of his medals" (Richthofen eventually garnered 23 decorations and two pilot badges), it is the only Richthofen postcard that portrays him in more than his usual *Pour le Mérite*, Iron Cross 1st Class, and Prussian Pilot's Badge. The latest award date of the six decorations displayed in S450 is 12 January 1917 for his *Pour le Mérite* (though he only received news of its bestowal on 16 January).[1] His next two medals, not seen in S450, were earned the following mid-April.[2] Richthofen was promoted to *Oberleutnant* on 23 March, but his epaulettes in the photo display his rank as *Leutnant*. It therefore follows that its date was sometime between mid-January and late March 1917 – and we are aware of only one trip to Berlin by Richthofen during this interval. He had assumed command of *Jasta 11* at La Brayelle (Douai) immediately after receiving his *Pour le Mérite*, and after serving several weeks at the Front paid a surprise visit to his mother in Schweidnitz on 4 February. She recalled that he had just come from a discussion of Albatros wing failures at the Inspectorate of Military Aviation in Berlin, and that it was the first

time that she had seen him wearing his new decoration.[3] Richthofen did not return to Berlin until 15 May 1917, so his early February trip there was the only opportunity he had to pose at Dühren's Berlin studio. This deduction finds final confirmation in a rare 1927 German calendar that marks the anniversary of Richthofen's death in April by providing an autographed photo of the flier above a poem (see S450: MVR1). The photo shows Richthofen standing in the very same Uhlan dress uniform he is wearing in S450, and it is signed "Manfred. 22.II.1917" (22 February 1917). Obviously, this picture and S450's must have been taken before that date.[4]

S503 is another Dühren photograph, probably taken the same time as S450 and MVR1. Richthofen may be wearing the same dark blue dress uniform beneath his overcoat, for the one visible button is smooth and unusually shiny and his uniform shade is considerably darker than the field grey tunics we otherwise see him wearing.[5] S503's photo can be seen in the 7 April 1917 edition of Berlin's *Die Woche*, which demonstrates that it was taken no later than March. As noted for S450, the only Berlin trip that Richthofen made that suits this timeframe was his early February visit. More tentative support is offered by a comparative examination of other Richthofen pictures. Several taken before February 1917 show him wearing an earlier style *Schirmmütze* (visored cap) with a patent leather chinstrap just above the visor.[6] Pictures taken around the time of his May leave and afterward display a later style without the strap.[7] One might question why photos from the same sitting would have been published as far apart as numbers S450 and S503. The gap, however, is not as wide as it seems because Sanke's series inexplicably stops at S451, then picks up again at S502 – so only two cards actually separate S450 from S503. Lastly, S450 and S503 are the only two photos credited to Dühren for Richthofen or any of the other German airmen other than his brother Lothar (S526). All things considered, the evidence points to S450, S503, and MVR1 as representing a set of photos taken in Berlin during Richthofen's visit there in early February 1917.

S509 captures Richthofen shaking hands with the commander of the German Air Force, *Generalleutnant* Ernst von Hoeppner. At least one other picture emerged from the same event: MVR2 (see S509). MVR2 shows Richthofen introducing Hoeppner to a lineup of the following *Jasta 11* members: *Lt.* von Hartmann (Adjutant), *Lt.* Konstantin Krefft (Technical Officer), *Lt.* Karl-Emil Schaefer, *Lt.* Otto Brauneck, *Lt.* Lothar von Richthofen, and *Lt.* Karl Esser. MVR2's date can be bracketed between 20 April 1917, when Brauneck joined *Jasta 11*, and 27 April 1917, when Schaefer left to command *Jasta 28*. Both the *Nachrichtenblatt der Luftstreitkräfte* (the Commander of the Air Force's weekly summary of activities) and Hoeppner's memoirs note that Richthofen and *Jasta 11* had distinguished themselves by bringing down their 100th official victory on 22 April 1917, so Hoeppner's visit probably occurred as a result of and shortly after this special achievement.[8]

Richthofen appears next in S511 in the company of four fellow *Jasta 11* pilots: *Vzfw.* Sebastian Festner, *Lt.* Karl Emil Schaefer, *Lt.* Lothar von Richthofen, and *Lt.* Kurt Wolff. MVR3 (see S511), the original image behind S511, establishes that someone touched up Festner's appearance by replacing his originally open mouth with a smirking one. The same group of airmen and Richthofen's dog, Moritz, are found in MVR4 (see S511), which was taken either immediately before or after S511/MVR3. MVR5 (see S511), which shows Richthofen sitting in the cockpit of an Albatros fighter behind 10 *Jasta 11* pilots, was also snapped around the same time. We know that among the 10 men shown, *Lt.* Otto Brauneck joined *Jasta 11* on 20 April 1917, *Vzfw.* Sebastian Festner was killed the morning of 25 April, and *Lt.* Karl-Emil Schaefer left *Jasta 11* for his new command two days later. Therefore, the image must have been taken during the period 20-24 April. Many similarities can be discerned between MVR5 and S511, but a particularly noteworthy one is the matching oil stain on the cloth legging wrapped around Festner's right leg. It is highly unlikely that the exact same pattern would have been formed by the various overlapping segments if the leggings had been used another day (i.e., unwrapped and rewound). Festner's, Schaefer's, and Lothar von Richthofen's outfits are practically identical, even down to the creases and folds in their visor caps. Only Wolff is different. Though his tunic and the high, white shirt collar beneath it are the same, he is wearing a visor cap and captured English flight coat in S511 as opposed to MVR5's stocking cap and sweater. An obvious explanation would be that Wolff simply changed clothes between photos. In any event, the next chapter will demonstrate that a multitude of photographs were taken of *Jasta 11* pilots over the course of a few days in late April 1917, many of which were later published as Sanke postcards.

Bloody April

"My father announced one day that he wanted to visit his two sons. My father is the local commandant of a small town in the vicinity of Lille and, consequently, was not far from us. I could often see him from above. He arrived by train at nine o'clock, and by nine-thirty was at our field. We had just come home from a pursuit flight and my brother was first to jump out of his crate and greet the 'old master': 'Hello, Papa, I have just shot down an Englishman.' After which I jumped out of my machine and said: 'Hello, Papa, I have just shot down an Englishman.' The old gentleman was very happy..." (Richthofen, *Red Baron*, p.87)

Major Albrecht von Richthofen chose a particularly noteworthy day to visit because before it was over Manfred had shot down no fewer than four enemy planes – a squadron and personal best. Albrecht could be equally proud of his other son, Lothar, who had brought down two of his own. Manfred had another reason to celebrate. He was about to go on a hunting trip and then home on an extended leave. Several surviving photos bear witness to the fact that a festive mood indeed prevailed in *Jasta 11* on 29 April 1917.

MVR6 shows Richthofen in the company of his father, *Lt.* Brauneck, *Lt.* Krefft, and *Lt.* Böhme, who had flown over from Fâmars near Valenciennes where he had been assigned to instruct fighter pilots. Four of them appear again in MVR7 to greet another visitor: *Lt.* Ernst von Althaus, knight of the Order *Pour le Mérite* and member of *Jasta 14*. A larger group is assembled in MVR8 that includes Richthofen (on a bicycle!), his father, Brauneck, and *Lt.* von Hartmann. Many of *Jasta 11*'s members are seated with Albrecht on the steps of Roucourt Château in MVR9, then standing without him near their airfield in MVR10. Lastly, MVR11 is a rare photo of the three Richthofens in front of Chateau Roucourt's steps. Several common denominators establish that all these photos were snapped the same day. The most obvious is Albrecht's presence in all but one, exhibiting the same outfit and in particular, the same stuffed, left tunic pocket. Manfred appears in them all, dressed in a generic M1915 *Bluse* tunic instead of his usual, double-breasted Uhlan tunic.[9] The outfits of the other pilots consistently match (e.g., Brauneck in MVR6, MVR8, MVR10; Lothar von Richthofen in MVR9-11; Krefft in MVR6, MVR7, MVR9, MVR10; Hintsch and Wolff in MVR9, MVR10). Even the chairs at the top of the steps are in the same position in MVR9 and MVR11. The date of the photo series is confirmed by a combination of factors. *Lt.* Brauneck's presence establishes 20 April 1917 as an early limit because that was when he first joined the squadron. *Lt.* Festner and *Lt.* Schaefer are conspicuously absent, pushing the date out further because Festner was killed and Schaefer left on 25 and 27 April, respectively. Albrecht von Richthofen is known to have paid his visit on 29 April and Manfred left on 1 May to return to Germany. Clearly, 29 April 1917 was "photo opportunity" day at *Jasta 11*.

Similarly, S509, S511, and MVR2-5 all may have been taken on the same day or group of days during 20-24 April. MVR2 and MVR5 offer the link. Specifically, the shape and creases in Richthofen's service cap are identical, Schaefer, Lothar von Richthofen, and Esser are wearing the same outfits, and Krefft is in his flight overalls in both images. Krefft, in full flight gear in MVR2, has unbuttoned his overalls and donned a service cap in MVR5; and Brauneck wears a turtleneck sweater instead of MVR2's tunic in MVR5. Such minor differences notwithstanding, these photos could have been taken on the same day but at different times.

Brauneck is wearing the turtleneck sweater we saw in MVR5, but is now standing near an Albatros fighter in S508. In addition, he has donned overalls and his footwear and service cap appear different. Festner is preparing for flight in S510, but the cloth legging stains and a tunic button observed in S511 and MVR3-5 are not present. Schaefer is photographed near a repaired Albatros in S512, possibly dressed the same as in S511, MVR2, and MVR5, but sans overcoat. Wolff strikes the same pose in a captured English flight coat in S513 and S511, but he has a white shirt collar and different cap folds in the latter. Nevertheless, there is no question that these Sanke photos were all taken within a short span of time at Roucourt airfield just like those above.[10]

In April 1917, *Jasta 11* downed 92 aircraft versus one loss of their own, and Richthofen's personal score stood at 52 – 12 more than the great Boelcke had amassed. Whether all the images discussed here were separated by a matter of minutes or days, they jointly testify that photographers gathered later that month at Roucourt airdrome to record Manfred von Richthofen and other *Jasta 11* airmen in action. They traveled there because they knew that *Jasta 11*'s unparalleled success story would appeal to the German public. Sanke knew this too and responded with a postcard series in their honor: S508 through S513.

MVR8

Opposite

Top: One of the series of pictures taken at Roucourt airfield on 29 April 1917 when the Richthofen brothers were visited by their father prior to Manfred's leave. Left to right: *Lt.* Otto Brauneck, *Rittm.* Manfred von Richthofen, *Maj.* Albrecht von Richthofen, *Lt.* Erwin Böhme (who had flown over from Valenciennes), *Lt.* Konstantin Krefft.

Bottom: Another picture taken at Roucourt on 29 April 1917. Left to right: unidentified, *Lt.* Konstantin Krefft, *Oblt.* Ernst von Althaus (then serving with *Jasta 4* in nearby Douai), *Rittm.* Manfred von Richthofen, *Lt.* Erwin Böhme (a visitor from Valenciennes), *Maj.* Albrecht von Richthofen.

Above: Roucourt airfield, 29 April 1917. Left to right: *Oblt.* Wolfgang Plüschow, *Rittm.* Manfred von Richthofen, *Lt.* Lothar von Richthofen, *Lt.* von Hartmann (adjutant), unknown (possibly *Lt.* Georg Simon), unknown (possibly *Lt.* Karl Esser), *Lt.* Otto Brauneck, *Maj.* Albrecht von Richthofen, unknown.

Jasta 11 pilots on the back steps of Chateau Roucourt, 29 April 1917. Left to right (back row): *Lt.* Carl Allmenröder, *Lt.* Lothar von Richthofen, *Oblt.* Wolfgang Plüschow, *Lt.* von Hartmann. Left to right (front row): *Lt.* Georg Simon, *Lt.* Kurt Wolff, *Rittm.* Manfred von Richthofen, *Maj.* Albrecht von Richthofen, *Lt.* Konstantin Krefft, *Lt.* Hans Hintsch.

Jasta 11 pilots at Roucourt airfield, 29 April 1917. Left to right: *Lt.* von Hartmann (adjutant), *Oblt.* Wolfgang Plüschow, *Lt.* Konstantin Krefft, *Lt.* Georg Simon, *Lt.* Kurt Wolff, *Lt.* Karl Esser, *Rittm.* Manfred von Richthofen, *Lt.* Lothar von Richthofen, *Lt.* Hans Hintsch, *Lt.* Otto Brauneck, *Lt.* Matthof, *Lt.* Carl Allmenröder.

MVR11

The Richthofens before the back steps of Chateau Roucourt on 29 April 1917. Left to right: Manfred, Albrecht, Lothar.

The Sanke Series Continued

Richthofen had to make one side trip before going home. On 30 April 1917, the eve of his departure, he had been "invited" to meet with the *Kaiser* at his Supreme Headquarters (or "the Great Shack" as Richthofen irreverently referred to it) in Bad Kreuznach, west of Frankfurt. The meeting was to take place on 2 May – Richthofen's 25th birthday – at the *Kurhaus* spa and casino complex, now the imperial residence. General Staff Headquarters was just down the road in the Hotel Oranienhof, and he was to report there first for an interview with *General* Erich Ludendorff. Naturally, Richthofen also met with German Air Force staff, including their chief, *Oberstleutnant* Hermann Thomsen, and their commander, *Generalleutnant* Ernst von Hoeppner. In fact, Hoeppner hosted a dinner on 2 May with Richthofen and *Generalfeldmarschall* Paul von Hindenburg as the guests of honor.

S519 is a group photo of Richthofen, Hoeppner, and Thomsen. Slightly different and poorer quality views of the same scene exist in MVR12 and MVR13 (see S519). All three may have originated from one of the early May functions mentioned above. First, Thomsen and Hoeppner are wearing their *Pour le Mérites*, so we know the picture is no earlier than the date of their joint award, 8 April 1917. Second, Richthofen's uniform is the same in this photo and another taken during his 3 May visit with the *Kaiser*'s wife in Bad Homburg (see S519: MVR14). Specifically, his tunic has the same pocket flaps, arced right shoulder board, flat left shoulder board, and angled alignment of his Iron Cross 1st Class and Prussian Pilot's Badge. Lastly, Sanke seems to have published his Richthofen photos in actual chronological order – probably the logical result of when they became available to him. Theoretically, the next time that Richthofen could

have been with Thomsen and Hoeppner was 15-18 May when, having just finished his hunting trip in the Black Forest, he traveled to Berlin to meet with the Inspectorate of Military Aviation. Indeed, we will see that the next Richthofen images, S532-34, were taken at that time. There is no record, however, of either Hoeppner or Thomsen being in Berlin then, and Richthofen is wearing a different tunic in S532-34 and another photo taken during the same period.[11] Moreover, MVR12 was published on the cover of the 16 May 1917 edition of the German aviation magazine, *Flugsport*, whereas MVR13 appeared in the 13 May 1917 edition of *Deutsche Kriegszeitung* – an almost certain indication that S519's picture originated from one of the earlier 1-2 May meetings.

In May 1917, Richthofen was home in Schweidnitz on a well-earned leave. His and his squadron's performance in April had made him the most celebrated airman in all of Germany. On Sunday, 20 May, Richthofen and his family politely stood outside their home for much of the day to greet the steady stream of admirers who had come there to catch a glimpse of their hero. His mother recalled:

"With great patience, Manfred had autographed all the postcards with his picture that the children and adults had brought. However, as one lady arrived with a hundred cards at one time for him to sign, he said harshly, 'I will not sign a single one.' Suspicious over this almost brusque tone of refusal, I looked at him with astonishment. He explained, still grumbling, that in another city someone had also asked him once to autograph fifty picture postcards. He did so. Afterwards he observed from his window as the fifty cards were sold on the street." (Fischer, *Mother of Eagles*, p.124)

We can deduce that the postcards referred to by Richthofen's mother must have been S450 and S503, because S509, S511, and S519 would have been published too late to have been presented at his home for signature in May. We know that S450 and S503 were photographed in Berlin. We also know that the next cards to feature Richthofen alone, S532-34, were taken there as well and originated from one sitting at the studio of Nicola Perscheid, the exclusive Berlin photographer who occasionally took pictures of only the most elite military personnel. What we have not known is when and why S532-34 were taken. Richthofen's *Pour le Mérite*, delivered to him around 16 January 1917, is present in these images whereas the head wound he suffered the following 7 July is not. To our knowledge, Richthofen was in Berlin four times between these dates: (i) in early February just before his trip home, (ii) on 15-18 May when he visited with the Inspectorate of Military Aviation and test flew aircraft at Johannisthal airfield, and (iii) during two brief stopovers on 31 May (to catch a train to Vienna) and around 10 June (on his way to attend Karl-Emil Schaefer's funeral). His next visit to Berlin came the following October. Richthofen was photographed by C.J. von Dühren during his early February visit, and it seems unlikely that he would have gone to Perscheid then as well. His brief stopovers on 31 May and 10 June were probably too short to accommodate such a session, so his 15-18 May stay in Berlin appears to be the most viable candidate. During this May visit, Richthofen met with the Ullstein publishing company. They wanted to print his story, and after he went home to Schweidnitz later that month, they sent a stenographer to meet him there and take down dictations. When the book, *Der rote Kampfflieger*, came out a few months later, its frontispiece and a major newspaper advertisement for it featured the same photograph: Perscheid's S532.[12] Though the Ullstein company could have struck a deal with Sanke for rights to the photo, it is equally plausible that they originally arranged the Perscheid photo session for use in their future publication and later licensed the photos to Sanke. The 15-18 May date for the S532-34 series finds support from another picture of Richthofen snapped during the same period. After a morning of test flying aircraft at Johannisthal, Richthofen attended the races at Berlin's Grunewald track where his picture was taken. He was dressed in the same tunic – it has no pocket flaps, the left shoulder board has the identical wavy pattern, and his Iron Cross 1st Class and Pilot's Badge are vertically aligned in the same pattern. This candid photo, MVR15, was later published in newspapers and also served as the basis for N6255.

S554 shows Richthofen and *Lt.* Werner Voss – two of the most successful German aces of the day – standing in their flight gear in front of an Albatros D.III. A series of pictures taken at the same occasion, including a fuller version of the one used in S554, can be found in other sources.[13] The heart and swastika insignia Voss employed to decorate his machine are partially discernible in some of them, so the D.III shown in S554 was his. Historians have agreed that these pictures were all taken during a visit to Krefeld where the Voss family lived, but several have incorrectly assigned their origin to April or May 1917. Though it is now surmised that Voss was on leave in Krefeld sometime between 8 April and 5 May (see p.38 and S506), Richthofen could not have been there too. He was at the Front

Rittm. Manfred von Richthofen (center) at Berlin's Grunewald racetrack, probably 15-18 May 1917.

during all of April, and was on official visits with the royal family and then a hunting trip in the Black Forest in early May. Richthofen did eventually go to Krefeld, but it was not until June 1917. After receiving word of Karl-Emil Schaefer's death on 5 June, Richthofen cancelled a trip to Schweidnitz to attend his friend's funeral. Schaefer was from Krefeld too, so Richthofen used the occasion to visit with the Voss family. Upon his return to the Front, Richthofen sent them a thank you note:

> "I would be grateful if I could learn the addresses of both of the charming young ladies. I think that within eight to fourteen days Werner will also become a leader of a *Jagdstaffel*. I have again taken command of my *Staffel* and feel very happy. Yesterday [I shot down] Number 53." (Kilduff, *Richthofen: Beyond the Legend*, p.141)

Voss had been transferred from *Jasta 2* to *Jasta 5* on 20 May following a dispute over his commanding officer's fitness to lead. His transgression might have resulted in more serious punishment had it not been for the fact that Voss was one of Germany's leading aces with 28 victories. Several more transfers followed: he stayed with *Jasta 5* until mid-June, briefly served with *Jasta 29* until 3 July, and was then shuffled to *Jasta 14* until he finally found a home with Richthofen's *Jagdgeschwader Nr.1* on 30 July as *Jasta 10*'s commanding officer. Voss, normally a consistent scorer, displayed only two significant gaps in his career's victory string.[14] The first was between 6 April and 7 May when he was home on leave (see S506). The second was during the period of his multiple transfers. The disruption caused by these transfers undoubtedly reduced his scoring chances in July, but they do not account for the gap in June.

After his arrival at *Jasta 5* on 20 May, Voss quickly brought down six aircraft between 23 May and 6 June. Though he continued to serve with the unit until 28 June, he did not score again. There is reason to believe that he was again home on leave. Josef Mai's diary discloses that Voss was slightly wounded by an explosive bullet during an air battle on 6 June.[15] He might have been sent home to recuperate or he might have traveled there to attend Schaefer's funeral – or both. In his thank you note, Richthofen acknowledged his June visit to the Voss family and his introduction to two "charming young ladies." Photos taken during that visit show Richthofen surrounded by the family, two young women, and Werner Voss. Unlike another set of pictures taken during a second visit with Voss, Richthofen bears no signs of the head wound he suffered on 7 July.[16] This combination of factors points to S554 being taken around 11-12 June when Richthofen was in Krefeld to attend Schaefer's funeral and visit the Voss family.

On 17 December 1916, *Jasta 2* was renamed *Jagdstaffel Boelcke* in recognition of its late leader. Similarly, *Kaiser* Wilhelm ordered that *Jasta 11* be called *Jagdstaffel Richthofen* from 26 April 1917 forward. This was a singular honor because naming a unit after its living leader was a distinction normally reserved for either royal or very senior officers. Official records indeed referred to *Jagdstaffel Richthofen* throughout most of the ensuing May (see also S511), but then returned to using *Jasta 11* thereafter. The distinction survived elsewhere though, because S606 is identified as a picture of "*Jagdstaffel Richthofen*."[17] The same group is seen in a different pose in MVR16. The service records of the 10 men surrounding Richthofen provide us with important information concerning when and where the photos originated:

Identity	Date of Service	Reason for Departure
Lt. Siegfried Gussmann	Nov 1917 – 7 Apr 1918	transfer to *FEA 5*
Fwlt. Fritz Schubert	Mar 1917 – 25 Aug 1918	
Lt. Hans-G von der Osten	10 Aug 1917 – 16 Mar 1918	transfer to *Jasta 4*
Lt. Werner Steinhäuser	Dec 1917 – 26 Jun 1918	killed in action
Lt. Karl Esser	Jan 1917 – 5 Jun 1918	transfer to *AFP 17*
Lt. Friedrich-W. Lübbert	Oct 1917 – 17 Feb 1918	wounded in action
Oblt. Hans-H. von Boddien	24 Jun 1917 – 29 Jan 1918	transfer to *Jasta 59*
Lt. Hans-K. von Linsingen	27 Nov 1917 – **24 Jan 1918**	injured
Lt. Eberhard Mohnicke	30 Apr 1917 – 8 Sep 1918	
Vzfw. Edgar Scholtz	**Jan 1918** – 2 May 1918	killed in action

Scholtz joined the unit in January 1918 and Linsingen was seriously injured later that month, so the pictures must have been snapped sometime in between for both men to have been present. Richthofen had been at Brest-Litovsk for peace talks with Russia's new revolutionary government during the first week in January, and was called away again on 19 January to attend fighter plane trials at Adlershof. He did not return to the Front until February. Consequently, S606 and MVR16 must have occurred at *Jasta 11*'s airfield at Avesnes-le-Sec sometime during 8-19 January 1918. Richthofen is wearing his M1915 *Bluse* tunic instead of his customary *Ulanka*, and we may once again surmise that it was because his Uhlan attire had been put aside in preparation for his upcoming trip (see footnote 9). If so, this would date the photos closer to 19 January. *Lt.* Hans-Georg von der Osten assumed temporary command of *Jasta 11* on 19 January, which may explain his position at the apex of the group in MVR16. MVR17 is a photo of Richthofen, his brother Lothar, *Lt.* Curt Wüsthoff, *Oblt.* Wilhelm Reinhard, and *Lt.* Erich Loewenhardt that is usually described as a grouping of *Jagdgeschwader Nr.1* commander Richthofen and his four *Jasta* leaders shortly before the March 1918 German offensive.[18] Richthofen's attire, however, is almost identical to that seen in S606

and MVR16: *Bluse* tunic without any decorations, sharply bent right shoulder board, softly angled left shoulder board, high white shirt collar, and dark trousers. Only his footwear is different (he is wearing leather "gators" and shoes in MVR16 and S606, and boots in MVR17). It appears then that all three images may have originated from the same period in mid-January. The collection of pilots with Richthofen was therefore more coincidental than others have believed, though later photographic evidence tells us that Loewenhardt and brother Lothar accompanied Richthofen to Adlershof on 19 January.[19]

S619 is a death card that places S534's image within a black border over an elegiac poem written by the same author of S377's, S393's, and S409's works. Obviously, it was created after Richthofen was shot down on 21 April 1918.

Liersch and NPG

True to form, Liersch offered no original photographs of Richthofen and only reprinted many of those already seen in various Sanke cards.[20] Conversely, NPG published two unique presentations: N6255 and N6306.

Opposite

Top: S606 - Sometime during 8-19 January 1918, nine pilots from *Jasta 11* and one from *Jasta 6* pose for a picture around their *Geschwaderkommandeur* Manfred von Richthofen near their airfield at Avesnes-le-Sec. From left to right: *Lt.* Siegfried Gussmann, *Fwlt.* Friedrich Schubert (*Jasta 6*), *Lt.* Hans-Georg von der Osten, *Lt.* Werner Steinhäuser, *Rittm.* Manfred von Richthofen, *Lt.* Karl Esser, *Lt.* Friedrich-Wilhelm Lübbert, *Oblt.* Hans-Helmuth von Boddien, *Lt.* Hans-Karl von Linsingen, *Lt.* Eberhard Mohnicke, *Vzfw.* Edgar Scholtz.

Bottom: A photograph taken at Avesnes-le-Sec during 8-19 January 1918 around the same time as S606. From left to right: *Lt.* Kurt Wüsthoff (*Jasta 4*), *Oblt.* Wilhelm Reinhard (*Jasta 6*), *Rittm.* Manfred von Richthofen (*Kommandeur* of *JG 1*), *Lt.* Erich Loewenhardt (*Jasta 10*), and *Lt.* Lothar von Richthofen (*Jasta 11*). Another version of this picture is often reproduced with drawings of *Pour le Mérite* medals added in for Manfred von Richthofen, Reinhard, and Loewenhardt. Reinhard never actually received the coveted decoration. (photo courtesy of UTD)

Right: A different arrangement of the same airmen seen in S606. From left to right: *Fwlt.* Friedrich Schubert (*Jasta 6*), *Vzfw.* Edgar Scholtz, *Lt.* Werner Steinhäuser, *Lt.* Hans-Karl von Linsingen, *Lt.* Karl Esser, *Lt.* Hans-Georg von der Osten, *Lt.* Eberhard Mohnicke, *Lt.* Friedrich-Wilhelm Lübbert, *Oblt.* Hans-Helmuth von Boddien, *Lt.* Siegfried Gussmann.

MVR16

The previous section already touched on N6255 by mentioning that it had originated from a candid photo of Richthofen attending horse races at Berlin's Grunewald track. *Hptm.* Erich von Salzmann, a friend of Richthofen's, described the scene:

> "Once we were together at the races in [the Berlin section] Grunewald and for a while he remained unnoticed. That morning he had been at Johannisthal, had test flown some new aircraft and his 'dress' was not really very elegant racecourse attire. In general, Richthofen was little inclined toward superficial appearances, although he did not seek to neglect the way he looked. Suddenly people recognized him. Then the photographers came. I have seen other young celebrities in such moments, as they put on airs and posed. None of that for Richthofen. His complete self-confidence was obvious. The young girls rushed toward him. He was asked to sign their programs as souvenirs." (Kilduff, *Richthofen: Beyond the Legend*, p.156)

The date was sometime within the period 15-18 May 1917. One particular picture, MVR15, was printed in the newspapers, and it was this one that NPG artists used for N6255.[21] They lifted Richthofen's image and superimposed it in front of the same crashed

BE.2c they had previously displayed in N5601 as Boelcke's last victory (see p.18). The fact that the scene was a complete fabrication did not seem to matter, as long as they could present Richthofen standing modestly before a vanquished foe.

N6306 offers a minor mystery. It undoubtedly is another photo from the Nicola Perscheid S532-34 series taken in Berlin during 15-18 May. Richthofen's pose is similar to S533's, except that the opposite hand is on his hip and his demeanor is decidedly glummer. Nevertheless, the picture is credited to "A. Müller" – a photographer whose name does not appear anywhere else among the Sanke, Liersch, and NPG cards except in the series N6304-6. N6304 is a picture of *Lt.* Curt Wüsthoff that lists Müller's studio location as Dresden-Loschwitz. The same studio information is printed on N6305, a photo of a certain *Lt.* von Ahlen who flew in the Balkan theater of operations. Little is known about Ahlen, but we do know that Wüsthoff was connected to Dresden.[22] Richthofen had no particular link to the city, and as stated earlier, N6306's original photo was actually taken by Perscheid in Berlin. Was the Müller credit a misprint carried over from the previous two cards, or did Dresden's Müller somehow obtain the photo from another source such as Perscheid or the Ullstein publishing house? For the time being, this mystery remains unsolved.

Notes

[1] In order of their award, they are: Prussia's Iron Cross 2nd Class (23 September 1914), Prussia's Iron Cross 1st Class (unknown, but probably soon after his first victory in September 1916), Saxe-Coburg and Gotha's Duke Carl Eduard Medal 2nd Class with Swords and Date (9 November 1916), Prussia's Royal Hohenzollern House Order Knight's Cross with Swords (11 November 1916), Austria-Hungary's Military Merit Cross 3rd Class with War Decorations (unknown) and the *Pour le Mérite* (12 January 1917). Several surviving examples attest to the fact that Richthofen indeed autographed S450 just as Bodenschatz described.

[2] They were Württemberg's Military Merit Order, Knight (13 April 1917) and Saxony's Military St. Henry Order Knight's Cross (16 April 1917).

[3] See Fischer, *Mother of Eagles*, p.116. On 23 January 1917, Albatros D.III lower wing failures caused the deaths of two of Richthofen's comrades from *Jasta Boelcke*: *Lt.* Hans Imelmann and *Vzfw.* Paul Ostrop. Richthofen himself experienced a cracked lower wing the next day, but escaped unharmed. The remaining Albatros D.III machines, which had only recently made their debut with these units, were temporarily removed from active duty for repairs. These events undoubtedly led to Richthofen's subsequent visit to the Inspectorate of Military Aviation to see what could be done about the recurring weakness.

[4] At that time, signing one's first name to a photograph was a highly personal dedication reserved for either family or only the closest associates. The photo itself has an intimate feel as well, because Richthofen, with a suppressed smile and hands clasped shyly, looks more like a young man barely containing his pride over his achievements than a heroic and seasoned warrior. The photo captures some of the excitement that drove Richthofen to rush home to show off his new decoration to his mother in the early hours of 4 February:

> "It is still early, the house sleeps, the bitter cold makes it good to be in bed. I believe I hear a sound. I turn on the light, the clock shows seven in the morning. Then, the door quickly opens, and Manfred stands in front of my bed, fresh and happy, no trace of fatigue after the long night's journey. The blue star glitters at his throat—the *Pour le Mérite*. I hold his hand, speak, as if praising the boy: Bravo, you have done well, Manfred. And ask: How did you get in? Was the garden gate open? No, it wasn't, but it didn't matter. The Knight of the *Pour le Mérite* climbed over the fence." (Fischer, *Mother of Eagles*, p.115)

Speculating that MVR1 may have been taken as a gift for Richthofen's mother, though purely conjectural, would be in concert with the events related above.

[5] The dark blue Uhlan dress uniform employed smooth, highly polished buttons, whereas the wartime field gray Prussian tunic used darkened or subdued buttons that carried an embossed royal crown.

[6] The chinstrap, originally intended to be used to keep the cap on during windy conditions or strenuous maneuvers such as horse riding, later became purely decorative. For photos of Richthofen with this style cap, see Ferko, *Richthofen*, p.9 (with *Kasta 8*, March-August 1916), Ibid., p.13 (with *Jasta 2*, September-November 1916), or the photos of Richthofen at Boelcke's funeral shown in the discussion of S363†.

[7] For pictures taken immediately before his May leave, see S509, S511, MVR6-11 (p.26-29 above), and Ferko, *Richthofen*, p.26; for during his May leave, see S519, S533, S534, MVR12-15 (see S519 and p.30 above), MVR18-19 (see S519), and C&C 10:2, p.112. The only post-February 1917 photos of Richthofen wearing a visored cap with chinstrap are from the *Kaiser* Military Parade held in Flanders on 20 August 1917 (e.g., see Ferko, *Richthofen*, p.51). The cap has a stiffer appearance than Richthofen's usual "crusher" look, and it also seems to be several sizes too big in order to accommodate the bandage covering Richthofen's head (he was wounded on 7 July 1917). It was probably borrowed for the occasion.

[8] See the discussion of S509 for *Nachrichtenblatt der Luftstreitkräfte No.10*'s and Hoeppner's recognition of this milestone.

[9] The double-breasted Uhlan tunic was called an *Ulanka*. Apart from this series of photos and a handful of others, Richthofen is usually seen wearing one. A practical explanation is that his Uhlan attire was being cleaned or had been packed or set aside in preparation for his trip to Berlin and that he owned a spare, more generic tunic for use under such circumstances.

[10] Since writing this section, a little known account written by war correspondent Alfred Richard Meyer has been discovered: *"Ein Besuch bei Rittmeister von Richthofen und seiner Staffel"* ("A Visit with Cavalry Captain von Richthofen and his Squadron") in the rare 1917 book *Fliegerbüchlein für*

deutsche Volk. Though its heading only states *"In Westen, April 1917,"* several internal references (e.g., Lothar von Richthofen's eight victories, Manfred's 46 victories, Schaefer's presence at *Jasta 11*) combine to establish a 17-21 April 1917 timeframe at Roucourt for the visit. Three photos accompany the report: the group shot seen in S511, the well-known lineup of *Jasta 11*'s and *4*'s Albatros fighters, and a view inside Richthofen's quarters. The 5 May 1917 edition of *Die Woche* had a two page pictorial essay entitled *"Ein Tag bei der Jagdstaffel des Rittmeisters Frhrn. von Richthofen"* ("A Day with Cavalry Captain Baron von Richthofen's Squadron") that included the same Albatros fighter lineup and view of Richthofen's quarters. It also printed snapshots of Manfred climbing into his Albatros, Lothar being helped down from his, and the same portraits of Festner, Schaefer, and Wolff seen in S510, S512, and S513 – all of which support the conclusion that many photos, including the Sanke series S508 through S513, were taken over the course of just a few days in late April at Roucourt aerodrome. For a detailed analysis, see Appendix I.

[11] There are distinct differences between the *Ulanka* tunics Richthofen wore in S519/MVR13 and S532-34/N6255. The tunic in S519 has pocket flaps while S532-34's does not. The right shoulder board in S519 has a wavy pattern compared with the smooth arc seen in S532-34. Lastly, S519's Iron Cross and Pilot's Badge decorations are aligned diagonally along the tunic flap as opposed to S532-34's vertical positioning. To avoid piercing the material, many officers chose to have small loops sewn on their tunics that would hold their decoration's attachment pin. The result was that their decorations were usually fixed in the same location on a particular tunic.

[12] See the cover of the 12 August 1917 edition of *Berliner Illustrirte Zeitung*.

[13] See Ferko, *Richthofen*, p.29 and C&C 18:3, pp.208-10.

[14] Voss' 1917 victories ran as follows:

1 Feb, 4 Feb, 10 Feb, 25 Feb (2), 26 Feb, 27 Feb (2)
4 Mar, 6 Mar, 11 Mar (2), 17 Mar (2), 18 Mar (2), 19 Mar, 24 Mar (2)
1 Apr, 6 Apr
7 May, 9 May (3), 23 May, 26 May, 28 May
4 Jun, 5 Jun, 6 Jun
10 Aug, 15 Aug, 16 Aug, 23 Aug
3 Sep, 5 Sep (2), 6 Sep, 10 Sep (3), 11 Sep (2), 23 Sep

[15] See OTF 11:3, p.234.

[16] See Ferko, *Richthofen*, p.31.

[17] Richthofen himself was no longer a member of *Jasta 11*. He was the commander of *Jagdgeschwader Nr.1*, which was comprised of *Jastas 4, 6, 10* and *11*. Of the ten other men shown in S606, nine served with *Jasta 11* and one (Schubert) with *Jasta 10*.

[18] Several authenticated Wüsthoff signatures demonstrate that he spelled his first name with a "C" rather than the more traditional "K". Carl Allmenröder had the same preference.

[19] See photos of the event published in Kilduff, *Richthofen: Beyond the Legend*, between pp.160 and 161, and Kilduff, *Illustrated Red Baron*, p.100.

[20] L7835 = S450, L7846 = S511, L7847 = S509, L7895 = S533, L7898 = S503, L7932 = S503†, L7933 = S533†. Once again, Liersch did not follow Sanke's original publication sequence. Copies of the Liersch and NPG postcards and associated photographs discussed herein will be presented in a future volume. The individual card numbers and other references cited here are included to allow readers who have access to them to make their own comparisons until that time.

[21] See Kilduff, *Illustrated Red Baron*, p.89 and the 24 June 1917 edition of the *Berliner Illustrirte Zeitung*. The same picture appeared between photos of two 20 May 1917 recipients of the *Pour le Mérite* (Georg Sick and Max von Boehn) on the back of a c.24 June 1917 edition of *Illustrierte Kriegs-Zeitung* (see Select Bibliography listing for approximate dating of this publication).

[22] Though born in Aachen in western Germany, Wüsthoff moved at some point to Dresden. In the first footnote of his brief biography of another Saxon pilot, Rudolf Windisch, Hannes Täger states: "Wüsthoff was born in Aachen but moved with his parents to Dresden, where he lived, learned, studied, and eventually died." (OTF 17:3, p. 230) Indeed, Wüsthoff's S586-88 series is credited to another Dresden studio. After being released from a French POW camp in 1920 he returned to Dresden to recuperate from the severely broken legs he had suffered in his 17 June 1918 crash behind enemy lines. He was killed there in 1926 during a flying exhibition that was held to raise funds for a memorial to Dresden-born Max Immelmann.

CHAPTER THREE

THE SANKE SERIES CHRONOLOGY

Immelmann, Boelcke, Richthofen

Now that we have a fairly accurate idea of when many of the Boelcke, Immelmann, and Richthofen photographs were originally taken, we can begin to deduce when the Sanke cards that featured them first appeared. The chronology of photo dates that we have assigned to Sanke's cards is followed for the most part by their numerical sequence:

Boelcke & Immelmann

Photo	Photo Taken	Year
S340	2 Aug – 9 Sep	1915
S342	15 Dec	1915
S347	15 Nov	1915
S360	17-19 Jan	1916
S361	"	"
S362	"	"
S363	"	"
S364	"	"
S369	"	"
S373	20 Jan	1916

Richthofen

Photo	Photo Taken	Year
S450	2-3 Feb	1917
S503	"	"
S509	23-26 Apr	1917
S511	20-24 Apr	1917
S519	1-2 May	1917
S532	15-18 May	1917
S533	"	"
S534	"	"
S554	11-12 Jun	1917
S606	8-19 Jan	1918

The cards themselves also contain clues that help pinpoint their probable publication dates. For example, they refer to the airmen by their different ranks: Immelmann as *Leutnant* or *Oberleutnant,* and Boelcke as *Leutnant, Oberleutnant,* or *Hauptmann.* Immelmann was promoted to *Oberleutnant* on 18 April 1916. His S340, S342, S347, S360-62, and S364 occur with both ranks, so the *Leutnant* versions

must have been published before mid-April 1916. S373 and S610 refer to him only as *Oberleutnant,* so they must have appeared after mid-April 1916. Boelcke was promoted to *Oberleutnant* in late January or very early February 1916 and again to *Hauptmann* on 21 May 1916. His S363 appears in *Leutnant, Oberleutnant,* and *Hauptmann* versions, so it was initially published in early 1916. S364 and S369 exist in both *Oberleutnant* and *Hauptmann* forms, so they initially appeared after early February and were reprinted after 21 May 1916. S373 and S409 only identify Boelcke as *Hauptmann* and therefore must have been published sometime after late May 1916. S450 initially identifies Richthofen as "*Freiherr*" ("baron") without a rank. A later version of S450 and the remainder of his Sanke series refer to him as "*Rittmeister*" ("cavalry captain"), which he became on 7 April 1917. This indicates that the earliest S450 may have been the only Richthofen card to come out before or around the time of his final promotion.

We also have obvious examples of posthumous publications where cards are marked either with a black border or a "†" symbol signifying "'deceased," or both. Immelmann's S361†, S377, and S610 were therefore published after his death on 18 June 1916, while Boelcke's S363† and S409 were printed following his fatal collision on 28 October 1916. Similarly, Richthofen's S503†, S532-34†, and S619 were published after he was killed on 21 April 1918.

Knowing the dates when certain events occurred is only half the battle. The transmission of news and pictures during World War I was not as efficient as it is today. Obtaining a photograph, editing it, setting it up for printing, then manufacturing and shipping the resulting postcard would have taken considerably longer, which brings us to a key point in our examination. What was the amount of time normally required before a particular event or photograph could be published as a Sanke postcard? An exhaustive survey of the earliest postmarks of mailed cards with a known event or photo date would provide the answer, but the extensive database required for such a survey is not currently available. Most of the surviving Sanke cards that appear in the trade, whether by collector preference or natural outcome, are postally unused examples. Fewer used or mailed cards have been preserved. The matter is further complicated by the fact that Sanke cards were often bought and mailed months (or even years) after their initial appearance – so even when mailed cards have survived, the odds are low that they reflect the earliest postmarked examples. Nevertheless, several cards in this writer's possession may collectively offer an answer. They represent the shortest time periods encountered to date between the occurrence of certain known events and the mailing of a related postcard. After Oswald Boelcke was killed in a mid-air collision on 28 October 1916, a funeral ceremony was held for him at Cambrai cathedral on 31 October. His body was later transported to Dessau for burial on 2 November. An example of his commemorative death card, S409, was mailed on 27 November 1916, a little over three weeks from the time of his burial. Walter Höhndorf is wearing the *Pour le Mérite* he won on 20 July 1916 in S381. One S381 card was mailed only six weeks later on 30 August 1916. We have already determined that the photos for Otto Brauneck's S508 and Karl-Emil Schaefer's S512 were taken in late April 1917. Brauneck signed and mailed one of his S508 postcards on 30 May 1917, only a little more than four weeks later. Schaefer's S512 was published within at least four weeks of the late April picture session because several autographed examples exist that must have originated before his death on 5 June 1917. Perhaps the most significant evidence occurs in the form of Carl Allmenröder's S543. A crude drawing of the *Pour le Mérite* that Allmenröder was granted on 14 June 1917 was superimposed on the postcard's photo. One surviving example has a handwritten and postmarked date of 27 June 1917, or just about two weeks after the award date that the card obviously commemorated. So S543 provides solid proof that Sanke was capable of producing a postcard as quickly as two weeks after a noteworthy event. Yet other postmarked examples and, as we shall soon see, other publication evidence suggest that such speed might have been more the exception than the rule. It is possible that in S543's case it was attributable to the comparative ease and efficiency of modifying an older, already existing photograph as opposed to waiting for a more current picture to become available.[1] Though S543's testimony should not simply be dismissed as some sort of singular aberration, the collective evidence indicates that as a general rule Sanke's postcards usually did not appear any earlier than three weeks after the events that inspired them.[2] Hopefully, this conclusion will suit the majority of cases. In the few remaining instances, where older photographs may already have been in Sanke's possession, the publishing timeframe may have been as fast as two weeks.

How do these conclusions hold up against a comparison of event and picture dates for other publications? Illustrated newspapers like the *Berliner Illustrirte Zeitung*, a pictorial magazine published weekly by the Ullstein firm, probably had relatively efficient access to photographs. A study of all its issues in 1916-18 demonstrates that with only a few exceptions, it usually reported on events about two to three weeks after their occurrence (as opposed to daily newspapers that reported events more contemporaneously but without photographs). For example, Boelcke's seventh victory on 5 January 1916 is not reported until the 16 January edition of *Berliner Illustrirte*

Zeitung. Similarly, Boelcke's 18th victim (21 May 1916) and Immelmann's 15th (16 May 1916) are not reported until 11 June. Notices of *Pour le Mérite* awards to Wintgens (1 July 1916), Mulzer (8 July), and Parschau (10 July) appear first in a 23 July edition, while Parschau's death on 21 July is not reported until 6 August. Even major events such as Boelcke's fatal accident (28 October 1916) or Richthofen's fall behind enemy lines (21 April 1918) appear in editions dated 12 November 1916 and 5 May 1918, respectively. The same holds true for *Die Woche*, another illustrated weekly newspaper. It did not report Boelcke's and Immelmann's *Pour le Mérite* awards (12 January 1916) until its 22 January edition. *Oblt.* Manfred von Richthofen's 30th victory was mentioned on 7 April 1917, but Richthofen had already added another six to his total and been promoted to *Rittmeister* by that date. Photographs generally experienced an even greater time lag. For example, Immelmann's picture near the wreckage of his seventh victim was taken on 15 December 1915 (see S342), but both story and snapshot were not published by *Berliner Illustrirte Zeitung* until 16 January 1916. Of the three photos mentioned earlier of Wintgens, Mulzer, and Parschau in the 23 July 1916 edition of *Berliner Illustrirte Zeitung*, only the one of Wintgens shows him wearing his *Pour le Mérite* (awarded 1 July). Reports and pictures covering the funerals of Wintgens and Mulzer, who died on 25 and 26 September, were published on 29 October and 22 October, respectively. A picture of Richthofen's grave, provided by the British a few days after his burial in France on 22 April 1918, was not printed until 2 June. There are a few faster examples, such as when Frankl's S384 *Pour le Mérite* picture (taken shortly after his receipt of the award on 12 August 1916) was printed in the 27 August edition of *Berliner Illustrirte Zeitung*. The photo of Hoeppner congratulating Richthofen in S509 was taken soon after 22 April and subsequently appeared in the 5 May 1917 edition of *Die Woche*. The majority of cases, however, show that it generally took three to four weeks for a new photograph to appear in a pictorial publication. Such a delay may seem inordinately long by today's standard of instant access via electronic media. But when placed in the context of a worldwide conflagration that still employed horses for transportation, it is more understandable. Our observation that most Sanke cards normally did not appear any sooner than three weeks after the event that inspired them seems to be in concert with the time delay usually exhibited by other illustrated publications.

If we subscribe to this general rule that at least three weeks were usually needed to publish a Sanke card following any particular event, we can begin to predict when many Sanke cards may have first been released to the public. A list of all versions of the earliest Sanke cards dealing with wartime airmen up through S381 follows:

Card#	Version	Photo or Event Date		First Published	
S340	*Lt* Immelmann	2 Aug – 9 Sep	1915	Dec/Jan	1915/16
S342	*Lt.* Immelmann	15 Dec	1915	Jan	1916
S347	*Lt.* Immelmann	15 Nov	1915	Jan/Feb	1916
S360	*Lt* Immelmann	17-19 Jan	1916	Feb	1916
S361	*Lt* Immelmann	17-19 Jan	1916	Feb	1916
S362	*Lt* Immelmann	17-19 Jan	1916	Feb	1916
S363	**Lt. Boelcke**	**17-19 Jan**	**1916**	**Feb**	**1916**
S363	*Oblt.* Boelcke	late Jan – early Feb	1916*	Mar – May	1916
S364	*Lt* Immelmann, *Oblt.* Boelcke	"	1916*	Mar – Apr	1916
S369	*Oblt.* Boelcke	"	1916*	Mar – Jun	1916
S364	*Oblt* Immelmann, *Oblt.* Boelcke	18 Apr	1916*	May	1916
S340	*Oblt.* Immelmann	"	1916*	May	1916
S342	*Oblt.* Immelmann	"	1916*	May	1916
S347	*Oblt.* Immelmann	"	1916*	May	1916

Card#	Version	Photo or Event Date		First Published	
S360	*Oblt.* Immelmann	"	1916*	May	1916
S361	*Oblt.* Immelmann	"	1916*	May	1916
S362	*Oblt.* Immelmann	"	1916*	May	1916
S363	**Hpt. Boelcke**	**21 May**	**1916***	**Jun**	**1916**
S364	**Oblt. Immelmann,**				
	Hpt. Boelcke	"	**1916***	**Jun**	**1916**
S369	**Hpt. Boelcke**	"	**1916***	**Jun**	**1916**
S371	**Hpt. Buddecke**	**mid-Apr– May**	**1916**	**May – Jun**	**1916**
S373	**Oblt. Immelmann,**				
	Hpt. Boelcke	**21 May**	**1916***	**Jun**	**1916**
S361†	**Oblt. Immelmann**	**18 Jun**	**1916****	**Jul**	**1916**
S377	**Oblt. Immelmann**	"	**1916****	**Jul**	**1916**
S378	**Lt. Wintgens**	**1-19 Jul**	**1916**	**Aug**	**1916**
S379	*Lt.* Mulzer	early in career		Aug	1916
S380	**Lt. Parschau**	**10-21 Jul**	**1916**	**Aug**	**1916**
S381	**Lt. Höhndorf**	**20 Jul – 13 Aug**	**1916**	**Aug**	**1916**

* promotion
** killed in action

Using our three-week rule, we can establish with relative certainty when many of the cards above first appeared. These instances are marked in **bold** print.

We have determined that the photo for S363 was taken 17-19 January 1916 at one of Boelcke's *Pour le Mérite* ceremonies. Applying the three-week rule yields an initial publication date of early February 1916. It makes sense that it did not come out much later because Boelcke was promoted to *Oberleutnant* in late January or early February 1916, and S363-*Oblt.* and S364, which did not come in a *Leutnant* version, followed soon after. This means that S363-*Lt.* was practically finished before news of Boelcke's promotion became widespread and led to future corrections. In fact, none of his other cards refers to him as *Leutnant*.

S373 identifies Boelcke only as *Hauptmann* and it occurs in the Sanke series before S377, Immelmann's death card. Boelcke was promoted on 21 May 1916 and Immelmann was killed on 18 June 1916. S373 probably first came out in June 1916 before or around the time of Immelmann's death because there is no indication ("†" symbol or black border) that he was already dead. Our three-week rule indeed supports an initial publication date sometime in mid-June – a period apparently verified by the 25 June 1916 postmark encountered on Buddecke's S371, which comes just two cards before S373. It follows that the *Hauptmann* versions of S363 and S369 came out around the same time.

S361† may have been published sooner than three weeks after Immelmann's death because it merely bordered the former S361 in black. The same could be true for S377 except that its addition of an elegiac poem to S360's photo probably took longer to create. Regardless, a first appearance in July 1916 would cover them both adequately; and we have an early, postmarked example of S377 dated 3 August 1916.

Finally, S378-81 pick up right where S377 leaves off. They commemorate *Pour le Mérite* awards to four other pilots in July 1916: *Lt.* Kurt Wintgens (1 July), *Lt.* Max Mulzer (8 July), *Lt.* Otto Parschau (10 July), and *Lt.* Walter Höhndorf (20 July). We have postmarked examples of 9 August 1916 for Parschau's S380 and 30 August 1916 for Höhndorf's S381 that confirm their August 1916 publication dates.

With these cards as our solid framework, we can go back and fill in the blanks for the remainder. The photos for S360-62-*Lt.* and S363-*Lt.* were taken soon after Immelmann and Boelcke were simultaneously awarded the *Pour le Mérite*. The postcards featuring them were probably published together in February 1916 as part of a series honoring the first two airmen to receive Prussia's highest combat honor.

S342's photo was taken on 15 December 1915, and the three-week rule would result in an initial publication date of early January 1916. S347, snapped before this on 15 November 1915, nevertheless had to have been offered between S342 and S360 because of its numerical position between them. Its initial publication date would then be somewhere in a January to February 1916 timeframe.

Where does this leave S340-*Lt.*? IMMEL2 shows Immelmann's name, rank, and "1915" date in his own handwriting. S340-*Lt.* copied the name and rank in the same handwriting but omitted the "1915." The year "1916" was not added until a new signature and *Oberleutnant* rank appeared in a later version. Though this might imply that the *Leutnant* version was printed toward the close of 1915 when a commitment to either 1915 or 1916 would have posed problems, it is equally possible that it made its first appearance in January 1916. Perhaps a postmarked example will come to light in the future and provide us with more solid evidence.

The first version of S364, depicting *Leutnant* Immelmann and *Oberleutnant* Boelcke, must have been issued sometime after Boelcke's promotion in late January or early February and before Immelmann's promotion on 18 April 1916. This would place its publication somewhere in March to April 1916. It was duly followed by an updated version listing both airmen as *Oberleutnante*, which must have appeared sometime after 18 April but before Boelcke's second advancement on 21 May 1916. It is likely then that it first came out in May 1916 along with all the other *Oberleutnant* reprints of prior Immelmann cards.

A chart of the cards surrounding Richthofen's S503, S509, and S511 follows:

Card#	Version	Photo or Event Date	First Published
S502	**Böhme**	**late Mar 1917**	**Apr 1917**
S503	**Richthofen**	**2-3 Feb 1917**	**Apr/May 1917**
S504	Thomsen	? – 8 Apr 1917	May 1917
S505	Hoeppner	? – 8 Apr 1917	May 1917
S506	**Voss**	**Apr 1917**	**May 1917**
S507	Schaefer	?	May 1917
S508	**Brauneck**	**late Apr 1917**	**May 1917**
S509	**Richthofen**	**late Apr 1917**	**May 1917**
S510	**Festner**	**late Apr 1917**	**May 1917**
S511	**Richthofen**	**late Apr 1917**	**May 1917**
S512	**Schaefer**	**late Apr 1917**	**May 1917**
S513	**Wolff**	**late Apr 1917**	**May 1917**

Once again, the cards whose first appearance can be established with relative certainty are marked in **bold**.

We have already discussed that the photos seen in S508-13 were taken at *Jasta 11*'s Roucourt airfield in late April 1917. There is no doubt that the postcards were published the following May because of a 30 May postmark on S508 and the existence of S512 examples autographed by Schaefer (killed on 5 June). We can now confirm that S506, a picture of *Lt.* Werner Voss that came out just before this series, had a May 1917 debut as well. The photo shows Voss sitting indoors near a wood mantel with his *Pour le Mérite* and its immediate predecessor, the Royal Hohenzollern House Order, in full display. Voss was awarded the *Pour le Mérite* on 8 April 1917 after having achieved 24 victories. He would not score again until the following 7 May – a seemingly inexplicable gap considering his run in February (eight victories), March (eleven victories), and the start of April (two victories on 1 and 6 April), as well as the tremendous success enjoyed by other German pilots later that month.[3] But Voss could not have scored if he was away from the Front. It was often the case that *Pour le Mérite* recipients were granted leave along with the award, and Voss was no exception. Proof of this rests in the form of the patterned quilt or afghan that Voss is sitting on in S506. The same item appears again in the bottom left corner of VOSS1 (see S506), a photo of Richthofen's later visit to the Voss family home. The patterned cover makes it clear that S506 was originally snapped at the Voss residence in Krefeld. It had to have been taken after 8 April, because he is wearing his *Pour le Mérite*, but before 7 May when his scoring streak resumed. This in turn is confirmed by a photograph given to Karl Bodenschatz and signed "Werner Voss, *Mai* 1917" (see S506). It is the same picture as S506, and was probably given to Bodenschatz upon Voss' departure from *Jasta 2* on 20 May 1917. Thus S506's photo was taken in April 1917 and the three-week rule would place its publication in May sometime before or around the later May appearance of the S508-13 series that came next.

We know the origin of S502 from a letter written by *Lt.* Erwin Böhme to his fiancée on 21 November 1917, one week before his death. After receiving a framed picture of her, he wrote:

"Enclosed immediately is a reciprocal gift. Yesterday while rummaging I came across a whole pile of picture postcards of 'Our successful fighter pilot *Leutnant* Böhme' based upon a photograph taken by Ella Kohlschein. They are from a Berlin art store that publishes a whole series of 'Heroes' Postcards. I am sending a dozen to you presently, so that you do not need to rob the Hamburg shop windows of their decorations." (OTF 11:1, p.15)

Ella Kohlschein was the wife of Professor Hans Kohlschein, a professional artist and the brother-in-law of Böhme's brother, Gerhard. Hans Kohlschein painted several portraits of Erwin Böhme, and the one that is most similar to the pose in S502 can be seen in BÖHME2 (see S502).[4] Ella apparently snapped several pictures of Böhme to assist her husband in his portrait efforts. Another letter from Böhme to his fiancée, dated 17 March 1917, tells us when this occurred:

"Yesterday I finally escaped from the physicians with a jump for joy. I even flew a consolation honor lap over the field today, but it went only moderately well. My arm is still stiff and cannot be completely straightened. As a result, I still have to go for follow-up treatment (orthopedic exercises) in the interior, in fact to Düsseldorf. I suggested that they send me to Hamburg, but the right kind of orthopedic specialist (a beautiful German word!) supposedly is not there. Nevertheless, I will go to Düsseldorf gladly, because there I will find my dear brother-in-law's folks, the Kohlscheins...Already tomorrow I will arrive at the Rhine [which flows through Düsseldorf]...Last Sunday, the General of the Air Force surprised me with a telegram reporting that the *Kaiser* had awarded me the Hohenzollern House Order with swords. I have been walking around almost one week now with this decoration." (Böhme, pp.97-98, trans. by this writer)

Böhme had been shot down and wounded in the left arm on 11 February 1917. As stated above, he was sent in March to Düsseldorf to complete his recovery. While there, he visited with the Kohlscheins and apparently had his picture taken by Ella for the portrait painted by Hans (note the caption in BÖHME2). The picture and portrait must have followed his award of the Royal Hohenzollern House Order, Knight's Cross with Swords because the decoration's ribbon is present in both.[5] His next letter, dated 5 April from Düsseldorf, explains that his leave was cut short and that he had to return to active service the next day.[6] He stayed a short while with *Jasta Boelcke* and then left to take command of the fighter school at Fâmars (near Valenciennes) later the same month. His photograph, taken in late March, would not have been available in Sanke card form until mid- to late April according to our three-week rule. This timing finds further support from the fact that the earliest dated example seen so far for the next card in the series, Richthofen's S503, is 26 April 1917.

Generalleutnant Ernst von Hoeppner, Commanding General of the Air Force, and *Oberstleutnant* Hermann Thomsen, his Chief of Staff, were both awarded the *Pour le Mérite* on 8 April 1917. Though their photos in S504 and S505 do not show them wearing the coveted awards, there is no doubt that the postcards commemorated the event because the next card in the series, S506, is a portrait of Werner Voss and his *Pour le Mérite*, awarded the same day. Thus their cards were probably published around the same time in May 1917.

Karl-Emil Schaefer's S507, by virtue of its appearance between S506 and S508, probably first came out in May 1917. Its image deserves further discussion though because it exists in several versions. The earliest is an original photo of Schaefer wearing buttonhole ribbons for the Iron Cross 2nd Class and Schaumburg-Lippe Cross for Faithful Service. SCHAEFER2 (see S507 reissue) is a later modification that appeared as the cover photo of a magazine shortly after Schaefer's death on 5 June 1917. In this version, drawings of an Iron Cross 1st Class and Pilot's Badge were added to his tunic. S507's photo was again altered to produce SCHAEFER4 (see S507-reissue), the frontispiece of a book about Schaefer published in early 1918. The book, *Vom Jäger zum Flieger*, includes a forward by Emil Schaefer, Karl's father, and was apparently written with the full cooperation of the Schaefer family. SCHAEFER4 shows that the original Iron Cross 2nd Class ribbon was extended into a dangling Royal Hohenzollern House Order above the Schaumburg-Lippe ribbon. A ribbon bar with nondescript, unidentifiable ribbons appears on his chest, and very crude drawings of a *Pour le Mérite* and Iron Cross 1st Class have been added as well. S507's reissued version replaces the original's buttonhole ribbons entirely with a Royal Hohenzollern House Order. It is accompanied by slightly better representations of the remainder of Schaefer's medals.[7] We know that the Schaefer family sent this card to well-wishers in 1918.[8] So it appears that S507 first came out in its simplest version in May 1917. The same photo was touched up shortly after 5 June 1917 for a newspaper memorial, again for a reissue of S507 after Schaefer's death, and once more for the early 1918 Schaefer book.

Conclusions – Immelmann, Boelcke, Richthofen

Apart from the specific information related above, we can also draw several general conclusions from our study of the Sanke, Liersch, and NPG postcards discussed so far. First, they all probably owe their existence to a personal device employed by their earliest subject, Max Immelmann. Immelmann used autographed photos and picture cards to respond to various contacts, including some that were the direct predecessors to S340, S342, and N5613. Indeed, IMMEL2 – essentially duplicated in S340 – may have been the card that sparked Sanke's entrepreneurial interest in this area. Sanke secured at least the postcard rights to several of these pictures and used them to launch his series on German combat aviators. When Immelmann and

Boelcke became knights of the Order *Pour le Mérite*, even the publicity-wary Boelcke had to capitulate to the German people's desire to see and celebrate their new heroes. Sanke fed this desire with a series of postcards, S360-63, that provided photographs taken at or very near the time of the airmen's award ceremony. Their popularity must have been enormous, because Sanke not only combined two of the images in his next card, S364, but he also reprinted and updated each one whenever Immelmann or Boelcke was promoted. Second, when it came to any particular pilot subject, Sanke's postcard sequence usually followed the chronological order of the photographs they displayed. That is, pictures taken early in Immelmann's, Boelcke's, and Richthofen's careers were normally published first with subsequent pictures rolled out in sequence. Liersch sometimes, but not unfailingly, did the same. NPG, who usually featured unique photos, did not publish them in any particular order, such as when Boelcke's N5619 followed N5601's "last picture" of him, or when Richthofen's N6306 came long after N6255 even though both were taken around the same time. Third, sources for the postcard publishers' photographs were many and varied. In some cases, they came from posed sessions at elite studios such as those of Berlin's C.J. von Dühren (S450, S503), Nicolas Perscheid (S532-34), or Anhalt's royal photographer, Julius Müller (N5579-80). On the other hand, some were candid pictures provided by an unknown photographer, such as Richthofen's S519 and N6255. On other occasions, the source might have been military, as in Immelmann's censored S347, Boelcke's N5619, their shared S373, or Richthofen's S606. Sometimes the pictures were originally intended for private use and came from the pilot or his family, such as Richthofen's S450 and S554, Böhme's S502, or Voss' S506. At other times, several originated from one particular event or time period, such as Sanke's "Bloody April" series, S508-13. Fourth, it appears that the challenges encountered during wartime in first learning of a news event and then pursuing a wide variety of sources to find a photograph representing it usually resulted in at least a three week delay before that photograph could appear in postcard form. Occasionally, in those few instances where Sanke already possessed the necessary image and needed to make only minor changes, the process could be completed in two weeks. We can now better appreciate that publishing a constant stream of combat pilot postcards throughout the last three years of the war must have been a complicated business requiring tenacity and ingenuity.

It is now time to apply what we have learned up to this point to an examination of the remainder of Sanke's airmen series in an effort to further discern when and why they were published. This volume, the first of three, will focus on Sanke cards S340 through S543.

Notes

[1] See the discussion of S543, where it is demonstrated that the image was taken during Allmenröder's Easter (8 April 1917) leave. Sanke may have already been close to publishing S543 when the news of Allmenröder's *Pour le Mérite* came out, prompting the crude and hasty addition of the decoration to his image.

[2] Another possible exception may be those cards that reprinted previously published photos with updated information (e.g., new rank or "†" death notice). Examples of N6004 and N6005, two NPG postcards that commemorated Boelcke's death on 28 October 1916, are postmarked 15 November 1916, or just about two weeks afterward. One Boelcke S363† example has survived with a 7 November 1916 postmark. Once again, the fact that cards such as these required only minor changes to pictures already in the publisher's possession may have led to their faster turnaround.

[3] For example, *Jasta 2* (*Boelcke*) squadron mate *Lt.* Otto Bernert shot down 15 aircraft in April 1917, including a remarkable five in one day on 24 April.

[4] The artist later added a *Pour le Mérite* and the inscription "*Böhme, Führer der Staffel Boelcke †29.11.17*" ("Böhme, Leader of Squadron Boelcke,

died 29 November 1917") to this painting. See the cover of OTF 11:1 for a color version of the revised portrait.

[5] Böhme's uniform and the relative locations of his Iron Cross 1st Class, Pilot's Badge, and ribbon bar are identical in BÖHME2 and S502. Curiously the artist – either because he was not familiar with military details or did not particularly care – confused the location of the Iron Cross 2nd Class ribbon on Böhme's ribbon bar, and painted what appears to be the ribbon for a Bavarian Military Merit Order 4th Class with Swords (which Böhme did not receive) next to it instead of the actual Prussian Royal Hohenzollern House Order. Evidently, he did not in this instance consult closely with the photograph.

[6] In the third installment of his series of articles on Böhme (OTF 17:2, p.142), *Dr. Ing.* Niedermeyer notes that Werner's book misreported the date of the letter as 4 April 1917 when it was actually written on 5 April.

[7] They are the *Pour le Mérite*, Iron Cross 1st Class, Pilot's Badge, and a medals bar depicting the Iron Cross 2nd Class, Schaumburg-Lippe Cross for Faithful Service 2nd Class, and the Bavarian Military Merit Order 4th Class with Swords.

[8] This writer possesses such a card with a handwritten dedication by Karl's father Emil on the back.

CHAPTER FOUR

THE SANKE SERIES GUIDELINES

The Sanke Series Guidelines – Guideline 1

Fortunately, several Sanke cards with both dateable events and postmarks have surfaced. When we add roughly three weeks to their event dates and compare the result against their mailing dates, we sometimes encounter a convergence of time. For example, S381 is an outdoor photograph of *Lt.* Walter Höhndorf wearing the *Pour le Mérite* bestowed on him on 20 July 1916. He was given the decoration in recognition of the 14 July downing of his eighth victim – the same count that brought Immelmann and Boelcke their awards. Another slightly different picture taken at the same time appears in the 13 August 1916 edition of *Berliner Illustrirte Zeitung*, so both pictures must have been taken between 20 July and 12 August 1916. Applying our three-week rule yields an earliest publication spread of mid-August to early September. An example of S381 exists that was written and postmarked on 30 August 1916, so we have corroborative evidence that the card probably first appeared that month. Another example is Gustav Leffers' S413-15, S417 series. These four cards recognized his receipt of the *Pour le Mérite*, which is shown in all of them, on 5 November 1916. Leffers was killed in action on 27 December, so the photos must have been taken between these dates. Adding three weeks points to an initial publication range of early December to mid-January, and we have a written example of S413 dated 13 December 1916.

At this point, it is helpful to plot the results of our publication date conclusions on some kind of visual aid. Chart 1 (see p.328) has an x-axis consisting of the months of the years 1916-17 and a y-axis formed by the numerical series of known Sanke cards. When we plot S381's August 1916 date and S413's mid-December date on this chart and connect their two points with a line, we can test whether that line, Guideline 1, will serve as a useful, approximate guide to the publication dates of the cards in between, i.e., S382 through S412. "Approximate" is the key word here. We do not know how Sanke timed the release of his cards. It might have been several at once, one at a time at an even pace, or some mixture of both. It is unlikely that his subjects' photos became available on a routine, steady basis, so we cannot assume that Sanke followed a strict pattern for publication, particularly under wartime conditions. We also have not factored in how the publication of Sanke's S900 and S1000 aircraft series might have impacted the combat aviators series' publication pace. Paper and other material shortages, holiday cards, special events, and other factors may have complicated the situation even further. Thus our connecting line should be interpreted only as an approximate guide and not as an absolute, rigid determinant.

Several postcards that relate to events or include items that determine their earliest possible publication dates have not yet been corroborated by postmarked examples. Nevertheless, they can play a helpful role in testing the validity of our projected guideline. For example, S383 shows *Oblt.* Ernst von Althaus wearing the *Pour le Mérite* he was awarded on 21 July 1916, the day he had reached eight total victories. The previous card, S382, also featured Althaus but was based on an older photo modified to include a drawing of his new decoration. *Lt.* Walter Höhndorf's S381, which immediately preceded the Althaus pair, celebrated his receipt of the coveted award one day before Althaus on 20 July 1916. HÖHNDORF1 (see S381), a picture of Althaus and Höhndorf in front of various members of *Feldflieger-Abteilung 23* and its fighter detachment, *KEK Vaux*, shows them wearing the same outfits they have on in S383 and S381. In fact, S381, S383, and HÖHNDORF1 may have been taken around the same time, with HÖHNDORF1 capturing a joint *Pour le Mérite* celebration. Althaus and Höhndorf figure prominently in the picture, wearing what appear to be large boutonnieres of some sort, and they flank another *Pour le Mérite* holder who had either recently joined or was just visiting their unit, *Lt.* Kurt Wintgens (awarded 1 July 1916).[1] Theoretically, the earliest such a picture could have been reproduced on a Sanke card would have been mid-August; and the postmark date of one S383 example proves it came out no later than 2 October 1916. Guideline 1 falls between these markers and predicts a debut in late August or early September.

The subject of the next card in the series, S384, is *Lt.* Wilhelm Frankl, another member of the highly successful *KEK Vaux*. His eighth victim, a prerequisite for winning the *Pour le Mérite* at that time, was either a two-seat Nieuport or a Caudron that fell along with his ninth on 9 August 1916. The decoration that came to him on 12 August 1916 can be seen dangling from his collar. The 27 August 1916 edition of *Berliner Illustrirte Zeitung* displays the same photograph, identifying it as Frankl's "*neueste Aufnahme*" ("latest picture"). It therefore follows that the picture must have been taken during the period 12-26 August. As we shall see in our discussion of Berthold's S402, the location was Vaux before *KEK Vaux* moved to Roupy to form *Jasta 4* on 1 September. Our three-week rule results in a publication spread of 2-16 September. Once again, our connecting line rests in between these dates and predicts an early September debut. A postmarked example dated 1 October points in that direction.

We have reason to believe that Höhndorf's S389 was based on a photograph taken during an August 1916 leave to Berlin (see S389). If so, the earliest appearance it could have made in Sanke card form would have been late August. If not, we can still be fairly certain that it debuted no earlier than that because of the established appearance of one of its predecessors, Höhndorf's S381, in late August. A 15 October 1916 postmarked example of *Lt.* Hartmut Baldamus' S390 – the card that immediately followed S389 – places an outer limit on S389's initial publication. Guideline 1 splits the difference and assigns S389's debut to mid-September.

We can apply similar logic to Baldamus' S390. Once again, it would not have come out earlier than S381's established late August date, and we have one S390 example postmarked 15 October. Guideline 1 rests between these markers and predicts a late September appearance – the period when a similar photo taken the same time as S390 was published in the c.24 September 1916 edition of *Illustrierte Kriegs-Zeitung* (see Select Bibliography listing for approximate dating of this publication).

As noted before, a photograph and poem honoring Oswald Boelcke appear on S393. The poem praises him in the present tense and makes no mention of his death. This supports Guideline 1's prediction of an early October publication before he was killed later the same month. It also suits the assumption that the card probably celebrated Boelcke's return to active duty in September as the commander of a new *Jagdstaffel* on the Western Front following his two-month tour of the Eastern Front. Indeed, this was the purpose behind the 30 September 1916 edition of *Berliner Illustrirte Zeitung* when it featured Boelcke's S363 photo on its cover.

Lt. Max Mulzer was awarded Bavaria's Military Max-Joseph Order on 21 August 1916. Two of the three photos in his S396-98 series contain an artist's replication of the order, which proves that they came out sometime afterward either in September or beyond. Our guideline projects an October publication.

Vzfw. Rudolf Windisch and *Oblt.* Maximilian von Cossel proudly display four new awards between them in S401. The pair had conducted a daring sabotage mission behind enemy lines on 2-3 October 1916. Under the cover of darkness in the early morning hours, Windisch flew Cossel over the lines to a drop-off point near a forested area adjacent to the Russian Rowno-Brody rail line. Cossel, carrying a 100-pound pack containing explosives and detonators, hiked to the rail line and placed his charges on a curved portion of the tracks. He detonated them shortly after midnight when a large freight train reached the proper spot. The train derailed and blocked the vital supply route. Cossel returned to the drop-off point and was retrieved by Windisch the next day. As a result, Cossel and Windisch immediately became national heroes. On 5 October, Cossel received Prussia's Royal Hohenzollern House Order, Knight's Cross with Swords and Waldeck's Merit Cross 3rd Class with Swords, while Windisch was awarded the Prussian Crown Order 4th Class with Swords and Waldeck's Honor Cross with Swords. That these decorations hang from their tunic buttonholes in S401 is an indication that they were recently bestowed. Though their service records list 5 October as the official award date, the *Kaiser* actually pinned his awards on them two days later on 7 October. The Saxon St. Henry Medal in Silver given to Windisch on 18 October does not appear in S401, so the image was probably taken during the earlier part of 7-18 October. Allowing three weeks for preparation of the card results in a publication spread of late October to mid-November, the period crossed by Guideline 1. We can at least be certain that S401 did not come out any later than one example postmarked 22 November.

Oblt. Rudolf Berthold's *Pour le Mérite* award was celebrated in S402 by adding a drawing of it to a snapshot taken months earlier. A close look at the photo shows that Berthold is sitting in the same chair and location depicted in Frankl's S384. We have already ascertained that Frankl's picture was taken 12-26 August 1916. The fact that Berthold is not wearing any sign of the Royal Hohenzollern House Order, Knight's Cross with Swords given to him on 27 August further suggests that S402 was taken around or at the same time as S384. We have independent verification that the location was Vaux, because the chair that Berthold and Frankl used appears once again in a group photo taken there between 21 July and 12 August 1916 (see S381, S384).[2] Clearly, S402's photo was taken before *KEK Vaux* moved to Roupy on 1 September. The *Pour le Mérite*'s addition to S402 dates the card's publication to sometime after Berthold's receipt of the award on 12 October. Our three-week rule yields an earliest publication date of 2 November that coincides with our guideline's projection.

S403 is a drawing of a German airplane dropping pine boughs and Christmas wishes to a peaceful hamlet below. Even though it does not feature a famous aviator, it is mentioned here because its subject matter supports the November to December period ascribed to the Sanke cards falling on either side of it. Numerous postcards celebrating Christmas during the war years testify that they were issued in November in anticipation of the holiday. Given the 2 December postmark date of the S408 example that follows, it seems that S403 was no exception.

S408 is a compilation of prior Sanke photos honoring the first 10 recipients of the *Pour le Mérite* and the famous duo, Cossel and Windisch. Berthold's *Pour le Mérite* award date of 12 October 1916 represents the latest event among them. *Lt.* Gustav Leffers, who received his *Pour le Mérite* on 5 November, does not appear on S408 even though he had been featured in the earlier S372. This indicates that the process for the card began sometime during the period 13 October to 5 November, giving us a theoretical publication spread of 3-26 November. This and a postmarked example of S408 dated 2 December comply with Guideline 1's prediction of a late November issuance.

Lastly, we come to S409: Boelcke's black-bordered death card that features his S363 portrait above an elegiac poem. Going forward three weeks from his death on 28 October 1916 results in an earliest publication date of 18 November. It is possible that the card came out earlier than that because it used a picture already in Sanke's possession. This seems to have been the case for Boelcke's S363†, where we have a postmarked example dated 14 November 1916. Conversely, it could have taken additional time to prepare the poem, so we may again be closer to the latter half of November. At any rate, we have an example of S409 postmarked 27 November 1916 that proves it was no later than then.

The Sanke Series Guidelines – Guideline 2

Correlating event and postmark dates for S381 and S413 provided solid anchors for the establishment of publication Guideline 1. A similar nexus occurs in the form of Manfred von Richthofen's S450. We have already seen how an early February 1917 trip to Berlin was the only opportunity for C.J. von Dühren to have taken the Richthofen portraits displayed in S450 and MVR1, and how Richthofen himself dedicated MVR1 to a family member or friend on 22 February 1917. It is therefore possible, in accordance with our three-week rule that S450 could have first emerged in early March 1917. A recent discovery – an S450 example carrying a message dated 10 March 1917 – is the earliest sample encountered to date and appears to offer further validation of our three-week rule. We can now establish Guideline 2 by connecting S413 to S450 and testing the suitability of the publication dates predicted for the cards falling in between.

S416 portrays *Lt.* Albert Dossenbach and the *Pour le Mérite* he received on 11 November 1916. The first two-seater pilot to win the award, he is wearing all the decorations he had received up to that point, but not the particularly noteworthy one that followed on 9 December: the Military Karl Friedrich Merit Order, Knight's Cross. This was his native Baden's premier decoration and it was awarded to only seven other aviation officers during the war. Its absence establishes the picture's origin to sometime between 11 November and 8 December. S416 would have appeared no earlier than three weeks later between 2 and 29 December, right where Guideline 2 is situated.

In S423, *Oblt.* Rudolf Berthold displays all his decorations including the *Pour le Mérite* awarded to him on 10 October 1916. His appearance is the same in BERTHOLD4 (see S423), a photo taken during a visit to his old unit, *Feldflieger-Abteilung 23*, at their Vaux airfield (they had remained there when their fighter detachment, *KEK Vaux*, had been detached and transferred to Roupy in September 1916). His particularly dark tunic, ribbon bar, white cuffs, and white collar match, as do the distinct bends in his shoulder boards and the chain bracelet on his left wrist. It is therefore likely that they were taken around the same time. A duty board that is discernible in BERTHOLD4's background records the date of his visit as 17 December 1916, so in this instance we know the exact date and location for a photograph. Three weeks later brings us to 7 January 1917, precisely the time that Guideline 2 indicates.

S425 and S426 portray *Oblt.* Hans Berr and the *Pour le Mérite* he received on 4 December 1916. BERR1 (see S426) is a photograph probably taken at the same sitting that was published in the 14 January 1917 edition of *Berliner Illustrirte Zeitung*. It seems likely then that the pictures were snapped during the early part of Berr's leave home, which began on 2 January 1917 and lasted one month. This in turn yields a projected publication period of late January to late February 1917 – very near the time that Guideline 2 indicates.

Sanke took a break from his pilot portraits and published seven pictures of German aircraft in the series S435-41. Two of them, S435 (DFW biplane) and S439 (Rumpler biplane) have been discovered with respective postmarks of 6 March and 8 March 1917. The fact that the prior Berr S425-26 could not have been published before the last half of February places an early limit on S435's and S439's appearances. Our guideline predicts their debut occurred somewhere in between.

After compiling seven victories with *Jasta 4* – three of them in one day on 9 November 1916 – two prestigious awards were bestowed on *Lt.* Fritz Otto Bernert. The first was Saxony's Albert Order Knight 2nd Class with Swords which was awarded on 5 January 1917. The second, Prussia's Royal Hohenzollern House Order, Knight's Cross with Swords, came to him on 25 January 1917. Bernert can be seen wearing them both in S442 and S443, but they are represented in two different ways. S442 has them fully displayed on his medals bar while S443 shows only their ribbons attached to his tunic's buttonhole. A closer examination of S443 discloses that those ribbons were in fact drawn in (e.g., under magnification, his button actually peeks through the ribbon drawn over it!), and that the tunic loops that held his *Grossordenschnalle* in S442 are visible but empty. This is curious because there is little doubt that S442 and S443 were taken at the same time. Despite being superficially differentiated by light and dark backgrounds, both display the same wicker chair and the same outfit worn by Bernert. Apart from the medals bar, all his other accoutrements are identical, even down to the leather gloves and creases in his service cap. The 25 February 1917 edition of *Berliner Illustrirte Zeitung* repeats S443, complete with drawn-in ribbons. Therefore, it appears that Bernert wore his *Grossordenschnalle* in one photograph and not in the other for some now unknown reason.[3] Someone later corrected this omission by adding his decorations back in ribbon form to S443. Both S442 and S443 can be dated to sometime between the award of his Saxon Albert Order, 25 January, and S443's publication in *Berliner Illustrirte Zeitung,* 25 February. Our three-week rule results in a publication timeframe of 15 February to 18 March 1917. The 10 March date for one postmarked example of the later S450 dictates that S442-43 could not have come out any later than that, so the timeframe is modified to 15 February-10 March, a span traversed by our predictive timeline.

While recuperating from a serious stomach wound that he had received in combat on 26 December 1916, *Vzfw.* Hans Müller became

a commissioned officer on 14 January 1917. S446-47 depict the recovered *Leutnant* during a visit to R. Dührkoop's studio in Berlin. Judging by his apparently fit condition, these photographs would not have been taken before February, which in turn means that S446-47's earliest appearance would have been in late February. S450's 10 March 1917 postmark establishes an outer limit for the pair, and Guideline 2 once again splits the difference.

The Sanke Series Guidelines – The Gap

This brings us to a mystery that has long plagued Sanke card students. The next card to follow *Lt.* Hermann Pfeifer's S451 is *Lt.* Erwin Böhme's S502. That is, a numerical gap of exactly 50 cards exists in the series where there are no extant examples of any Sanke postcards numbered S452 to S501. The reason for this gap is not known, but we now have evidence that it may have been more than just numerical. We predicted an early March 1917 debut for Manfred von Richthofen's S450 that was confirmed by a postmarked example sent on 10 March 1917. We also determined that the photograph for Erwin Böhme's S502 (just two cards later) was taken between 18 and 31 March 1917 and that the earliest it could have appeared in Sanke card form would have been mid-April – at least a full month after our postmarked S450. It seems improbable that this separation is a function of S450 representing the last of March's offerings and S502 the beginning of April's, because it seems fairly clear that S503-13 made their initial appearances in late April to May. Therefore, the spaced timing of S450 and S502, which fall on either side of a numerical gap of 50 cards, may reflect an actual interruption in publication schedule as well. As cautioned earlier, we should not rely too heavily on the precision of a set of predictive guidelines that could very well represent the average of what may have been a non-linear or inconsistent publication pattern. Still, the evidence for S452-501's numerical gap coinciding with some kind of time interruption seems conclusive. A portion of our mystery nevertheless remains unsolved: we still cannot adequately explain why Sanke simply did not numerically pick up from where he left off – that is, just continue on with a "452" despite any break in his publication timeline.

The Sanke Series Guidelines – Guideline 3

Lt. Erwin Böhme's 21 March 1917 letter to his fiancée helped us pinpoint S502's portrait date to between 18 and 31 March 1917 (see p.38). This would yield an earliest publication timeframe of 8-21 April that is supported by one example of the next card, Richthofen's S503, dated 26 April. Without a postmarked S502 as confirmation however, we must turn to the "Bloody April" series running from *Lt.* Otto Brauneck's S508 through *Lt.* Kurt Wolff's S513 to help reestablish our timeline. Their photographs probably originated during a 20-26 April 1917 timeframe, which would assign them a theoretically earliest publication range of 11-17 May. An autographed example of S508 postmarked 30 May 1917, as well as several authentic autographed S512 examples that must have been signed before Schaefer's death on 5 June, lend corroborative support to this range.

We find another anchor in the form of *Lt.* Carl Allmenröder's S543. Allmenröder was awarded the *Pour le Mérite* on 14 June 1917, and S543 clearly recognized this by adding a drawing of the decoration to an older photo. The postcard therefore came out after the announcement. We have a postmarked example dated 27 June 1917, which proves that Sanke on at least one occasion was able to publish a card within two weeks of a known event.

Connecting the S508-13 series to Allmenröder's S543 produces Guideline 3. Guideline 3's slope is slightly steeper than Guideline 2's, which in turn is just a little greater than Guideline 1's – a possible indication that Sanke's publication pace accelerated as the war progressed.

Evidence supporting the May publication of *Lt.* Werner Voss' S506 was presented on p.38. Its picture was snapped while Voss was home on leave in April following his receipt of the *Pour le Mérite* earlier that month. It would not have emerged later than the S508-13 "Bloody April" series from which one 30 May 1917 postmarked example has survived. This information helps corroborate Guideline 3, which is positioned in the early part of May.

Lt. Walter Göttsch shot down a British RE.8 near Amiens for his 20th victory on 10 April 1918. Normally, this would have brought him the *Pour le Mérite*, but in this instance the RE.8 put in a telling burst of its own and both victor and vanquished tumbled from the sky. Göttsch's chance to win the *Pour le Mérite* (a decoration that was not bestowed posthumously) was extinguished along with his life. S518 shows Göttsch about a year earlier when he was still an *Offizier-Stellvertreter*. Exactly when he was promoted to *Leutnant* is somewhat of a mystery. Franks, Bailey, and Guest (*Above the Lines*, p.118) states that Göttsch "returned in April as a Lieutenant," but the later Franks, Bailey, and Duiven (*Jasta War Chronology*, p. 56) ranks him as an *Offizier-Stellvertreter* up through his 11th victory on 4 May. The *Nachrichtenblatt der Luftstreitkräfte* also identifies him as an *Offizier-Stellvertreter* when it reports his 12th score on 5 May.[4] It is only by the time of his 13th on 17 July that all sources finally agree that he had become a *Leutnant*. If Göttsch had been promoted in late April, we would expect any card issued after that to have referred to him as *Leutnant*. But if his promotion came in later May or even June, S518 could still have identified him as an *Offizier-Stellvertreter* and Guideline 3's prediction of a late May publication date would be correct. We at least know that it came out no later than one example dated 24 June. Final verification will perhaps occur if and when Göttsch's promotion date is finally established, or if an earlier postmarked example is discovered.

The records state that *Lt.* Otto Bernert was granted his *Pour le Mérite* on 23 April 1917, even though the victory list recited by Franks, Bailey, and Guest (*Above the Lines*, p. 70) shows that he was one short of the usual 20 plane requirement.[5] No matter, because the very next day his record five enemy planes shot down in a single engagement would answer any doubts about his qualification. S521 shows him with the medal at his neck, so its image clearly originated after he had been decorated. Three weeks from his award produces an early limit of mid-May for S521, whereas the 27 June postmarked example of the later Allmenröder S543 provides an outer limit. Guideline 3 indicates that S521 was issued in the first part of this range around the beginning of June 1917.

Only one pilot amassed a better record than Manfred von Richthofen's 21 victories during "Bloody April" 1917, and that was *Lt.* Kurt Wolff with 22. Wolff, along with Karl-Emil Schaefer and Carl Allmenröder, were Richthofen's star pupils in *Jasta 11*. By June 1917, they were Germany's fourth, fifth and sixth ranked aces respectively, each having gained 30 or more victories as well as the *Pour le Mérite*. Kurt Wolff's S522-23 photos were unquestionably taken after his *Pour le Mérite* award on 4 May 1917 because they include his decoration. Wolff was named *Staffelführer* of *Jasta 29* two days later on 6 May, and gained his 30th victory on 13 May – both of which indicate that he remained at the Front for a short time after his award. After this, there is a gap in his scoring record up until 27 June. Like Voss (see p.38), Gontermann, Udet, and others, this gap is a strong indication that Wolff was away from the Front on several weeks' leave that had been granted as part of his reward.[6] It is likely then that S522-23's photos were taken during this period. Adding three weeks to the theoretical start of his leave brings us to 4 June, and the 27 June example of Allmenröder's later S543 cements the establishment of S522-23's June debut. Guideline 3 points to the beginning of the month.

Lt. Lothar von Richthofen won his *Pour le Mérite* on 14 May 1917 after having served as a fighter pilot for only a little less than 10 weeks – a remarkable achievement that was never matched by any other German pilot, including his famous older brother.[7] Lothar had been shot down and wounded the day before, and was convalescing in a Douai hospital when he learned of the award. It would be some time before a picture could be taken of a recovered Lothar wearing the elite decoration, so Sanke added a drawing of it to an older photograph to create S526. Going forward three weeks from his award date brings us to 4 June, almost exactly where Guideline 3 rests.

Lt. Heinrich Gontermann gained his *Pour le Mérite* on 14 May 1917 as well, was granted one month's leave, and returned to the Front on 19 June. The photographs in S527-29 were taken during this period because they include his new decoration and are attributed to Nicola Perscheid's Berlin studio (Manfred von Richthofen's S532-34 were taken around this time at the same studio). Three weeks later gives us a range of 4 June to 10 July for their earliest publication, yet the 27 June example of Allmenröder's S543 forces this back to June alone. A handwritten note on the back of one surviving copy of S529 reads: "*Lt. Heinrich Gontermann schoss bisher (Juli 17) 23 feindl. Flugzeuge ab und wurde mit dem* Pour le Merite *ausgezeichnet.*" ("Second Lieutenant Heinrich Gontermann up to now (July 1917) has shot down 23 enemy aircraft and has been awarded the *Pour le Merite*"). Gontermann bagged his 23rd on 27 June and his 24th on 16 July, so the card appears to have been written in the first half of July.[8] Guideline 3 projects that S527-29 were issued in the early part of June, about a month before.

Evidence has already been presented that Manfred von Richthofen's S532-34 photos came from a visit to Nicola Perscheid's Berlin studio sometime during 15-18 May 1917 (see p.30). Our three-week rule would place their earliest publication at 5-8 June, just a few days before Guideline 3's prediction.

On 13 June 1917, *Hptm.* Ernst Brandenburg led 17 Gotha G.IV aircraft from *Kampfgeschwader 3* to conduct the first heavier-than-air bombing raid over London. After inflicting heavy damage, and despite almost 100 sorties by responding British fighters, all the bombers under his command were brought back safely. In recognition of this feat, Brandenburg was awarded the *Pour le Mérite* the very next day on 14 June 1917. While returning from the award ceremony on 19 June, his airplane crashed and he was seriously injured, suffering the loss of one of his legs. Understandably, photos of him actually wearing the decoration would have been difficult to obtain at this time, so Sanke took two earlier pictures of Brandenburg and added *Pour le Mérite* drawings to them to create S536 and S541. According to our three-week rule, their earliest publication would have been early July; yet Guideline 3 indicates a June debut within a week or two of his award. When we recall what we observed regarding the delay usually experienced in publishing news events and photographs, such an appearance within a week of his award would have been exceptionally fast. We can reconcile this by deducing that like S508-13, S536 through S543 were not issued individually; rather, they came out together as a block offering in very late June. There are other reasons to suspect this, because Brandenburg and Allmenröder shared the same *Pour le Mérite* award date and drawn-in decorations on their postcards. Brandenburg's S536 and Allmenröder's S543 therefore provide evidence that Sanke may have issued his postcards in groups as opposed to the gradual publication of individual cards. They also demonstrate that Sanke could occasionally issue postcards close to two weeks after an event – at least in cases where he had an older picture that he could modify to suit his needs.

The Sanke Series Guidelines – Before Guideline 1

Now that we have a better understanding of the nature of Sanke's work when he was in relatively full gear, we can take a step back and look at the more intermittent publication of those cards that immediately preceded Guideline 1's initial anchor, Höhndorf's S381. *Hptm.* Hans-Joachim Buddecke is featured in S371. His fighting career began with *Feldflieger-Abteilung 23* on the Western Front, where he attained three victories in the fall of 1915. In December he was sent to Turkey to fly a Fokker *Eindecker* fighter with Ottoman *Feldflieger-Abteilung 6*. He was officially credited with four more victories in January 1916 – a most impressive feat considering the comparatively crude conditions and smaller number of combat aircraft in the Turkish theater at the time. Unofficially, he was said to have shot down an incredible total of nine more enemy aircraft by the end of January. Whatever the actual count, Buddecke was recalled to Germany to enjoy a well-deserved leave at home. He was awarded the *Pour le Mérite* on 14 April 1916, and S371 shows him wearing the decoration at the collar of his Turkish military uniform. Theoretically, S371 could have had an earliest publication date of early May – three weeks after Buddecke's *Pour le Mérite* award. Yet S373, just two cards later, could not have appeared any earlier than June because of its reference to Boelcke only as *Hauptmann* (promoted 21 May 1916). Though this could be evidence of a publication gap similar to that seen between S451 and S502, all we can firmly conclude is that S371's publication occurred sometime between mid-May and mid-June. *Lt.* Kurt Wintgens' S378 offers additional testimony. Wintgens, silhouetted against a black background, is wearing the *Pour le Mérite* awarded to him on 1 July 1916, but not the Saxon Albert Order Knight 2nd Class awarded 19 July. The same picture, but with its original outdoor backdrop, appeared in the 23 July 1916 edition of *Berliner Illustrirte Zeitung*. Both point to an earliest S378 publication date of late July to early August, i.e., three weeks after 1-18 July. S378's immediate predecessor, S377, probably came out about two to three weeks after Immelmann's death on 16 June 1916. If we draw a line from Höhndorf's S381 to a theoretical mid-May date for Buddecke's S371, mid-July is predicted for the publication of Wintgens' S378 – a date too early for what we have otherwise surmised. Yet if we draw a line (see Guideline A) from Höhndorf's S381 to the 25 June postmark for Buddecke's S371, it coincides with the late July to mid-August projection for S378. So far, no postmark earlier than 25 June 1916 has been found for S371.

S380 depicts *Lt.* Otto Parschau shortly after his receipt of his *Pour le Mérite* on 10 July 1916. The photo must have been taken 10-20 July because he was killed in action only 11 days later on 21 July. Our line projects S380's earliest appearance to have been the latter part of August, about four weeks after his demise.

The Sanke Series Guidelines – An Exception that Proves the Rule?

We have established what seems to be a fairly reliable system for predicting when the various postcards in Sanke's airmen series were first published. Before moving on to the detailed examination of

cards S340-543, we should ask if there any instances where that system fails. The answer is yes, in the case of S444.

S444 is a portrait of Max Müller, the diminutive Bavarian who, in company with Manfred von Richthofen and Erwin Böhme, was one of the founding members of Boelcke's *Jasta 2*. Guideline 2 projects that S444 first appeared in February 1917. The problem is that S444 identifies Müller as a *Leutnant*, and his promotion to that rank indisputably occurred on 25 August 1917 – about six months later. S444 came from MÜLLER1, a photo that originally depicted Müller in the guise of an *Offizier-Stellvertreter*.[9] Someone touched up that photo to ensure that S444 conformed to Müller's new rank: his non-commissioned officer (NCO) collar insignia were blanked out to represent an officer's stand-up collar, and his field-gray, tress-trimmed NCO shoulder boards were converted into an officer's metal cord pattern. To further confuse things, N6271, NPG's version of MÜLLER1, altered the original photo in a similar but different manner. N6271 also changed his shoulder boards into a metal cord pattern; but instead of blanking out his collar completely, it added officer's *Litzen* (braid) there and to his left sleeve (but not the right!). Finally, a crudely drawn *Pour le Mérite* was added in recognition of its award to him on 3 September 1917. There can be no question that these cards were issued after his promotion on 25 August, and at least one of them after his *Pour le Mérite* award a short while later. Nevertheless, we have enough examples of postcards before and after S444 whose postmarks pre-date his promotion to prove that S444 was for some reason produced out of sequence. Was it a later version, similar to those seen for Schaefer's S507 or Bolle's S657? Unlike those two, an example of S444's "earlier" version has yet to be discovered. Müller's later series, S552-53, employs two images taken at the same sitting as S444's, and they display the same modifications to reflect his officer's rank. Was S444 supposed to have been S554, the next card in the series, but fell prey to a typographical error? But then, where was the real S444 that would have preceded it? Was S444 a number that had initially gone unused until someone finally decided to fill the void? Müller's S444 presents a mystery that might never be solved.

The Sanke Series Guidelines – Conclusions

The first step we took in attempting to determine Sanke's publication sequence was to establish several cards as anchor points where known, dateable events corresponded to postmark evidence. Connecting those anchors created guidelines that were tested and validated by our knowledge of several of the other cards that they fell across. If these guidelines are accepted as reliable indicators of Sanke's publication chronology, we can then reverse the process and use their path to help us determine when many of the remaining postcards' photographs were taken and why they were published. With this in mind, we can proceed with our examination of Sanke's series on an individual, card-by-card basis.

Notes

[1] Wintgens had earned his *Pour le Mérite* while serving with *KEK Falkenhausen*. He was then transferred to either *KEK Vaux* (see Franks, Bailey, and Guest, *Above the Lines*, p.231) or *KEK Bertincourt* (see O'Connor, *Aviation Awards VII*, p.429) later the same month.

[2] Althaus is shown with his *Pour le Mérite*, awarded 21 July, while Frankl is without his, awarded 12 August. Therefore, it is believed the picture was taken sometime in between.

[3] A close look at S442 shows that though the medals themselves were slightly touched up by someone, the ribbons were not. L7826's rendition of the same photo is more faithful and portrays the untouched medals, so they are completely authentic and the medals bar was not added later.

[4] See OTF 16:3, p.275 for a translation of *Nachrichtenblatt der Luftstreitkräfte No.15*. The *Nachrichtenblatt* is not always reliable either, for it calls Göttsch an *Offizier-Stellvertreter* on 3 May, a *Vizefeldwebel* on 4 May, and an *Offizier-Stellvertreter* again on 5 May.

[5] For further details, see the discussion of Bernert's S521.

[6] Wolff's 22 downed aircraft in April 1917 established a record that remains the best for all German pilots during any month of the war. Wolff continued his streak and downed two more aircraft on 1 May and a third on 13 May after he joined *Jasta 29* at Juniville. As noted, he would not score again until 27 June, but then gained two more victories on 6 and 7 July before being wounded and put out of action on 11 July. During this gap, three pilots from his *Jasta 29* scored on 15 May, 30 May, and 1 June before the squadron moved to another sector on 21 June. Three pilots from *Jasta 9* (Hermann Pfeifer, Heinrich Kroll, and Otto von Breiten-Landenberg), stationed only 11 miles away at Leffincourt, brought down five aircraft on 14, 19, 20, and 25 May.

Jasta 14, located at nearby Marchais, reported six victories by three of its pilots (Hans Bowski, Josef Veltjens, and Otto Gerbig) on 29, 31 May and 1, 2, 3, 15 June. So it does not appear that Wolff's scoring gap was attributable to either bad weather or a lack of enemy activity in the region.

[7] Hans Kirschstein came the closest. His first assignment as a fighter pilot was with *Jasta 6* on 13 March 1918, and just under 14 weeks later, he received the *Pour le Mérite* on 24 June.

[8] The same writer later made (with a different pencil) two additional entries on the back:

" *6. Aug.1917 25. Sieg*"
"*18. " " den 13. u. 14. feindl. Fesselballon*"

" 6 August 1917, 25th victory"
"18 August 1917, the 13th and 14th enemy balloon"

Each of the dates is late by one day when compared to Gontermann's official record. Otherwise, the information is accurate.

[9] The decorations on his medals bar also verify that the photo was taken when he was an *Offizier-Stellvertreter*. He is wearing the Bavarian Prince-Regent Luitpold Medal in Bronze (prewar award), Iron Cross 2nd Class (awarded 13 September 1914), Bavarian Military Merit Cross, 3rd Class with Crown and Swords (14 January 1915), Iron Cross 1st Class (27 April 1915), Bavarian Bravery Medal in Silver (18 February 1916) and Bavarian Long Service Medal, 9 years (1916, since he joined the army in 1907), but not any of the decorations he won after 1916.

SANKE CARDS S340-S543

Key to Abbreviations

AH	Austria-Hungary
Anh	Anhalt
Bad	Baden
Bav	Bavaria
BH	buttonhole; ribbon worn in tunic buttonhole
Brun	Brunswick
Ham	Hamburg
Hes	Hesse
Lüb	Lübeck
MB	medals bar; decoration on *Grossordenschnalle*
Meck-Sch	Mecklenburg-Schwerin
Old	Oldenburg
Ott	Ottoman Empire
Publ	published
RB	ribbon bar; ribbon on *Feldschnalle*
Sax	Saxony
Sax-Weim	Saxe-Weimar
SCG	Saxe-Coburg and Gotha
Sch-L	Schaumburg-Lippe
SD	Saxon Duchies
Wald	Waldeck
WR	wearing; decoration worn separately on tunic
Würt	Württemberg
/ Sw	with Swords

Note: All decorations without a particular designation after them are Prussian.

S340
IMMELMANN
Max
Leutnant

Taken: 2 August to 9 September 1915
Douai/Lille
Publ: December 1915 to January 1916
Reason: victory score

Decorations:
WR: Iron Cross, 1st Class
MB: None
RB: None
BH: None

Other Cards:
S342, S347, S360-62, S364, S373, S377, S408, S610
(L7705, L7713, L7716-20, L7793; N5613-14, N5632, N5690, N6004)
Note: Immelmann is not wearing his Pilot's Badge

Key Dates:

1 Aug 1915	victory #1
2 Aug 1915	awarded Iron Cross 1st Class
10 Sep 1915	awarded Albert Order, Knight 2nd Class/ Sw (Sax)
15 Dec 1915	victory #7
16 Jan 1916	photo of victory #7 published in *Berliner Illustrirte Zeitung* 3, p.32

S340 was the direct descendant of IMMEL1 and IMMEL2. Both predecessors display a telltale tapestry as S340's original backdrop and therefore confirm Lille or Douai as their location (the tapestry's significance is discussed in detail on pp.10-12). Significantly, Immelmann's only decoration in the photos is a prominently displayed Iron Cross 1st Class. There is no sign of the Iron Cross 2nd Class that preceded it, nor is he wearing his Pilot's Badge. Immelmann was given the Iron Cross 1st Class on 2 August 1915, the day after his first victory. Dr. Ernst Sieverts, who served with Immelmann in *Feldflieger-Abteilung 62*, recalled: "He loved to have himself photographed each time he got a new medal." (O'Connor, *Aviation Awards VI*, p.376) Immelmann indeed expressed how pleased he was with his latest decoration:

> "Yesterday I received the First Class of the Iron Cross as a mark of distinction. So now I have the nicest decoration any young officer can get." (Immelmann, *Eagle of Lille*, p.120)

The picture was taken sometime between 2 August 1915, when he received his Iron Cross, and 10 September 1915, the date of his next award, the Saxon Albert Order (which he is not wearing). Dr. Sieverts' observation makes it likely that it was taken soon after 2 August in celebration of "the nicest decoration any young officer can get."

We have already established the usual publication pattern for photographs of a particular event. That is, they generally appeared three to four weeks afterward in newspapers and similarly took three weeks or more to come out in the form of a Sanke postcard. S340 was closely followed by S342 – a picture of Immelmann beside his seventh victim, brought down on 15 December 1915. A slightly different picture of the same scene was published in the 16 January 1916 edition of *Berliner Illustrirte Zeitung*. This, according to the publication pattern noted above, was around the time that S342 could have made its earliest appearance. The implication is that S340, which would have come out a little earlier by virtue of its number, perhaps

debuted in early January 1916. On the other hand, though S340 faithfully copies IMMEL2's signature and handwritten rank, it does not repeat IMMEL2's 1915 date – nor does it include the 1916 date seen on the later version of S340 that was issued after Immelmann's promotion to *Oberleutnant* in April. We might construe this as signifying that S340's *Leutnant* version was first published in late 1915, when "1915" would have been inappropriate so close to the upcoming new year and "1916" would have been premature. A publication timeframe of December 1915 to January 1916 covers both possibilities.

We might also consider that S340 was issued as a direct result of Immelmann's receipt of the *Pour le Mérite* on 12 January 1916. That is, this older image was used to acknowledge the event pending the availability of photos of him actually wearing the decoration. This would move S340's publication date out to February 1916. At least three things, however, argue against this. First, we know from their personal letters that both Immelmann and Boelcke had been receiving a great deal of attention from the press in 1915 (e.g., see the excerpts printed on p.13). There is no reason to believe that Sanke would have lagged behind his associates and competitors and delayed the publication of an available Immelmann picture into February 1916. It should also be noted that S340 followed closely upon S338, a card featuring Anthony Fokker and the *Eindecker* airplane that Immelmann and Boelcke were making famous in late 1915. Second, IMMEL2 is proof that a postcard of Immelmann was already in use in 1915 – before his receipt of the *Pour le Mérite* – whose photo served as the basis of Sanke's S340. Third, Boelcke's S363 exists in both *Leutnant* and *Oberleutnant* versions. Our examination of S363 notes that Boelcke was promoted in late January or early February 1916, and that S363-*Lt.* therefore must have been issued before that time. If S340 had come out in February, then all the cards from S340 to Boelcke's S363-*Lt.* would have to have been February publications as well.[1]

Note

[1] Examples of S340, S342-43, S345, S347-50, S353-55, S357, and S359-63 have been observed and catalogued by collectors. Seven cards (i.e., S341, S344, S346, S351, S352, S356, and S358) remain unaccounted for and we do not know their subjects. In fact, we cannot be certain that cards with those numbers ever existed.

A print of the original photograph that served as the basis of *Lt.* Max Immelmann's S340. Similar to BOELCKE1-2, it may have been taken soon after Immelmann's first victory and his subsequent receipt of the Iron Cross 1st Class on 2 August 1915.

A postcard of *Lt.* Max Immelmann published in 1915 by Emil Richter of Oschatz, Saxony. Richter sometimes used the flag with the "E-R-O" letters seen at the bottom left as his mark.

S340
(reissue)
IMMELMANN
Max
Oberleutnant

Taken: 2 August to 9 September 1915
Douai/Lille
Publ: May 1916
Reason: promotion

Decorations:
WR: Iron Cross, 1st Class
MB: None
RB: None
BH: None

Other Cards:
S342, S347, S360-62, S364, S373, S377, S408, S610
(L7705, L7713, L7716-20, L7793; N5613-14, N5632, N5690, N6004)
Note: Immelmann not wearing Pilot's Badge

Key Dates:
18 Apr 1916	promoted to *Oberleutnant*
18 Jun 1916	killed in action

In April 1912, Max Immelmann resigned from *Eisenbahn-Regiment Nr.2* to study mechanical engineering at Dresden's Technical University. With this act, his formal military career seemed to have come to a close and he automatically became a member of the military reserves. When the war began, he reenlisted but retained his status as an ensign in the reserves until he was promoted to *Leutnant der Reserve* on 15 July 1915. By the end of March 1916, Immelmann – now a famous combat pilot – had reconsidered his military future:

"When I began to get known, the determination to remain an officer-pilot after the war matured within me gradually, and it was partly based on purely superficial reasons. The more known I became, the more I liked the idea. When I was with the Crown Prince of Saxony, we came to speak on that point. He showed visible pleasure when I said I was contemplating the idea of applying for reinstatement on the active list and told me my commission would certainly be well ante dated. So I made my application and lo! it was granted only 18 days after I sent it in, and I was promoted from subaltern to [first] lieutenant. The King is said to have been counting on my application and to have remarked:'Of course we'll make him a full lieutenant at once!' So now I have re-entered the ranks of my former comrades…Then we had a bit of a festivity in the mess that evening. To celebrate my promotion, they engaged a band, which played all through the meal. Hundreds of soldiers stood in the street and listened. Naturally they also ascertained the reason of the serenade. Then they all shouted enthusiastically: 'Immelmann, Hurrah! Hurrah! Hurrah!' After that we sang the airmen's march and 'Deutschland über alles'. When the strains of the latter died away, I called for three cheers for His Majesty, in which hundreds of male voices joined enthusiastically. Altogether it was a happy occasion." (Immelmann, *Eagle of Lille*, pp.192-93)

Following Immelmann's promotion to *Oberleutnant* on 18 April 1916, Sanke released a new version of S340. A simple repeat of S340 may have been performed quickly, but the inscription at the bottom of S340-*Oblt.* is different: the facsimile signature is not the same and it is accompanied by Immelmann's new rank and the year "1916" in his own handwriting. It likely took a little longer to obtain this updated inscription, so S340-*Oblt.* probably followed the usual three-week pattern and was first published in May 1916. A postmarked example of Immelmann's S362-*Oblt.* dated 20 May 1916 supports this conclusion. In the absence of any direct confirmation from a postmarked S340 however, it should be noted that S340-*Oblt.* technically could have emerged at any point up to or around Immelmann's death on 18 June. We can be fairly certain that its initial appearance was no later than that because it is not marked with a "†" or a black border as seen in Immelmann's S361† or Boelcke's S363†.

Above: *Offz-Stv.* Max Immelmann in an *FFA 62* LVG C.I airplane that might be C.162/15 – the aircraft that squadron-mate *Lt.* Oswald Boelcke was flying when he and his observer, *Lt.* Heinz-Hellmuth von Wühlisch, gained their first victory on 4 July 1915. Three days later, Boelcke switched to the unit's first Fokker *Eindecker* and his former C.I aircraft was passed on to Immelmann. Immelmann flew it up until just before his first combat (and victory) in a Fokker *Eindecker* on 1 August 1915 (see Immelmann, *Eagle of Lille*, pp.106-16 and Werner, *Knight of Germany*, pp.108-15).

Right: *Lt.* Max Immelmann in late summer 1915. He is wearing the Iron Cross 1st Class (awarded 2 August 1915) and ribbons for two prior decorations (Iron Cross 2nd Class, Saxony's Friedrich August Medal in Silver), but not the Albert Order, Knight 2nd Class that he received on 10 September 1915.

S342
IMMELMANN
Max
Leutnant

Taken: 15 December 1915
Valenciennes
Publ: January 1916
Reason: victory score

Decorations:
WR: None
MB: None
RB: None
BH: Royal Hohenzollern House Order, Knight's Cross/ Sw

Other Cards:
S340, S347, S360-62, S364, S373, S377, S408, S610
(L7705, L7713, L7716-20, L7793; N5613-14, N5632, N5690,
N6004)
Note: postcard also issued without a number

Key Dates:
9-11 Nov 1915	awarded Royal Hohenzollern House Order, Knight's Cross/ Sw
15 Dec 1915	victory #7
16 Jan 1916	similar photo of victory #7 published in *Berliner Illustrirte Zeitung* 3, p.32

This is one of the relatively rare instances where we know the actual day that a Sanke card photograph was taken. S342 shows Immelmann standing next to the collected remains of his seventh victim. In a long letter home, dated 20 December, Immelmann described the fight:

"The next day it was fairly foggy. The clouds appeared to hang pretty low. But you can never trust an Englishman, and so I took off in spite of the uncertain weather. It was fairly dark when I started, but half an hour later it was quite bright. I was up to about 200 metres when I saw the flashes of bursting shells or shrapnel in the far distance. They came from the direction of Lille, and the flare of the bursting shells stood out quite clearly against the dark sky. So off I went to Lille. When I was 10 kilometres away from the town I saw the enemy high above me to northward and on my right. I was only 1,200 metres up then, and he was 2,800, so that I was not able to attack him at the moment.

I am making you a little sketch of my pursuit. If you have a map, you will be able to follow it more exactly. I am sketching the whole thing from memory, so I make no claim to accuracy.

When he saw me, he did not fly southward, as was probably his original intention, but bore away from me in an eastward direction. I went into a turn and flew alongside him, although still much lower. He tried to reach the salvation of the lines by a right hand turn. I promptly flew towards him, although still somewhat lower and so unable to attack. I had climbed to 2,600 by then, but he was at 2,800. The feint attack I made on him misled him into abandoning his westward course and flying further south-east. Again he tried to reach his lines, but with a similar lack of result.

Now we were both at the same height, but I nevertheless let my machine climb a bit more. He did the opposite, for he put his machine down and thus obtained such a great speed that he almost disappeared from my view. I could only see him as a faint grey smudge on the distant horizon. He certainly hoped I had lost him, because he went into a right hand turn and headed for Douai.

Leutnant Immelmann
an den Trümmern eines von ihm abgeschossenen engl. Eindeckers.

I was now 3,200 metres up, while he might have been 2,600-2,700. As his line of flight was now about perpendicular to my own, my greater height enabled me to approach him at very fast speed. When we were still 500-600 metres apart, he opened a furious fire on me. The distance was too great for him to have any chance to succeed. He fired at least 500 rounds while I was coming up from 500-150 metres of him.

Then I too began to shoot. First I gave him a series of 40 rounds. The enemy flew gaily on; why not? Now there was only 100 metres between us, then 80 and finally 50. I saw the enemy observer fiddling at his machine gun. Probably he had a jam.

I had to use the moment. Without allowing the pause of even a fraction of a second, I let off 150 rounds. Suddenly the enemy monoplane reared up; with its propeller pointing skyward and its steering surfaces earthward, it stood on its tail for several seconds. Then it turned over by the right wing and whirled down in a nose-dive.

My efforts to catch another glimpse of it during the fall were useless. I flew a circle round the scene of the fray and then went off home.

Then I received a jubilant welcome, for a telephone message had already come through: 'In an airfight over Valenciennes a Fokker monoplane shot an enemy monoplane down. The latter turned over several times and crashed near Raismes, north-east of Valenciennes. Further details are lacking. The German monoplane went off in the direction of Douai.'

The section knew who was the victor, because I was the only one who had been up.

I asked our section-leader for permission to proceed to Valenciennes at once, which he granted. When I arrived there, I learnt that the wreckage had been cleared away and the bodies (Lieutenants Hobbs and Johnston) already buried.

I ascertained the following details from eye-witnesses. After dropping vertically for some distance, the machine turned over several times. In one of these turns the observer fell out when the machine was about 100 metres from the ground. He fell on to a tree. The branches pierced his body, which then dropped to the ground. There were several bullet wounds in his head and neck, so that his death must have been instantaneous.

The machine and pilot were found about 500 metres away from this tree. The pilot had a couple of bullet wounds in his head, in addition to one in his chest and another in a leg. The machine crashed on to the wall of a house and was smashed to bits.

No gun was found in the machine. But I induced the men to make a further search, because I had heard the enemy's shots. Finally they discovered the machine gun a long way to one side; it had fallen out.

Then it became clear to me why the Englishman ceased fire. One of my bullets went through his barrel, while another destroyed the loading mechanism. These facts I naturally could not know when I was still in the air. After receiving congratulations from all sides, I returned to Douai." (Immelmann, *Eagle of Lille*, pp.161-64)

Immelmann's victims were Lt. Alan Hobbs and 2nd Lt. Charles Tudor-Jones, the occupants of RFC No.3 Squadron's Morane Parasol No.5087. A German pilot dropped an account of their final fight behind the British lines. They were buried in Raismes Communal Cemetery in France.

IMMEL3 is the original photo that served as the basis for S342. IMMEL4 is another original picture taken at the same time that shows Immelmann standing next to the wreckage with the ruined machine gun in hand. Several pictures of the downed plane at its crash site have also survived. IMMEL5-10 are earlier shots of the wreck soon after its discovery. IMMEL5 is a clear picture of the fuselage and tail number. IMMEL6-8 offer different views of the same scene: the broken fuselage and collapsed wing lying in front of the brick wall that Immelmann described. IMMEL9 and IMMEL10 were taken while the wreckage was being cleared away. IMMEL3 and IMMEL4 were taken later after the wreckage had been moved away from the crash site (presumably to Valenciennes) and the missing machine gun had been discovered.

According to our three-week rule, the earliest that S342 would have made its initial appearance would have been mid-January 1916, around the time that the 16 January 1916 edition of *Berliner Illustrirte Zeitung* published an edited version of IMMEL4 that purposely obscured the background. We at least know that it was no later than 19 February 1916 because of an existing postmarked example with that date. It is doubtful that this was the time of its debut, however, because of the same reasons given in the discussion of S340-*Lt*.

Opposite

Top: An original picture of Immelmann standing next to the wreckage of his seventh victim after it had been cleared away to a German military site near Valenciennes. Note the German sign in the background that reads: "*Das unbefugte Betreten diese Halle ist streng verboten*" ("Unauthorized entry into this shed is strictly prohibited"). The top of that sign was etched out on Sanke's postcards, presumably to ensure a dark background for their white print.

Bottom: Immelmann, who has removed his flying helmet and replaced it with his *Schirmmütze* (service cap), now holds the machine gun that fell out during the fight and was subsequently recovered "a long way to one side" of the wreckage.

IMMEL3

IMMEL4

Several views of Immelmann's seventh victory at its crash site near Raismes: "The machine crashed on to the wall of a house and was smashed to bits." Note that the roundel on the right side of the fuselage, initially smashed in upon impact, later became exposed. It looks as though the pilot's leather flight helmet and goggles were removed and placed on the tail of the airplane (see IMMEL7 and IMMEL9). The sequence ends with a portion of the wings and the fuselage being carried away over a timber post wall.

IMMEL5

IMMEL6

IMMEL7

IMMEL8

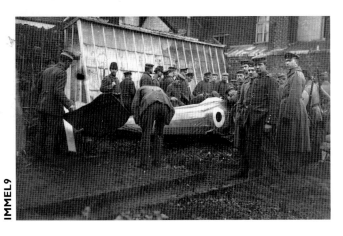

IMMEL9

IMMEL10

Leutnant Immelmann
Trümmern eines von ihm abgeschossenen engl. Eindeckers.

A rare version of Sanke's S342 that was issued without a number. Rarer still is the fact that this particular example was double struck with a lighter, upside-down imprint of the same scene.

S342
(reissue)
IMMELMANN
Max
Oberleutnant

Taken: 15 December 1915
Valenciennes
Publ: May 1916
Reason: promotion

Decorations:
WR: None
MB: None
RB: None
BH: Royal Hohenzollern House Order, Knight's Cross/ Sw

Other Cards:
S340, S347, S360-62, S364, S373, S377, S408, S610
(L7705, L7713, L7716-20, L7793; N5613-14, N5632, N5690, N6004)

Key Dates:
18 Apr 1916   promoted to *Oberleutnant*
18 Jun 1916   killed in action

Following Immelmann's promotion to *Oberleutnant* on 18 April 1916, Sanke released updated versions of S340, S342, S347, S360-62, and S364. The images were identical to those of their predecessors, so it appears that their purpose was to recognize his new rank. They probably came out faster than the usual three weeks after an event because they were not dependent upon the attainment and preparation of new photographs.[1] A 20 May 1916 postmarked example of S362-*Oblt.* supports a May debut for these reissues. In the absence of any direct confirmation, however, it should be noted that S342-*Oblt.* technically could have emerged at any point up to or around Immelmann's death on 18 June. We can be fairly certain that its initial appearance was no later than that because it is not marked with a "†" or a black border as seen in Immelmann's S361† or Boelcke's S363†.

Note
[1] A possible exception is S340-*Oblt.*, which employed a new signature and handwritten date.

S347
IMMELMANN
Max
Leutnant

Taken: 15 November 1915
Lille
Publ: January to February 1916
Reason: victory score

Decorations:
WR: Iron Cross, 1st Class; Pilot's Badge
MB: None
RB: Military St. Henry Order, Knight's Cross (Sax); Albert Order, Knight 2nd Class/ Sw (Sax); Friedrich August Medal in Silver (Sax); Iron Cross, 2nd Class
BH: None

Oberleutnant Immelmann an den Trümmern eines von ihm abgeschossenen engl. Eindeckers.

Leutnant Immelmann
an seinem Fokker-Flugzeug

347
Postkartenvertrieb W. Sanke
BERLIN N. 37.
Nachdruck wird gerichtlich verfolgt

Other Cards:
S340, S342, S360-62, S364, S373, S377, S408, S610
(L7705, L7713, L7716-20, L7793; N5613-14, N5632, N5690,
N6004)
Note: postcard also issued without a number

Key Dates:

13 Oct 1915	awarded Military St. Henry Order, Knight's Cross (Sax)
9-11 Nov 1915	awarded Royal Hohenzollern House Order, Knight's Cross/ Sw
15 Nov 1915	King of Saxony inspects *Feldflieger-Abteilung 24*

Here we once again have the rare satisfaction of knowing the precise day when one of Sanke's photographs was taken. An Immelmann letter dated 17 November 1916 provides the precise origin of S347's photo:

"The King intended to inspect Flying Section 24, a Saxon section led by Captain Rosenmüller, on the following morning. I was ordered to go out there and give a demonstration of flying…I arrived at No.24's aerodrome at 10 a.m. Two photographers promptly rushed at me and begged for the honour of taking my photo. I was very gracious to them. I was snapped about twenty or thirty times and then filmed. The films will appear in all German cinemas in about three weeks' time. So you must go to the pictures diligently so as not to miss this film. I was first filmed with the fourth English machine I shot down, then with Captain Rosenmüller and finally in conversation with the King of Saxony.

All the machines of Flying Section 24 were drawn up in parade order. First came the English machine, then my monoplane and finally the ten machines of No.24. The King arrived at 10:30 a.m. He went straight up to me, inspected and expressed surprise at Englishman No.4, and then took a photo of myself standing in front of this machine – just imagine, the King snapped me himself. Several generals and excellencies did the same, but it no longer made such a great impression on me…When the King passed on, I donned my leather kit and prepared to take off. His Excellency von Wilsdorf had previously asked me to do no stunts and confine myself to ordinary flying.

When His Majesty had seen all the machines, I took off. I managed to make my machine leave the ground just in front of His Majesty. Then I went into several turns and glides, fired about 80 rounds in the air, made a short nose-dive and a steep climb, flew close above the ground in front of the King, saluting as I passed him, and then landed.

When the machine came to a standstill, the King snapped me again. Then he came up to me and expressed his appreciation of what he had seen. Suddenly he grew plainly embarrassed and said: 'It's really fine what you did, hm, hm, hm, hm. I've brought you something as well. Hm, hm, hm. There's a monoplane on it, haha, a monoplane.' And with that he handed me a plate of Meissen porcelain, on which there was a charming picture of a fight between a German 'Taube' and an enemy biplane. It is really quite nicely done." (Immelmann, *Eagle of Lille*, pp.153-55)

IMMEL12 is a picture of *Feldflieger-Abteilung 24*'s lineup exactly as Immelmann described it. IMMEL13 is one of the photos taken that day of Immelmann in front of the wreckage of his fourth victory,

BE.2c No.2033 of RFC No.16 Squadron. The observer, Lt. David Leeson, survived and was taken prisoner of war. His pilot, 2nd Lt. John Gay, was not as fortunate and died shortly after impact. Immelmann, holding the Meissen plate mentioned above, is standing next to the King of Saxony in L7713 and IMMEL14. Immelmann's attire in IMMEL13, L7713, and IMMEL14 is identical to what he is wearing in S347 and IMMEL11 – two snapshots of him in front of his *Eindecker* fighter. Moreover, the same trees are visible in the background of most of these images, so it is certain that S347's picture originated from the King of Saxony's visit to *Feldflieger-Abteilung 24*'s airfield on 15 November 1915.

Unlike IMMEL11, someone touched up S347's photo to hide the details of the *Eindecker*'s engine and machine gun. It should also be noted that there is no sign in any of these photographs of the Royal Hohenzollern House Order that Immelmann had been awarded beforehand. In the letter quoted above, Immelmann relates that "several days" before 14 November, he had received a telegram informing him of the honor, but then says nothing of its actual, physical receipt. He goes on to remark on what a rarity it was because only one other Saxon officer and one other airman (Boelcke) had won it. From what we know of Immelmann, he would have worn the decoration if he had possessed it, so it evidently had not yet reached him.

S347 is one of the few examples of Sanke not following the actual chronological order of events. That is, S342, taken on 15 December, precedes S347, taken one month earlier. S347's numerical position between S342 and the later *Pour le Mérite* series, S360-62, indicates that it was first brought out in late January or early February 1916.

IMMEL11

This snapshot of *Lt.* Max Immelmann in front of his Fokker *Eindecker* shows the machine gun and motor details that were removed from its companion, S347. Both originated from the King of Saxony's inspection of *FFA 24* near Lille on 15 November 1915.

Above: *FFA 24*'s aircraft awaiting inspection by the King of Saxony on 15 November 1915. From left to right: the remains of Immelmann's fourth victim, Immelmann's Fokker *Eindecker*, six of the unit's two-seater aircraft.

Right: *Lt.* Max Immelmann strikes a nonchalant pose in front of what remains of the nose of BE.2c No.2033.

7713
Verlag von
GUSTAV LIERSCH & C°
BERLIN S.W.

Oberleutnant Immelmann
empfängt an der Front den Besuch des
Königs von Sachsen.

A. Grohs phot.

IMMEL14

Opposite

Top: L7713 captures *Lt.* Max Immelmann holding the Meissen plate given to him by the King of Saxony (center) during the king's inspection of *FFA 24* near Lille on 15 November 1915. This postcard was published much later, after Immelmann's receipt of the *Pour le Mérite* (added to the picture) and his promotion to *Oberleutnant*.

Bottom: Taken within minutes of L7713's photograph, this is another view of the same scene. Note that it does not have a drawn-in *Pour le Mérite* for Immelmann.

Below: The King of Saxony inspected the wreckage of Immelmann's fourth victory during his visit to *FFA 24* on 15 November 1915. This is a series of pictures of the plane at its crash site. BE.2c No.2033 of RFC No.16 Squadron had been manned by 2nd Lt. John Gay (pilot) and Lt. David Leeson (observer). Gay was killed in the air but Leeson survived the ensuing crash. The first three scenes are of the back of the airplane, and the next two show its nose poking through the tree line it had smashed into. The sixth picture (top of page 62) is actually an artist's rendering of the wreckage's removal that incorrectly identified the plane as "*französische*" or "French."

Ein von Leutnant Immelmann
heruntergeschossenes französisches Flugzeug.

A 377

Leutnant Immelmann
an seinem Fokker-Flugzeug.

Postkartenvertrieb W. Sanke
BERLIN N. 37.
Nachdruck wird gerichtlich verfolgt.

This is a rare example of S347 that was issued without a number. See S342 for a similar occurrence.

S347
(reissue)
IMMELMANN
Max
Oberleutnant

Taken: 15 November 1915
Lille
Publ: May 1916
Reason: promotion

Decorations:
WR: Iron Cross, 1st Class; Pilot's Badge
MB: None
RB: Military St. Henry Order, Knight's Cross (Sax); Albert Order, Knight 2nd Class/ Sw (Sax); Friedrich August Medal in Silver (Sax), Iron Cross, 2nd Class
BH: None

Other Cards:
S340, S342, S360-62, S364, S373, S377, S408, S610
(L7705, L7713, L7716-20, L7793; N5613-14, N5632, N5690, N6004)

Key Dates:

18 Apr 1916	promoted to *Oberleutnant*
18 Jun 1916	killed in action

Following Immelmann's promotion to *Oberleutnant* on 18 April 1916, Sanke released updated versions of S340, S342, S347, S360-62, and S364. The images were identical to those of their predecessors, so it appears that their purpose was to recognize his new rank. They probably came out faster than the usual three weeks after an event because they were not dependent upon the attainment and preparation of new photographs.[1] A 20 May 1916 postmarked example of S362-*Oblt.* supports a May debut for these reissues. In the absence of any direct confirmation, however, it should be noted that S347-*Oblt.* technically could have emerged at any point up to or around Immelmann's death on 18 June. We can be fairly certain that its initial appearance was no later than that because it is not marked with a "†" or a black border as seen in Immelmann's S361† or Boelcke's S363†.

Note
[1] A possible exception is S340-*Oblt.*, which employed a new signature and handwritten date.

Oberleutnant Immelmann an seinem Fokker-Flugzeug

This page and opposite: Various views of BE.2c No.4197 of RFC No.6 Squadron that Immelmann downed on 13 March 1916 for his 11th victory. Both of its occupants, Lt. Gilbert Grune (pilot) and 2nd Lt. Brian Glover (observer), were killed. Their bodies are just visible on the ground under the relatively intact tail of the plane in the second photo, and in the fourth they are resting to the left of the tail. This sequence also illustrates that the wreck was progressively stripped of its fabric, presumably by souvenir hunters.

S360
IMMELMANN
Max
Leutnant

Taken: 17 to 19 January 1916
Douai/Lille
Publ: February 1916
Reason: *Pour le Mérite* award

Decorations:
WR: *Pour le Mérite*; Iron Cross, 1st Class; Pilot's Badge
MB: None
RB: Military St. Henry Order, Knight's Cross (Sax); Albert Order, Knight 2nd Class/ Sw (Sax); Friedrich August Medal in Silver (Sax), Iron Cross, 2nd Class; Royal Hohenzollern House Order, Knight's Cross/ Sw; Military Merit Order, 4th Class/ Sw (Bav)
BH: None

Other Cards:
S340, S342, S347, S361-62, S364, S373, S377, S408, S610 (L7705, L7713, L7716-20, L7793; N5613-14, N5632, N5690, N6004)
Note: Taken same time as S361-62
Pour le Mérite has "pie-slice" attachment

S361
IMMELMANN
Max
Leutnant

Taken: 17 to 19 January 1916
Douai/Lille
Publ: February 1916
Reason: *Pour le Mérite* award

Decorations:
WR: *Pour le Mérite*; Iron Cross, 1st Class; Pilot's Badge
MB: None
RB: Military St. Henry Order, Knight's Cross (Sax); Albert Order, Knight 2nd Class/ Sw (Sax); Friedrich August Medal in Silver (Sax), Iron Cross, 2nd Class; Royal Hohenzollern House Order, Knight's Cross/ Sw; Military Merit Order, 4th Class/ Sw (Bav)
BH: None

Other Cards:
S340, S342, S347, S360, S362, S364, S373, S377, S408, S610 (L7705, L7713, L7716-20, L7793; N5613-14, N5632, N5690, N6004)
Note: Taken same time as S360, S362
Pour le Mérite has "pie-slice" attachment

S362
IMMELMANN
Max
Leutnant

Taken: 17 to 19 January 1916
Douai/Lille
Publ: February 1916
Reason: *Pour le Mérite* award

Decorations:
WR: *Pour le Mérite*; Iron Cross, 1st Class; Pilot's Badge
MB: None
RB: Military St. Henry Order, Knight's Cross (Sax); Albert Order,
Knight 2nd Class/ Sw (Sax); Friedrich August Medal in Silver (Sax),
Iron Cross, 2nd Class; Royal Hohenzollern House Order, Knight's
Cross/ Sw; Military Merit Order, 4th Class/ Sw (Bav)
BH: None

Other Cards:
S340, S342, S347, S360-61, S364, S373, S377, S408, S610
(L7705, L7713, L7716-20, L7793; N5613-14, N5631, N5690,
N6004)
Note: Taken same time as S360-61
Pour le Mérite has "pie-slice" attachment

Key Dates:
12 Jan 1916	awarded *Pour le Mérite*
17 Jan 1916	*Pour le Mérite* award ceremony at Lille
20 Jan 1916	Boelcke sends "new photos" home
21 Jan 1916	Boelcke departs from *Feldflieger-Abteilung 62*

Lt. Oswald Boelcke and *Lt.* Max Immelmann were the first German
airmen to be awarded Prussia's premier combat decoration, the *Orden
Pour le Mérite*. In separate engagements on 12 January 1916, the
official date of their awards, both men had shot down their eighth
airplane – an unparalleled achievement at that point of the war.
Boelcke described what followed later the same evening:

"We were just sitting down to dinner when I was called to
the telephone. There the chief's adjutant announced himself and
congratulated me upon receiving the 'Pour le Mérite.' I thought
he was having a joke with me, but he informed me that the
order had been bestowed on Immelmann and myself by a
telegram from His Majesty. Great were my surprise and joy.
Then I went in to the diningroom, but said nothing and just sent
Captain Kastner to the telephone. He came back and made a
public announcement about our decorations; at first everyone
was very astonished, then there was great rejoicing." (Werner,
Knight of Germany, pp.142-43)

Immelmann wrote:

"As is the custom when the section celebrates a joyful
event, our leader spoke a few words, but this time his speech
was livelier and gayer than usual. I cannot remember everything
he said, because I was too excited with my pleasure. I did not
really listen until at the end of his short speech. He said
something about a milestone in the history of aviation and a
turning point and recognition in high places, but finally the big
word came out: 'His Majesty the Emperor has been graciously
pleased to confer the highest war order, the "Pour le Mérite",
on the two victors in aerial warfare.'
I was dumb. I should have thought it a joke if my section-
leader had not said it in front of all our officers. I couldn't eat or

drink anything that day; I didn't know whether I was awake or
dreaming." (Immelmann, *Eagle of Lille*, p.169)

Congratulations poured in from all over the country by telephone
and telegram. Boelcke and Immelmann were invited to Lille to dine
with the King and the Crown Prince of Bavaria on the 14th. As would
so often be the case in such matters, they did not actually receive
their decorations until days later, as Boelcke related on 20 January:

"Immelmann and I were summoned to lunch again with
the Crown Prince of Bavaria on the 17th. Before the meal he
gave us our orders with some very nice words and helped us to
pin them on properly with his own hands. I sat on the prince's
right hand at table; he is very nice to talk to. Yesterday we were
invited to H.Q.; the general nearly killed himself with affability
and expressed the wish that we might soon return to his corps.
I enclose a couple of the new photos. If the 'Woche' is
absolutely determined to have one, send it along as far as I am
concerned – as a knight of the 'Pour le Mérite' I can no longer
keep myself out of the press." (Werner, *Knight of Germany*,
p.148)

The background tapestry that established the Lille/Douai location of
several snapshots of *Feldflieger-Abteilung 62* airmen (see pp. 10-

12) is present in Boelcke's S363 and S369. He is wearing the decoration he received on 17 January in both photos, and is known to have made his final departure from *Feldflieger-Abteilung 62* four days later on 21 January. This schedule and the fact that he sent home "a couple of the new photos" on 20 January led us to conclude that those pictures were probably the ones produced later as S363 and S369, thereby assigning their origin to a 17-19 January 1916 period. Immelmann's S360-61 photos incorporate the same tapestry and like Boelcke, portray him in his best dress field uniform. S362, taken the same time as S360-61, has Immelmann posing outdoors in the same dress outfit with his dog, Tyras. Immelmann's S360-62 and Boelcke's S363 were consecutively issued, so it is highly likely that Immelmann's pictures were taken during the same period as Boelcke's. Boelcke's S363-*Lt.* version must have been published in February before the news of his promotion to *Oberleutnant* became well known (see S363-*Lt.*). This in turn implies that Immelmann's S360-62, which immediately preceded S363, first emerged in February 1916 as well.

The details present in S360 provide instructive examples of how the camera film of the day often translated color into black-and-white. The piping that trims Immelmann's collar *Litzen* (braid) and the vertical flap of his tunic was red, but appears dark gray or black here. The cornflower blue enamel of his *Pour le Mérite* and the darker blue enamel of his Bavarian Miltary Merit Order come out light gray. The ribbons for his Saxon Military St. Henry Order, Saxon Friedrich August Medal, and Bavarian Military Merit Order were light blue with yellow side stripes, yellow with light blue side stripes, and white with thin black outer side stripes/dark blue inner side stripes, respectively. In S360 they look like light gray with medium gray side stripes, medium gray with light gray side stripes, and white with thin black outer side stripes/light gray inner side stripes.

S361 offers a tantalizing but tenuous link to the *Kaiser*. A copy of S361's original photograph (not a Sanke card) was discovered among Boelcke's personal documents and put up for sale in December 2002 (see Thies, *Historische Sammlungsgegenstände*, p.28). Signed "M. Immelmann, Leutnant" on the front, the reverse relates its origin to "Adolf Jessen Schleswig." The same Jessen is listed on Cossel and Windisch's S401 as owning the photo's copyright. S401 was probably taken soon after the *Kaiser* had personally pinned his awards on the airmen during a visit to the Eastern Front. The *Kaiser* had many connections to Schleswig including the fact that it was his wife's birthplace; so it is speculated that S401's picture was taken by Jessen or one of his photographers who had accompanied the *Kaiser* on his trip. But what was Jessen's association with S361? There is no question that S361 was taken in Douai or Lille and not Schleswig. In addition, it was the Crown Prince of Bavaria who pinned the *Kaiser*'s decoration on Boelcke and Immelmann, not the *Kaiser*. Was one of the *Kaiser*'s royal photographers sent to the ceremony to record the bestowal of what came to be regarded as the German Empire's highest award, or was the negative simply procured from a local photographer by Jessen? Obviously, at least one copy of Jessen's photocard was given to Immelmann who autographed and gave it out. But we still do not know exactly how it came into Jessen's possession beforehand. Though it is tempting to name Jessen as the photographer behind S360-63, we probably should not do so until a less circumstantial case can be presented.

S362 includes Immelmann's dog, Tyras. He purchased the dog in October 1914 in Berlin, shortly after being promoted to *Offizier-Stellvertreter*:

> "As this nomination to acting-officer also carries the advantage that I now draw 110-120 marks a month, it is undoubtedly a reason for acquiring a dog, and I have done so. I have bought Tyras, a German mastiff (of the type that Bismarck

Tyras and his new owner in Berlin in 1914 when Immelmann was still serving with *Eisenbahn-Regiment Nr.2*.

Opposite left - Top: This picture, found on a postcard entitled *"Familie Immelmann,"* is normally interpreted to include Max, his dog Tyras, his mother, and his sister. Max Immelmann's other photographs, however, demonstrate that he parted his hair slightly higher on the right side of his head – not the left as shown here – and that none of his various uniforms displayed the particular style of collar *Litzen* seen here. In addition, the women appear to be dressed in mourning clothes. If the photo's negative was not somehow reversed, then the young man might actually be Max's brother Franz, who Oswald Boelcke noted was "very like our Immelmann in both appearance and character…" (Werner, *Knight of Germany*, p.178). In this case, the picture most likely is of the Immelmann family after Max's death. Bottom: Another early portrait of Immelmann and his dog, Tyras.

used to keep) with a field-grey skin, so big that he can just touch the table with his chin, about a year and a half old and trained as a watchdog – a dear beast. Yesterday I took him out in the Grunewald from 2:30 to 7:30. He is very docile and likes his lessons. He only cost me six marks. I bought him from the Tierasyl, and as I did not know his name, I simply knocked the 'yl' off Tierasyl, so that he is now named Tieras, or, more correctly, Tyras." (Immelmann, *Eagle of Lille*, p.45)

Tierasyl is German for "animal pound." Shortly afterward, Immelmann sent a picture of his new pet home (see IMMEL15). IMMEL16 is another image of Tyras from a postcard entitled *"Familie Immelmann"* ("Immelmann family").

IMMEL I 6

S360
(reissue)
IMMELMANN
Max
Oberleutnant

Taken: 17 to 19 January 1916
Douai/Lille
Publ: May 1916
Reason: promotion

Decorations:
WR: *Pour le Mérite*; Iron Cross, 1st Class; Pilot's Badge
MB: None
RB: Military St. Henry Order, Knight's Cross (Sax); Albert Order, Knight 2nd Class/ Sw (Sax); Friedrich August Medal in Silver (Sax), Iron Cross, 2nd Class; Royal Hohenzollern House Order, Knight's Cross/ Sw; Military Merit Order, 4th Class/ Sw (Bav)
BH: None

Other Cards:
S340, S342, S347, S361-62, S364, S373, S377, S408, S610
(L7705, L7713, L7716-20, L7793; N5613-14, N5632, N5690, N6004)

Oberleutnant Immelmann

Note: Taken same time as S361-62
Pour le Mérite has "pie-slice" attachment

S361
(reissue)
IMMELMANN
Max
Oberleutnant

Taken: 17 to 19 January 1916
Douai/Lille
Publ: May 1916
Reason: promotion

Decorations:
WR: *Pour le Mérite*; Iron Cross, 1st Class; Pilot's Badge
MB: None
RB: Military St. Henry Order, Knight's Cross (Sax); Albert Order, Knight 2nd Class/ Sw (Sax); Friedrich August Medal in Silver (Sax), Iron Cross, 2nd Class; Royal Hohenzollern House Order, Knight's Cross/ Sw; Military Merit Order, 4th Class/ Sw (Bav)
BH: None

Other Cards:
S340, S342, S347, S360, S362, S364, S373, S377, S408, S610 (L7705, L7713, L7716-20, L7793; N5613-14, N5632, N5690, N6004)
Note: Taken same time as S360, S362
Pour le Mérite has "pie-slice" attachment

S362
(reissue)
IMMELMANN
Max
Oberleutnant

Taken: 17 to 19 January 1916
Douai/Lille
Publ: May 1916
Reason: promotion

Decorations:
WR: *Pour le Mérite*; Iron Cross, 1st Class; Pilot's Badge
MB: None
RB: Military St. Henry Order, Knight's Cross (Sax); Albert Order, Knight 2nd Class/ Sw (Sax); Friedrich August Medal in Silver (Sax), Iron Cross, 2nd Class; Royal Hohenzollern House Order, Knight's Cross/ Sw; Military Merit Order, 4th Class/ Sw (Bav)
BH: None

Other Cards:
S340, S342, S347, S360-61, S364, S373, S377, S408, S610 (L7705, L7713, L7716-20, L7793; N5613-14, N5632, N5690, N6004)
Note: Taken same time as S360-61
Pour le Mérite has "pie-slice" attachment

Key Dates:
18 Apr 1916   promoted to *Oberleutnant*
18 Jun 1916   killed in action

Following Immelmann's promotion to *Oberleutnant* on 18 April 1916, Sanke released updated versions of S340, S342, S347, S360-62, and S364. The images were identical to those of their predecessors, so it appears that their purpose was to recognize his new rank. They probably came out faster than the usual three weeks after an event because they were not dependent upon the attainment and preparation of new photographs.[1] A 20 May 1916 postmarked example of S362-*Oblt.* verifies that at least the S360-62 series was available in May.

Note
[1] A possible exception is S340-*Oblt.*, which employed a new signature and handwritten date.

Oberleutnant Immelmann

Top right: A candid shot of Immelmann showing that he had his lighter moments.

Right: An informal photo of Immelmann in flight gear.

Above: Number 13 for Immelmann. A German soldier lounges near the remains of BE.2c No.4116 of RFC No.15 Squadron, brought down on 30 March 1916. The pilot, 2nd Lt. Geoffrey Lightbourn Welsford, was killed by Immelmann's first pass. His observer, Lt. Wayland Joyce, who also had a pilot's license, managed to crawl into the cockpit and regain enough control to prevent a headlong plunge into the ground. He survived the crash landing and finished out the war as a prisoner.

Immelmann posing in front of a Fokker *Eindecker*.

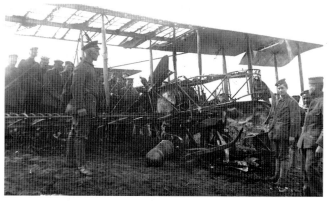

Two at right and below: Three views of Vickers FB.5 No.5079 of RFC No.11 Squadron, brought down by Immelmann on 23 April 1916 to bring his tally to 14. The first displays clear evidence of the still-smoldering fire set by the plane's occupants, Lt. William Mortimer-Phelan (pilot) and 2nd Lt. William Scott-Brown (observer), after their emergency landing. The other two show it after the nose-mounted gun, various other parts, and additional fabric pieces had been removed.

S361 (†)
(memorial)
IMMELMANN
Max
Oberleutnant

Taken: 17 to 19 January 1916
Douai/Lille
Publ: July 1916
Reason: memorial

Decorations:
WR: *Pour le Mérite*; Iron Cross, 1st Class; Pilot's Badge
MB: None
RB: Military St. Henry Order, Knight's Cross (Sax); Albert Order, Knight 2nd Class/ Sw (Sax); Friedrich August Medal in Silver (Sax), Iron Cross, 2nd Class; Royal Hohenzollern House Order, Knight's Cross/ Sw; Military Merit Order, 4th Class/ Sw (Bav)
BH: None

Other Cards:
S340, S342, S347, S360, S362, S364, S373, S377, S408, S610 (L7705, L7713, L7716-20, L7793; N5613-14, N5632, N5690, N6004)
Note: Taken same time as S360, S362
Pour le Mérite has "pie-slice" attachment

Key Dates:
18 Apr 1916	promoted to *Oberleutnant*
18 Jun 1916	killed in action

Max Immelmann was killed on 18 June 1916 while attacking several FE.2b aircraft from RFC No.25 Squadron. Eyewitnesses on the ground observed that shortly after downing one of the planes, his Fokker *Eindecker* suddenly started to make strange, tumbling movements – at first rearing straight up and hanging on its nose, then falling off steeply, then violently pulling up again – until the tail section broke away. A wing tore off next and the fuselage section that carried the hapless Immelmann dove steeply into the ground from about 2000 meters. An alleged eyewitness, whose account was printed in the 5 July 1916 edition of the German aviation magazine *Flugsport*, described the scene immediately afterward:

"Ich also, so schnell mich meine Füsse tragen, der Unfallstede zu. Der Motor hatte sich tief in die Erde eingegraben und lag mit dem unteren Teil nach oben, den Führer unter sich begrabend.

Unter den sich rasch versammelnden Soldaten liefen die verschiedenartigsten Gerüchte um. 'Ein Franzose ist es!' – 'O nein, leider ein Deutscher!' – 'Was?' entrüstet drohende Blicke treffen den zuletzt Sprechenden. 'Ein Franzose ist es, nichts weiter!' – 'Ja, ja,' schreien alle durcheinander, 'ein Franzose muss es gewesen sein!' Wie ist es den anders möglich!

Mitterweile haben wir mit vieler Mühe den Motor umgedreht. Mehrere Offiziere erscheinen und beaufsichtigen die Durchsuchung des Toten. – Wer mag es sein, Engländer, Franzose, oder Deutscher? Jeder ergeht sich in Vermutungen, niemand weiss bestimmtes.

Endlich hat man dem Toten den Lederrock geöffnet und findet als erstes – den 'Pour le mérite'*! – Immelmann? Bölcke? – Irgend jemand sprach es, wie ein Lauffeuer ging es weiter, und plötzlich entstand eine beängstigende Stille.*

Dann fand man das E.K., und dann kam die traurige Gewissheit, das Monogramm in der Wäsche – 'M.I.' – 'Unser armer Immelmann!' sprach ein anwesender höherer Offizier, und wir sprachen es traurig nach." (p.367)

"I therefore ran as fast as my feet could carry me to the crash site. The engine had buried itself deep in the earth and lay with its underside up with the pilot buried underneath.

All sorts of rumors circulated among the rapidly assembling soldiers. 'It's a Frenchman' – 'Oh no, unfortunately a German' – 'What?' outraged, menacing looks reacted to the last utterance. 'It's a Frenchman, that's all!' – 'Yes' everyone cried out in disorder, 'it must have been a Frenchman!' How could it be anything else!'

In the meantime, we turned the engine over with a great deal of difficulty. Several officers appeared and supervised a search of the dead man's body. – Who would it be, an Englishman, Frenchman, or German? Everyone had their guess, but no one knew for sure. Finally, someone opened the dead man's leather coat and found – a *Pour le Mérite*! – Was it Immelmann? Boelcke? – Possibly someone spoke this aloud [because] it spread like wildfire, and then a frightening silence suddenly developed.

Then someone found the Iron Cross, and finally the monogram 'M.I.' on his clothing confirmed the sad news. 'Our poor Immelmann!' said a high-ranking officer who was there, and we sorrowfully repeated the same sentiment." (trans. by this writer)

Following this event, Sanke released a memorial version of S361-*Oblt.* that added a "†" symbol below his name and was bordered in black. It is likely that this card made its first appearance in July 1916 within weeks of Immelmann's death (e.g., see Boelcke's S363†).

No similarly marked versions of S340, S342, S347, S360, or S362 have been reported.

Six different views from among the many that have survived of the remains of Immelmann's Fokker E.III 246/16 after it crashed on 18 June 1916. No fabric remains on this section of the plane (except for one wheel cover) and it exhibits signs of charring, indicating that it burned either on the way down or upon impact.

The relatively intact tail of Immelmann's Fokker E.III 246/16 that was discovered some distance away from the main wreck.

S363
BOELCKE
Oswald
Leutnant

Taken: 17 to 19 January 1916
Douai/Lille
Publ: February 1916
Reason: *Pour le Mérite* award

Decorations:
WR: *Pour le Mérite*; Iron Cross, 1st Class; Pilot's Badge
MB: None
RB: None
BH: Royal Hohenzollern House Order, Knight's Cross/ Sw; Life Saving Medal

Other Cards:
S364, S369, S373, S393, S408, S409
(L7720, L7721, L7761, L7776, L7785, L7793; N5579, N5580, N5601, N5619, N5690, N6004, N6005, N6225)
Note: Taken same time as S369. Name given as "Bölcke" instead of the airman's preferred spelling, "Boelcke."

Key Dates:

12 Jan 1916	awarded *Pour le Mérite*
17 Jan 1916	*Pour le Mérite* award ceremony at Lille
20 Jan 1916	sends "new photos" home
21 Jan 1916	departs from *Feldflieger-Abteilung 62*
2 Feb 1916	promoted to *Oberleutnant* by this date

See the discussion of Immelmann's S360-62-*Lt.* where it is demonstrated that this photo must have been taken between Boelcke's receipt of his *Pour le Mérite* during a luncheon celebration on 17 January and his mailing of "a couple of the new photos" home on 20 January 1916. BOELCKE4 is the original source of S363's image.

Boelcke's promotion to *Oberleutnant* plays an important role in determining when S363 was published, though the exact date of that event is unknown. His biographer, Professor Johannes Werner, indicated that it was before 2 February 1916 around the time of Boelcke's departure from *Feldflieger-Abteilung 62* on 21 January:

> "The new mission was connected with the great Verdun offensive, which was still a dead secret at that time and eventually started on Feb. 2nd. As in September, 1915, Boelcke was again transferred to the Metz 'pigeons'…but Oswald did not go to Metz; having been advanced to [first] lieutenant, he was sent from Montmédy direct to the artillery flying section, No. 203 at Jametz, north of Verdun, to act as escort to machines engaged on artillery spotting." (Werner, *Knight of Germany*, p.148)

We have independent evidence that it occurred after he left *Feldflieger-Abteilung 62* because one of the items described in a 2001 auction of Boelcke memorabilia was a postcard sent by *Leutnant* Boelcke on 21 January 1916. Unfortunately, one of Immelmann's letters confuses the issue: "Boelcke has been a full lieutenant since February 18th, which was about the time when he shot down his 9th." (Immelmann, *Eagle of Lille*, p.183) Boelcke's ninth victim fell on 14 January, and his next did not come until 12 March; so Immelmann's date appears to have been incorrect. The 2001 auction mentioned above offered another letter, this time from *Oberleutnant* Boelcke, that was dated 12 February 1916, so we can be certain that he was promoted before then. We also know that Professor Werner

Leutnant Bölcke.

363
Postkartenvertrieb W. Sanke
BERLIN N. 37.
Nachdruck wird gerichtlich verfolgt.

had complete access to Boelcke's personal papers while compiling the airman's biography and that he generally related their contents accurately.[1] Therefore, we should allow that Werner was most likely aware of the facts and that Boelcke was promoted sometime between 21 January and 2 February 1916, as Werner related.

Our general Sanke postcard publication rule projects that S363 would not have been published much earlier than 10-12 February 1916, or three weeks after the taking of its photograph. It appears that Boelcke had been promoted a few weeks before, so why did S363 still call him a *Leutnant*? First, given the one or two weeks that it took at that time for news to become widespread, it is difficult to say exactly when Sanke would have become aware of Boelcke's new rank. Second, it is equally hard to predict when such news would have caused him to react in his publications. That is, at what point would Sanke have interrupted S363's publication process to make a correction? Normally, Sanke was quite attentive to details including an airman's rank – a fact demonstrated by the very next card, S364, where Boelcke is only identified as an *Oberleutnant* (and later, *Hauptmann*). We can at least surmise that S363-*Lt.* would not have been issued beyond late February 1916. By then, it is likely that Boelcke's new rank would have become more common knowledge and that Sanke would have accurately reflected it as he did in its successor, S364.

Note

¹ Werner's book referred to many of the letters and other items that appeared in the 2001 auction of Boelcke memorabilia. A comparison of some of those original letters to Werner's versions demonstrates that although he sometimes abridged them by omitting purely personal or somewhat extraneous passages, the overall content was generally faithfully reported.

A print from the original photograph used for Boelcke's S363.

Above and two below: On 11 August 1915, *Lt.* Oswald Boelcke wrote that "Lieut. von John, who is in hospital here with an injured knee, came along to visit me with two nursing sisters." (Werner, *Knight of Germany*, p.119) He also stated that he took the two nurses up for joyrides from Douai airfield in his Fokker *Eindecker.* One of them, identified as "Nurse Blanka," can be seen sitting in the cockpit behind Boelcke in the first two photographs and standing next to him in the third. The third picture shows, from left to right: *Lt.* von John (note the bandaged knee beneath his trousers), Nurse Blanka, Boelcke, unidentified nurse, unidentified soldier.

BOELCKE 4

On 5 January 1916, *Lt.* Oswald Boelcke successfully attacked BE.2c No.1734 of RFC No.2 Squadron, crippling the plane's observer, Lt. G.C. Formilli, and severing several control wires. The pilot, 2nd Lt. W.E. Somervill, signaled Boelcke that he wished to set down and surrender, which he did in a barely controlled crash. Boelcke landed nearby and found the wreck surrounded by German soldiers. When he visited the wounded observer two days later, he "brought him some English papers and photos of his wrecked machine." (Werner, *Knight of Germany*, p.140) These three snapshots – the first capturing Boelcke in front of his seventh victim – may have been among them.

S363
(reissue)
BOELCKE
Oswald
Oberleutnant

Taken: 17 to 19 January 1916
Douai/Lille
Publ: February to May 1916
Reason: promotion

Decorations:
WR: *Pour le Mérite*; Iron Cross, 1st Class; Pilot's Badge
MB: None
RB: None
BH: Royal Hohenzollern House Order, Knight's Cross/ Sw; Life Saving Medal

Other Cards:
S364, S369, S373, S393, S408, S409
(L7720, L7721, L7761, L7776, L7785, L7793; N5579, N5580, N5601, N5619, N5690, N6004, N6005, N6225)
Note: Taken same time as S369. Name given as "Bölcke" instead of the airman's preferred spelling, "Boelcke."

Key Dates:

21 Jan 1916	departs from *Feldflieger-Abteilung 62*
2 Feb 1916	promoted to *Oberleutnant* by this date
21 May 1916	promoted to *Hauptmann*

Oberleutnant Bölcke

363
Postkartenvertrieb W.Sanke
BERLIN N.37

S363-*Lt.* already discussed how Boelcke's promotion to *Oberleutnant* probably occurred sometime between 21 January and 2 February 1916. Indeed, his new rank appears in the return address of this letter to his mother, dated 12 February 1916:

"Liebe Mütter!
Zu Deinem Geburtstage wünsche ich Dir von Herzen alles Gute und Gottes Segen. Leider kann ich selber nicht da sein und Dir Glück wünschen, ich hätte, wenn's möglich gewesen ware, gern zu diesen Tagen Urlaub genommen.
Ich nehme an dass Du jetzt wieder von Diener Reise aus Berlin zurück bist und das Max sein Scheinergespenst, das Fähnrichs examen, glücklich hinter sich hat. Ihr müsst mir darüber gleich schreiben, da ich oder neugierig darauf bin.
In dem vorletzten Brief meinst, l[iebe] Mütter, dass ich auf dem Bilde schmal aussehe. Da kannst Du ganz unbesorgt sein. Bei meiner jetzigen Tätigkeit, wo ich fast gar keine körperliche Bewegung habe, dafür aber viel schlafe und esse, muss ich ja dick werden. Zu tun habe ich hier in letzter Zeit gar nicht gehabt, der wir fast nur schlechtes Wetter hatten. In der Zeit, die ich hier bin, bin ich nur 4-5 Mal zum Fliegen gekommen. Und wenn man hier fliegt, dann lohnt es auch gar nicht, da die Franzosen gar nicht mehr [he]rüberkommen. Nur einmal habe ich ganz kurz an der Front einen Farman-Doppeldecker zu fassen bekommen, doch ist der sofort schleunigst ausgerückt.
Das Leben ist hier in der Abt[ei]l[un]g ganz erträglich. Der Hptm. Vogl ist ein sehr vernünftiger, ordentlicher und klugen Mann. Das Dorf bietet sehr wenig Reize. Ein alles Drecknest, besonders in den jetzigen Regentagen. Zivilbevölkerung gibt es kaum noch. Nur noch wenige Leute. Die Zeit vertreibe ich nur durch Rumbummeln, Mitvorfahren zur Artillerie oder durch Lesen, Schreiben und Lernen in meinem Zimmer, was jetzt sehr gemütlich eingerichtet ist. Ich schicke Euch gleichzeitig einige Bilder mit, die Ort pp. zeigen, ausserdem wieder eine Anzahl Briefe pp., die ich mitschicke, damit Ihr sehr, womit ich jetzt

überschwemmt werde. – Der Unteroffz. Kestner ist bei nur eingetroffen und hat mir die von Euch mitgegebenen Sachen überbracke. Vielen Dank fur alles. Hemden habe ich jetzt genug. – Meine Zahne habe ich nur vor kurzem erst in Douai nachsehen lassen. Es ist nach alles in Ordnung. – Die Bilder von mir aus Douai sind immer noch nicht eingetroffen. Sie müssen aber bald kommen. Ich lasse Euch auch direkt von Douai welche zuschicken.
Ich schicke Dir, liebe Mütter, gleichzeitig durch Postanweisung eine Kleinigkeit, welche Du nach Deinem Wünsch anlegen kannst.
Mit herzlichsten Grüssen an Dich und Vater,

Oswald"

"Dear Mother,
From my heart I wish you God's blessings and everything good on your birthday. Unfortunately, I can't be there to wish you a happy birthday in person; I would like to have taken leave at this time if it had at all been possible.
I take it that you have just returned from your trip to Berlin and that Max is a 'glowing spirit', happy to have the Officer Candidate examination behind him. You must write me about that since I'm quite curious about it.

In the letter before last you thought, dear Mother, that I looked thin in the photo. You can put your mind at ease about that! With my current occupation, where I have virtually no physical activity but eat and sleep a lot instead, I'm going to get fat. Not much has been going on here lately, because we almost always have bad weather. I've only flown 4-5 times since I've been here. And when one does get to fly, it's hardly worth it because the Frenchmen don't come over here anymore. Only once did I very briefly tangle with a Farman two-seater at the Front, but then he quickly disengaged.

Life here in the flying section is quite bearable. Captain Vogt is a very sensible, orderly and shrewd man. The village offers very few attractions. It's a dirty little place, particularly during the current rainy weather. There's hardly any civilian population left; only just a few people. I spend the time by taking long strolls, tagging along with the artillery, or by reading, writing and studying in my room, which is now furnished quite comfortably. I'm enclosing some pictures that show you this place along with a large number of letters, which now constantly inundate me. Corporal Kestner just arrived and has delivered to me the items you sent along with him. Thank you for everything. I now have enough shirts – I quite recently had my tooth checked in Douai. It's all right after all. – The pictures of me didn't arrive yet from Douai. They should come soon though. I will have them sent to you directly from Douai as well.

A portrait of Oswald Boelcke and his ground crew in front of his Fokker E.IV. The accompanying closeup discloses that the top of the airplane's cowling bore the entwined initials "O.B."

I am simultaneously sending you, dear Mother, the small matter of a money order, which you can spend in accordance with your own wishes.

With warmest regards to you and Father,

Oswald" (trans. by this writer)

Though the pictures he refers to could not have included S363's (which had already been published before or around the time of Boelcke's promotion), his farewell photo posed with *FFA 62* that later appeared in S373 may have been among them.

Sanke reissued S363 sometime after Boelcke's promotion to *Oberleutnant* with no changes other than its updated rank. Though it seems likely that this card would have been issued soon after S363-*Lt.* and around the same time as S364, it technically could have come out at any point between then and Boelcke's next promotion to *Hauptmann*. Perhaps the matter will be settled in the future by reliable postmark evidence.

A candid portrait of Oswald Boelcke. Several other photos of him either just before or after a combat patrol similarly display his white shirt collar worn outside the tunic. Good combat pilots constantly swiveled their heads, scanning the skies looking for other aircraft. Presumably, Boelcke arranged his collar in the manner shown here either to help minimize neck chafing (similar to the later use of silk scarves) during patrols or for generally improved comfort.

S363
(reissue)
BOELCKE
Oswald
Hauptmann

Taken: 17 to 19 January 1916
Douai/Lille
Publ: June 1916
Reason: promotion

Decorations:
WR: *Pour le Mérite*; Iron Cross, 1st Class; Pilot's Badge
MB: None
RB: None
BH: Royal Hohenzollern House Order, Knight's Cross/ Sw; Life
Saving Medal

Other Cards:
S364, S369, S373, S393, S408, S409
(L7720, L7721, L7761, L7776, L7785, L7793; N5579, N5580,
N5601, N5619, N5690, N6004, N6005, N6225)
Note: Taken same time as S369. Unlike S363-*Lt.* and S363-*Oblt.*,
name given as "Boelcke" in accordance with the airman's preferred
spelling.

Key Dates:
21 May 1916   promoted to *Hauptmann*
28 Oct 1916   killed in action

Oswald Boelcke did not learn of his promotion to *Hauptmann* through
the normal channels:

> "On the night of that victorious day and evening Boelcke
> started for home on a leave that had been granted some time
> previously. It began with a most joyful surprise. When he
> reached Köthen on the following afternoon, he had to wait for a
> connection to Dessau, and [when he] went for a stroll in the
> street he read the latest communiqué in a shop window: '[First]
> Lieutenant Boelcke shot down his 17th and 18th opponents south
> of Avocourt and the Mort Homme respectively. His Majesty
> the Emperor has shown his appreciation of this superb flying
> officer's services by promoting him to captain.'" (Werner,
> *Knight of Germany*, p.171)

Sanke reissued S363 once again sometime after this promotion. Like
S363-*Oblt.* before it, there are no changes to its appearance other
than its updated rank. Theoretically, it could have made its debut
any time from June 1916 until Boelcke's death in October 1916 (after
which S363† was issued). The postmarked example of Immelmann's
S362-*Oblt.*, however, indicates that such cards were issued relatively
soon after the airman's promotion.

An odd variant of S363-*Hptm.* also exists. Though it displays
the same photograph and "*Hauptmann* Boelcke" title as well as the
information "363" and "W. Sanke, Berlin N.37," all the wording is
arranged differently and "*Postkartenvertrieb*'" is omitted along with
Rotophot's R-P-H symbol and the usual phrase warning against
copying the card. Was this a rare instance where Sanke worked with
another printer, or was it a counterfeit produced from Sanke's
original?

Above right: Oswald Boelcke, who was touring Turkey and the Balkans at the time, sits as a passenger in the back of an unarmed LVG airplane. He wrote on 30 July: "After a hasty lunch I flew back to Chanak with Meinecke, who came to fetch me; then we went back to St. Stefano along the northern coast of the Sea of Marmora. It was a fine flight as far as Rodosto, after which it became boring. But in this fashion I got back to Constantinople in three hours instead of the twenty-six taken by steamer." (Werner, *Knight of Germany*, p.96) The man in front is Emil Meinecke, one of the *Eindecker* pilots of *FA6*. Note that Boelcke is wearing his *Schirmmütze* (service cap), reversed and secured by its chinstrap, instead of a flying helmet. (photo courtesy of UTD)

A rare variant of S363-*Hptm*.

Toward the end of his summer 1916 tour of the Eastern Front, *Hptm*. Oswald Boelcke traveled to Kovel (Ukraine) where his brother Wilhelm was CO of *Kampstaffel 10*. This photograph was taken at that time and includes Oswald (marked with "xx"), Wilhelm standing to Oswald's right, and a captured Russian pilot (marked with "x"). *Leutnante* Erwin Böhme and Manfred von Richthofen served with *Kampfstaffel 8*, also located in Kovel, and it was during this visit that Boelcke asked them to join his newly-formed *Jasta 2* on the Western Front.

Two at right: On 17 July 1916, *Hptm*. Oswald Boelcke traveled to a port near Istanbul, Turkey, to see the German battle cruisers "Goeben" and "Breslau". "After seeing over both ships and dining on board the 'Goeben' I listened to a concert on deck in the glorious summer night. When I left, Captain Ackermann, the commanding officer of the Goeben, called for three cheers for me, and the sailors hoisted me on their shoulders." (Werner, *Knight of Germany*, p. 192) The first image is a snapshot of Boelcke on the sailors' shoulders and the second shows him with the ship's officers.

S363 (†)
(memorial)
BOELCKE
Oswald
Hauptmann

Taken: 17 to 19 January 1916
Douai/Lille
Publ: November 1916
Reason: memorial

Decorations:
WR: *Pour le Mérite*; Iron Cross, 1st Class; Pilot's Badge
MB: None
RB: None
BH: Royal Hohenzollern House Order, Knight's Cross/ Sw; Life
Saving Medal

Other Cards:
S364, S369, S373, S393, S408, S409
(L7720, L7721, L7761, L7776, L7785, L7793; N5579, N5580,
N5601, N5619, N5690, N6004, N6005, N6225)
Note: Taken same time as S369

Key Dates:
21 May 1916   promoted to *Hauptmann*
28 Oct 1916   killed in action

Sanke brought out S363† as a memorial card in November 1916
following the airman's death on 28 October 1916. It is marked with
a black border and has the "†" death symbol next to his name. Here
we have a definite example of a reissued Sanke card being published
sooner than the three-week rule generally observed by cards
exhibiting new photographs, because one representative has survived
that was used as early as 7 November 1916.

Lt. Josef Jacobs wrote the following in his diary entry of 30
October 1916:

> "The rumor circulated yesterday evening that *Hptm.*
> Boelcke had fallen. After an enquiry to headquarters we were
> informed that he had been fatally wounded in combat yesterday.
> It is reported to have happened this way. Boelcke chased a
> French biplane and forced it to the ground. Shortly before
> landing, the Frenchman is said to have fired for the last time
> whereupon Boelcke's machine ran into the French aircraft.
> Outside of some small damage both machines landed safely.
> Boelcke had been hit in the head and was instantly killed while
> the Frenchman was captured." (OTF 9:4, p.331)

Apart from the facts that Boelcke collided with another machine
and that he was dead, nothing else contained in the rumor turned out
to be true. Manfred von Richthofen, an eyewitness to Boelcke's fall,
wrote:

> "On the twenty-eighth of October we flew once again under
> the leadership of the great man. We always felt secure when he
> was along. There was only one Boelcke. The weather was very
> stormy, with many clouds. Other pilots did not fly that day,
> only fighter pilots.
> From a great distance we saw two impudent Englishmen
> over the Front, apparently having fun in the bad weather. We
> were six against their two. If they had been twenty we would
> not have been surprised to receive the signal of attack from
> Boelcke.

> The usual battle began. Boelcke went after one, and I the
> other. Close to Boelcke flew a good friend of his. It was an
> interesting fight. Both fired, and at any moment the Englishman
> had to fall. Suddenly an unnatural movement was observed in
> both German airplanes. The thought flashed through my brain:
> collision! I had never seen a collision in the air, although, like
> many others, I had imagined it. But this was not a collision;
> rather, it was a mere touching. But at the great speed of an
> airplane, even a slight touching is a violent concussion.
> Boelcke immediately pulled away from his intended victim
> and fell to earth in great spiraling curves. I still did not have the
> feeling he would crash, but as he glided below I noticed that a
> section of his wings was broken. I could not observe what
> happened next, but in the clouds he lost a whole wing. His
> airplane became uncontrollable and he plunged down,
> accompanied all the way by his faithful friend. When we got
> home, the report was already there: 'Our Boelcke is dead!' One
> could hardly conceive of it.
> It was most grievous, of course, to the one who survived
> the accident." (Richthofen, *Red Baron*, pp.57-58)

Boelcke's "faithful friend" was *Lt.* Erwin Böhme. Boelcke had
personally invited both Böhme and Richthofen, then with
Kampfstaffel 8, to join his new *Jasta 2* fighter squadron during an

August 1916 visit to Kovel. Though both men and many others who served with Boelcke would claim his friendship, Richthofen noted that Böhme was perhaps the closest to Boelcke of them all. Böhme related his story to his fiancée, Annamarie Brüning, on 31 October 1916:

"On Saturday afternoon we were sitting around our small airfield quarters on combat alert. I had just begun a game of chess with Boelcke. We were then called shortly before four o'clock during an infantry attack on the front. Boelcke himself led us, as usual. We came into contact over Flers very quickly with a number of English aircraft, fast single-seaters, that skillfully defended themselves.

In the ensuing wildly gyrating melee in which we could always only get into range for brief moments, we attempted to force our opponents downward by alternately blocking their path, as we had previously so often done with success. Boelcke and I had the same Englishman between us, as another opponent being chased by our friend Richthofen cut in front of us. In our abrupt mutual efforts to dodge, with both Boelcke and my views hindered by our wings, we did not see each other for a moment. Here is where it happened.

How can I describe my feelings from that moment on, when Boelcke suddenly appeared just a few meters to my right, how he dove, how I jerked upward, and how we nevertheless grazed each other, and both plummeted downward! It was only a light touch, but at such breakneck speeds that also meant a strong impact. Fate is usually so horribly irrational in its choice. Only a portion of my undercarriage was torn away. He lost the outermost portion of his left wing.

After falling a couple of hundred meters, I regained control of my aircraft and could follow Boelcke's. I saw his aircraft in a gradual glide, left wing drooping a bit, drifting toward our lines. First, in a layer of clouds in lower regions, where his aircraft was buffeted by strong winds. Then, he went into an ever steepening glide, and I saw before the landing how he could no longer keep his plane facing straightforward, and how he struck the ground near a gun battery.

People immediately hurried out of the battery dugout in order to help. My attempts to land near my friend were of no avail because of the shell holes and trenches. So I flew hurriedly back to our field. They told me only the other day that I nosed over on landing. I was completely unaware of the fact. I was totally distracted, but I still had some hope. However, as we arrived in an auto, they brought the corpse to us. He was immediately killed at the moment of impact. Boelcke never wore a crash helmet and also did not buckle himself firmly into his Albatros. Otherwise, he might have survived the actually not powerful impact." (OTF 5:1, pp.47-49)

Richthofen, in a letter home to his mother, further elaborated that Boelcke's skull had been crushed upon impact. Böhme was tormented by his role in Boelcke's fall – one can imagine the pressing guilt that plagued him knowing that he had contributed, albeit accidentally, to the death of his friend, mentor, and the Air Service's greatest ace – and a suicide watch was reportedly posted around him. On 12 November 1916, he again wrote to his fiancée:

"I have now regained a superficial control of myself. But in the silent hours my eyes see once again that ghastly moment when I had to watch my friend and master fall from beside me. Then the torturing question comes up once more: Why was he, the irreplaceable, doomed to be the victim of this blind destiny – for neither he nor I bore any blame for the calamity!" (Werner, *Knight of Germany*, pp.230-31)

Böhme, with the support of his friends and Boelcke's parents (who corresponded with him regularly after their son's funeral), eventually overcame the tragedy and went on to serve his country with great distinction.

S363 (†)
(memorial)
BOELCKE
Oswald
Hauptmann

Taken: 17 to 19 January 1916
Douai/Lille
Publ: November 1916
Reason: memorial

Decorations:
WR: *Pour le Mérite*; Iron Cross, 1st Class; Pilot's Badge
MB: None
RB: None
BH: Royal Hohenzollern House Order, Knight's Cross/ Sw; Life Saving Medal

Other Cards:
S364, S369, S373, S393, S408, S409
(L7720, L7721, L7761, L7776, L7785, L7793; N5579, N5580,
N5601, N5619, N5690, N6004, N6005, N6225)
Note: Taken same time as S369

Key Dates:
21 May 1916   promoted to *Hauptmann*
28 Oct 1916   killed in action

Sanke issued yet another S363 memorial card following Boelcke's 28 October 1916 fall in combat. Like S363†, it is bordered in black. Unlike S363†, the airman's printed identity has been replaced with a handwritten "Boelcke, *Hptm.*" The handwriting resembles Boelcke's and presumably was copied from an original document. In addition, Sanke's label and Rotophot's R-P-H symbol have traded positions when compared to all the other S363 versions. In the absence of any corroborating postmarks, this memorial version theoretically could have been issued anytime after Boelcke's demise. Nevertheless, it most likely came out closer to November 1916.

A funeral service was held for *Hptm.* Oswald Boelcke in Cambrai Cathedral on 31 October 1916. This was the first time that a German hero had been honored at one of the venerable cathedrals of northern France (see Werner, *Knight of Germany*, p.233), and as the following series of photographs demonstrate, the ceremony was conducted on a massive scale. This first set of three pictures show his coffin as it lay in state, gradually accumulating more flowers, wreaths, and other adornments as time progressed.

Two below: These two pictures show the Boelcke family climbing the stairs to enter the cathedral. Professor Max Bölcke (he preferred this spelling) and his wife, Mathilde, are dressed in black and are accompanied by Wilhelm, Max, and another of their sons (either Heinrich or Martin).

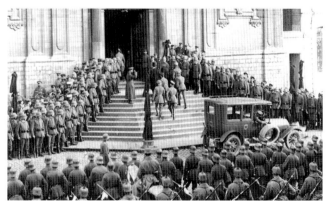

The funeral procession emerges from the cathedral. The first photo shows the empty gun carriage awaiting Boelcke's coffin. The next four include Manfred von Richthofen (with fur collar) carrying Boelcke's *Ordenskissen* (the black pillow that bore a dead serviceman's decorations) in front of the draped coffin. The final picture shows the coffin headed toward the gun carriage, with Manfred von Richthofen at the extreme right.

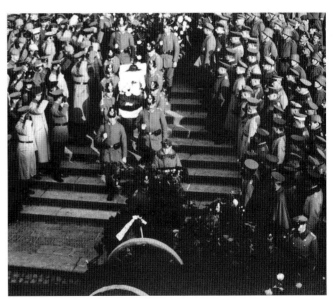

The Boelcke family follows Oswald's remains as they are loaded onto the gun carriage. In the center of the first picture, just to the right of the draped coffin, we see *Frau* Mathilde Bölcke. Above and to her right are Oswald's brothers Wilhelm, either Heinrich or Martin, and Max. Professor Max Bölcke stands in front of them in the second snapshot.

Above and opposite: "Bathed in rays of light, the procession…passed onward to the station through a long lane formed of lancers and footguards, while German airmen circled round in the sky above." (Werner, *Knight of Germany*, p.234)

The funeral procession files past the Boelcke family and through Cambrai on its way to the train station.

Opposite and above: Boelcke's funeral cortège arrives at the train station. The first photo in this series shows Manfred von Richthofen at the head of the procession carrying Boelcke's decorations on an *Ordenskissen*. Final tributes were delivered by *Gen.* von Below (Commander of the 1st Army, representing the Kaiser) and *Oblt.* Stefan Kirmaier (Boelcke's replacement as *Staffelführer* of *Jasta* 2). Kirmaier, with hands clasped and apparently delivering his oration, can be seen standing alone in the center of the third photograph. Manfred von Richthofen (with fur collar and service cap) is just in front of the short, dark tower to the left. From Cambrai station, a special train carried Boelcke's body home to Dessau.

S364
BOELCKE
Oswald
Oberleutnant

IMMELMANN
Max
Leutnant

Taken: 17 to 19 January 1916
Douai/Lille
Publ: late February to April 1916
Reason: post-*Pour le Mérite*

93

Decorations:
see Immelmann S361 and Boelcke S363

Other Cards:
See Immelmann S361 and Boelcke S363
Note: see Immelmann S361 and Boelcke S363. Name given as
"Bölcke" instead of the airman's preferred spelling, "Boelcke."

Key Dates:

21 Jan 1916	Boelcke departs from *Feldflieger-Abteilung 62*
2 Feb 1916	Boelcke promoted to *Oberleutnant* by this date
18 Apr 1916	Immelmann promoted to *Oberleutnant*

See the discussion of Boelcke's S363-*Lt.* where it was concluded
that he was promoted to *Oberleutnant* sometime between his 21
January departure from *Feldflieger-Abteilung 62* and 2 February
1916.

S364 is an obvious compilation of S361's and S363's photos
that was intended to honor Immelmann and Boelcke's simultaneous
investitures as knights of the Order *Pour le Mérite*. Of particular
interest is that it identifies Boelcke only as an *Oberleutnant* after its
predecessor, S363, had ranked him as *Leutnant*. In addition,
Immelmann is listed as a *Leutnant,* which he remained until 18 April
1916. This information, which helped us pinpoint S363-*Lt.*'s initial
appearance to February 1916, provides us with bookends for S364's
publication – that is, late February (a few weeks after Boelcke's
promotion) to April 1916 (Immelmann's promotion).

S364
(reissue)
BOELCKE
Oswald
Oberleutnant

IMMELMANN
Max
Oberleutnant

Taken: 17 to 19 January 1916
Douai/Lille
Publ: May to early June 1916
Reason: promotion

Decorations:
See Immelmann S361 and Boelcke S363

Other Cards:
See Immelmann S361 and Boelcke S363
Note: see Immelmann S361 and Boelcke S363. Name given as
"Bölcke" instead of the airman's preferred spelling, "Boelcke."

Key Dates:

| 18 Apr 1916 | Immelmann promoted to *Oberleutnant* |
| 21 May 1916 | Boelcke promoted to *Hauptmann* |

Like Immelmann's other cards to this point, S364 was reissued to
reflect the new rank he had attained on 18 April 1916. It continues to
list Boelcke as an *Oberleutnant,* which indicates that it was not
published any later than early June 1916, when the news of Boelcke's
21 May promotion would have been generally widespread.

Similar to S364, Boelcke and Immelmann were often featured together as the
"dynamic duo" of the German Air Service. This composite of portions of
IMMEL16 (see S362) and BOELCKE2 (see p.11) was used to announce their
simultaneous *Pour le Mérite* awards on the cover of the 23 January 1916 edition
of Frankfurt's *Das Illustrierte Blatt*. Note the misspelling of Boelcke's name.

S364
(reissue)
BOELCKE
Oswald
Hauptmann

IMMELMANN
Max
Oberleutnant

Taken: 17 to 19 January 1916
Douai/Lille
Publ: June 1916
Reason: promotion

Decorations:
See Immelmann S361 and Boelcke S363

Other Cards:
See Immelmann S361 and Boelcke S363
Note: see Immelmann S361 and Boelcke S363. Unlike prior S364
versions, name given as "Boelcke" in accordance with the airman's
preferred spelling.

Key Dates:

| 18 Apr 1916 | Immelmann promoted to *Oberleutnant* |
| 21 May 1916 | Boelcke promoted to *Hauptmann* |

Below and right: A commemorative plate, commissioned by the *Deutscher Luftflotten-Verein* ("German Airfleet Association") and manufactured by Rosenthal of Bavaria, was issued "in memory of our two heroes" in 1917. An advertisement for the plate appeared in the November/December 1917 issue of the association's magazine, *Die Luftflotte*. Note that its appearance in the ad is slightly different than the actual item.

Unsere Flieger-Helden

Hauptmann Boelcke

Oberleutnant Immelmann

S364 was reissued once again to reflect Boelcke's 21 May 1916 promotion to *Hauptmann*. Though the card technically could have been published any time after mid-June 1916 up until Boelcke's death, a postmarked example of Immelmann's updated S362-*Oblt.* indicates that this card most likely came out quite soon after Boelcke's promotion.

S369
BOELCKE
Oswald
Oberleutnant

Taken: 17 to 19 January 1916
Douai/Lille
Publ: late February to early June 1916
Reason: post-*Pour le Mérite*

Decorations:
WR: *Pour le Mérite*; Iron Cross, 1st Class; Pilot's Badge
MB: None
RB: None
BH: Royal Hohenzollern House Order, Knight's Cross/ Sw; Life Saving Medal

Other Cards:
S363, S364, S373, S393, S408, S409
(L7720, L7721, L7761, L7776, L7785, L7793; N5579, N5580, N5601, N5619, N5690, N6004, N6005, N6225)
Note: Taken same time as S363

Key Dates:

12 Jan 1916	awarded *Pour le Mérite*
17 Jan 1916	*Pour le Mérite* award ceremony at Lille
20 Jan 1916	sends "new photos" home
21 Jan 1916	departs from *Feldflieger-Abteilung 62*
2 Feb 1916	promoted to *Oberleutnant* by this date
21 May 1916	promoted to *Hauptmann*
25 Jun 1916	postmark on Buddecke's S371

S369 was a contemporary of S363. They share the familiar Douai/ Lille tapestry and the same chair in the background (see S363's original source, BOELCKE1). As noted during the examination of S363-*Lt.*, these photographs must have been snapped after Boelcke had received his *Pour le Mérite* but before he had sent "a couple of the new photos" home (on 20 January) and left Douai (21 January). His attire is identical in S363 and S369, so they probably originated from the same sitting.

Unlike S363, there is no known example of a *Leutnant* version of S369. This makes sense, given that S364 only refers to Boelcke as an *Oberleutnant* or *Hauptmann*. This also means that S369, like S363-*Oblt.*, was first published sometime from late February to May 1916. Here, however, it is likely that S369 was issued in the latter part of that range because it is numerically proximate to Buddecke's S371, which is thought to have first appeared in later May or early June. Possible support may be offered by one postmarked example written 27 June 1916.

S369
(reissue)
BOELCKE
Oswald
Hauptmann

Taken: 17 to 19 January 1916
Douai/Lille
Publ: June 1916
Reason: promotion

Decorations:
WR: *Pour le Mérite*; Iron Cross, 1st Class; Pilot's Badge
MB: None
RB: None
BH: Royal Hohenzollern House Order, Knight's Cross/ Sw; Life Saving Medal

Other Cards:
S363, S364, S373, S393, S408, S409
(L7720, L7721, L7761, L7776, L7785, L7793; N5579, N5580, N5601, N5619, N5690, N6004, N6005, N6225)
Note: Taken same time as S363

Key Dates:
21 May 1916   promoted to *Hauptmann*
28 Oct 1916   killed in action

Sanke reissued S369 sometime after Boelcke's promotion to *Hauptmann*. There are no changes to its appearance other than its updated rank. Theoretically, it could have made its debut any time from June 1916 until Boelcke's death in October 1916 (after which S363† was issued). One postmarked example of Immelmann's S362-*Oblt.* tells us that such cards were probably published soon after the airman's promotion. Nevertheless, without reliable postmark evidence, we are currently unable to designate a narrower timeframe with any certainty.

Oblt. Oswald Boelcke pays his respects at the burial of *Oblt.* Werner von Bake, *Staffelführer* of *KG 4*. Bake and his pilot, *Lt.* Georg Schultz, were shot down near Avoucourt on 16 May 1916 and died of their wounds two and three days later, respectively. This was right before Boelcke left for home on 21 May and discovered that he had been promoted to *Hauptmann*. The pilot in line behind

Boelcke accompanies him again in the second picture. The next man in line, wearing an Observer's Badge, bears a striking resemblance to Eberhard Mohnicke (e.g., see MVR16), who we know served with *KG 2* in 1916. Did he also spend some time with *KG 4?*

S371
BUDDECKE
Hans-Joachim
Hauptmann

Taken: mid- to late April 1916
Turkey, by Addie Kah
Publ: mid-May to June 1916
Reason: *Pour le Mérite* award

Decorations:

WR: *Pour le Mérite*; Iron Cross, 1st Class; Pilot's Badge (Ott);
Golden Liakat Medal/ Sw (Ott)
MB: None
RB: None
BH: None

Other Cards:

S408, S433, S434
(L7793, L7825; N5600)
Note: Turkish uniform with Turkish Air Service insignia on black
lambskin *kalpak* hat

Key Dates:

14 Apr 1916	awarded *Pour le Mérite*
6 May 1916	S371 photo published in *Die Woche* 19, p.657; credited to "Phot. Addie Kah"
7 May 1916	visits Vaux airfield
8 May 1916	visits Charleville headquarters
24 May 1916	S371 photo published in *Flugsport* 11, p304
25 Jun 1916	S371 postmarked example

Hauptmann Buddecke

371
Postkartenvertrieb W.Sanke
„ BERLIN N. 32. „
Nachdruck wird gerichtlich verfolgt

Though the leafy wallpaper in S371's background seems to suit a European location, the 6 May 1916 edition of *Die Woche* credits the photograph to "Addie Kah" – a name that is neither Turkish nor German.[1] *Die Woche* featured a wider view of S371's picture that shows part of a mirror to Buddecke's right. BUDDECKE1 was published in the 21 January 1917 edition of *Berliner Illustrirte Zeitung* and though poor in quality, appears to have come from the same sitting. BUDDECKE2 is a picture taken around the same time that appeared in Buddecke's biography, *El Schahin (Der Jagdfalke)*. This time, we see a tapestry curtain in the background that could be either German or Turkish. We do not know if Buddecke received his *Pour le Mérite* in Turkey or after he was recalled to Germany; but we do know that he was back in Germany in early May because of a brief reference in one of Oswald Boelcke's letters home and certain photographic evidence. On 9 May 1916, Boelcke wrote:

> "Yesterday we went to Charleville together to visit the chief; we also met Buddecke there, who flies in Turkey. He told me some very interesting tales." (Werner, *Knight of Germany*, p.167)

A photo taken during a visit with his former unit, *Feldflieger-Abteilung 23*, shows Buddecke standing with a group of men in front of Chateau Vaux (BUDDECKE3). The date "7 May 1916" is written at the top of a blackboard duty roster in the background. Charleville is only 35 miles east of Vaux, so Buddecke could easily have traveled there the next day to run into Boelcke. We also have a picture of Buddecke standing in front of a Fokker D.I in the company of Anthony Fokker and *Hptm.* Albert Mühlig-Hofmann at Fokker's airfield in Schwerin-Gorries (BUDDECKE4). Some sources have theorized that it was taken in August 1916, yet it is equally possible that it was snapped in April or May 1916, shortly after Fokker had entered his D.I in the fighter trials held at Adlershof on 15 April

1916. The aircraft seen in the picture fits the description of his D.I prototype, No.140/16. Schwerin-Gorries is 115 miles northwest of Berlin, and Buddecke, a native of the capital and presumably home on leave around this time, would have had good reason to see Fokker's latest offering firsthand. In any event, Buddecke is dressed in the same, rather distinctive outfit in S371 and BUDDECKE1-4. In particular, he is wearing the Golden Liakat Medal as his only Turkish decoration in all of them. We know it is not the similar-looking Imtiaz Medal that he subsequently earned because the Imtiaz Medal is noticeably larger than the Liakat. The 12 February 1916 edition of *Die Woche* tells us that he had won the "*Goldenen Liakatmedaille*" for recent actions over the Dardanelles. If he had received the more prestigious Golden Imtiaz Medal before the *Pour le Mérite*, he surely would have worn it instead of the Liakat Medal, as seen in later pictures of him (e.g., see the photo with *General* Liman von Sanders below and S434's BUDDECKE5). Evidently, the Golden Imtiaz Medal came to Buddecke only after his return to Turkey in the summer.[2]

The *Pour le Mérite* recipients before and immediately after Buddecke earned their decorations by bringing down eight aircraft. Buddecke is considered to have been an exception to this rule, because his eighth official victory is listed as having fallen on 6 September – much too late to have been the qualifying factor (see Franks, Bailey, and Guest, *Above the Lines*, p.88). Consequently, it has been offered that German officials recognized that victories were tougher to come by in the Turkish theater that Buddecke served in, and that the seven confirmed and twelve unconfirmed kills that he had achieved by 27 January were considered close enough. Yet a 14 April award date seems a little late to have recognized this record. Two more unconfirmed victories occurred on 30 March and 4 April 1916, and their proximity to Buddecke's award date makes it at least equally possible that one of them was counted as his eighth at that time.

Buddecke's gravestone and service record list him as an *Oberleutnant*, though S371 calls him *Hauptmann*. This is because German Air Service pilots were often granted a temporary promotion while serving with the Turkish military. Buddecke's shoulder boards indeed display the two "pips" of a captain, so Sanke accurately referred to him as such.

The fact that Buddecke is wearing his *Pour le Mérite* (awarded 14 April) and that this image was published in a 6 May German newspaper points to an original photography date of mid- to late April 1916. Normally, we would deduce from this that S371 could have made its initial appearance as early as three weeks later, or early May. Yet Boelcke and Immelmann's S373, just two cards later, could not have come out earlier than June by virtue of its reference to Boelcke as *Hauptmann*, which he became on 21 May. Thus it seems more likely that S371 made its debut close to S373's in June. The earliest postmark encountered so far for S371, 25 June 1916, supports this. So does the course of a line drawn from the late August 1916 appearance of Höhndorf's S381 back to S371's proposed debut. If the line ends up at mid-May, it projects that Wintgen's S378 was published faster than any other card we have seen (i.e., within two weeks of his *Pour le Mérite* photograph). If it ends in June, it conforms to the late July to mid-August debut otherwise predicted for S378. It is also possible, however, that a publication gap of some sort, like that observed between S451 and S502, occurred some time after S371 and before S378. In such a case, S371 and S378 still could have come out respectively in mid-May and late July without running afoul of each other. Hopefully, future postmark evidence will settle the matter.

Notes

[1] According to one expert, most of the photographers in Turkey at this time were foreigners from many different parts of the world. Thus the name could well have been non-Turkish. Peter Kilduff, however, has offered a more interesting suggestion (personal correspondence). The letters "ADK" are pronounced "ah-day-kah" in German. Perhaps the photographer or his organization had these initials and were phonetically represented as such.

[2] This notion is contradicted by a transcript of the memoirs of *Maj.* Erich Serno (chief of the German Air Service in Turkey), a copy of which can be found in the History of Aviation Collection housed at the University of Texas at Dallas. Under the heading of "The Closing Battles of Gallipoli," Serno notes that "the Great Golden Imtiaz was presented to Buddecke by Enver Pasha on the battlefield of Gallipoli itself." (p.I/24) The Gallipoli campaign drew to a close during the period August-December 1915. Nevertheless, given *Die Woche*'s 12 February 1916 notice of Buddecke's receipt of the lesser Golden Liakat Medal around this time and the photographic evidence that shows it as the only Turkish award accompanying his *Pour le Mérite* (awarded 14 April 1916), one wonders if the two awards became confused in Serno's memory.

BUDDECKE I

A newspaper photograph of *Hptm.* Hans-Joachim Buddecke that appears to have been taken the same time as S371. In both images, Buddecke's Golden Liakat medal is approximately level with his second tunic button – a higher position than usual (see next images).

On 20 July 1916, Oswald Boelcke arrived in Smyrna and wrote: "Lunched with Excellency Liman von Sanders, who was very nice and had his photo taken with Buddecke and myself." (Werner, *Knight of Germany*, p.193) From left to right: Buddecke, Sanders, Boelcke. Note that Buddecke is now wearing the larger Golden Imtiaz medal.

BUDDECKE2

BUDDECKE3

Four photos of *Hptm.* Hans-Joachim Buddecke. His Turkish uniform and the presence of his *Pour le Mérite* and Golden Liakat decorations indicate that they were snapped between 14 April 1916 and his return to Turkey sometime before Oswald Boelcke met him there on 20 July 1916. The first seems to have originated from Turkey, perhaps at the time of Buddecke's *Pour le Mérite* investiture. The second was taken when he visited *FFA 23* at Vaux on 7 May 1916. Note that his Golden Liakat medal hangs lower here than in any of the other photos. The next photo shows, from left to right, Anthony Fokker, *Hptm.* Albert Mühlig-Hofmann, and Buddecke in front of a Fokker D.I. The last is of Buddecke alone, perhaps at the same airfield location (his medal positions are precisely the same).

BUDDECKE4

ribbon (see O'Connor, *Aviation Awards IV*, p.108 and *Aviation Awards VI*, p.305). A later photo, taken 10-20 July 1916, shows him in possession of both Oldenburg awards (see O'Connor, *Aviation Awards VI*, p.86). So we at least have photographic evidence that brackets their receipt to sometime between February and July 1916. This seems correct, given that S372 came out right after Buddecke's S371, which first appeared within a mid-May to June timeframe. Our guideline assigns the first publication of Leffers' S372 to no later than the end of June. Pushing back three weeks from that point places the picture's origin within a timeframe ranging from mid-February to late May 1916.

LEFFERS1, a nearly identical but cropped photograph taken the same time as S372's, was later published in the 20 August 1916 edition of *Berliner Illustrirte Zeitung* in recognition of Leffers' fifth victory on 9 July.

Note
[1] *KEK B*'s name was changed to *Abwehr-Kommando-Nord* (*AKN*) in late June or early July 1916, and again to *Kampfeinsitzer-staffel Bertincourt* (*Kest B*) a few weeks later.

This newspaper publication's image is almost identical with Leffers' S371 portrait. Even the reflective light patterns on his service cap's visor and chinstrap appear to match. Leffers' face, however, is turned slightly more toward the camera in S371 (e.g., compare the angle of the bridge of his nose or the relative position of his chin in both pictures), which tells us that they are two separate images that came from the same sitting.

A pre-*Pour le Mérite* picture of *Lt.* Gustav Leffers, probably taken in early 1916.

LEFFERS1

Opposite: Three views of *Lt. Gustav Leffers'* first confirmed victory on 5 December 1915, BE.2c No. 2049 of RFC No.13 Squadron. Both the pilot, 2nd Lt. Arthur Browne, and his observer, Air Mechanic 1st Class William Cox, were killed. Their bodies lie in the foreground of the first picture, covered by fabric from their airplane.

Right: The aftermath of Gustav Leffers' fourth victory. RFC No.15 Squadron lost 2nd Lt. James Cunningham (pilot), Air Mechanic 1st Class John Newton, and BE.2c No.4153 when they fell together in flames on 14 March 1916.

S373
BOELCKE
Oswald
Hauptmann

IMMELMANN
Max
Oberleutnant

and other members of *FFA 62*

Taken: 20 January 1916
Douai
Publ: July 1916
Reason: post-*Pour le Mérite*

Decorations:
See Immelmann S361 and Boelcke S363

Other Cards:
See Immelmann S361 and Boelcke S363

Key Dates:

21 Jan 1916	Boelcke departs from *Feldflieger-Abteilung 62*
18 Apr 1916	Immelmann promoted to *Oberleutnant*
21 May 1916	Boelcke promoted to *Hauptmann*
11 Jun 1916	portion of S373 photo published in *Berliner Illustrirte Zeitung* 24, p.353
18 Jun 1916	Immelmann killed in action

Immelmann's biographer, his brother Franz, included S373's picture in *Der Adler von Lille* and labeled it: *"Abteilung 62 am 20.I.16"* ("Section 62 on 20 January 1916"). Boelcke's personal copy of the same photograph (BOELCKE10) lists the name of each man on the back in Boelcke's own handwriting. The photograph had special significance because it marked the last day of Boelcke and

Hauptmann Boelcke und Oberleutnant Immelmann im Kreise ihrer Kameraden.

Immelmann's successful partnership in the same flying unit. Boelcke departed the next day for Montmédy and later to Jametz to take part in preparations for the Verdun offensive. He would not return again to Douai until the following June when he attended Immelmann's funeral services.

It is perhaps just possible that S373's photograph was among those that Boelcke sent home with his 20 January letter (see Boelcke's S363). Observation units had their own photographic development capabilities, so Boelcke's farewell picture could have been prepared in time for his letter home, particularly if it had been taken by one of the unit's men. This would have been very fast work, however. It is more likely that the group photo was among those referred to by Boelcke as not yet having arrived from Douai in his 12 February 1916 letter (see S363-*Oblt.*). Of course, he could have had it delivered independent of either of these two occasions.

Note that both Immelmann and Boelcke are dressed somewhat more casually than they are in S360-63. Boelcke's trousers do not display the crisp creases seen in S363, and Immelmann is wearing the Royal Hohenzollern House Order ribbon in his buttonhole instead of his *Grossordenschnalle*. This supports the notion that S360-63 were taken earlier at a more formal function, and perhaps quite soon after the aces' *Pour le Mérite* investitures on 17 January.

S373 includes three other pilots who would appear in later Sanke cards. The first is *Lt.* Max Mulzer who had only recently arrived from *Feldflieger-Abteilung 5b.* Immelmann became Mulzer's mentor and helped him achieve his first victory two months later. The two men, nicknamed "Bavarian Max" and "Saxon Max," often flew in action together and shared a professional and personal bond that was later symbolized by Mulzer carrying Immelmann's decorations at his funeral. The second future Sanke airman is observer *Oblt.* Maximilian von Cossel who, along with then *Vzfw.* Rudolf Windisch, would gain fame during a daring sabotage mission behind enemy lines the following October. *Lt.* Ernst Hess, who had shot down his first plane in the company of Oswald Boelcke on 5 January 1916, is the third:

> "The sky having clouded over meanwhile, I drove into the town. I had hardly sat down to lunch when ten enemy aircraft appeared over Douai. I jumped into a car and drove out to the aerodrome. When I got there, all ten were just unloading bombs on our aerodrome. Consequently all the mechanics had crawled into the dug outs – I bellowed like a bull until at last one came out. Unfortunately Immelmann, who stayed on the aerodrome over lunchtime, had taken off in my new 160 H.P. Fokker – he could not get the hang of its gadgets – so that I was left with an old 80 H.P. reserve machine. Consequently, I could not overhaul the enemy squadron, but only got near a single machine that lagged behind the others. But this was already picked off by another Fokker—our Lieut. Hess. The pair of them were doing gymnastics all round each other. To help a bit, I dived on the Englishman and put about one hundred and fifty rounds into his machine. Then the fellow saw he could not do anything against the two of us and preferred to make a quick landing at Vitry – with the both of us at his heels." (Werner, *Knight of Germany*, pp.140-41)

This telling passage reveals two facets of Boelcke's personality. His expression of frustration with Immelmann suggests that their relationship was not always cordial – something that we have only recently begun to recognize. We also see the supportive and generous side that served Boelcke well as a leader and teacher. Even though Hess was credited with this victory, one suspects that Boelcke's attack helped more than just "a bit."

The cover of the 11 June 1916 edition of *Berliner Illustrirte Zeitung* published a composite image of Boelcke and Immelmann that was created from S373's scene (BOELCKE11). In this version, all the other men were removed, the background was replaced with an artificial one, and Boelcke and Immelmann were repositioned shoulder-to-shoulder. The caption notes that the two airmen had collectively achieved 33 victories (18 for Boelcke, 15 for Immelmann). Considering the original picture's 20 January date, June might seem a little late for an appearance in the newspapers. Our guideline, however, similarly predicts that S373 was not published until early July. These factors seem to indicate that the photo was not made available for publication until around this time. Now comes the question of what prompted S373's publication – the victory celebration expressed by the magazine version or Immelmann's death on 18 June? That S373 has no "†" or other indication of Immelmann's demise seems to favor something along the line of the former, although the postcard alternately could have been too far into its publication process by the time the news of the ace's fall became widespread. Though it is true that unmarked cards of dead pilots were issued later on in the series (e.g., Kirmaier's S445, Schulte's S547, Keudell's S555-56, and Wendelmuth's S594), we would expect that the death of a pilot of Immelmann's stature, as demonstrated by S361†, S377, and the later S610, would have been noted on any subsequent card.

BOELCKE10

Oswald Boelcke himself identified the airmen of *FFA 62* on the back of this personal copy of the original photo used for S373. Front row, from left to right: Salffner, Meding, (*Lt.* Albert) Oesterreicher, Boelcke, (*Hptm.* Hermann) Kastner, (*Lt.* Max) Immelmann, von Krause, (*Lt.* Ernst) Hess. Back row, from left to right: (*Lt.* Max) Mulzer, von Schilling, (*Oblt.* Maximilian) von Cossel, Fromme, (*Oblt.*) von Gusnar.

BOELCKE II

These two images were based on the figures found in S373. The first cleverly attached Immelmann's body and left hand to *Hptm.* Hermann Kastner's left arm to make it appear that Immelmann stood next to Boelcke. The second removed Kastner completely and inserted a drawing of Boelcke's left arm to give the same impression.

S377
(memorial)
IMMELMANN
Max
Oberleutnant

Taken: 17 to 19 January 1916
Douai/Lille
Publ: July 1916
Reason: memorial

Decorations:
WR: *Pour le Mérite*; Iron Cross, 1st Class; Pilot's Badge
MB: None
RB: Military St. Henry Order, Knight's Cross (Sax); Albert Order, Knight 2nd Class/ Sw (Sax); Friedrich August Medal in Silver (Sax), Iron Cross, 2nd Class; Royal Hohenzollern House Order, Knight's Cross/ Sw; Military Merit Order, 4th Class/ Sw (Bav)
BH: None

Other Cards:
S340, S342, S347, S360-62, S364, S373, S377, S408, S610
(L7705, L7713, L7716-20, L7793; N5613-14, N5632, N5690, N6004)

Note: Taken same time as S360-61
Pour le Mérite has "pie-slice" attachment

Key Dates:
18 Jun 1916   killed in action

To this day, controversy still surrounds the death of Max Immelmann. German accounts state that during the final burst of machine gun fire that brought down 2nd Lt. John Savage and Air Mechanic 2nd class T. Robinson in FE.2b No.4909 (RFC No.25 Squadron), the interrupter gear on Immelmann's Fokker E.III malfunctioned, resulting in some of his own bullets sawing off at least one of his propeller blades. This in turn caused violent vibrations that led to the eventual breakup of his machine in midair and his fatal crash. The British, on the other hand, claim that he was brought down by the marksmanship of Corporal J. Waller in another FE.2b flown by 2nd Lt. G. McCubbin. In his correspondence with *Popular Flying* magazine in October 1935, McCubbin recalled:

> "At about 9.00 in the evening, we both saw three Fokkers at the back of Lens. Savage and I were quite a distance apart, but we signaled to each other that we were going to engage these Fokkers.

Savage, whilst proceeding towards them suddenly signaled that he was returning. He was much nearer the Fokkers than I was, and they apparently noticed this as well, and one dived on him immediately. I was flying much higher than they were and immediately dived on the one that was by this time on Savage's tail, but did not open fire. The other two got on my tail, with the result that you had a string of machines all diving down.

Savage's machine suddenly got out of control, as the Fokker had been firing at it, and Savage's machine went down. By this time I was very close to the Fokker and [the pilot] apparently realized we were on his tail, and he immediately started to do what I expect was the beginning of an 'Immelmann' turn. As he started the turn we opened fire and the Fokker immediately got out of control and went down to earth."

Some writers have theorized that the German explanation had been concocted to "sustain the myth of Immelmann's invincibility" from enemy skills. Such a conclusion, however, ignores three facts. First, Immelmann had barely survived a similar incident only a few weeks before while flying a Fokker E.IV on 31 May 1916. His brother Franz described the incident:

"In his efforts to protect Heinemann and divert these two opponents to himself my brother opened a continuous fire from far too great a distance. Then his Fokker suddenly reared up with a terrible jerk, which was followed by a horrible shaking and jolting. His hands performed the right actions instinctively – gas off – ignition out.

Weird tremors accompanied the final revolutions of the engine which went round very irregularly with the driving force of its 14 cylinders and only half a propeller, until at last a violent jerk brought it to a standstill, and at the same moment the machine whirled down into the depths over its left wing." (Immelmann, *Eagle of Lille*, pp.201-02)

Immelmann managed to bring the stricken craft down safely; and upon later examination on the ground, it was determined that his "half a propeller" was due to a failure of the machine gun interruptor mechanism.

Second, photographic evidence seems to support the German account. IMMEL17 is a picture of the wreckage of Immelmann's plane after it had been placed in temporary strorage in a hangar. One propeller blade exhibits signs of what may be bullet hole penetrations at precisely the level where the machine gun's barrel was aligned (compare to IMMEL18 and IMMEL19).

Third, when Boelcke traveled to Douai to attend Immelmann's funeral, he most likely viewed the wreckage and talked with investigators himself. In a 4 July 1916 letter home, he told his family:

"Immelmann lost his life by a silly chance. All that is written in the papers about a fight in the air, etc. is rot. A bit of his propeller flew off; the jarring tore the bracing wires connecting up with the fuselage, and then that broke away." (Werner, *Knight of Germany*, p.178)

Indeed, IMMEL17 and another photo (see S361†) display the relatively intact portion of the rear fuselage that was reported to have torn away. Boelcke's letters amply demonstrate that he was truthful and accurate in his reporting and there is no reason to believe that he would have taken part in a conspiracy to "sustain the myth of Immelmann's invincibility" in a private letter home. There is no reason to mistrust McCubbin's testimony either, so the truth probably resides within both accounts. Franz Immelmann's description of his brother's mishap on 31 May noted that the machine "suddenly reared up" after the propeller blade had been shot off and then "whirled

down into the depths over its left wing." McCubbin stated that right after Immelmann had shot down Savage and Robinson's plane, "he immediately started to do what I expect was the beginning of an 'Immelmann' turn." At that moment McCubbin and Waller opened fire "and the Fokker immediately got out of control and went down to earth." Both accounts describe similar events. What may have happened is that Immelmann, during the course of his attack on Savage and Robinson, once again sheared off his propeller with his own bullets. His machine jerked up in response, stalled, and fell down over its wing just as it had on 31 May. From the perspective of McCubbin and Waller, who had just opened fire at this point, he had attempted an escape maneuver and then gone down as a result of their return fire.

S377 is unique in that the entire background of the card is black. Immelmann's S360 picture is placed above a poem written by Barbara Goede that is roughly translated as:

With a Geman eagle's strength and certainty,
You guided your airplane, through danger and adversity,
Floated through the air, so calm and graceful,
Conqueror of the clouds, unreachable!
In years so young, with courage unmatched,
Laurel wreath flowering in your grasp!
Immelmann, of fliers boldest!

Immelmann, of victors proudest!
How your pair of wings so radiant
Brought fear and terror to your opponent.
How you – fighting your foes,
From dizzying heights to a deep grave below,
Vanquished them all, defying death –
Inspired song with your success.
Immelmann, of fliers boldest!
Immelmann, of victors proudest!

Today our sorrow weighs heavy and full,
He flies no more, our pride, our eagle!
His heart suddenly stopped in his victory run,
In his flight up to the radiant sun!
His decoration, a green laurel wreath,
Blooms proudly from the grave beneath,
Gratefully and sadly with loving hand,
It is cared for and guarded by the Fatherland!
Immelmann, boldest fighter
Lives on in the people ever brighter.
(trans. by this writer)

The collected remains of Immelmann's Fokker E.III 246/16. With regard to the German claim that Immelmann shot himself down, the upright propeller blade in the center foreground of the first photo is of particular interest because it displays evidence of being sawn in two by bullets. Compare the location of its break to the next two pictures. The first shows the results of a similar incident with another *Eindecker*, while the second gives a better perspective on the machine gun's level relative to the propeller blade. If one uses the circular, metal propeller hub plate as a scale reference, it can be seen that the break in Immelmann's propeller occurred right at machine gun level.

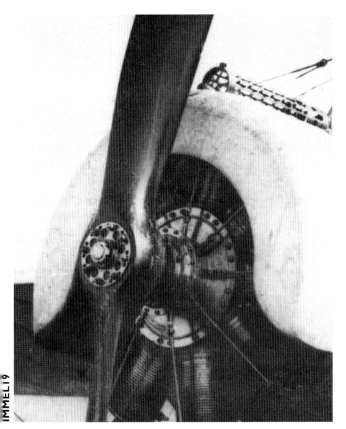

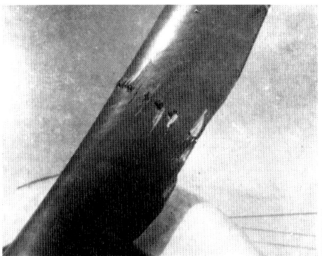

Our guideline places S377's debut in July 1916, about four weeks after Immelmann's death. Indeed, we have one S377 example that is postmarked 22 July 1916. We have an analogous situation involving Boelcke. Following his death on 28 October 1916, both Sanke and Liersch issued S409 and L7776 that featured Boelcke's S363 portrait above a poem mourning his loss. One surviving example of S409 is

postmarked 27 November 1916, while one of L7776 is dated 13 November 1916. Sanke and Liersch did the same thing after Immelmann's demise, issuing S377 and L7705 that combined poetic tributes with his S360 portrait; and we have an L7705 example postmarked 3 August 1916.

Right: "…wreaths in honour of the 'Gallant and Chivalrous Opponent' were dropped behind the German lines by representatives of the Royal Flying Corps and various British squadrons as soon as his death became known on their own side." (Immelmann, *Eagle of Lille*, p.218). This is one of them, delivered by Lts. Allister McMillen and Howard Long on 1 July 1916.

Below: "The coffin lay in state in the garden of the hospital in Douai, in the centre of a grove of laurels and cypresses, where it was surrounded by wreaths and covered with a sea of roses. It was flanked by four pillars, crowned with iron braziers, from which glowing flames rose up to heaven." (Immelmann, *Eagle of Lille*, p.219)

The coffin, held aloft by pall bearers, is led out of the hospital garden by *Lt.* Max Mulzer, bearer of Immelmann's *Ordenskissen*.

Above and next page: The funeral procession leaves the hospital grounds in the first photo, then wends its way through the streets of Douai. Max Mulzer, with white hat band, can be seen following the flag-draped coffin in the third and fifth pictures.

The cortège, led by a military band, arrives at Douai's train station. In the third through seventh pictures, Immelmann's coffin is brought to the special train car that will carry it to Dresden. Once again, Mulzer (with distinctive white hat band) can be observed accompanying his friend's coffin. The final image records the presiding chaplain and other attendees conferring with one another after the train with Immelmann's body had departed.

After the arrival of Immelmann's coffin at Dresden's train station, his mother and sister (center) are greeted by an officer while another mourner pays her respects in the funeral car.

"Thousands awaited him in silent mourning, thousands lined the streets, thousands accompanied the dead airman on his last journey from the station to the Tolkewitz cemetery." (Immelmann, *Eagle of Lille*, p.220)

S378
WINTGENS
Kurt
Leutnant

Taken: 1 to18 July 1916
Publ: August 1916
Reason: *Pour le Mérite* award

Decorations:
WR: *Pour le Mérite*; Iron Cross, 1st Class; Pilot's Badge
MB: None
RB: None
BH: Royal Hohenzollern House Order, Knight's Cross/ Sw; Iron Cross, 2nd Class; Miltary Merit Order, 4th Class/ Sw (Bav)

Other Cards:
S391, S392, S400, S408
(L7729, L7793)
Note: Wearing eyeglasses

Key Dates:

30 Jun 1916	victory #8
1 Jul 1916	awarded *Pour le Mérite*
19 Jul 1916	awarded Albert Order, Knight 2nd Class/ Sw (Sax)
23 Jul 1916	S378 photo published in *Berliner Illustrirte Zeitung* 30, p.452

On 22 June 1916, *Lt.* Kurt Wintgens wrote a friend:

"Dear Karl:
At the time you wrote your last letter you had already been asked for eight days previously at *Idflieg*. If this organization would really work correctly, everything should have been all right by now. Once again I'll try to speed up things a bit.

This afternoon my 160hp engine goes to Oberursel. Yesterday it collected a bullet in a too strenuous chase of a Farman with 1420 rpm. It has earned its cooper up in the factory reasonably, for now it has downed one Clerget, two Le Rhône and lastly a 16-cylinder Renault. That last one was placed in a Farman biplane, which was my sixth. It was a wonderful fight. He exploded marvellously. He was already behind the French lines when the pilot, who hung dead over the right side, apparently touched the rudder in some way. The machine turned and fell burning into the German lines, greeted by a thunderous hurrah from the whole of the Front.

A couple of hundred meters next to me, Höhndorf fought a Nieuport. The French thereupon wrote in their announcement: 'In Lorraine, four of our machines gave battle to four Fokkers. Two of the latter fell down, one of them afire. One of our machines had to land.'

The one who fell in flames was supposed to be me. I had rather slid down somewhat, but as an old hand at stunt flying, had flattened out elegantly over the French lines. The flames mentioned were those of my opponent, whose landing took place at a negative angle." (C&C 26:2, pp.103-04)

The day after writing this letter, Wintgens brought down American Victor Chapman from Escadrille N.124. Wintgens' all-important eighth victory, which qualified him for the *Pour le Mérite*, followed a week later when he shot down another Farman near Chateau-Salins.

In S378, Wintgens proudly displays the *Pour le Mérite* that he was subsequently awarded on 1 July 1916, but there is no sign of the Saxon Albert Order, Knight 2nd Class that he received soon afterward on 19 July 1916. This places the origin of the photograph to 1-18 July, a timeframe confirmed by the original picture's appearance (complete with leafy background) in the 23 July 1916 edition of *Berliner Illustrirte Zeitung* (WINTGENS1). It is likely then that the picture was snapped on or nearer the day of his actual investiture, because it often took several weeks or more for photographs to make it into such publications.

Our publication guideline predicts that S378's appearance as a Sanke postcard followed in late July 1916 or early August, which would comply with our three-week rule. We know it was no later than 2 September 1916, the date of one postmarked example.

WINTGENS I

The original image behind S378 before the leafy background was erased and Wintgens' signature was added.

An early portrait of Kurt Wintgens, published in the journal *Illustrierte Geschichte des Weltkrieges*. At the time this photo was taken, he was serving with *Telegraphen-Bataillon Nr.2*, whose insignia is evident on his shoulder board.

Lt. Kurt Wintgens seated in what appears to be a Fokker M.5L (A.II) *Eindecker*. That particular model was used for reconnaissance and artillery-spotting duties and had openings in the wings adjacent to the fuselage to allow for a better downward view. Note too that it was unarmed.

Wintgens being greeted while in a Fokker M.8 (A.I), another unarmed reconnaissance model. It carried two men in tandem, and the airman in flight gear to the right may have been accompanying Wintgens. Whether Wintgens flew the M.8 and M.5L for training purposes or on actual missions is unknown.

Lt. Kurt Wintgens at the controls of another motorized vehicle. The time and place are unknown, but the cowling and part of the fuselage of a Fokker *Eindecker* can be seen in the background behind the man sitting on the automobile's hood. (photo courtesy of Jeffrey Sands)

Escadrille N.68 lost a Nieuport 12 and its crew, *MdL*. Beauchamps and *Sous-Lt.* Debacker, to Wintgens' guns on 20 May 1916. It was Wintgens' fourth victory and his report that the airplane was not marked with the usual cockades is confirmed by this photograph.

S379
MULZER
Max (*Ritter* von)
Leutnant

Taken: late 1915 to early 1916
Memmingen, by Hans Weis
Publ: August 1916
Reason: Pour le Mérite award

Decorations:
WR: None
MB: None
RB: None
BH: Iron Cross, 2nd Class

Other Cards:
S373, S385, S396, S397, S398, (possibly S399), S408
(L7720, L7727, L7793; N5630, N5690)

Key Dates:
20 Aug 1915	transfers to Air Service
13 Dec 1915	first assignment with *FFA 4b*
17 Apr 1916	awarded Military Merit Order, th Class/ Sw (Bav)
8 Jul 1916	awarded *Pour le Mérite*
23 Jul 1916	S379 photo published in *Berliner Illustrirte Zeitung* 30, p.452

Lt. Max Mulzer, later *Ritter* von Mulzer by virtue of his Military Max-Joseph award, is wearing the winged propeller insignia of the *Fliegertruppe* on the shoulder boards of his Bavarian *Chevauleger-Regiment Nr.8* dress tunic. The Iron Cross 2nd Class ribbon attached to his buttonhole was earned with that regiment on 10 October 1914. Mulzer transferred from the cavalry to the Air Service on 20 August 1915, so we at least have an early limit for the photograph's date. After he completed his pilot training at Schleissheim, north of Munich, he reported for active duty with *Feldflieger-Abteilung 4b*. There is no sign in S379 of the Military Merit Order (Bavaria) that he was awarded on 17 April 1916. As a Bavarian, he almost certainly would have displayed it in such a formal photograph, so the photo must have been snapped before then. Unfortunately, that is about all that S379 tells us, so the best we can do is assign it to a late 1915 to early 1916 timeframe.

Unser erfolgreicher Kampf-Flieger, Leutnant Mulzer

379
Postkartenvertrieb W.Sanke,
BERLIN N.37.
Nachdruck wird gerichtlich verfolgt.

N5630, a duplicate of S379 (but less cropped) with a drawn-in *Pour le Mérite*, credits the photo to the H. Weis studio in Memmingen. Mulzer was born in nearby Kimratshofen bei Kempten and spent his early years in Dietmannsried, but then the family moved to Memmingen in 1906. Thus the picture was most likely taken when he was visiting home, either sometime during his flight training near Munich or during a subsequent trip from the Front.

The 23 July 1916 edition of *Berliner Illustrirte Zeitung* used S379's portrait to announce Mulzer's addition to the ranks of the knights of the Order *Pour le Mérite*. Given its position between Wintgens' S378 *Pour le Mérite* picture (awarded 1 July 1916) and Parschau's S380 *Pour le Mérite* photo (awarded 10 July 1916), it is clear that S379 was intended for the same purpose and that it came out about three weeks after Mulzer's investiture. Mulzer was officially granted the *Pour le Mérite* on 8 July, the day he brought down his eighth opponent and one day before his 23rd birthday. He was the first Bavarian airman, and only the sixth Bavarian military man, to win the prestigious award.

Just three weeks earlier, on 18 June, Mulzer had reached the halfway mark by achieving his fourth victory. Yet there seems to be some confusion with regard to exactly which airplane it was and how it was earned. First, several authors have stated that the victory actually belonged to Max Immelmann – the second of two that he brought down that day. Due to his subsequent death however, he was prevented from putting in the claim, which was instead either awarded to or usurped by Mulzer. Though anything is possible, this explanation has some inherent problems. For example, if the military had decided to make use of Immelmann's two unclaimed victories, why would they have assigned only one and not both to someone else? For those that suspect propaganda as the underlying motive, one would think that the heroic image of Immelmann bringing down not one but two opponents before his ultimate sacrifice would have had more value than giving one away to a then relatively unknown pilot. Moreover, the notion that another man's victory was assigned to one who had nothing to do with it does not seem in keeping with the personal or military codes of conduct in practice at the time. It is difficult to imagine Mulzer either accepting or stealing his dead friend's victory under such circumstances; and it is equally hard to picture the military either condoning an unwarranted claim or forcing it upon Mulzer. Second, several of the same authors list Mulzer's fourth as FE.2b No.6940 of RFC No.25 Squadron, identifying it as the aircraft Immelmann had attacked right before falling to his death. In some cases, this is supported by photos of the downed plane (named "Baby Mine") including one with Mulzer standing next to it. The trouble is that "Baby Mine" – definitely manned by Savage and Robinson, the last airmen to come under Immelmann's fire (see S377) – possessed serial number "4909." "6940" was the number of another RFC 25 Squadron airplane that Immelmann had attacked, and some say shot down, earlier the same day. Given this realization, another explanation of why Immelmann was never credited with either FE.2b becomes possible. We know that Immelmann's Fokker E.IV sustained enough damage from the first engagement (with No.6940) that he had to use an older E.III for the second ("Baby Mine," No.4909). It is conceivable that though he might have been responsible for the hits intially inflicted on No.6940, it was Mulzer who administered the *coup de grâce*, particularly if Immelmann had been forced to break away because of the damage his E.IV had suffered. Under such circumstances, Mulzer's claim would have been justifiable and proper. Only "Baby Mine," No.4909, would have remained unclaimed because its conqueror, Immelmann, was no longer alive to complete the process.

Opposite and this page: Three photographs from the time when *Uffz.* Wolfgang Heinemann received Brunswick's War Merit Cross from his Duke, Ernst August. Heinemann had been among Germany's earliest airmen, earning Pilot's License No. 667 on 11 February 1914. A few years later he was serving with Max Immelmann and Max Mulzer in *FFA 62* as a Fokker *Eindecker* pilot. The unit was split up on 12 June 1916. The two-seaters went to Russia and were replaced by a Bavarian unit, *FFA 5b*, while the single-seat fighters remained behind in Douai and were redesignated as *KEK 3*. A caption under the first image above states that Duke Ernst August was visiting Bavarian *FFA 4b* (probably an error for *5b*) and identifies Max Immelmann with an "x" (far right) and Heinemann with an "xx" (center). It also notes that Heinemann was the son of "*Hofschauspielers* Heinemann, *Braunschweig*" ("Brunswick's royal court actor Heinemann"). Max Mulzer, wearing his distinctive, light-banded *Chevauleger-Regiment* service cap, can also be seen in attendance, fifth from the left. The second picture's caption relates that the Duke was there to decorate Heinemann with the War Merit Cross (neither Immelmann nor Mulzer appear in this image). The final photo shows Immelmann (left) saluting the Duke at a place described as a Bavarian *Feldflieger-Abteilung*. This means that the pictures were taken after *FFA 5b*'s arrival on 12 June; so within a few days of these photos, Immelmann was dead. A little over a month later, on 21 July, Heinemann joined him.

This series of pictures demonstrates that the FE.2b dubbed "Baby Mine" attracted a great deal of attention after being brought down, perhaps because it was *Oblt.* Max Immelmann's final, though unofficial, victory. The eighth and ninth images above prove that it carried serial number 4909 and not 6940, which was credited to Mulzer as his fourth.

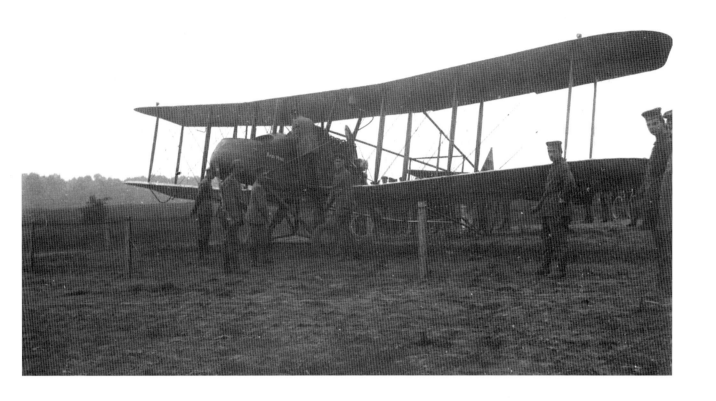

Engl. Flieger abgeschossen am 18.6.16. (bei Noyelles)

S380
PARSCHAU
Otto
Leutnant

Taken: 10 to 20 July 1916
Flanders
Publ: August 1916
Reason: *Pour le Mérite* award

Decorations:
WR: *Pour le Mérite*; Iron Cross, 1st Class; Pilot's Badge; Pilot's Badge (AH)
MB: Iron Cross, 2nd Class; Royal Hohenzollern House Order, Knight's Cross/ Sw; War Merit Cross, 2nd Class (Brun); Military Merit Cross, 3rd Class/war decoration (AH)
RB: None
BH: None

Other Cards:
S408, S556
(L7731, L7793)

Key Dates:

3 Jul 1916	awarded Royal Hohenzollern House Order, Knight's Cross/ Sw
9 Jul 1916	transferred to *FFA 32*
10 Jul 1916	awarded *Pour le Mérite*
21 Jul 1916	killed in action
6 Aug 1916	S380 photo published in *Berliner Illustrirte Zeitung* 30, p.476

Lt. Otto Parschau had only a little more than one week to live after this photograph was taken. He is wearing his recently-awarded *Pour le Mérite* and is posed with his dog in front of *Kagohl 1*'s train car living quarters. The same train section, marked "*Schlafwagen*" ("sleeping car"), also served as the backdrop of another Parschau picture (with a different dog) dated before 3 July 1916 (see O'Connor, *Aviation Awards VII*, p.57). Parschau was transferred to *Feldflieger-Abteilung 32*'s fighter detachment the day he brought down his eighth victory: a balloon north of Grévillers on 9 July 1916. The next day he was given the *Pour le Mérite*. By 14 July 1916, he was in command of the independent fighter unit initially called *Abwehr-Kommando-Nord* (AKN) and then *Kampfeinsitzerstaffel B* (the "B" standing for its airfield, Bertincourt) after his death. S380's image was taken after Parschau's *Pour le Mérite* award but evidently during a visit back to his former unit, *Kagohl 1*. PARSCHAU1 is a snapshot of the airman and his dog after their arrival at Bertincourt in the company of various *Feldflieger-Abteilung 32* and *AKN* personnel.

The upper portion of S380's image was used in the 6 August 1916 edition of *Berliner Illustrirte Zeitung* for the dual announcement of Parschau's *Pour le Mérite* award and his death in combat. The timing of S380's publication suggests that it was issued for the same combination of reasons, because Guideline A projects that it first appeared around three weeks after the airman's death; and we have an S380 example written on 9 August 1916 that coincides with this projection. We also have what is believed to be the original photograph behind the Sanke and *Berliner Illustrirte Zeitung* publications: PARSCHAU2. The following brief, typewritten account is attached to its back:

"*Zum Tode des Fliegerleutnant Parschau. Leutnant Parschau stieg am Abend des 21.Juli zu einem Luftkampf mit 6 französischen und englischen Flugzeugen auf, in einer Höhe von 3000 Metern erhielt er von einem Engländer einen Bauch-*

schuss, hatte jedoch noch die Energie hinter den deutschen Stellungen zu landen, nach 3 Stunden starb er. Er hatte 8 feindliche Flugzeuge heruntergeschossen und war der jüngste Ritter des Pour le merite."

"Regarding the death of pilot 2nd Lieutenant Parschau: On the evening of 21 July, 2nd Lieutenant Parschau went up to an aerial combat with six French and English airplanes. At a height of 3,000 meters he received a stomach wound from one of the Englishmen, but still had the energy to land behind the German lines, and died three hours later. He had shot down eight enemy planes and was the most recent knight of the *Pour le Mérite*." (trans. by this writer)

If PARSCHAU2 were Sanke's source, then this notation most likely confirms that it was only made available soon after the flier's fall. The reverse bears the stamp, "No.2466, Copyright, A. Grohs, Illustrations Verlag, Berlin SW.68, Zimmerstr.48." The A. Grohs Illustration Company was a major source of wartime photographs used by newspapers, books, and other publications. This writer is fortunate to possess several such images, and unlike many that are marked with the phrase "*Alle Rechte vorbehalten*" ("all rights reserved"), PARSCHAU2 specifically states instead that A. Grohs owned its copyright. It is therefore likely that both Sanke and the *Berliner Illustrirte Zeitung* had to obtain A. Grohs' permission to use it. Yet as we shall see in our discussions of S447 and S502, this does not necessarily mean that Grohs was actually responsible for the picture. The firm, like Berliner Illustrations Gesellschaft, often bought the rights to pictures taken by independent photographers, and then controlled their distribution and use.

Bezwinger der Luft (Conquerors of the Air), a book published in either late 1916 or early 1917, relates a similar, more or less contemporaneous account of Parschau's final battle and its aftermath:

> *"Parschau stieg am Abend des 21. Juli 1916 ganz allein zum Luftkampf mit sechs französischen und englischen Flugzeugen auf. Er schoss einen der Gegner glatt herunter. Dann erhielt er in dreitausend Meter Höhe von dem Maschinengewehr eines Feindes einen schweren Bauchschuss.*
>
> *Wie schon gesagt wurde, hatte er noch die Energie, zu landen, starb dann aber drei Stunden später.*
>
> *Die feierliche Beisetzung des Helden erfolgte am Sonntag den 23. Juli auf dem Militärfriedhof in St. Quentin unter grossen militärischen Ehren. Als Vertreter des Kaisers schritt der Feldflugchef hinter dem Sarge mit dem älteren Bruder des Gefallenen, der ebenfalls Flugzeugführer ist. Ferner waren Abordnungen von Offizieren fast sämtlicher Fliegertruppen des Westens erschienen. Eine Ehrenkompagnie erwies die Trauerbezeugungen.*
>
> *Parschau wurde übrigens zugleich mit dem Fliegerleutnant Schramm beigesetzt, der während der ganzen Dauer des Krieges fast immer mit Parschau zusammengewesen war. Er war am gleichen Tage wie Parschau ehrenvoll im Luftkampf gefallen.*
>
> *Beim Leichengottesdienst der beiden Helden sprachen ein evangelischer und ein katholischer Geistlicher. Am offenen Grabe hielt dann noch der Feldflugchef eine warm empfundene Ansprache, in der er der Trauer der Armee um die beiden gefallenen Bezwinger der Luft Ausdruck verlieh."* (pp.166)

Flieger-Leutnant PARSCHAU †
Ritter des Ordens Pour le mérite

Berliner Illustrirte Zeitung used S380's image to simultaneously announce Parschau's *Pour le Mérite* award and his death in its 6 August 1916 edition.

"On the evening of 21 July 1916, Parschau went up alone to an aerial combat with six French and English airplanes. He shot one of the opponents straight down. Then at 3,000 meters he received a serious stomach wound from an enemy machine gun.

As was already stated, he still had the energy to land [behind our lines], but then died three hours later.

The solemn funeral of the hero took place with great military honors on Sunday, 23 July, at St. Quentin's military cemetery. The Chief of the Air Force [Thomsen] walked behind the coffin as the *Kaiser*'s representative alongside the dead warrior's brother, who is also a pilot. Delegations of officers from nearly all the air units on the Western Front also turned out. An honor guard provided the funeral escort.

Incidentally, Parschau was buried along with pilot 2nd Lt. Schramm, who had served with Parschau throughout most of the war. He had fallen in aerial combat the same day as the noble Parschau. A Protestant clergyman and a Catholic priest spoke at the funeral service of the two heroes. The Chief of the Air Force delivered a heartfelt speech at the open graves, in which he expressed the Army's great sorrow over [the loss of] the two fallen conquerors of the air." (trans. by this writer)

This account and the A. Grohs notation evidently relate what was the accepted version of Parschau's final combat. Yet today, no one is really sure about the details. Though it is unlikely that six English and French aircraft actually flew together in one formation, squadrons from both countries did participate in actions against Parschau's

Right: This photograph was copyrighted by A. Grohs Illustrations Verlag and assigned No.2466.

PARSCHAU2

sector that day. This is reflected by the fact that his demise has been variously credited to either Maj. John O. Andrews of RFC No.24 Squadron or the great French ace, Lt. Charles Nungesser. *Lt.* Werner Schramm, who had accompanied Parschau from *Kagohl 1* to *AKN*, was killed the same evening in a fight with RFC Squadrons 22 and 24. Several photographs of the joint funeral procession (see O'Connor, *Aviation Awards VII*, p.63) have survived to confirm the tremendous military tribute paid to the nation's sixth aviation recipient of the *Pour le Mérite* and his comrade.

PARSCHAU I

Lt. Otto Parschau, wearing his newly-awarded *Pour le Mérite*, in the company of personnel from *FFA 32* and *AKN* in Bertincourt. In the front row, starting second from the left, are *Lt.* Hohberg (*FFA 32*), Parschau (*AKN*), *Hptm.* Ritter (*FFA 32*), *Lt.* Max Mulzer (*AKN*), *Lt.* Gustav Leffers (*AKN*), *Lt.* Alfred Schott (*FFA 32*), and *Lt.* Burkhard Lehmann (*FFA 32*). Parschau's dog, also seen in S380, rests at his feet.

Opposite
Top left: A portrait of *Lt.* Otto Parschau before his receipt of the *Orden Pour le Mérite*.

Top right: Otto Parschau in front of an *Eindecker*, time and place unknown. He was a pilot before the war, having earned Pilot's License No.455 on 4 July 1913, and was later tapped by Anthony Fokker to introduce and demonstrate his *Eindecker* to various military units including Boelcke's and Immelmann's *FFA 62* in the summer of 1915. (photo courtesy of UTD)

Bottom left: Parschau and Oswald Boelcke.

Bottom right: This stamp, issued to raise money for a pilots' charity fund, used a portion of S380's photo and credited "W.Sanke" as owning the copyright.

S381
HÖHNDORF
Walter
Leutnant

Taken: 21 to 31 July 1916
Vaux
Publ: August 1916
Reason: *Pour le Mérite* award

Decorations:
WR: *Pour le Mérite*; Iron Cross, 1st Class
MB: None
RB: None
BH: None

Other Cards:
S389, S408
(L7730, L7755, L7793; N5679, N5690)
Note: Höhndorf not wearing Pilot's Badge
Iron Cross 1st Class is "screwback" type

Key Dates:

20 Jul 1916	awarded *Pour le Mérite*
12 Aug 1916	S381 photo published in *Illustrirte Zeitung* 3815, p.176
13 Aug 1916	S381 similar photo published in *Berliner Illustrirte Zeitung* 31, p.492
30 Aug 1916	S381 postmarked example

KEK Vaux's *Lt.* Walter Höhndorf was awarded the *Pour le Mérite* on 20 July 1916, and squadron mate *Oblt.* Ernst von Althaus received his the very next day. The unit's first knight of the order, *Lt.* Kurt Wintgens, had joined them earlier that month, so *KEK Vaux* could now boast of three members who sported Prussia's highest decoration. HÖHNDORF1 is believed to be a picture of the squadron's joint celebration of Höhndorf's and Althaus' awards at Chateau Vaux around 21 July.[1] Wintgens sits center stage and is flanked by Höhndorf and Althaus, who are adorned with special boutonnieres.[2] This image was certainly taken before 12 August 1916 because *Lt.* Wilhelm Frankl, standing in the background, is not wearing the *Pour le Mérite* he won on that date. Höhndorf and Althaus are dressed identically in HÖHNDORF1, S381, and S383, so it is likely that they all originated from the same period. It is particularly noteworthy that Höhndorf is not wearing his Pilot's Badge in either S381 or HÖHNDORF1, unlike the more formal portrait of him with both Pilot's Badge and dress belt in front of Chateaux Vaux in HÖHNDORF2. S381's photo appeared in the 12 August 1916 edition of *Illustrirte Zeitung*, while HÖHNDORF3, a photo taken only minutes apart from S381, was printed in the 13 August 1916 edition of *Berliner Illustrirte Zeitung*. We have already seen that photographs often experienced a lag of several weeks from the time they were recorded until they appeared in newspaper publications (see p.36), so it seems that S381, HÖHNDORF3, and probably HÖHNDORF1were taken at Vaux during the last week in July 1916.

S381 serves as Guideline 1's first anchor because its predicted appearance in the last half of August 1916 – three weeks after the date of its photograph – has been corroborated by a surviving postmarked example dated 30 August 1916.

Unser erfolgreicher Kampf-Flieger Leutnant Höhndorf.

381
Postkartenvertrieb W.Sanke
BERLIN N 87.
Nachdruck wird gerichtlich verfolgt.

Notes

[1] O'Connor, *Aviation Awards VII*, p.429, relates that one knowledgeable German historian believes that Wintgens never served with *KEK Vaux*, but went directly from *KEK Falkenhausen* to *Abwehr-Kommando-Nord* (*AKN*) in early July. If so, he must have been visiting the nearby unit to welcome the latest members of the *Orden Pour le Mérite* when HÖHNDORF1was snapped.

[2] *Illustrierte Geschichte des Weltkrieges* 119, p.340 printed this picture above a caption stating that it was a *Pour le Mérite* party but did not name the recipient(s).

HÖHNDORF1

HÖHNDORF3

Above: Members of *KEK Vaux* and *FFA 23* celebrate the presence of three recent knights of the Order *Pour le Mérite: Lt.* Walter Höhndorf, *Lt.* Kurt Wintgens, and *Oblt.* Ernst von Althaus (seated left to right in the foreground). Directly behind Wintgens is the CO of *FFA 23, Hptm.* Hermann Palmer. In the same row and at the extreme right, sits *Oblt.* Rudolf Berthold and behind him stands *Lt.* Wilhelm Frankl. *Vzfw.* Josef Veltjens is in the back row, second from the left.

Right: A companion portrait to S381's photo. Note the book in Höhndorf's hands and the absence of his Pilot's Badge in both images.

Below: Another shot of *KEK Vaux* and *FFA 23* personnel outside Chateau Vaux. *Vzfw.* Josef Veltjens is at the far right. The fifth person away from him in the front row is *Lt.* Wilhelm Frankl, followed by *Hptm.* Hermann Palmer, Höhndorf, and *Lt.* Kurt Wintgens.

HÖHNDORF2

Walter Höhndorf as a civilian pilot and engineer before the war. He was granted Pilot's License No.582 on 3 November 1913. (photo courtesy of Jeffrey Sands)

Lt. Walter Höhndorf poses in front of the wreckage of his seventh victim. Caudron No.1202 of Escadrille C.9 fell to his guns on 25 June 1916. Manned by *Cpl.* Bresch and *Sous-Lt.* Joseph Ransom, the plane crashed in flames north of Nomeny.

S382
ALTHAUS
Ernst *Freiherr* von
Oberleutnant

Taken: November 1915 to mid-May 1916
Publ: August 1916
Reason: *Pour le Mérite* award

Decorations:
WR: Iron Cross, 1st Class, Pilot's Badge
MB: None
RB: Military St. Henry Order, Knight's Cross (Sax); Iron Cross, 2nd Class; War Merit Cross, 2nd Class (Brun); General Honor Decoration for Bravery (Hes)
BH: None

Other Cards:
S383, S408, S430, S431
(L7751, L7793)
Note: Cipher for former unit, *Husaren-Regiment (1. sächsisches) Nr.18*, on shoulder boards

Key Dates:

6 Aug 1915	promoted to *Oberleutnant*
23 Oct 1915	awarded War Merit Cross, 2nd Class (Brun)
28 May 1916	S382 photo published in *Berliner Illustrirte Zeitung* 22, p.328.
21 Jul 1916	awarded *Pour le Mérite*
30 Jul 1916	S382 photo published in *Berliner Illustrirte Zeitung* 31, p.463.

A portion of S382's picture was printed in the 28 May 1916 edition of *Berliner Illustrirte Zeitung* above the caption "the flier who has been mentioned several times in military reports." By that time, Althaus had amassed six victories while serving with *KEK*s *Sivry* and *Vaux*. The image was recorded after he had received the Brunswick War Merit Cross on 23 October 1915, but before he had been given Prussia's Royal Hohenzollern House Order, Knight's Cross sometime in the summer of 1916.[1] The tree in the background bears little or no foliage, which helps narrow the time of the photo down to winter or spring. It could well be that the image was taken expressly for newspaper publication purposes around the time of his fifth and sixth victories, which he attained on 30 April and 3 May 1916, because at that time he was Germany's fourth highest scorer behind Boelcke, Immelmann, and Buddecke. This supposition, however, lacks concrete support and we must assign the picture's

Unser erfolgreicher
Kampfflieger
Oberleutnant
Freiherr von Althaus.

Unser erfolgreicher
Kampfflieger
Oberleutnant
Freiherr von Althaus.

origin to a more conservative November 1915 to mid-May 1916 timeframe.

Berliner Illustrirte Zeitung used S382's photo again when its 30 July 1916 edition announced Althaus' *Pour le Mérite* award. Höhndorf's S381 and Althaus' S383 – the cards on either side of S382 that display the *Pour le Mérite* decorations won by both airmen on 20 and 21 July 1916, respectively – confirm that Sanke issued S382 for the same reason. Our guideline projects that it came out a little over three weeks later in late August.

Note

¹ O'Connor, *Aviation Awards VII*, pp.45-46 tells us that on 23 October 1915, while Duke Ernst August of Brunswick and Prince August Wilhelm of Prussia were visiting *Feldflieger-Abteilung 23*'s airfield near St. Quentin, British planes were observed in the area. *Lt.* Hans-Joachim Buddecke and Althaus took off in pursuit and chased the enemy away after Buddecke had shot one of them down. Deeply appreciative of their actions, Duke Ernst August personally gave Brunswick's War Merit Cross to the two airmen shortly before his departure later that day.

S383
ALTHAUS
Ernst *Freiherr* von
Oberleutnant

Taken: 21 to 31 July 1916
Vaux
Publ: August 1916
Reason: *Pour le Mérite* award

Decorations:
WR: *Pour le Mérite*; Iron Cross, 1st Class, Pilot's Badge
MB: None
RB: None
BH: Royal Hohenzollern House Order, Knight's Cross/ Sw

Other Cards:
S382, S408, S430, S431
(L7751, L7793)
Note: Cipher for former unit, *Husaren-Regiment (1. sächsisches) Nr.18*, on shoulder boards

Key Dates:
21 Jul 1916   awarded *Pour le Mérite*

This time Sanke had a portrait of Althaus wearing his *Pour le Mérite* that was taken within a week or so of his investiture. ALTHAUS1 is another image taken around the same time as S383: his tunic, medal arrangement, curved shoulder boards, and service cap folds are identical. The Royal Hohenzollern House Order ribbon that he is wearing in S383, however, is not present in ALTHAUS1. Refer to Höhndorf's S381 to review how it was determined that S381, S383, and HÖHNDORF1 (where both airmen are attending a party celebrating their consecutive receipt of the award) were all taken during the last days of July 1916. Sanke issued S382 and S383 about three weeks later toward the end of August.

The following account, published in the 1917 work, *Unsere Luftwaffe*, and ascribed to Althaus himself, reported the events that led up to his fourth victory:

> "*Anschliessend noch eine Schilderung eines kurzen, aber aufregenden Luftkampfes: Eines Nachmittags kam telephonisch die Meldung, ein französischer Doppeldecker fliege von der Front aus nach der deutschen Stadt O.u. Bald hatte ich seine Höhe—3200 Meter—und ihn selber auf Schussweite erreicht. Es war ein französisches Grosskampfflugzeug mit zwei Motoren. Ich jagte ihm, von hinten angreifend, eine Serie von etwa 80 Schuss auf den Pelz. Etwa 30 Meter von ihm entfernt bog ich nach rechts in einer starken Kurve aus, um mich wieder hinter ihn zu fetzen. In dem Augenblick, wo meine Maschine auf dem Flügel stand, geriet ich in den Luftstrom der beiden Propeller des Gegners. Im nächsten Augenblick überschlug sich mein Fokker zwei- bis dreimal und stürzte, keinem Steuerdruck mehr gehorchend, senkrecht in die Tiefe. Mein Motor hatte unglücklicherweise ausgesetzt, besann sich aber wieder, und mit seiner Hilfe gelang es mir, nach einem Sturz von 600 Metern, den Apparat wieder in die Hand zu bekommen und aufzurichten. Sofort suchte ich nach meinem Gegner. Auch er war, durch meinen Schuss getroffen, zugleich mit mir abgestürzt, hatte etwas unter mir seine Maschine ebenfalls wieder gefangen und strebte eiligst der französischen Front zu. Ich stiess sofort wieder auf ihn herunter, und nach kurzem Endkampf stürzte er zerschmettert in unsere Linien ab. Es war der vierte Gegner, den ich erledigte, und ich hatte dadurch die grosse Freude, seinerzeit zum erstenmal im Heeresbericht erwähnt zu werden.*" (pp.99-100)

"A description of a short but exciting aerial combat follows: One afternoon a telephone message came that a French biplane was flying from the Front toward a German city. I soon reached its height – 3200 meters – and came within firing range. It was a French bombing machine with two engines. I shot a series of about 80 rounds into him, attacking from the rear and right on his tail. When I was about 30 meters away from him I curved out to the right so that I could swing back and fasten onto him from behind once more. At the precise moment that my machine stood on its wing, I entered the prop wash of my enemy's two propellers. Suddenly, my Fokker turned itself over two or three times and dove straight toward the ground, no longer obeying the controls. My engine, which had unfortunately cut out, came to life once again and helped me regain control of my machine after a fall of 600 meters. I immediately looked for my opponent. He, struck by my fire, had fallen the same time I had, and was now just below me heading fast toward the French lines. I dove down upon him at once, and after a short, final struggle he smashed into our lines. He was my fourth victory, and I had the tremendous joy of being mentioned in the Army Report for the first time because of it." (trans. by this writer)

Lt. Fritz Otto Bernert (holding dog) and *Oblt.* Ernst von Althaus (center) during a visit with *Lt.* Rudolph Hermann of *FFA 64*. Althaus' dog, named Mousse, is at his feet. Hermann can be seen again, this time with squadron mate *Oblt.* Oskar Kuppinger, in another photo published in O'Connor, *Aviation Awards IV*, p.43.

A pleasing portrait of a relaxed Althaus. (photo courtesy of UTD)

This action occurred on 19 March 1916, and the Caudron G4 that had nearly cost Althaus his life was reported to have crashed west of the road between Meharicourt and Lihons.

ALTHAUS1

S384
FRANKL
Wilhelm
Leutnant

Taken: 12 to 18 August 1916
Vaux
Publ: September 1916
Reason: *Pour le Mérite* award

Decorations:
WR: *Pour le Mérite*; Iron Cross, 1st Class; Pilot's Badge
MB: None
RB: None
BH: None

Other Cards:
S408, S420, S421
(L7752, L7793)

Key Dates:

12 Aug 1916	awarded *Pour le Mérite*
27 Aug 1916	S384 photo published
	in *Berliner Illustrirte Zeitung* 35. p.516
2 Sep 1916	S384 photo published
	in *Die Wochenschau* 36, p.1145
1 Sep 1916	*KEK Vaux* moves to Roupy and forms *Jasta 4*

Oblt. Ernst von Althaus, flanked by two other officers, stands in front of an AGO C-type airplane. The man to the right bears a strong resemblance to Althaus and may have been a relative. (photo courtesy of UTD)

Lt. Wilhelm Frankl is sitting in the same kind of chair that *Lt.* Rudolf Berthold occupies in S402 and HÖHNDORF1 (see S381 and HÖHNDORF1b below). In fact, S384, S402, and FRANKL1 (which shares the same foliage in its background) seem to have been taken relatively concurrently in the same spot just outside Chateau Vaux. All these photos originated before *KEK Vaux*, the fighter unit that adopted its name, moved to Roupy on 1 September to form one of the new *Jagdstaffeln, Jasta 4*. Frankl is wearing the *Pour le Mérite* that he officially won on 12 August 1916, so S384's image must have been recorded between those two dates. The picture's appearance in the 27 August 1916 edition of *Berliner Illustrirte Zeitung* narrows the timeframe down even further to within a week of the award, because we have seen that it often took about two weeks or more for a news story and its photograph to be published in newspapers. *Berliner Illustrirte Zeitung* was not exaggerating when it labeled the photo as Frankl's "*neueste Aufnahme*" ("newest picture"). It also appears that Sanke wasted little time in publishing S384 about three weeks later in early September.

The 1 July 1917 edition of *Der Feldzug 1914/17*, a magazine that compiled daily highlights of the war as well as press stories from various sources, included a portion of S384's image (p.499) along with several other aviator portraits. Though most of them were credited to "W. Sanke," S384's source was listed as "A. Mocsigay," who was known to have operated a photographic studio in Hamburg. The 2 September 1916 edition of *Die Wochenschau* also credited "Arnold Mocsigay" as the photo's source. Frankl was born in Hamburg, but later moved to Frankfurt and then Berlin-Charlottenburg; so his connection with Mocsigay's Hamburg studio is unclear, particularly when the picture itself was undoubtedly taken at Chateau Vaux.

FRANKL I

Top left: This enlarged section of HÖHNDORF1 (see S381) shows Rudolf Berthold sitting in the same kind of chair seen in S384, which demonstrates that Frankl's snapshot also originated from Chateau Vaux.

Above: This photograph, a portion of which was published in Leipzig's *Illustrirte Zeitung Nr. 3819* on 7 September 1916, was almost certainly taken the same time as S384's image.

Left: Frankl is warmly greeted by a crowd of people as he emerges from the cockpit of an *Eindecker*.

132

Above: A formally attired *Lt.* Wilhelm Frankl strikes a casual pose at the waterfront.

Top right: Wilhelm Frankl, former student of Germany's pioneer female aviator Amelie "Melli" Beese, received Pilot's License No. 490 on 20 August 1913. At the outbreak of the war, he was accepted in the Air Service and posted to *FFA 40*. He achieved his first victory with them when he brought down a Voisin, purportedly with his carbine rifle, on 10 May 1915. He was later promoted to *Vizefeldwebel*. In the photo above, Frankl, now an officer wearing the *Pour le Mérite*, visits with members of his former unit, *FFA 40*. (photo courtesy of UTD)

Right and pages 134-135: Still flying with *FFA 40*, but now in a Fokker *Eindecker*, *Vzfw.* Wilhelm Frankl attacked Voisin 4 No. 991 on 10 January 1916 and forced it to land near Woumen (south of Dixmude). The crew, *Sgt.* Parent and *Fus.* Bonnier, were taken prisoner. The plane, nicknamed "*Boum*" ("Bang") because of the large cannon it carried, came down relatively intact and was later put on display in Germany. The first five images above show the captured plane at its landing site, where burlap bags and other cloth materials were used to obscure the national insignia on its wings. The last five pictures were taken after *Boum* had been moved to a German military site. (final photo courtesy of UTD)

S385
MULZER
Max (*Ritter* von)
Leutnant

Taken: 22-31 August 1916
Memmingen, by Karl Müller
Publ: September 1916
Reason: *Pour le Mérite* award

Decorations:
WR: *Pour le Mérite*; Iron Cross, 1st Class; Pilot's Badge (Bav)
MB: None
RB: None
BH: None

Other Cards:
S373, S379, S396, S397, S398, (possibly S399), S408
(L7720, L7727, L7793; N5630, N5690)
Note: Taken same time as S396-98

Key Dates:

8 Jul 1916	awarded *Pour le Mérite*
21 Aug 1916	awarded Military Max-Joseph Order, Knight's Cross (Bav)
6 Sep 1916	Military Max-Joseph Order, Knight's Cross (Bav) award ceremony at La Brayelle airfield

S385 and the later S396-98 Mulzer series are intriguing in that each of them has distinct, distinguishing characteristics despite having been taken at the same time in the same place. Their simultaneous origin is well demonstrated by the matching appearance of the subtle impressions and curve in his tunic collar, the slight protrusion of his white shirt collar underneath, the hang of his *Pour le Mérite*, the position of his belt just overlapping the fifth row of buttons, and all the bends and angles of his shoulder boards. In S396-98, his *Grossordenschnalle*'s Bavarian Military Merit Order and Royal Hohenzollern House Order overlap his Iron Cross in precisely the same manner – which brings us to S385's distinguishing characteristic. Why is his medals bar missing from it? A look at Mulzer's tunic under magnification discloses a patch that has a different, artificial texture when compared with the surrounding area. Moreover, the patch covers the exact spot where his *Grossorden-*

schnalle would have hung. Evidently, it *had* been there originally, but someone later erased it and camouflaged its disappearance as best as they could. Even though S379 had been issued in recognition of Mulzer's receipt of the *Pour le Mérite*, S385 was the first card to show him actually wearing it. Perhaps then the motivation behind this curious alteration was that someone felt that the medals bar was an unnecessary distraction from the card's intended purpose of featuring Mulzer with Prussia' highest decoration.

The presence of his *Pour le Mérite* (awarded 8 July 1916, following his eighth victory) and the absence of his Bavarian Miltary Max-Joseph Order (physically given to him on 6 September 1916) help us ascertain when the photo was taken. If our guideline is correct and S385 was first issued in September 1916, the three-week time period required for publication would further bracket the picture's origin to sometime around mid-July to late August 1916. MULZER1 is an original photo of Mulzer and his father that was taken in the same studio (note the identical painted background in S385 and S396) and probably at the same time as the S385, S396-98 series. Once again, various characteristics of Mulzer's outfit match right down to the curve of his shoulder boards and the glove he holds in his left hand. In this instance, however, he is not wearing his medals bar and there is no sign that it was "brushed out." The photographic studio's identity is disclosed by the stamp "K. Müller, Memmingen" on the bottom right corner, which undoubtedly refers to the Karl Müller who founded a company dedicated to sheet film production and film enlargement in Memmingen in 1896. Mulzer's father relocated the family to Memmingen in 1906 and later had his son's body returned there for burial. The identification therefore confirms that these photographs were taken while Mulzer was back home in Bavaria. Several weeks leave customarily accompanied the award of the *Pour le Mérite*, but four items in Memmingen's archives demonstrate that this was not the case for Mulzer. First, a 29 July letter that he wrote from France to the local newspaper, thanking his hometown for its congratulations and good wishes, indicates that he remained at the Front for some time after the 8 July award. Second, a local newspaper recorded that Mulzer (and his father) came home for a short leave following his award of the Military Max-Joseph Order on 21 August. This explains why that decoration's award ceremony did not occur until over two weeks later – after Mulzer's return to the Front – on 6 September.[1] Third, a letter dated 8 September 1916 from "Karl Müller, Hofphotograph, Memmingen" to the City Council, states that he had taken a photograph of Mulzer "*in den letzten Tagen*" ("recently") and would be pleased to provide a copy to the Council for their use. Last, Elizabeth Schobacher of Kempten (near Mulzer's birthplace) wrote a short 1917 biography of Mulzer that included S397's original picture (see S398) with the caption: "*Aufnahme während seines letzten Urlaubs*" ("photograph during his last leave"). Consequently, it is almost certain that the Karl Müller photographs originated in late August 1916 when Mulzer was home on leave.

Note

[1] A photograph of the award ceremony, held at La Brayelle's field, can be seen in the inside cover of Imrie, *German Air Aces* (though the date he gives is incorrect) or O'Connor, *Aviation Awards V*, p.288.

Unser erfolgreicher Kampf-Flieger Leutnant Mulzer.

385
Postkartenvertrieb W.Sanke
BERLIN N.37.
Nachdruck wird gerichtlich verfolgt.

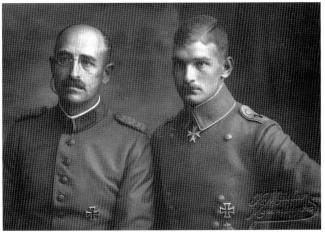

MULZER1

Opposite

Top: A rare photograph of *Lt.* Max Mulzer, seated in the cockpit of his Fokker *Eindecker*.

Bottom: Two portraits of Mulzer taken by H. Hoffmann of Munich.

A portrait of father and son. *Lt.* Max Mulzer and his physician father, also named Max, pose together during a photo shoot at Karl Müller's studio in Memmingen. Dr. Mulzer is wearing the military medical insignia of blue collar patches and a single snake entwined around a straight staff on his shoulder boards.

S388
GERLICH
Martin
Oberleutnant

Taken: 1916
Publ: September 1916
Reason: victory score

Decorations:
WR: Iron Cross, 1st Class; Observer's Badge
MB: None
RB: None
BH: None

Other Cards:
(L7753; N6335)

Key Dates:

9 Apr 1916	Walz & Gerlich victory
21 May 1916	Walz & ? victory
3 Jul 1916	Walz & Gerlich victory
9 Jul 1916	Walz & Gerlich victory
15 Jul 1916	Walz & ? victory
29 Jul 1916	Walz & ? victory
30 Jul 1916	Walz wounded in action

Oberleutnant Gerlich

388
Postkartenvertrieb W.Sanke
BERLIN N.37.
Nachdruck wird gerichtlich verfolgt.

Martin Gerlich was interred in none other than Berlin's Invalidenfriedhof – a cemetery for some of the country's greatest war heroes including aviators Manfred von Richthofen, Hans-Joachim Buddecke, Ernst Udet, and Oliver Beaulieu-Marconnay.[1] He therefore must have had a distinguished military career, though little about it appears in existing publications. His gravestone tells us that he was born on 28 October 1892 and that he entered the war as a member of *Grenadier-Regiment 'Kronprinz (1. ostpreussisches)' Nr. 1*. Other sources inform us that he transferred to the Air Service and trained as an observer, going to *Kasta 4* of *Kampfgeschwader 1* in February 1916 and then *Kasta 2* the following July. Gerlich, nicknamed "*Spatz*" ("sparrow") by his closer colleagues, then went to *Kampfgeschwader 3* in 1917 as its adjutant, first under *Hptm.* Ernst Brandenburg and later with *Hptm.* Rudolf Kleine. After the war, Gerlich became a *Hauptmann* with the Berlin Security Police and served as the organization's Department Manager. He died a short time later, however, on 26 February 1920.

Our first hint regarding why Sanke featured Gerlich in his postcard series comes in Norman Franks' informative *Sharks Among Minnows* (p.80) where it was disclosed that then *Leutnant* Gerlich flew as *Oblt.* Franz Walz's observer in *Kampfgeschwader 1*. Walz commanded one of the unit's fighting detachments, *Kasta 2*, and gathered six victories as a two-seater pilot before being severely wounded on 30 July 1916. This was a remarkable tally at the time and made him one of the earliest pilot recipients of the Royal Hohenzollern House Order, Knight's Cross with Swords the following September.[2] Franks (pp.167-68) also informs us that Walz was partnered with Gerlich for at least three of his six victories. Unfortunately, the observer's name was not recorded for the remaining three. Was Gerlich with Walz on one or more of those occasions as well? Successful pilot and observer teams often remained together over the course of several months, as in the case of Fahlbusch (S418) and Rosencrantz (S419), or Dossenbach (S416) and Schilling. So it is not implausible that Gerlich, who accompanied Walz during his 9 April, 3 July, and 9 July victories, also flew with him in between these dates. There is no record of Gerlich having received the Royal Hohenzollern House Order, so he might not have been with Walz for all six victories. Nevertheless, a count of four or

five would have earned Gerlich special mention in military despatches and a certain amount of notoriety. Indeed, *Bezwinger der Luft*, a book published in late 1916 or early 1917, ranks both Gerlich and Walz as tied for eighth place among German airmen with four victories each as of 1 August 1916.[3] This count also probably brought him the honor of being the subject of one of Sanke's postcards. Gerlich was only the third airman to appear in Sanke's series who did not hold the *Pour le Mérite* at the time of his postcard; and the two before him, Immelmann (S340) and Leffers (S372), had been included because of their victory totals.

If Gerlich's record was the reason for his inclusion, then we might ask why Walz never appeared on a Sanke card. Not all of Germany's high scorers in the fall of 1916 were represented in the series (e.g., Hans Schilling – 8 victories, Renatus Theiller – 7, Hans Schüz – 6, Kurt Haber – 5); so Walz may have been a similar case. There is also another intriguing, though purely speculative, possibility. No example of any "S387" – the card that would have preceded Gerlich's S388 – has been uncovered to date. Had this spot been reserved for Walz, but later abandoned and forgotten when no picture was forthcoming?

The Gerlich-Walz team was broken up when Walz was wounded on 30 July. Our guideline projects that Gerlich's S388 first appeared a little over six weeks later in September 1916.

Notes

[1] Other famous *Fliegertruppe* personnel who were buried at Invalidenfriedhof: Rudolf Berthold, Paul Billik, Gustav Doerr, Leo Leonhardy, Ulrich Neckel, Hermann von der Lieth-Thomsen, and Emil Thuy.

[2] His six victories tied him for seventh place among all German fighter pilots in July 1916 behind *Pour le Mérite* aces Boelcke (19), Immelmann (15), Wintgens (12), Höhndorf (11), Mulzer (9), Althaus (8), Buddecke (8), and Parschau (8).

[3] Modern records show that four victories actually would have placed Gerlich in a tie for 10th place as of the end of July 1916. Walz had compiled six victories by then and was tied for eighth place. *Illustrierte Geschichte des Weltkriegs* 119 (p.338) lists Walz with six victories and Gerlich with four as of 15 September 1916.

A rare photograph of *Lt.* Martin Gerlich (right) and his flying partner, *Oblt.* Franz Walz. Gerlich's dog, Prinz, also seen in S388, sits on the wing behind his master. (photo courtesy of UTD)

Above and below: Martin Gerlich converses with other members of *Kampfgeschwader 1*. In the first photo, from left to right: *Oblt.* Hans-Ulrich von Trotha, Gerlich, *Lt.* Turk, *Hptm.* Rudolf Kleine. In the second photo, Gerlich is at far right with two unidentified comrades. *KG 1* used the train cars seen in the background for living and dining quarters. We know that Gerlich and Kleine served with *KG 1* before moving on to *KG 3*, and the first photo tells us that the same was also apparently true for Hans-Ulrich von Trotha. He was the *KG 3* pilot who was ferrying *Hptm.* Ernst Brandenburg back from his *Pour le Mérite* ceremony when their plane crashed, killing Trotha and injuring Brandenburg. (photos courtesy of UTD)

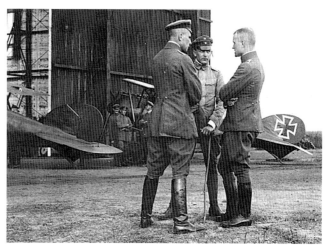

Oblt. Martin Gerlich (center) is engaged in a conversation between his CO, *Hptm.* Rudolf Kleine (left), and *Rittm.* Manfred von Richthofen. The site is *KG 3*'s airfield at Gontrode. To the left of the men is an Albatros D.V, apparently completely overpainted in red, that is believed to have been Richthofen's. The D.V model was not supplied to *Jasta 11* until late June 1917 and Richthofen shows no sign of the head wound he received a little later on 6 July. Therefore, the photo was taken sometime around 24 June 1917, the time that Richthofen was given command of Germany's first fighter wing, *Jagdgeschwader Nr. 1*. Kleine had been placed in command of bomber wing *Kampfgeschwader 3* only one day earlier, so perhaps this image captures the two *Geschwaderführers* conferring about their new responsibilities.

Above: Gerlich (left) and *Lt.* Otto Parschau (right) of *KG 1* are both wearing turtleneck sweaters in this photo taken near the wreckage of BE.2c No.2074 of RFC No.12 Squadron. Parschau brought the airplane down on 19 December 1915 for his second victory, and both occupants, Lt. Norman Gordon-Smith and Lt. Duncan Cunningham-Reid, were killed.

Below: *Oblt.* Martin Gerlich, standing fourth from the right, raises his cigar over the head of a member of *Kampfstaffel 17*. The officers of *Kasta 17*, one of *KG 3*'s flights, assembled for this picture along with their *Geschwaderführer, Hptm.* Rudolf Kleine. Kleine stands in the center of the back row to the right of a woman identified as *Freifrau* von Schichting (holding a dog).

Right: The gravestone for the Gerlich brothers, Martin and Theodor, in Berlin's Invalidenfriedhof cemetery. When Martin was interred there, the family added a memorial inscription for Theodor, who had been killed early in the war at Lake Hancza on 6 October 1914.

S389
HÖHNDORF
Walter
Leutnant

Taken: 1 to 22 August 1916
Berlin-Schöneberg, by Karl Wahl
Publ: September 1916
Reason: post-*Pour le Mérite*

Decorations:
WR: *Pour le Mérite*; Iron Cross, 1st Class, Pilot's Badge, Pilot's Badge (AH)
MB: None
RB: None
BH: Royal Hohenzollern House Order, Knight's Cross/ Sw; Iron Cross, 2nd Class; Hanseatic Cross (Ham)

Other Cards:
S381, S408
(L7730, L7755, L7793; N5679, N5690)

Key Dates:
2 Jun 1916	victory #4
17 Jun 1916	victory #5
22 Jun 1916	victory #6
25 Jun 1916	victory #7
15 Jul 1916	victory #8
19 Jul 1916	victory #9
20 Jul 1916	awarded *Pour le Mérite*
21 Jul 1916	victory #10
30 Jul 1916	victory #11
23 Aug 1916	assigned to *Jasta 1*
17 Sep 1916	victory #12

Unlike S381 and HÖHNDORF3, where the airman struck a more casual pose outdoors with book in hand, S389 formally captures Höhndorf in his full dress uniform. Apart from the fact that he is wearing his *Pour le Mérite*, which dates the photo to post-20 July 1916, we have another clue regarding when it might have been taken that does not appear on S389 itself. Rather, it appears at the bottom right hand corner of N5679, a snapshot taken at the same sitting. There we see the name and location of the photographer: Karl Wahl of Berlin-Schöneberg.[1] Höhndorf came from Prutzke, about 60 miles northeast of Berlin. Before the war, he had worked on aircraft design and construction at the Union-Flugzeugwerke in Teltow near Berlin. He continued his association with the aircraft industry during the war and was recalled to Germany for test-flying duties on several occasions. In particular, he worked with the AEG factory in Henningsdorf near Berlin. Obviously, S389 and N5679 must have originated either during a trip home or while he was back in the Berlin area for consulting work. A 15 October 1916 postmarked example of the next card in the series, Baldamus' S390, and our three-week publication rule determine that S389's image would not normally have been available any later than mid-September or so. In fact, our predictive guideline projects a mid-September publication for both S389 and S390, which would push the latest date of their photos back to the end of August. Höhndorf's victory list proves that he was at the Front until at least 30 July. We know he was there again when he was assigned to help form the new *Jasta 1* on 23

Unser erfolgreicher Kampf-Flieger
Leutnant Höhndorf.

389
Postkartenvertrieb W.Sanke
, BERLIN N. 37.
Nachdruck wird gerichtlich verfolgt.

Left: A photograph taken the same time as S389, published by NPG as card No.5679.

Below: *Lt.* Walter Höhndorf and company engineer Westphal in front of a Kondor W.I airplane. Its interplane struts were unusual in that they formed a "V" when viewed from the front. The picture may have been taken at Kondor Flugzeugwerke, which was located at Rotthausen-Gelsenkirchen near Essen. (photo courtesy of UTD)

Bottom: *Lt.* Walter Höhndorf visits *Jasta 14* and their CO, *Hptm.* Rudolf Berthold, in March 1917. Berthold is the center of attention, flanked by Höhndorf (left) and *Lt.* Josef Veltjens (right), a former *Jasta 4* squadron mate who had just transferred to *Jasta 14. Lt.* Walter Kypke, with light reflecting off his glasses, stands second from the right in the back row. (photo courtesy of UTD)

Opposite
Top: Höhndorf (standing in the center wearing his *Pour le Mérite*) and Berthold (seated below Höhndorf) partying again at an unknown time and location. Judging from the expression, however, on the face of the captured British officer seated next to Berthold (behind the wine bottle), this was not a "good time had by all." (photo courtesy of UTD)

Bottom: Walter Höhndorf was killed on 5 September 1917 at Iré-le-Sec while test flying the AEG D.I that he had helped design. His *Ordenskissen*, seen in this photo of his coffin lying in state, displayed all the decorations attributed to him by Neal O'Connor (see *Aviation Awards II*, p.234) plus one more: the star-shaped Turkish War Medal. (photo courtesy of UTD)

142

August. Had he gone to Berlin sometime in between? Other evidence, though circumstantial, supports this notion. First, a trip home would have been the customary reward for his *Pour le Mérite* achievement – indeed, we know that many subsequent *Pour le Mérite* recipients were given leave soon after their investiture. Second, despite an impressive run-up of victories in June and July, his guns were silent in August, even though squadron mates Wintgens and Frankl had four victories and other units in the vicinity claimed three more aircraft in the first two weeks of August (bad weather hampered most of the third week's activities). All things considered, it is possible that Höhndorf was in Berlin in August 1916 and that S389 and N5679 were taken at that time.

Note

[1] Recently, it has been discovered that S389's image was also attributed to "Phot. Karl Wahl" in a book published in late 1916 (see Funk, *Unsere Luftwaffe*, opp. P.32).

Unser erfolgreicher
Kampfflieger
Leutnant Baldamus

S390
BALDAMUS
Hartmut
Leutnant

Taken: March to early September 1916
Dresden, by Hugo Erfurth
Publ: September 1916
Reason: victory score

Decorations:
WR: Iron Cross, 1st Class; Pilot's Badge
MB: None
RB: None
BH: Iron Cross, 2nd Class; Albert Order, Knight 2nd Class/ Sw (Sax)

Other Cards:
S432
(L7754; N6204)
Note: Taken same time as S432

Key Dates:

21 Feb 1916	awarded Albert Order, Knight 2nd Class/ Sw (Sax)
15 Mar 1916	victory #1 with *Feldflieger-Abteilung 20*
24 May 1916	victory #2
24 Jul 1916	victories #3 & 4
29 Jul 1916	victory #5
27 Aug 1916	transferred to *Jasta 5*
c.24 Sep 1916	S390 similar photo published in *Illustrierte Kriegs-Zeitung (Das Weltbild)* 112, p.8
7 Oct 1916	transferred to *Jasta 9*
31 Mar 1917	S390 photo published in *Berliner Illustrirte Zeitung* 13, p.174

Our guideline projects that *Lt.* Hartmut Baldamus' S390 appeared sometime during the last half of September 1916. The publication of BALDAMUS1, another picture from the same sitting, in the c. 24 September 1916 edition of the pictorial *Illustrierte Kriegs-Zeitung* newspaper seems to have coincided with this. The earliest postmarked example of S390 uncovered to date at least tells us that it emerged no later than 15 October 1916. By this time, Baldamus had run up a score of five downed planes while serving with *Feldflieger-Abteilung 20* (an armpatch bearing the number "20" is just visible on his left sleeve). Two had come in one day on 24 July 1916 – a particularly noteworthy achievement at this point in the war. The ribbon for his

Saxon Albert Order peeks out from underneath his Iron Cross 2nd Class ribbon, so the pictures can be dated to sometime shortly after his receipt of that award (21 February 1916) to two weeks or so before the newspaper's date (22 September). A tally of five by the close of August 1916 placed Baldamus among Germany's top scorers behind Gustav Leffers, Rudolf Berthold, and Franz Walz (all with six) and nine *Pour le Mérite* holders.

The diary of *Lt.* Josef Jacobs provides us with an interesting anecdote about Baldamus along with a glimpse of the celebrity he had achieved by this time. The entry for 9 September 1916 reads:

"*Ltn.* Tegetau and *Ltn.* Birk, who had flown to Vouziers, told us they met Baldamus there. He had no Fokker or any other single-seat fighter. A pilot with 5 aircraft to his credit: 3 Caudrons and 2 Voisin, who cannot even be given a 100 h.p. Fokker because of machine scarcity…what a bad state of affairs." (OTF 9:4, p.324)

Baldamus had been sent to *Jasta 5* to serve as a fighter pilot on 27 August. He never scored with that unit and we now have at least one possible explanation as to why.

S390 was taken the same time as the photo used in his later S432. The distinct wallpaper pattern seen behind Baldamus in S432 also appears in Wüsthoff's S564 and S566 (which belonged to his disjointed S560, S563-44, S566 series). Baldamus was born in

Dresden and Wüsthoff moved there before the war. Indeed, Wüsthoff's later S586-87 series names "Hugo Erfurth, Dresden" as the photographer, so it seems reasonable to conclude that Dresden was the common thread between the pictures. S587's light background and S586's mottled background are similar to Wüsthoff's earlier S563 and S560, respectively, but no conclusive match is evident. The definitive link, however, is finally found in the 31 March 1917 edition of *Berliner Illustrirte Zeitung* where S390's photo is credited to a "Hugo Erfurt." So it is through this rather circuitous route that we now know that all these photos came from Hugo Erfurth's Dresden studio.

S391
WINTGENS
Kurt
Leutnant

Taken: August to early September 1916
Minden, by Karl Zinne
Publ: September 1916
Reason: post-*Pour le Mérite*

Decorations:
WR: *Pour le Mérite*; Iron Cross, 1st Class; Pilot's Badge

A picture of *Lt.* Hartmut Baldamus taken the same time as the one published as S390.

MB: None
RB: Royal Hohenzollern House Order, Knight's Cross/ Sw; Iron Cross, 2nd Class; Miltary Merit Order, 4th Class/ Sw (Bav); Albert Order, Knight 2nd Class/ Sw (Sax)
BH: None

Other Cards:
S378, S392, S400, S408
(L7729, L7793)
Note: Taken same time as S392
Wearing eyeglasses

S392
WINTGENS
Kurt
Leutnant

Taken: August to early September 1916
Minden, by Karl Zinne
Publ: September 1916
Reason: post-*Pour le Mérite*

Decorations:
WR: *Pour le Mérite*; Iron Cross, 1st Class; Pilot's Badge
MB: None

RB: Royal Hohenzollern House Order, Knight's Cross/ Sw; Iron Cross, 2nd Class; Miltary Merit Order, 4th Class/ Sw (Bav); Albert Order, Knight 2nd Class/ Sw (Sax)
BH: None

Other Cards:
S378, S391, S400, S408
(L7729, L7793)
Note: Taken same time as S391
Wearing eyeglasses

Key Dates:

Pre-Jun 1916	awarded Iron Cross 1st and 2nd Class
Jun 1916	awarded Royal Hohenzollern House Order, Knight's Cross/ Sw
1 Jul 1916	awarded *Pour le Mérite*
19 Jul 1916	awarded Albert Order, Knight 2nd Class/ Sw (Sax)
25 Sep 1916	Wintgens killed in action

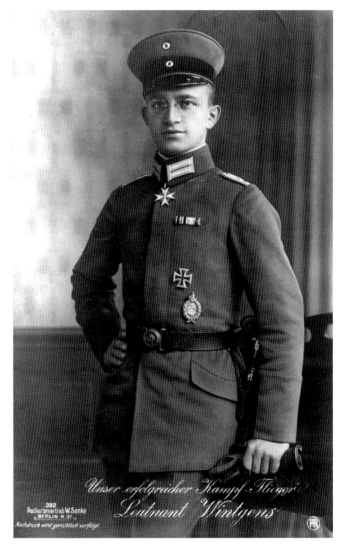

The *Feldschnalle* (ribbon bar) that *Lt.* Kurt Wintgens is wearing in S391-92 points us toward their photographic origin. The ribbons of four of his awards are displayed in the order prescribed by official military protocol: The Prussian Royal Hohenzollern House Order, Knight's Cross with Swords (black ribbon with white side stripes and crossed swords device), Prussian Iron Cross 2nd Class (black ribbon with white side stripes), Bavarian Military Merit Order 4th Class with Swords (white ribbon with black and blue side stripes with crossed swords device), and Saxon Albert Order, Knight 2nd Class with Swords (green ribbon with white side stripes and crossed swords device).[1] The Albert Order's presence dates the photos to after his receipt of that award on 19 July. Yet other photos of him ascribed to July 1916 show a different *Feldschnalle* arrangement that is not easily explained. WINTGENS2 and HÖHNDORF1 (see S381) display a ribbon bar with three awards in this order: a dark ribbon with light side stripes, a light ribbon with thin dark side stripes, and a dark ribbon with light side stripes. The middle one unquestionably is for the Bavarian Military Merit Order. But how do we explain the two on either side of it, given the sequence in which they appear? Prussian orders usually came first on ribbon and medals bars, though natives of Saxony and Bavaria sometimes placed their kingdom's awards ahead of Prussian ones. But in such instances, each kingdom's medals were customarily grouped together and not divided by another kingdom's. So it would have been odd indeed if Wintgen's Bavarian Military Merit Order had come between his Prussian Hohenzollern and Iron Cross awards.[2] It is therefore unlikely that the dark ribbons with light side stripes were both Prussian. If the first ribbon was for the Albert Order, we must question why a non-Saxon would have placed it so, and furthermore why a Prussian order would have been placed last behind both Saxon *and* Bavarian orders. This leaves the conclusion that the first ribbon was a Prussian one and that the third represented his Albert Order. The Albert Order, however, was awarded after the other three decorations, so why would Wintgens have added it to his *Feldschnalle* without also adding the missing Prussian award that had preceded it? A possible explanation is based on an assumption derived from other photographic evidence. The Royal Hohenzollern House Order, which came on the same ribbon as the Iron Cross 2nd Class and other Prussian awards, was usually distinguished from them by the addition of a crossed swords device (often with crown) pinned to the ribbon. Several Sanke cards indicate that once the Royal Hohenzollern House Order was awarded, it took the prior position of the Iron Cross 2nd Class' ribbon without the further addition of a replacement. That is, the crossed swords device was placed on the Iron Cross ribbon without another black and white ribbon being added (e.g., see Boelcke's S363 and S369,

Althaus' S383, Berr's S425-26, Fricke's S607, Loerzer's S651, Göring's S654, Heldmann's S664). These examples, however, involve ribbons worn from tunic buttonholes rather than those on the *Feldschnalle*. Two other cards provide more direct, supportive evidence. Brandenburg's S541 shows only the Royal Hohenzollern House Order on his ribbon bar even though he was certainly entitled to display the Iron Cross 2nd Class as well (i.e., it was the prerequisite award for the Iron Cross 1st Class that is pinned on his tunic). Kissenberth's S595 quite conveniently exhibits the same type of ribbon bar display that is now theorized for WINTGENS2 and HÖHNDORF1: Royal Hohenzollern House Order, Bavarian Miltary Merit Cross, Saxon Albert Order. Though signs of a crossed swords device on the first ribbon in WINTGENS2 seem to be present under magnification, the identification is uncertain.

It is clear that Wintgens later replaced his somewhat unusual three-medal *Feldschnalle* with the four-place one seen in S391-92. It also appears that he acquired a new tunic around the same time. Many earlier photos, including WINTGENS2 and HÖHNDORF1, portray him in an M1910 tunic with its eight-button front. His four-ribbon *Feldschnalle*, with one exception (see WINTGENS3), is seen only in later pictures like S391-92 where he dons an M1915 tunic that concealed its buttons beneath a flap. One of them (see S400, WINTGENS7) was originally signed and dated 14 September 1916 by Wintgens on the back.

HÖHNDORF1 is believed to commemorate *KEK Vaux*'s joint celebration of the consecutive 20 and 21 July 1916 bestowals of the *Pour le Mérite* on Walter Höhndorf and Ernst von Althaus (note the special boutonnieres that they are wearing). Another picture of Wintgens with his older M1910 tunic and three-place ribbon bar (WINTGENS4), was taken beside the wreckage of his 13th victim on 2 August 1916. Accordingly, it seems that Wintgens acquired his new tunic and *Feldschnalle* and had his pictures snapped wearing them sometime afterward in August or early September for S391-92 to have been published in late September 1916, as our guideline predicts.

WINTGENS5 displays S391's image, but offers a slightly wider and taller field of vision; so it could not have been copied from S391. It is labeled as an original photograph and its lower right hand corner is imprinted with the mark "Karl Zinne, Minden." Wintgens was born in "Neustadt a. S." (probably Bad Neustadt an der Saale) but his family later moved to Minden. His remains were transferred from St. Quentin to Minden's Nordfriedhof cemetery after the war, and the town still possesses a street named "Wintgensstrasse." It seems likely then that Wintgens visited Karl Zinne's studio and had this picture taken there while on leave.

Notes

[1] Strictly speaking, the Iron Cross 2nd Class ribbon should have come before the Royal Hohenzollern House Order's, but their placement before Bavaria's and Saxony's orders was correct for a Prussian officer.

[2] This writer has seen only one such example in Buckler's S631, where it appears that his Hessian General Honor Decoration comes between his Prussian *Goldenes Militär-Verdienstkreuz* (Golden Military Merit Cross) and Iron Cross 2nd Class ribbons.

Lt. Kurt Wintgens was serving with *KEK Falkenhausen* when he won his *Pour le Mérite* on 1 July 1916. This picture shows Wintgens with the unit's namesake, *Generaloberst* Ludwig von Falkenhausen (center). *Lt.* Walter Höhndorf stands on the other side of the general and *Vzfw.* Walter Kypke is to the far left.

WINTGENS2

Lt. Kurt Wintgens and his brothers pose together before the camera. This is the only photo known to this writer that shows Wintgens wearing his four-place *Feldschnalle* with his older M1910 tunic. It may be a transitional picture taken between his receipt of the new ribbon bar and the purchase of his new M1915 tunic. On the other hand, Wintgens simply may have retained his older tunic and used it occasionally as a spare. (photo courtesy of UTD)

WINTGENS3

WINTGENS4

Lt. Kurt Wintgens poses behind the remains of his 13th victim, Morane BB biplane No.5177 of RFC No.60 Squadron, shot down on 2 August 1916. The observer, 2nd Lt. Henry Newton, died instantly, and the pilot, Lt. John Ormsby, expired a few days later.

On 21 July 1916, *Lt.* Albert Oesterreicher of *KEK 3* made the initial attack on BE.2c No.2100 of RFC No.12 Squadron. Though his bullets hit the machine, it was *Lt.* Kurt Wintgens who swooped in and badly wounded the pilot, 2nd Lt. R.M. Wilson-Browne, forcing him to crash land and thus be credited to Wintgens as his 10th victory. Wilson-Browne, seen here on the ground surrounded by several German soldiers, died later that day. He was avenged by the loss of *KEK 3*'s *Vzfw.* Wolfgang Heinemann during the same engagement (see S379).

WINTGENS5

S393
BOELCKE
Oswald

Taken: 17 to 19 January 1916
Douai/Lille
Publ: October 1916
Reason: victory score

Decorations:
WR: *Pour le Mérite*; Iron Cross, 1st Class; Pilot's Badge
MB: None
RB: None
BH: Royal Hohenzollern House Order, Knight's Cross/ Sw; Life Saving Medal

Other Cards:
S363, S364, S369, S373, S408, S409
(L7720, L7721, L7761, L7776, L7785, L7793; N5579, N5580, N5601, N5619, N5690, N6004, N6005, N6225)
Note: Taken same time as S369

Key Dates:
18 June 1916   Immelmann killed in action

Jul 1916	Boelcke begins enforced leave and tour of Eastern Fronts
10 Aug 1916	*Jagdstaffel 2* created
20 Aug 1916	Boelcke returns to Dessau
27 Aug 1916	*Jasta 2* assembled in Bertincourt under Boelcke's command
2 Sep 1916	victory #20

S393 displays S363's photograph above a poem written by Barbara Goede – the same author of the poetic eulogy found on Immelmann's S377. This time her work is a laudatory celebration of Boelcke, "*König der Lüfte*" ("King of the Skies"), who strikes terror in enemy hearts:

High up in the glistening clouds
Reigns boldness! Our Boelcke!

High above in the ether's azure flow,
Like an eagle he crosses over the meadows below!
Terror suddenly takes hold of the enemy
When he violates the Falcon's territory!

Underneath—grey evil-flows,
Above him—the sun glows,
Ahead—ghostly and fey
The enemy falls into death's domain!
Terribly beautiful battle sight!
Victory upon victory in God's heights!
Which, high up where only the stars could see,
Each one done with bravery,
Force even the enemy himself, though full of wrath
To acknowledge respect in your behalf!
The King of the Sky watches over
German honor, German power!

High up in the glistening clouds
Reigns boldness! Our Boelcke!

Boelcke had been ordered to stop flying following Immelmann's death and opted to visit Austria, Bulgaria, the Balkans, Turkey, and the Russian Front instead of "cooling his heels" at a desk behind the lines. He cut his trip short and returned to Germany in late August after news reached him that he was to be placed in command of one of the German Air Service's new fighter squadrons. He and *Jasta 2* settled into Bertincourt on 27 August, and only six days later Boelcke demonstrated that he had not lost his touch by bringing down the unit's first victim on 2 September. *Jasta 2* proceeded to shoot down 21 more aircraft that month, nine of them by Boelcke. He was back in a big way, and the 30 September 1916 edition of *Berliner Illustrirte Zeitung* celebrated this and his 26th victory (achieved on 15 September) by featuring his S363 photo on its cover. S393, which our guideline says came out around the same time, was no doubt intended to do the same.

A seldom-seen portrait of *Hptm.* Oswald Boelcke. He is dressed in the lightweight summer uniform he often wore during his July-August 1916 tour of the Eastern Front.

Above: Boelcke in conversation with a group of officers, time and place unknown.

Right: Boelcke relaxing with an unidentified officer who bears some resemblance to Hermann Göring. We know that Göring flew two-seaters in the Verdun region with *FFA 25* and an *Eindecker* with *KEK Stenay* when Boelcke was serving with nearby *KEK Sivry* (March through June 1916). In addition, Boelcke mentioned flying with Göring's good friend, Bruno Loerzer, at *KEK Jametz* during February through March 1916; so it is conceivable that they met through Loerzer at that time. Nevertheless, there is no direct evidence, other than the possibility this photograph presents, that Göring and Boelcke ever met.

Two more rare snapshots of *Hptm.* Oswald Boelcke. They were taken upon the occasion of a visit by his former observer, Heinz-Hellmuth von Wühlisch. (first photo courtesy of Jeffrey Sands)

S394
FRIEDRICH
Alfred

Taken: May 1915 to September 1916
Berlin-Schöneberg, by Karl Wahl
Publ: October 1916
Reason: prewar aviator

Decorations:
WR: Iron Cross, 1st Class; Pilot's Badge; Merit Cross (Sax)
MB: None
RB: None
BH: Iron Cross, 2nd Class

Other Cards:
S395
(N6024)
Note: Taken same time S395

S395
FRIEDRICH
Alfred

Taken: May 1915 to September 1916
Berlin-Schöneberg, by Karl Wahl
Publ: October 1916
Reason: prewar aviator

Decorations:
WR: Iron Cross, 1st Class; Pilot's Badge; Merit Cross (Sax)
MB: None
RB: None
BH: Iron Cross, 2nd Class

Other Cards:
S394
(N6024)
Note: Taken same time as S394

Key Dates:
None

Alfred Friedrich was a famous prewar pilot who had been featured in several early Sanke cards (S106, S137, S140, S200, and two unnumbered cards). *Ingenieur* (engineer) Friedrich received German Pilot License No.149 on 11 January 1912 and soon gained the reputation of a daredevil pilot through his pioneer performance of *die Figur "Korkenzieher"* (the "Corkscrew" figure) at airshows, a maneuver that later became known as a *"Trudeln,"* or "spin." On 3 September 1913, he and navigator Dr. Hermann Elias took off from Berlin in an Etrich Taube and flew to Paris with only four stops in between (Hannover, Gelsenkirchen, Brussels, and Salle à Bruyère). He left Paris on 13 September, accompanied this time by his airplane's designer Igo Etrich, and flew over the English Channel to London – the first time that a pilot with a passenger had performed such a feat. Friedrich completed his roundtrip journey to Berlin on 20 September and was met with international acclaim.

Illustrierte Kriegs-Zeitung Nr. 40 (c. 9 May 1915) announced that Friedrich had been awarded the Iron Cross 1st Class for his outstanding flying accomplishments. Other than this, little has been uncovered to date regarding his military career. FRIEDRICH1 shows him wearing his new Iron Cross medal as well as the ribbons for the Iron Cross 2nd Class and Saxon Merit Cross. He is adorned with the same decorations in S394-95. It is interesting to note that his Saxon

Merit Cross is not "with swords," an indication that it may actually have been awarded before the war. We can also see from his left shoulder board that he served with a unit numbered "1." By the time S394-95's photos were taken, Friedrich had been promoted to *Vizefeldwebel*. Unfortunately, we have no other information with regard to when this might have occurred. Therefore, the most that can be said about S394-95 is that they were snapped at some point between May 1915 and three weeks before their projected publication date of October 1916.

N6024 offers a touched-up version of S395 where the indicators of Friedrich's *Vizefeldwebel* rank have been replaced with those of a *Leutnant*. N6024 followed Boelcke's N6005 memorial card, so we know that it had to have first appeared in December 1916 or later. Once again, we have no further information on when his promotion took place. N6024, however, does provide us with its origin, and therefore the origin of S394-95. It notes that its picture was taken by Karl Wahl of Berlin-Schöneberg. This is the same studio that another prewar aviator, Walter Höhndorf, had visited for his S389 picture. Perhaps both men had been acquainted with Wahl's services before the war when they had been at nearby Johannisthal – the cradle of German aviation.

FRIEDRICH I

This photo accompanied *Illustrierte Kriegs-Zeitung*'s c. 9 May 1915 announcement of Friedrich's receipt of the Iron Cross 1st Class.

N6024, NPG's version of S395. Friedrich's rank was "artistically" updated to *Leutnant*.

ALFRED FRIEDRICH und seine ETRICH - MERCEDES - TAUBE, mit der er im Jahre 1913 als erster Deutscher von Berlin nach Paris und London flog.

Above and opposite top: Five pre-war postcards featuring Alfred Friedrich – four were produced by Sanke, above right by an independent publisher.

Alfred Friedrich
Flog als erster Deutscher
Berlin-Paris-London-Berlin.

Alfred Friedrich.

Alfred Friedrich.

S396
MULZER
Max (*Ritter* von)
Leutnant

Taken: 22-31 August 1916
Memmingen, by Karl Müller
Publ: October 1916
Reason: Military Max-Joseph Order award or post-death

Decorations:
WR: *Pour le Mérite*; Iron Cross, 1st Class; Pilot's Badge (Bav)
MB: Military Max-Joseph Order, Knight's Cross (Bav); Military
Merit Order, 4th Class/ Sw (Bav); Iron Cross, 2nd Class; Royal
Hohenzollern House Order, Knight's Cross/ Sw; Hanseatic Cross
(Ham); Friedrich Cross, 2nd Class (Anh)
RB: None
BH: None

Other Cards:
S373, S379, S385, S397, S398, (possibly S399), S408
(L7720, L7727, L7793; N5630, N5690)
Note: Taken same time as S385, S397 and S398

S397
MULZER
Max (*Ritter* von)
Leutnant

Taken: 22-31 August 1916
Memmingen, by Karl Müller
Publ: October 1916
Reason: Military Max-Joseph Order award or post-death

Decorations:
WR: *Pour le Mérite*; Iron Cross, 1st Class; Pilot's Badge (Bav)
MB: Military Max-Joseph Order, Knight's Cross (Bav); Military

Unser erfolgreicher Kampf-Flieger
Leutnant Mulzer

396
Postkartenvertrieb W.Sanke
BERLIN N 37
Nachdruck wird gerichtlich verfolgt.

Merit Order, 4th Class/ Sw (Bav); Iron Cross, 2nd Class; Royal Hohenzollern House Order, Knight's Cross/ Sw; Hanseatic Cross (Ham); Friedrich Cross, 2nd Class (Anh)
RB: None
BH: None

Other Cards:
S373, S379, S385, S396, S398, (possibly S399), S408 (L7720, L7727, L7793; N5630, N5690)
Note: Taken same time as S385, S396 and S398

S398
MULZER
Max (*Ritter* von)
Leutnant

Taken: 22-31 August 1916
Memmingen, by Karl Müller
Publ: October 1916
Reason: Military Max-Joseph Order award or post-death

Decorations:
WR: *Pour le Mérite*; Iron Cross, 1st Class; Pilot's Badge (Bav)

MB: Military Merit Order, 4th Class/ Sw (Bav); Iron Cross, 2nd Class; Royal Hohenzollern House Order, Knight's Cross/ Sw; Hanseatic Cross (Ham); Friedrich Cross, 2nd Class (Anh)
RB: None
BH: None

Other Cards:
S373, S379, S385, S396, S397, (possibly S399), S408 (L7720, L7727, L7793; N5630, N5690)
Note: Taken same time as S385, S396 and S397

Key Dates:
8 Jul 1916	awarded *Pour le Mérite*
21 Aug 1916	awarded Military Max-Joseph Order, Knight's Cross (Bav)
6 Sep 1916	Military Max-Joseph Order, Knight's Cross (Bav) award ceremony at La Brayelle airfield
26 Sep 1916	killed in accident

To fully understand the distinguishing characteristics of Mulzer's S385, S396-98 series (see S385), we need to turn first to its final card, S398. There and in MULZER2 (a picture taken at the same time) we see what was undoubtedly the actual *Grossordenschnalle* that Mulzer wore at the time all these pictures were taken. It spans from his left side to the middle of his chest and does not include the Military Max-Joseph Order (Bavaria). The patch denoting the erasure of this medals bar in S385 covers precisely the same area. S396 and S397 extend the medals bar beyond the middle of his chest with the addition of the Military Max-Joseph Order. An examination of S397 under magnification discloses that all its decorations are genuine except for the Military Max-Joseph Order, which is a cleverly drawn-in fabrication. Curiously, S396's entire appearance is close to that of a drawing, but a careful comparison to S397 and S398 demonstrates that an artist merely touched up the highlights of an underlying, actual photo (e.g., the manner in which the medals overlap one another is consistent throughout S396-98). On the basis of S398's authenticity, we can once again surmise that S396's Military Max-Joseph Order was the only object added in. In summary, S398 is the only untouched photograph of the lot. Where S385 expunged Mulzer's medals bar completely, an artist's impression of the Military Max-Joseph Order was added to S396 and S397. The same artist presumably touched up all of S396's highlights, perhaps to help disguise his handiwork or to improve upon an original lack of photographic clarity.

We have already determined that S385's picture was taken sometime during Mulzer's leave in Memmingen following his receipt of the Military Max-Joseph Order. By association, this must be true for S396-98 as well. This explains why the Max-Joseph Order was drawn into two of them, because though the decoration was technically awarded on 21 August, Mulzer did not physically receive it until after his return to the Front on 6 September.

The ultimate motivational factor behind S396-98's publication is not as easily discernible because their nature and timing suit several possibilities. S396-98 clearly came out after Mulzer's receipt of the Military Max-Joseph Order in late August 1916. Yet if this event had been the reason for their publication, why was that decoration omitted from S398? The fact that none of the postcards refers to Mulzer by the "*Ritter* von" title that automatically accompanied Bavaria's highest decoration further complicates matters. Mulzer died in the crash of an Albatros D.I he was test flying at Fâmars (near Valenciennes) on 26 September. If this had been the driving force, the October 1916 publication date projected by our guideline would be just about right according to our three-week rule. Unlike Immelmann's or Boelcke's memorial cards though, S396-98 are not marked by a black border or death cross to confirm this. But neither are Kirmaier's S445, Schulte's S547, Keudell's S555-56, Wendelmuth's S594, Tutschek's S650, or Schreiber's S661, which were definitely issued after each subject's death.[1] Perhaps a combination of events contributed to the origin of S396-98. That is, while they were being prepared for a Max-Joseph Order celebration, news of Mulzer's death may have interrupted the process. This may have spurred their hasty publication and led to the omission of the Max-Joseph Order from the last card in the series and the "*Ritter* von" title from all of them. With no clear choice available, both reasons are listed as possibilities behind the publication of S396-98.

Note

[1] Other probable posthumous publications were Nathanael's S537, Hess' S590, Eisenmenger and Gund's S636, and Collin's S669.

MULZER 2

Top: Another portrait from Mulzer's visit to Karl Müller's studio in late August 1916 that appeared on the cover of the 1 February 1918 edition of *Das Bayerland, Illustrierte Halbmonatsschrift für Bayerns Land und Volk*.

Right: The original portrait behind S397 that appeared in a 1917 biography of Max Mulzer.

On 1 October 1916, the body of *Lt.* Max *Ritter* von Mulzer lies in state in the same hospital courtyard in Douai where the remains of his friend, Max Immelmann, had rested a few months earlier.

Army parson Stadler (to the left in front of the dais) conducts Mulzer's service at *Kriegslazarett A*, Douai.

Above and two below: An officer pays tribute to Max *Ritter* von Mulzer. His coffin is carried from the courtyard in back of *Kriegslazarett A* to a waiting gun carriage that transports it through the streets of Douai to the train station.

S400
WINTGENS
Kurt
Leutnant
(with Anthony Fokker)

Taken: August 1916
Publ: October 1916
Reason: post-death

Decorations:
WR: *Pour le Mérite*; Iron Cross, 1st Class; Pilot's Badge
MB: None
RB: Royal Hohenzollern House Order, Knight's Cross/ Sw; Iron Cross, 2nd Class; Miltary Merit Order, 4th Class/ Sw (Bav); Albert Order, Knight 2nd Class/ Sw (Sax)
BH: None

Other Cards:
S378, S391, S392, S408
(L7729, L7793)
Note: Taken same time as S391
Wearing eyeglasses

Key Dates:

1 Jul 1916	Wintgens awarded *Pour le Mérite*
19 Jul 1916	Wintgens awarded Albert Order, Knight 2nd Class/ Sw (Sax)
Sep 1916	Wintgens transferred to *Jasta 1*
25 Sep 1916	Wintgens killed in action
8 Oct 1916	S400 photo published in *Berliner Illustrirte Zeitung* 41, p.603
11 Oct 1916	S400 photo published in *Flugsport* 21, p.562

Mulzer's *Ordenskissen* – the pillow that displayed his decorations.

See S391-92 for a discussion of Wintgens' appearance in a new M1915 tunic with four-place *Feldschnalle* (ribbon bar) in August 1916. He is wearing the same items in S400 and two other photographs, WINTGENS6 and WINTGENS7. WINTGENS6 depicts him in a motorcar with *Oblt.* Hans-Joachim Buddecke, who had returned to France from Turkey to take command of *Jasta 4* – a new fighter squadron created on 25 August 1916 from *KEK Vaux*, the unit that Höhndorf and Frankl had made famous. Buddecke and Wintgens are at an unknown airfield that seems somewhat more extensive and established (note the lineup of fixed hangars) than Vaux might have been, and some experts are convinced it was taken at Fokker's Schwerin factory and airfield. WINTGENS7 has an airplane in the background and may have been taken the same day at the same airfield. S400 could provide the link. Wintgens, this time standing next to Anthony Fokker, looks the same as he does in WINTGENS6 and 7. Though this is pure speculation, it is possible that all three photos were therefore taken at Fokker's Schwerin factory. With regard to time, we can be fairly certain that at least WINTGENS6, and possibly WINTGENS7 and S400, were taken in August 1916 because in early September, Wintgens was sent to another newly formed unit, *Jasta 1*, so that its commander, *Hptm.* Martin Zander, could draw on his veteran experience. Wintgens maintained a full schedule there and indeed brought down six more planes with *Jasta 1* before being killed in action later that month.

S400's photo was published in the 8 October 1916 edition of *Berliner Illustrirte Zeitung*, along with the caption, "*Letzte Aufnahme des Fliegerleutnants Wintgens, der jüngst im Luftkampf fiel...*" ("The last picture of Lt. Wintgens, who recently fell in air combat..."). Three days later, *Flugsport* announced Wintgens' death with the same picture. Sanke probably issued S400 with similar intentions, given the card's projected November publication date. Though a black border around the card or "†" next to Wintgens' name would have given us confirmation, we will see that these devices were absent from many Sanke cards that were issued after a pilot's death (e.g., Kirmaier's S445, Schulte's S547, Keudell's S555-56, Wendelmuth's S594, Tutschek's S650, and Schreiber's S661). It is somewhat ironic that Anthony Fokker was present in the airman's "last picture." Though they had figured largely in each other's celebrity, in the closing weeks of his life Wintgens had abandoned Fokker's *Eindecker* because it had become outclassed by newer Allied aircraft. He achieved his final victories and most likely flew to his end in a Halberstadt D.II.

WINTGENS6

Lt. Kurt Wintgens (center) sits in a Stoewer model staff car with fellow *Pour le Mérite* holder, *Oblt.* Hans-Joachim Buddecke (in backseat), possibly at Fokker's Schwerin airfield.

Wintgens looking at a Fokker E.IV *Eindecker*. (photo courtesy of UTD)

2nd Lt. L.N. Graham was piloting Martinsyde G100 No.7471 of RFC No.27 Squadron when it was shot down by *Lt.* Kurt Wintgens on 30 July 1916. Graham managed to land safely near Péronne where he was captured and this photograph was taken.

WINTGENS7

The back of this pleasant portrait of Wintgens bears his autograph and the date 14 September 1916. (photo courtesy of UTD)

The funeral service held for Kurt Wintgens on 27 September 1916 in St. Quentin. In front of the coffin is a wreath shaped like a *Pour le Mérite* (see next photo).

S401
COSSEL
Maximilian von
Oberleutnant
(with Rudolf Windisch)

Taken: 7 to 18 October 1916
Perespa, by Adolph Jessen
Publ: October 1916
Reason: sabotage mission

Decorations:
WR: Merit Cross, 3rd Class/ Sw (Wald); Royal Hohenzollern House
Order, Knight's Cross/ Sw; Iron Cross, 1st Class; Observer's Badge
MB: None
RB: Iron Cross, 2nd Class; Hanseatic Cross (Lüb)
BH: None

Other Cards:
S373, S408, S424
(L7720, L7756, L7783, L7793; N6003)
Note: Cossel only airman to be awarded Merit Cross, 3rd Class/ Sw
(Wald)

S401
WINDISCH
Rudolf
Vizefeldwebel
(with Maximilian von Cossel)

Taken: 7 to 18 October 1916
Perespa, by Adolph Jessen
Publ: October 1916
Reason: sabotage mission

Decorations:
WR: Honor Cross/ Sw (Wald); Crown Order, 4th Class/ Sw; Iron
Cross, 1st Class; Pilot's Badge
MB: None
RB: Iron Cross, 2nd Class
BH: None

Other Cards:
S408, S576, S662
(L7756, L7784, L7793; N6003)
Note: Windisch only airman to be awarded Crown Order, 4th Class/
Sw

Key Dates:
2-3 Oct 1916	conduct mission behind enemy lines
5 Oct 1916	receive Waldeck awards
7 Oct 1916	receive Prussian awards from *Kaiser*
18 Oct 1916	Windisch awarded St. Henry Medal in Silver (Sax)

When the men of *Feldflieger-Abteilung 62* assembled for dinner on
7 May 1916, they heard their commanding officer, *Hptm.* Hermann
Kastner, recount some of their unit's most impressive
accomplishments. Just four months earlier, Oswald Boelcke and Max
Immelmann, the stars of their highly successful fighter detachment,
had earned Prussia's highest decoration. Though Boelcke had moved
on to another assignment in the Verdun sector, Immelmann still
remained to continue setting an example for them and the entire
German Air Service. Their comrades, two-seater pilots and observers,

A funeral wreath in the form of a *Pour le Mérite* rests upon Wintgen's grave in
the military cemetery just outside St. Quentin. A close look discloses that the
wreath's arms were marked the same as the medal: crowned "F" on the top
cross arm, "Pour" on the left arm, "le Mé" on the right, and "rite" on the bottom.
(photo courtesy of UTD)

had carried out equally dangerous duties with matching, though perhaps less publicized, courage and success. They had flown 1,000 sorties that had covered over 55,000 miles of terrain, bringing down twenty-five enemy aircraft while losing only two of their own. Kastner's message could not have been lost on the group: *FFA 62* had established a tradition of success that they were expected to maintain. Sitting in the audience were *Lt.* Max Mulzer, *Lt.* Maximilian von Cossel, and newcomer *Fw.* Rudolf Windisch, who had joined the unit just six days earlier – and none would disappoint Kastner. Mulzer, who with two victories already to his credit had received his Pilot's Badge the day Windisch arrived, would go on to earn yet another *Pour le Mérite* for the group. As for Cossel and Windisch, their collaboration during an especially daring mission would enhance *FFA 62*'s reputation even more.

On 12 June 1916, *FFA 62*'s reconnaissance and fighter units were separated. The two-seater crews were sent to the Eastern Front while the fighter pilots remained behind under the new designation, *KEK Douai*. Cossel, an *Oberleutnant* since 6 June, and *Fw.* Windsich were among those who made the arduous four-day journey to Ukraine, and after their arrival at their new Perespa airfield they began flying combat missions together. July brought Windisch a series of rewards in rapid succession: his Pilot's Badge on 10 July, the Iron Cross 2nd Class on 12 July, and a promotion to *Vizefeldwebel* on the 13th. He and Cossel enjoyed their first taste of success as a team in August when they downed a Russian balloon on the 25th. But it was October that brought them national recognition. The following summary of their famous mission is based on Cossel's narrative entitled, "*Eine Bahnunterbrechung im Rücken der Russen*" (see Neumann, *In der Luft unbesiegt*, pp.101-106).

Orders were issued to the fliers to disrupt a key railway supply line that linked the main Russian base to the Front. Cossel and Windisch figured that aerial bombardment would be ineffective, so they devised a daring behind-the-lines sabotage mission instead. Fearing discovery by spies, they covertly obtained the supplies and special munitions they needed and made secret preparations for their journey. At 4:45 am on 2 October, they took off in their Roland C.II *Walfisch* and flew toward a wooded area south of their designated target. Windisch landed in a nearby clearing and dropped off Cossel and the over 100 pounds of explosives and related gear he elected to carry. Cossel knew that being caught as a spy would mean certain execution, so he chose to remain in uniform. Nevertheless, he took great pains to disguise his appearance by donning an overcoat of common appearance, removing the cockades from his service cap, and smearing parts of himself with mud. The purpose was for him to look more like a native, at least from afar. He traveled several miles by foot toward his destination, passing several farmers tending their fields along the way, until he finally arrived at the rail line. A guarded block house was within view, so he waited until dark to begin his work. Even then, the appearance of passing trains forced him to retreat several times into the tall grass nearby to avoid detection. After several hours of effort, he finally placed the charges and readied the detonator. Cossel wanted to give the Russians as little time as possible to find him after the explosion, so he did not strike until the last hour before he would be in danger of missing his pre-arranged rendezvous with Windisch back at the drop-off point. Then, as a train approached, he set off an explosion that derailed the engine and some of its cars. While the alarm sounded at the block station, Cossel reeled in the detonator cables and dropped a recent copy of *The Times* of London nearby in an attempt to obscure the real culprits. To hasten his escape, he decided to follow a direct line through a village toward the rendezvous spot. Fortunately, pouring rain helped disguise him and discourage the occupants' curiosity. After reaching his destination, he grew concerned that the very same rain that had aided him would jeopardize Windisch's ability to return and collect him. But all he could do at this point was set down ground markers as guides for

Windisch and wait. Around 5:00 am, almost exactly 24 hours after their mission had begun, Cossel spotted a plane flying just below the clouds. Windisch had braved the foul weather after all, and Cossel watched with considerable relief and joy as his partner landed safely in the sodden field. After reloading Cossel's gear into the plane, the two lit celebratory cigars and escaped back to friendly territory and the gratitude of a nation.

Despite the military's initial desire for secrecy, the German press caught wind of the duo's daring mission and trumpeted it broadly within a few days of their return (so much for Cossel's attempt to direct suspicions at the English). On 5 October, Cossel was informed that he and Windsich had been awarded Waldeck's Merit Cross 3rd Class with Swords and its Honor Cross with Swords, respectively. Though Cossel was a Prussian and Windisch was a Saxon, the Prince of Waldeck-Pyrmont was in charge of one of the units assigned to their area and he chose to recognize their mission as supportive of his own. The awards themselves arrived later the same day – much faster than usual. Not to be outdone, the *Kaiser*, who happened to be touring their portion of the Front, gave notice that he was giving Cossel his Royal Hohenzollern House Order, Knight's Cross with Swords, and Windisch his Crown Order 4th Class with Swords. He pinned them on their chests himself during a 7 October ceremony. All four decorations were exceptional at that time. Cossel was the only airman, and Windisch was the first of only two airmen, to receive such Waldeck awards. Cossel's Royal Hohenzollern House Order was solid gold, and as O'Connor speculated, appears to have come from the *Kaiser*'s personal stock. Yet it was the bestowal of the Crown Order on Windisch that was the most extraordinary of all. Orders were for officers, not non-commissioned personnel – and so it was for the remainder of the war, for no other NCO ever received the Crown Order again. Tellingly, these are the four decorations that are prominently displayed in S401.

S401's picture was probably taken soon after the *Kaiser*'s award ceremony on 7 October because Cossel and Windisch, with new decorations pinned to their tunics and wearing belts and gloves, appear to have come from a formal function. The other indication that it originated from a royal award ceremony comes in the form of the inscription found at the card's lower right hand corner: "Copyright Adolph Jessen Schleswig." The *Kaiser* had many ties to Schleswig-Holstein including his wife, who was born there, and we have already seen where Jessen had attended another royal visit (see Immelmann's S362-*Lt.*). It appears then that S401's photo was taken by a (royal?) photographer who had accompanied the *Kaiser* on his trip to the Eastern Front, and who later licensed its use on a postcard to Sanke. Technically, the picture could have occurred any time from 7 October to when Windisch received the Saxon St. Henry Medal in Silver (which he is not wearing) on 18 October. Therefore, a range of 7 to 18 October has been assigned. The earliest that the image could have appeared in the form of a Sanke card, at least in accordance with our three-week rule, would have been late October – the very timeframe predicted by our guideline.

Practically identical, COSSEL1 is a photograph taken the same time as S401. Its perspective is only slightly to the right of S401, as if two photographers had been standing side-by-side for the same shot.[1] Curiously, the airmen are not donning their belts in COSSEL1. A close look at it under magnification reveals that someone, for some now unknown reason, went to a great deal of trouble to erase them from the photograph.

Note
[1] Several factors illustrate this. For example, compare the positions of the loop at the end of Cossel's riding crop, the edge of the bush behind Cossel, the view of Cossel's left trouser leg with respect to his left hand, the location of the trees behind Windisch's head, and the angle of Windisch's shoes.

COSSEL I

A snapshot taken the same time as S401. Curiously, the airmen's belts were studiously erased from this image. Even the buttons that had been obscured by them were drawn back in. (photo courtesy of UTD)

Oblt. Maximilian von Cossel (left) and *Fw.* Rudolf Windisch.

Lt. Maximilian von Cossel (far left) poses at the nose of an LFG Roland C.II Walfisch next to a pilot identified as *Offz-Stv.* Müller. Cossel and then *Vzfw.* Müller both received a special commendation from General Max von Boehn on 20 March 1916 (see O'Connor, *Aviation Awards VII*, p.362). The team was cited again on 9 May for having completed nearly 80 successful flights at the Front, and it was simultaneously announced that Müller had been awarded the Iron Cross 1st Class. Múller is not wearing that Iron Cross in this photo, yet he had been promoted to *Offizier-Stellvertreter*, which must have occurred after the 20 March citation when he was still a *Vizefeldwebel*. Therefore, this photo was probably taken in April or early May 1916 at *FFA 62*'s Douai airfield.

Opposite

Top: A closer look at an LFG Roland C.II *Walfisch*, the type of plane Cossel and Windisch used for their renowned sabotage mission.

Bottom: An artist's rendering of Cossel and Windisch's mission as published in the 18 November 1916 edition of *Die Wochenschau*.

S402
BERTHOLD
Rudolf
Oberleutnant

Taken: 12 to 19 August 1916
Vaux
Publ: November 1916
Reason: *Pour le Mérite* award

Decorations:
WR: *Pour le Mérite*, Iron Cross, 1st Class; Pilot's Badge
MB: None
RB: None
BH: None

Other Cards:
S408, S423, S629
(L7793)

Key Dates:

25 Apr 1916	crashes and goes to hospital
24 Aug 1916	victory #6 with *KEK Vaux*
27 Aug 1916	awarded Royal Hohenzollern House Order, Knight's Cross/ Sw
1 Sep 1916	*KEK Vaux* moves to Roupy airfield as *Jasta 4*
12 Oct 1916	awarded *Pour le Mérite*
c. 5 Nov 1916	S402 published in *Illustrierte Kriegs-Zeitung (Das Weltbild)* 118, p.8
5 Nov 1916	S402 photo published in *Berliner Illustrirte Zeitung* 45, p.671

Unser erfolgreicher Kampf-Flieger Oberleutnant Berthold.

Rudolf Berthold was an observer with *Feldflieger-Abteilung 23* when the war broke out, but by January 1915 he had become a pilot. Almost a year later he got his own single-seater to fly, and on 10 January 1916 he claimed a victory over a French Voisin that went unconfirmed. The next day, on 11 January 1916, *Feldflieger-Abteilung 23*'s fighter detachment was formed under the name *KEK Vaux*. Berthold claimed another Voisin on 2 February, and this time it counted. Just three days later he brought down number two, and by 16 April he had five victories to his credit. He crashed in his Pfalz *Eindecker* on 25 April and was sent off to a hospital for recovery. He was back at *KEK Vaux* when a party was held for the unit's most recent *Pour le Mérite* recipients, *Lt.* Walter Höhndorf (20 July) and *Oblt.* Ernst von Althaus (21 July). HÖHNDORF1 (see S381), a picture of that celebration, shows Berthold sitting off to the right in the same type of chair that appears in S402; and S384 and S402 capture Frankl and Berthold in the same chair and spot near a leafy hedge outside the steps to Chateau Vaux. The hedge appears once again in the background of BERTHOLD1, a photo undoubtedly taken the same time as S402 (e.g., his service cap exhibits the exact same creases and folds in both). Apparently, the photographer took the opportunity to snap pictures of Frankl and Berthold, if not other members of *KEK Vaux*, at one time and setting.

We have already determined that the photograph used in Frankl's S384 was recorded 12-19 August 1916. This in turn would date Berthold's S402 to the same period, which seems about right considering there is no visible sign of the Royal Hohenzollern Order Berthold was awarded on 27 August, and that the unit left Vaux for Roupy on 1 September. We also have BERTHOLD2, a copy of the original image behind S402. BERTHOLD2 states that its copyright was held by Berliner Illustrations Gesellschaft. Indeed, both of the November 1916 newspaper editions cited above named B.I.G. as their photo's source. An early November debut for S402 is similarly designated by our guideline, so it is likely that Sanke had to obtain his rights to the image from the same firm. We saw a similar situation in our discussion of Parschau's S380, except in that case A.Grohs Illustrations Verlag owned the rights.[1]

In BERTHOLD2 (and for that matter, BERTHOLD1) the airman is not adorned with the *Pour le Mérite* that was so obviously drawn into S402. It therefore follows that S402 was created from this older image that was modified to celebrate his award of the *Pour le Mérite* on 12 October 1916.

Note

[1] If it is eventually confirmed that Frankl's S384 and Berthold's S402 were originally snapped by A. Mocsigay of Hamburg (see S384), we should remember that Berliner Illustrations Gesellschaft often obtained its photographs from independent sources.

Above: A companion portrait to S402. Note the similarity in poses between S402/BERTHOLD1 and S384/FRANKL1. It is believed that both sets originated around the same time, if not the same day, in August 1916.

Top right: This is a print from S402's original photograph (note the lack of a drawn-in *Pour le Mérite*), labeled as No.20085 in Berliner Illustrations Gesellschaft's company files. This number and the accompanying caption, which noted that Berthold had brought down two enemy airplanes in one day according to a 17 September army report (the action had taken place the day before), assign this particular print's origin to October 1917. Indeed, the same image, accredited to "B.I.G.", appeared on the cover of the c.14 October 1917 edition of *Illustrierte Kriegs-Zeitung*.

Right: *Lt.* Erwin Tütschulte (left) and *Rittm.* Max Schueler von Krieken of *FFA 23* flank two white terriers. One of the terriers posed with Berthold in S402. Both dogs appear in another *FFA 23* photo seen in O'Connor, *Aviation Awards VII*, p.55.

Above: Rudolf Berthold (center right) and Hans-Joachim von Seydlitz-Gerstenberg (far right) when both were serving with *FFA 23*. (photo courtesy of UTD)

Right: *Oblt.* Rudolf Berthold (left), and *Lt.* Walter Gnamm of *FFA 23*. Gnamm is wearing the ribbon for his Gold Military Merit Medal (Württemberg), awarded on 2 August 1915, but not the Observer's Badge he won a little over one month later on 5 September. This probably pinpoints the picture to sometime between those dates. At that time, Berthold was piloting a large, twin-engined AEG "Battle Plane" and had not yet moved on to single-seaters. Note that Gnamm is wearing some kind of material inside his tunic collar, probably to prevent chafing of the neck. (photo courtesy of UTD)

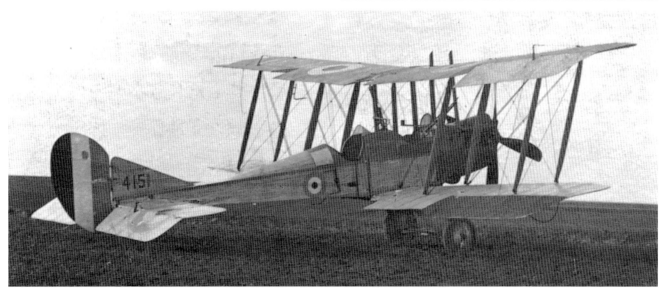

On 13 March 1916, Berthold and two other Fokker *Eindecker* pilots attacked four BEs headed toward Cambrai. BE.2c No.4151 of RFC No.8 Squadron was hit by a burst from Berthold's gun and forced down near Bourlon, where this picture was snapped. A wounded 2nd Lt. M.A.J. Orde and his fellow crewman, P. Shaw, were taken prisoner. After the war, Orde related that two German airmen had landed near his downed plane and waited with them until other Germans arrived. Orde believed the German airmen came from a two-seater, but other witnesses stated that they saw two Fokkers set down. Norman Franks (*Sharks Among Minnows*, p.68) has speculated that Berthold may have been one of them.

S407
ZANDER
Martin
Hauptmann

Taken: 1915 to August 1916
Publ: November 1916
Reason: *Staffelführer* and victory score

Decorations:
WR: Iron Cross, 1st Class; Pilot's Badge
MB: None
RB: None
BH: Iron Cross 2nd Class

Other Cards:
None

Key Dates:

25 Sep 1915	victory #1 with *Feldflieger-Abteilung 9b*
11 Oct 1915	victory #2
14 Dec 1915	unconfirmed victory
22 Aug 1916	CO of *Jasta 1*
25 Aug 1916	victory #3
17 Sep 1916	victory #4
10 Oct 1916	victory #5
10 Nov 1916	CO of *Jastaschule I*
17 Dec 1916	becomes ill, sent to hospital

Like Franz Walz, Wilhelm Fahlbusch (S418) and Albert Dossenbach (S416), *Hptm.* Martin Zander was a successful two-seater pilot in the early years of the war. In fact, Zander had two (and possibly three) victories six months before any of the others – quite a feat in 1915. His accomplishments brought him the notice of High Command, and on 22 August 1916 he was afforded the honor of being placed in charge of the first of the new fighter units, *Jasta 1*. He was in distinguished company because *Hptm.* Oswald Boelcke (*Jasta 2*), *Oblt.* Hans-Joachim Buddecke (*Jasta 4*), and *Oblt.* Hans Berr (*Jasta 5*) were given their commands close to the same time. *Offz-Stv.* Hans Reimann (S429) of Zander's unit opened the scoring for all the new *Jagdstaffeln* on 24 August. True to form, Zander did not waste much time in catching up and brought down an FE.2b from RFC No.22 Squadron the next day. *Jasta 1*, with *Oblt.* Hans Bethge, *Lt.* Gustav Leffers (S372), *Lt.* Hans von Keudell (S555), and *Lt.* Kurt Wintgens (S378) on its roster, went on to roll up a total of 17 enemy aircraft (three of them Zander's) by the close of September. Zander then added what turned out to be his final victory on 10 October. One month later, he was placed in charge of another first-of-its-kind outfit, *Jastaschule I* at Fâmars near Valenciennes. *Lt.* Josef Jacobs explained the school's origin and purpose in his diary:

> "The French recognized that pilots of fighter aircraft with their different ways of doing battle can best impart their skills by sending them to a school for fighter pilots where they can teach and mutually share their experiences with the students. At the same time a *Jastaschule* would show the student the latest in technical advancements thus allowing instructors to explain the newest in aircraft construction to all the officers who in turn could then share their knowledge with their comrades when they returned to their front-line *Jastas*. One cannot promote a single method of fighting, therefore no standards can be taught due to the wide variations of weapons in use, such as machine guns, on the various battle fronts.

> Through these reciprocal discussions at the *Jastaschule* and the later practical application of this knowledge at the front it may be possible that some not-so-well-known aspects of fighting would be grasped by the fighter pilots. For this reason alone the *Jastaschule* was the brainchild of none other than *Hptm.* Boelcke. As far as I know it was he who instigated a school like this back of the lines where various fighter pilots from the Somme had an opportunity to become further informed through discussion and the practical testing of standard fighter tactics at the *Jastaschule* which was established in November 1916..." (OTF 9:4, p.333)

Jacobs arrived there as an instructor on 16 December. Zander, however, ruptured a blood vessel the next day during a formation flying exercise and was sent to the hospital in Valenciennes. *Oblt.* Hans Berr of *Jasta 5* took over the reins temporarily while Zander recovered. We know that by April 1917, Zander had returned to his duties at the *Jastaschule*; but from the start of 1918 on he disappears (at least from us) into the fog of war. He apparently never saw active combat again, and little more is known about what happened to him except that he met an early death on 6 September 1928 when the Bodensee Aero Lloyd Fokker F.III he and two others were flying in crashed at Heroldsbach, Germany. His body was laid to rest at Düsseldorf's Nordfriedhof cemetery in a now-unmarked grave.

S407 and ZANDER1 are pictures of Zander in his *Feldflieger-Abteilung 9b* days, as attested to by the number "9" on his armpatch, and he is adorned with both classes of the Iron Cross. At this stage of the war, the Iron Cross 1st Class was often, but certainly not always, awarded to a pilot following his first victory – that is, if he had not already won it in the trenches. Zander's first victim fell on 25 September 1915, so these photos may postdate that event. We really have very little else to help us date them, however, so they have been assigned the broad timeframe of 1915 to August 1916 (before his *Jasta 1* service).

The November 1916 publication date indicated by our guideline suggests that S407 came out as a result of Zander's role as the *Staffelführer* of *Jasta 1*, Germany's first and by October, highly successful, fighter squadron. His personal contribution of three victories to its record during the period August-October may have been a contributory factor as well. His assignment as the first commander of a *Jastaschule* appears to have come too late for that to have been the inspiration behind this postcard.

Few other photographs of Martin Zander have been published to date. ZANDER2, however, first seen in the final volume of Neal O'Connor's masterly series on Germany's World War I aviation awards and the men who earned them (*Aviation Awards VII*, p.410) shows Zander standing between two British POWs in the company of other German soldiers at *Armee-Flug-Park 2* in 1916. Though not identified by O'Connor as such, there is reason to believe that it is a snapshot of Zander's third official victory on 25 August 1916. First, the fact that Zander is still in his flight gear and has his arms linked with those of the POWs flanking him implies that they were his prisoners. Second, the two Englishmen seem reasonably fit. The crew manning Zanders' fourth victory were killed in action, while the men of his fifth came down wounded. Third, all his other victories had occurred in a two-seater in 1915. There is no sign of an observer with Zander and the picture is said to have come from 1916. If so, we now have a photographic record of the second victory ever achieved by Germany's *Jagdstaffeln*. The POWs would then be Lt. R.D. Walker and 2nd Lt. C. Smith who had been flying FE.2b No.4285 of RFC No.22 Squadron before being brought down and taken prisoner. Herbert Bayard Swope, a reporter from *The New York World*, encountered these two men during a visit to Cambrai prison in late August/early September 1916. His 1917 book, *Inside the German Empire*, related the circumstances:

A companion image to the one produced on S407.

"It was a matter of ammunition that, after two years of chivalry among the knights of the air, threatened to lead to great bitterness. The Germans accused the English fliers of using incendiary bullets in their machine-guns. These cartridges, slightly larger than the usual rifle-shell, carry an explosive chamber that ignites in flight and inflames the substance against which it is shot. As aëroplane wings are oil-coated, they are highly combustible, and several disasters overtook German fliers in this way…It was in this connection that it became my good fortune to be of service in possibly saving the lives of two young English flying officers. They had just been captured and when the prison-yard commandant at Cambrai gave me permission to speak with them, he added that I might tell them that they were to be court-martialed, and probably shot, on the ground that they had been using the so-called illegal ammunition. I was unwilling to be the bearer of such unhappy news, and I did not tell them. Instead, as I had not been placed under any confidence by the German officers, I informed Ambassador Gerard of their danger, when I returned to Berlin, as he is charged with the British interests in Germany. Through the Foreign Office the ambassador immediately requested permission to have the Englishmen represented by counsel at their trial. This permission was granted, although it had been declined in the case of Captain Fryatt. Before I left Germany, I was given to understand that even if the two men were court-martialed, it was highly improbable that they would be executed. They were Ronald Walker, first lieutenant of the Royal Flying Corps, of March Rectory, Cambridgeshire, and Lieutenant C. Smith of Cemetery Road, York. When I spoke with them their first request was to notify their families, and their second for chocolate and cigarettes." (pp.237-39)

ZANDER2

Above: This picture is a record of only the second victory to be scored by one of Germany's newly organized *Jagdstaffeln*. On 25 August 1916, *Jasta 1* leader *Hptm.* Martin Zander forced down FE.2b No.4285 of RFC No.22 Squadron near Gueudecourt. Its crew, Lt. R.D. Walker and 2nd Lt. C. Smith, are on either side of Zander who is still in his flight gear (center). (photo courtesy of UTD)

Left: *Hptm.* Martin Zander, Commanding Officer of *Jastaschule I*, is visited by his former *Jasta I* squadron mate, *Lt.* Gustav Leffers. The men, from left to right, are *Lt.* Willy Rosenstein, *Lt.* Helmut von Schütz, Leffers, Zander, unknown naval pilot, *Lt.* Friedrich Mallinckrodt, unknown naval pilot. Leffers was awarded the *Pour le Mérite* on 16 November 1916 – about one week after Zander had been posted to the school – and was killed in action on 27 December. Rosenstein, a pre-war pilot at Johannisthal, was sent to the *Jastaschule* as an instructor on 9 November 1916 and returned to his unit (*Jasta 9*) on 14 December. Mallinckrodt was another instructor, serving from 11 November to 12 December; so this picture originated during that time period. (photo courtesy of UTD)

Two above: Having already removed the wings, German soldiers continue to dismantle FE.2b No.4852 for transport elsewhere. *Hptm.* Martin Zander shot this plane down on 17 September 1916 for his fourth victory. Though it appears relatively intact, Franks, Bailey, and Duivan (*Jasta War Chronology*, p.11) relate that both occupants, Sgt. B. Irwin and 2nd Lt. F.G. Thierry of RFC No.23 Squadron, were killed.

Right: After recovering from a wound received on 11 February 1917, *Lt.* Erwin Böhme was assigned as an instructor to *Jastaschule I* in early April. Here he sits on the steps of the school's billet, Chateau Fâmars, along with the school's CO, *Hptm.* Martin Zander (left), and *Lt.* Burkhard Lehmann (right). This photo probably was taken after Böhme had left the school, however, because each man's attire is the same in another picture of them next to a Morane Parasol that Böhme dropped off in July 1917 (see below). Lehmann served under Zander as one of the original members of *Jasta I*, and up to now it has been thought that he remained with *Jasta I* until his transfer to *Jasta 12* on 28 July 1917. This photo and the next three, however, combined with two others showing him seated in captured Sopwith Pup and Nieuport 17 fighters at the school's airfield (see OTF 17:2, p.146) indicate that he probably did a stint there with his former commander in the summer of 1917 before going to *Jasta 12*. (photo courtesy of UTD)

Opposite
Top and middle: Two snapshots of *Jastaschule I*'s lineup of captured aircraft in German markings. Starting from the right is FE.8 No.7624 from RFC No.40 Squadron (downed by Erwin Böhme on 9 November 1916), two Sopwith Pups, two Spad 7s, two Nieuport 17s, a Nieuport 11, and another Nieuport 17. The FE.8 and Nieuport 17s appear to have retained their original color schemes; however, the Pups, Spads, and Nieuport 11 were overpainted with a color that some sources contend was red. *Lt.* Burkhard Lehmann appears in both these photos dressed in a light-colored *Litewka* tunic. (first photo courtesy of Helge Dittmann)

Bottom: Several pilots cluster around a Morane Parasol in German markings at *Jastaschule I*. The Parasol had been captured on 10 July 1917, and *Dr. Ing.* Niedermeyer, who had access to Erwin Böhme's papers and other memorabilia, has reported that it was Böhme (*Staffelführer* of *Jasta 29* since the end of June) who delivered it to the training grounds (see OTF 17:2, p.155). From left to right we have Böhme in conversation with *Lt.* Burkhard Lehmann, *Hptm.* Zander appearing just over Lehmann's shoulder, unknown, and a *Lt.* Biesel. By the look of the leather flight gear on the plane's horizontal stabilizer and Lehmann's flight coat, it appears that this image was snapped soon after or just before his piloting of the plane. Lehmann was posted to *Jasta 12* on 28 July (where he was killed in action just nine days later on 5 August), so this particular picture was taken in the last half of July 1917. (photo courtesy of Helge Dittmann)

Top: Martin Zander, in the light tunic, poses in front of *Jastaschule I*'s array of an Albatros D.III, a Halberstadt D.II, and a captured Spad 7. All appear to have been similarly overpainted, perhaps in red. The man to the right leaning against the Spad's wing is *Oblt.* Erich Hahn, another original member of *Jasta 1* and its temporary commander when Zander was first sent to the fighter school. Unlike *Lt.* Burkhard Lehmann, there is no evidence that Hahn was at Fâmars for anything other than a visit with his former CO. (photo courtesy of UTD)

Above: In this picture, Zander is front and center on the steps of Chateau Fâmars and *Lt.* Fritz Kempf is standing in the back row just to the right of

Zander. We know that Kempf was sent to *Jastaschule I* on 20 October 1917 to instruct future fighter pilots, so we might have assigned this photo to late 1917 if not for the presence of the ubiquitous *Lt.* Burkhard Lehmann at far right (see S380's PARSCHAU1 for another snapshot of Lehmann in a similar pose). As mentioned earlier, Lehmann left the school for *Jasta 12* at the end of July 1917 and was killed nine days later, so this image could not have originated from when Kempf was an instructor. Perhaps Kempf attended the school to pick up single-seat fighter tips around the time he was relieved of two-seater duties and joined *Jasta Boelcke* on 28 March 1917. (photo courtesy of UTD)

S408
10 *POUR LE MÉRITE* PILOTS;
COSSEL & WINDISCH

Taken: composite of photos taken at various times in 1916
Publ: November 1916
Reason: year-end celebration

Decorations:
See S361, S363, S371, S380, S383, S384, S389, S392, S397, S401, S402

Other Cards:
(L7793)

Key Dates:
12 Oct 1916	Berthold awarded *Pour le Mérite*
5 Nov 1916	Leffers awarded *Pour le Mérite*

Entitled *"Unsere Flieger-Helden"* ("Our Flier-Heroes"), S408 incorporates select segments of 11 previously published Sanke postcards: S361, S363, S371, S380, S383, S384, S389, S392, S397, S401, and S402. The Air Service's first 10 *Pour le Mérite* recipients and the famous pilot and observer team, Cossel and Windisch, were

W. Sanke Berlin, N. 37.   408

their subjects. The original backgrounds of all these pictures except S401 were brushed out; so too the little dog that sat in Berthold's lap in S402. Berthold's card was the most recent of the 11 and it marked his receipt of the *Pour le Mérite* on 12 October 1916. *Lt.* Gustav Leffers, whose impressive record led to his appearance in S372 and whose *Pour le Mérite* was later awarded on 5 November, is absent from S408's montage. The next card in the series, S409, mourns Boelcke's death – an event that occurred on 28 October 1916. S408 bears no indication of Boelcke's demise. The collective implication is that S408's publication process was put in motion around the time of Boelcke's death but before Leffers' investiture, thereby preventing his inclusion. A postmarked example of S408 dated 27 November upholds our guideline's prediction of a November 1916 publication.

Though it is not a card that features a particular aviator, S403 helps verify the November-December timeframe assigned to Sanke's early S400 series. It depicts the occupants of a German two-seater dropping Christmas wishes (and pine boughs from its precariously perched tree) to a small town below. Obviously, this seasonal card was brought out to celebrate the upcoming Christmas holiday. The dates of many other wartime Christmas postcards confirm that they were issued as early as November throughout Germany.

Left: S403, a Sanke Christmas card for 1916. The airplane is dropping leaflets with the expressions "Herzlichen Weihnachtsgruss" ("Warm Christmas Greetings") and "Frohes Fest" ("Happy Christmas") on them.

S409
(memorial)
BOELCKE
Oswald
Hauptmann

Taken: 17 to 19 January 1916
Douai/Lille
Publ: November 1916
Reason: memorial

Decorations:
WR: *Pour le Mérite*; Iron Cross, 1st Class; Pilot's Badge
MB: None
RB: None
BH: Royal Hohenzollern House Order, Knight's Cross/ Sw; Life Saving Medal

Other Cards:
S363, S364, S369, S373, S393, S408
(L7720, L7721, L7761, L7776, L7785, L7793; N5579, N5580, N5601, N5619, N5690, N6004, N6005, N6225)
Note: Taken same time as S369

Key Dates:
28 Oct 1916   killed in action

Sanke called once more upon the talents of Barbara Goede, the poet whose verses had adorned Immelmann's mournful S377 and Boelcke's celebratory S393. This time she composed a poetic eulogy that sang Boelcke's praises following his death from a tragic accident on 28 October 1916:

O proud ruler of the realm of flight,
Sky-king Boelcke, who is your like?
The greatest courage you invoked,
To face each day's new venture.
You carried the honor of our Folk
Through troubled, stormy weather.

As the brightest star of those above,
That every German knows and loves,
Your youth bore the hero's boldness
That miracle after miracle makes.
Through thunder and lightning, light and darkness,
Your victor's beam breaks!

Below: After Oswald Boelcke's memorial service was held in Cambrai on 31 October 1916, his body was transported back home to Dessau. The coffin arrived the evening of 1 November and was placed before the altar of St. John's Church to lie in state.

And we peer into it, bent with pain,
This bright light of your fame!
Future, joyful generations will see
What you were to this nation of ours!
No one can match your luminosity
Sky-king Boelcke, in the realm of stars!

Guideline 1 predicts a late November 1916 debut for S409 and we have one example postmarked 27 November 1916.

Above and right: Members of the Boelcke family arrive at St. John's Church in Dessau on the morning of 2 November 1916. The first picture shows, from left to right, Oswald's father Max, his mother Mathilde, brother Wilhelm, and the oldest of the Boelcke siblings, sister Louise.

Two at left: Boelcke's coffin is carried out of St. John's Church by an honor guard consisting of decorated NCO pilots, then placed on a waiting gun carriage for transport to the cemetery. Ironically, if Boelcke had worn something like the padded flying helmet placed on top of his coffin, he might have survived the crash that fractured his skull.

Above and right: Several accounts state that almost all of Dessau's citizens turned out for the final farewell to their native son. Here we see three images of the funeral procession wending its way through Dessau and the attending crowd on its way to the Ehrenfriedhof cemetery south of town.

"Here, as in Cambrai, airmen circled over the church." (Werner, *Knight of Germany*, p.235) One of them took this photograph of the funeral cortège proceeding toward the cemetery from St. John's Church.

Above and below: The coffin arrives at Boelcke's special burial site, across the street from the civilian cemetery. The final image captures the Boelcke family at graveside, just to the right of a group of clergymen, one of whom was Pastor Karl Bölcke, Oswald's uncle. The family's emotions are touchingly represented by younger brother Max bringing a handkerchief to his eyes.

The final resting place of *Hptm.* Oswald Boelcke.

S411
MEYER
Carl
Flugmeister

Taken: 1916, before December
Publ: December 1916
Reason: victory score

Decorations:
WR: Iron Cross, 1st Class; Naval Pilot's Badge
MB: None
RB: None
BH: Iron Cross, 2nd Class

Other Cards:
None
Note: See S412

Key Dates:

17 Jul 1916	victory #1 (with Boenisch)
2 Aug 1916	victory #2 (with Boenisch)
5 Aug 1916	victory #3 (with Boenisch)
7 Sep 1916	unconfirmed victory (with Boenisch)
1 Oct 1916	victory #4
1 Oct 1916	unconfirmed victory
23 Oct 1916	victory #5

In 1916, *Flgm.* Carl Meyer was in Zeebrugge serving with *Seeflugstation Flandern 1*. There he teamed up with observer *Lt. z. See* Erich Boenisch (who already had two victories to his credit flying with other pilots), and in rather rapid succession the pair brought down three enemy planes in July and August 1916. They claimed another victory together on 7 September, but it went unconfirmed. Meyer was on patrol with a different observer, *Flugmaat* Karl Elsasser, when they reported the downing of two aircraft on 1 October, but only one of them was allowed. Meyer was finally officially credited with his fifth victory on 23 October, making him the German Naval Air Service's first pilot ace and second ace overall (Boenisch, his former observer, was the first).[1] It was shortly after this, according to our guideline, that Meyer's S411 was issued in sequence with his former observer Boenisch's S412.

Meyer did not score again until 1 February 1917 when he brought down a Sopwith Pup relatively intact. It was later flown and studied under German markings. His best known victory came next with the destruction of British coastal airship "C 17" on 21 April 1917. The DH.4 that he overcame on 22 June 1917 was his eighth and final victory. On 6 November, Meyer (now an *Oberflugmeister*) became only the third airman to be given the *Goldenes Militär-Verdienstkreuz* (Golden Military Merit Cross) – Prussia's highest bravery award within the ranks (i.e., NCOs). But he did not live to see 1918, for on 31 December 1917 he died in Leipzig of injuries suffered during a flying accident.

We have no reliable indication of when S411's photograph was taken. We do not know when Meyer became a *Flugmeister*, nor do we know the dates of the awards he is wearing. We might speculate that his Iron Cross 1st Class was bestowed, as with many other pilots, after his first victory. This would date the image to after 17 July 1916. Others, however, also gained this award under entirely different circumstances, so a more conservative estimate of sometime in 1916 will have to suffice.

Note

[1] Though a pilot with five victories is recognized as an ace today, the Germans did not follow such a standard in World War I. Four victories seemed to be the level at which a pilot was initially singled out in military reports.

Right: Carl Meyer of Marine Feldjasta I stands in front of his Albatros D.V 2144/17, nicknamed "Gussy."

S412
BOENISCH
Erich
Leutnant zur See

Taken: 1916, before mid-October
Publ: December 1916
Reason: victory score

Decorations:
WR: Iron Cross, 1st Class; Naval Observer Badge
MB: None
RB: None
BH: Iron Cross, 2nd Class

Other Cards:
None
Note: See S411

Key Dates:

5 May 1916	victory #1
8 Jun 1916	victory #2
17 Jul 1916	victory #3 (with Meyer)
2 Aug 1916	victory #4 (with Meyer)

A portrait of *Oberflugmeister* Carl Meyer in a naval aviator's lightweight summer tunic.

5 Aug 1916	victory #5 (with Meyer)
7 Sep 1916	unconfirmed victory (with Meyer)
17 Oct 1916	injured during test flight

Lt. z. See Erich Boenisch scored his first two victories with different pilots at the controls – one with *Oblt.* Kurt Reinert and the next with *Flgm.* August Ponater. After that he teamed up with *Flgm.* Carl Meyer, the subject of S411. Together, they made Boenisch the German Naval Air Service's first ace on 5 August 1916. Despite the team claiming another aircraft on 7 September, Boenisch's fifth proved to be his last official score. While testing Brandenburg LW Seaplane No.571 on 17 October 1916 with *Lt.* Hans Rolhoven (who would later command the *Seeflugstation*), Boenisch crashed and sustained injuries that ended his flying career. He survived the war, and like so many other former *Fliegertruppe* heroes, was tapped by Third Reich officials to help build the *Luftwaffe* in the 1930s. In 1938, *Oberst* Boenisch was named commander of the new air force base at Neumünster.

Not much more is known about Boenisch today, so it is difficult to pinpoint when S412's photo was taken. Like Meyer's S411, we can speculate that it originated sometime after Boenisch's first victory in May 1916 because of the presence of his Iron Cross 1st Class; but it is also possible that he won that award for some other achievement. Until other, more substantial evidence turns up, all we can really

Unser erfolgreicher See-Kampfflieger
Leutnant z. S. Boenisch

Postkartenvertrieb W.Sanke
. BERLIN N.37.
412
Nachdruck wird gerichtlich verfolgt.

offer is that S412 was probably taken sometime in 1916 before Boenisch's career-ending crash.

Our guideline projects a December publication date for S412, and there seems little doubt that its appearance, like S411's before it, celebrated the German Naval Air Service's highest scoring aces of the war.

Above: A more formal pose for Erich Boenisch.

Top right: A candid snapshot of a cigar-smoking *Lt. z. See* Erich Boenisch.

Right: A rare image of then *Flugobermaat* Carl Meyer and *Lt. z. See* Erich Boenisch inspecting what little remained of the French FBA flying boat they brought down off Middlekerke on 5 August 1916. It counted as Boenisch's fifth and Meyer's third.

S413
LEFFERS
Gustav
Leutnant

Taken: 9 to mid-November 1916
Publ: December 1916
Reason: *Pour le Mérite* award

Decorations:
WR: *Pour le Mérite*; Friedrich August Cross, 1st Class (Old); Iron Cross, 1st Class; Pilot's Badge
MB: Iron Cross, 2nd Class; Royal Hohenzollern House Order, Knight's Cross/ Sw; Friedrich August Cross, 2nd Class (Old)
RB: None
BH: None

Other Cards:
S372, S414, S415, S417
(L7728, L7801, L7802)
Note: Taken same time as S414, S415, and S417

S414
LEFFERS
Gustav
Leutnant

Taken: 9 to mid-November 1916
Publ: December 1916
Reason: *Pour le Mérite* award

Decorations:
WR: *Pour le Mérite*; Friedrich August Cross, 1st Class (Old); Iron Cross, 1st Class; Pilot's Badge
MB: Iron Cross, 2nd Class; Royal Hohenzollern House Order, Knight's Cross/ Sw; Friedrich August Cross, 2nd Class (Old)
RB: None
BH: None

Other Cards:
S372, S413, S415, S417
(L7728, L7801, L7802)
Note: Taken same time as S413, S415, and S417

S415
LEFFERS
Gustav
Leutnant

Taken: 9 to mid-November 1916
Publ: December 1916
Reason: *Pour le Mérite* award

Decorations:
WR: *Pour le Mérite*; Friedrich August Cross, 1st Class (Old); Iron Cross, 1st Class; Pilot's Badge
MB: Iron Cross, 2nd Class; Royal Hohenzollern House Order, Knight's Cross/ Sw; Friedrich August Cross, 2nd Class (Old)
RB: None
BH: None

Other Cards:
S372, S413, S414, S417
(L7728, L7801, L7802)
Note: Taken same time as S413, S414, and S417

See S417 for discussion

S416
DOSSENBACH
Albert
Leutnant

Taken: 11 to 30 November 1916
Frankfurt am Main, by Prof. A. Krauth
Publ: December 1916
Reason: *Pour le Mérite* award

Decorations:
WR: *Pour le Mérite*; Iron Cross, 1st Class; Pilot's Badge; Military Merit Cross, 1st Class (Meck-Sch)
MB: None
RB: Iron Cross, 2nd Class; Military Merit Cross, 2nd Class (Meck-Sch); Order of the Zähringer Lion, Knight 2nd Class/ Sw (Bad)
BH: Royal Hohenzollern House Order, Knight's Cross/ Sw

Other Cards:
(L7803; N6149)

Key Dates:
21 Oct 1916	awarded Royal Hohenzollern House Order, Knight's Cross/ Sw
11 Nov 1916	awarded *Pour le Mérite*

9 Dec 1916	awarded Military Karl-Friedrich Merit Order, Knight's Cross (Bad)

Lt. Albert Dossenbach earned rapid promotion, both classes of the Iron Cross, and Baden's Order of the Zähringer Lion, Knight 2nd Class while serving with the army in the early years of the war. In November 1915, he underwent observer training at Gotha, and then moved on to pilot training at Pozen in December. On 1 June 1916, he was assigned to *Feldflieger-Abteilung 22* at Flesquieres airfield near Bapaume. There he met up with *Oblt.* Hans Schilling, an observer who had already brought down an enemy plane on 10 January 1916. By August 1916 Dossenbach had attained four victories while Schilling had three to his credit. The exact dates of these early victories and whether they flew together for any of them is unknown. Existing records, however, do show that they shot down four aircraft as a team between 13 August and 27 September. The last of these returned the favor, however, and set their victor's plane on fire with a parting burst. Dossenbach and Schilling suffered minor burns on the way down but were able to land without further mishap. Both men received the Royal Hohenzollern House Order, Knight's Cross on 21 October, and a short while afterward, they claimed another victim on 3 November. On 11 November 1916, Dossenbach's accomplishments were recognized with the *Pour le Mérite*. Several authors have found it curious that Schilling was not similarly honored at the same time. The discussion of Berr's S425-26, however, explains that the victory total that automatically brought the *Pour le Mérite* to airmen may have been increased from eight to sixteen as of the end of October 1916. If so, Schilling, whose eighth came on 3 November, and others who reached that level in November (e.g., Kirmaier, Richthofen, Keudell) would not have qualified.

Dossenbach was not with his teammate when Schilling was killed on 4 December during a fight with the noted French ace, Charles Nungesser. Perhaps Dossenbach was home on leave, as was the custom following many *Pour le Mérite* awards. Whatever the case, their partnership ended abruptly on an all too final note.

It was around this time that Dossenbach's career as a two-seater pilot came to a close. In early 1917, he switched over to single-seat fighter duties and in February trained with *Jasta 2* (also called *Jasta Boelcke* in honor of its deceased leader). On 22 February, he was placed in command of a new fighter squadron, *Jasta 36*. He bagged *Jasta 36*'s first score on 5 April and brought down four more enemy aircraft that month before being wounded on the ground during a bombing raid. After his recuperation, he was given command of *Jasta 10* on 21 June. He scored his 15th and final victory just six days later. On 3 July, while in pursuit of several enemy two-seaters, his aircraft caught fire and he fell (or leaped) from it to the ground. The tables had been turned on the first two-seater pilot to be honored with the *Pour le Mérite*.

Friend and fellow Badener, *Lt.* Hans Schröder, related this alleged eyewitness account of Dossenbach's final hours:

> "July 3rd was a murky day, with no weather for flying. About 5 p.m. Dossenbach rang me up. 'I say, what's going on at the front?' he inquired. 'I feel like putting in a bit more flying. By the way, did you see that balloon I shot down yesterday?' [writer's note: an apparent reference to Dossenbach's final victory over a balloon on 27 June, not 2 July.]
>
> 'Of course I did; congratulations! Simply marvellous! They must have opened their eyes a bit when they suddenly saw you attack from below. But man alive, do take a bit more care of yourself! What's the good of running such risks? Well, look here, there's nothing doing at the front at present; not an Englishman in the sky. Visibility bad; I wouldn't advise you to take off. I promise I'll ring you up as soon as I see an Englishman.'

> 'Good; I'm counting on you. Good luck!'
> 'Good luck, old man!'
>
> Ten minutes later there was a whirr of wings in the air. They were German Fokkers [writer's note: Jasta 10 was actually flying Albatros fighters at this time]; Dossenbach and his pilots were flying low over La Montagne. He stretched an arm out and waved to me; then he pointed in the direction of Ypres.
>
> 'There's six Englishmen coming along over there, Herr Lieutenant,' announced a corporal.
>
> I saw Dossenbach's Staffel climbing in the direction indicated. Lucky fellow, I thought, and made ready to view the coming fight through the telescope.
>
> They spiralled up over Gheluvelt, and a few minutes later they attained the level of their English opponents, who appeared to be waiting for them. Dossenbach headed for the leader of the enemy formation; it was only a matter of a few seconds before they came to grips.
>
> Oh Heaven, what's that? A jet of flame spurts out from Dossenbach's Fokker, which seems to stand still in the air. And what of the pilot?
>
> Dossenbach was a real man. I saw him stand up calmly in the burning machine. He knew there was no hope for him, and so he jumped. Although still alive, his earthly account was closed, but in those last seconds of life, he robbed death of the initiative when by his own free will he leapt out to fall through 4,000 metres of airspace. He came down before the burning wreckage of his machine; I watched, but not until he reached the ground, somewhere in the neighbourhood of Zonnebek, did the hoarse scream escape my throat. Albert Dossenbach – dead!
>
> How did it happen? The Englishman must have used a telescopic sight, for he opened fire at more than 500 metres distance – a distance at which none of our scouts would dream of firing.
>
> I rang up the squadron to report my observations. There was great dismay at my news – Dossenbach shot down! One of the best pilots!
>
> When on the following day I walked behind his coffin, on the way to the goods siding where the corpse was to entrain for its journey to South Germany, I remembered that only a fortnight before I had walked beside him when we followed the coffin of an officer belonging to Richthofen's Jagdstaffel 11 [writer's note: presumably the funeral of *Lt.* Walter Bordfeld, killed in action over Zandvoorde on 18 June 1917]. Then Dossenbach said to me thoughtfully: 'Every one of us has to go sooner or later. We scouting pilots are all doomed to death. I'd only like to know who will be the next of us.'" (*An Airman Remembers*, pp.227-28)

S416's portrait was one of a series. S416 and DOSSEN1 display nearly identical poses, while DOSSEN2 shows him wearing his service cap. All three were taken indoors against the same wood-panelled wall. DOSSEN3 was taken at the same spot but at a different time (note the difference in his service cap in DOSSEN2). S416 gives credit to "Prof. Krauth" – presumably the "Prof. A. Krauth" listed on another Dossenbach postcard, N6149.[1] Our guideline projects that S416 was published in late December or early January. Subtracting three weeks takes us back to at least late November or early December, or shortly after Dossenbach's receipt of the *Pour le Mérite* on 11 November. This timeframe suits the fact that the Military Karl-Friedrich Merit Order, Knight's Cross that Dossenbach was awarded on 9 December does not appear in any of the photos.

Note
[1] *Illustrierte Geschichte des Weltkrieges* 197, p.343 situated Krauth's studio in Frankfurt am Main.

DOSSEN1

DOSSEN3

DOSSEN2

Two at left: Two photos of *Lt.* Albert Dossenbach that were taken the same time as S416's image by Professor A. Krauth.

Above: Another portrait of Albert Dossenbach that, like S416, was taken by Prof. A. Krauth but at a different time. This particular print bears the stamp of Dossenbach's first command, *Jasta 36*. The handwritten note refers to his having been wounded during a bombing raid on 2 May 1917. (photo courtesy of UTD)

Opposite
Top left: Dossenbach and his partner at *FFA 22*, *Oblt.* Hans Schilling, at or near the time of their simultaneous receipt of the Royal Hohenzollern House Order, Knight's Cross on 21 October 1916. The medals are looped through their tunic buttonholes, as was the norm when first awarded (e.g., see Cossel and Windisch's S401 or Hirth's S422). On the wall behind them is what appears to be a montage of aerial photographs taken by them or their unit.

Top right: A picture of *Lt.* Albert Dossenbach that was published in the 10 December 1916 edition of *Berliner Illustrirte Zeitung* to announce his receipt of the *Pour le Mérite*.

Bottom: *Oblt.* Hans Schilling's first victim, Morane 5091 of RFC No. 1 Squadron, brought down on 10 January 1916. The crew, 2nd Lts. John McEwen and F. Adams, were taken prisoner. This was the only victory Schilling had without Dossenbach at the controls.

Abgesch. Franz. Flugzeug
bei Tournai am 10. Jan. 16.

S417
LEFFERS
Gustav
Leutnant

Taken: 9 to mid-November 1916
Publ: December 1916
Reason: *Pour le Mérite* award

Decorations:
WR: *Pour le Mérite*; Friedrich August Cross, 1st Class (Old); Iron Cross, 1st Class; Pilot's Badge
MB: Iron Cross, 2nd Class; Royal Hohenzollern House Order, Knight's Cross/ Sw; Friedrich August Cross, 2nd Class (Old)
RB: None
BH: None

Other Cards:
S372, S413, S414, S415
(L7728, L7801, L7802)
Note: Taken same time as S413-15

Key Dates:

17 Oct 1916	victory #8
5 Nov 1916	awarded *Pour le Mérite*
26 Nov 1916	S372 similar photo published in *Berliner Illustrirte Zeitung* 48, p.718
13 Dec 1916	S413 postmarked example
27 Dec 1916	killed in action
7 Jan 1917	S372 similar photo published in *Berliner Illustrirte Zeitung* 1, p.2

Unser erfolgreicher Kampf-Flieger Leutnant Leffers

417
Postkartenvertrieb W.Sanke
BERLIN N.37.
Nachdruck wird gerichtlich verfolgt.

The official award date for Leffers' *Pour le Mérite* is 5 November 1916, although it has been said that he did not actually receive confirmation of it until 9 November – the day he scored his ninth and final victory (see O'Connor, *Aviation Awards VI*, p.317). A postmarked example of the first card in this series, S413, was written on 13 December 1916. Applying our three-week rule would move the photograph's origin back to at least around 22 November, leaving us with a fairly compact window for when it was taken: 9-22 November 1916. Leffers appears to be dressed in his finest uniform, and it is plausible that these photos were taken at or soon after his *Pour le Mérite* award ceremony. The same is true for S417, despite its different, white background. S417 otherwise shares all the same attributes as S413-15 and its pose is only slightly different than S413's. Sanke may have secured exclusive rights to this series because none of them shows up in either of the popular Berlin magazines, *Berliner Illustrirte Zeitung* or *Die Woche*. The former merely reprinted the same photo that was taken the same time as S372 when reporting his *Pour le Mérite* investiture and funeral.

Right and opposite: Three pictures from *Lt.* Gustav Leffers' 4 January 1916 funeral at his hometown, Wilhelmshaven. The first is a close-up of his flag-draped coffin lying in state, while the second shows it being carried to a horse-drawn carriage for transportation to the cemetery. The person carrying Leffers' *Ordenskissen* can be seen directly underneath the caption. Note that the German navy, which had a major base in Wilhelmshaven, supplied the honor guard that surrounds the horses and carriage. The last picture captures the funeral procession as it begins its passage through Wilhelmshaven.

Fliegerleutnant Fahlbusch

418
Postkartenvertrieb W.Sanke
BERLIN N. 37.
Nachdruck wird gerichtlich verfolgt.

Fliegerleutnant Rosencrantz

419
Postkartenvertrieb W.Sanke
BERLIN N. 37.
Nachdruck wird gerichtlich verfolgt.

S418
(memorial)
FAHLBUSCH
Wilhelm
Leutnant

Taken: 1916
Publ: December 1916
Reason: memorial

Decorations:
WR: Iron Cross, 1st Class; Pilot's Badge
MB: None
RB: None
BH: Iron Cross, 2nd Class

Other Cards:
None
Note: See S419

See S419 for discussion

S419
(memorial)
ROSENCRANTZ
Hans
Leutnant

Taken: 1916
Publ: December 1916
Reason: memorial

Decorations:
WR: Iron Cross, 1st Class; Observer Badge
MB: None
RB: None
BH: Iron Cross, 2nd Class

Other Cards:
None
Note: See S418

Key Dates:
31 Aug 1916	victory #5
2-3 Sep 1916	unconfirmed victory
6 Sep 1916	killed in action
8 Oct 1916	Rosencrantz photo published in *Berliner Illustrirte Zeitung* 41, p.607.

5 Nov 1916   S418 photo published in *Berliner Illustrirte Zeitung* 45, p.671.

Like Walz and Gerlich, Meyer and Boenisch, and Dossenbach and Schilling before them, Fahlbusch and Rosencrantz were a highly successful two-seater crew for the period in which they operated. Little is known about their careers except for the few appearances Fahlbusch makes in Josef Jacobs' war diary. The entry for 19 May 1916 notes that a *Vzfw.* Fahlbusch came from an aircraft park to serve as a pilot with *Feldflieger-Abteilung 11*. On 27 May, it is told that now *Lt.* Fahlbusch and his observer experienced a harrowing flight over the Front and that their aircraft lost its undercarriage upon landing. At some point after this, Fahlbusch moved to *Kampfstaffel 1* (which along with Walz's and Gerlich's *Kampfstaffel 2* was attached to *Kampfgeschwader 1*) and teamed up with Rosencrantz. Few details have survived regarding their early victories together, but they probably were the crew that conquered 2nd Lt. C.V. Hewson of RFC No.21 Squadron on 9 July. Their fifth and final official victory came on 31 August 1916, though some sources indicate that they may have brought down a sixth unconfirmed airplane afterward on either 2 or 3 September. They were killed just a few days later on 6 September in a fight with RFC No.70 Squadron's Sopwith 1 1/2 Strutters. American correspondent Herbert Bayard Swope related some of the details of this fatal encounter in a contemporaneous newspaper account. While touring the Somme Front near Bapaume in September 1916, Swope visited with Oswald Boelcke and reported:

"...that there is more to Boelke's record than mere luck is shown by the fact that on the day following his twentieth prize two of his companions were killed trying to stop an English raiding party of eight aeroplanes that flew over the German lines bombarding railroad stations. The fight was at 5:30 Wednesday afternoon, and showed the exceptional courage of the Germans in taking on a fight with such a superior force." ("Boelke, Air Hero" in *The New York Times*)

In a 1917 book that revisited the interview, Swope clarified that Boelcke's companions were named "Rosencrantz and Falbusch." He further explained that the Germans had claimed that the two had been downed by the use of incendiary bullets:

"The German military authorities resented the new tactics, and talked of making an example of captured Englishmen who had employed what Germany held to be an unfair and illegal method. Rosencrantz and Falbusch were shot down in this way." (*Inside the German Empire*, p.238)

The Germans apparently did pursue this matter further with two captured Englishmen who had been brought down shortly before on 25 August by *Hptm.* Martin Zander (see Zander's S407).

The appearance of pilot-observer teams was relatively rare in Sanke's series, but even rarer was the black border seen in S418 and S419 – a sure sign of posthumous publication. This device was otherwise reserved for only the most famous: Immelmann (S361†), Boelcke (S363†, S409) and Richthofen (S503†, S532†, S533†, S534†, S619). Swope's account of their heroic and controversial end may explain why they were treated in such a special manner by Sanke.

ROSEN1 is the observer's picture, published in the 8 October 1916 edition of *Berliner Illustrirte Zeitung*, that noted his death in combat. Fahlbusch's S418 photo was published in the 5 November 1916 edition of *Berliner Illustrirte Zeitung*. Unfortunately, the caption only notes that he had brought down five enemy aircraft and gives no other reason for his photo's appearance two months after his death.

There is little in either S418 or S419 to tell us when their images might have been taken. Though S418 is heavily touched up, it looks as though Fahlbusch's shoulder boards, collar *Litzen*, and Iron Cross 1st Class (and possibly even his Pilot's Badge) were added in, indicating that the photo may have been snapped when he was still an NCO. S419 is a more authentic picture but again reveals very little regarding its origin. A broad assumption of 1916 has therefore been offered.

ROSEN1

A picture of *Lt.* Hans Rosencrantz that appeared in the 8 October 1916 edition of *Berliner Illustrirte Zeitung,*.

S420
FRANKL
Wilhelm
Leutnant

Taken: September to early November 1916
Publ: January 1917
Reason: post-*Pour le Mérite*

Decorations:
WR: *Pour le Mérite*; Iron Cross, 1st Class; Pilot's Badge
MB: None
RB: None
BH: Hanseatic Cross (Ham)

Other Cards:
S384, S408, S421
(L7752, L7793)
Note: Taken same time as S421

S421
FRANKL
Wilhelm
Leutnant

Taken: September to early November 1916
Publ: January 1917
Reason: post-*Pour le Mérite*

Decorations:
WR: *Pour le Mérite*; Iron Cross, 1st Class; Pilot's Badge
MB: None
RB: None
BH: Hanseatic Cross (Ham)

Other Cards:
S384, S408, S420
(L7752, L7793)
Note: Taken same time as S420

Key Dates:
12 Aug 1916   awarded *Pour le Mérite*
1 Sep 1916   *KEK Vaux* moves to Roupy and forms *Jasta 4*
12 Dec 1916   *Jasta 4* moves to Hivry-Circourt

At first glance, S384 and S420 look like they may have been taken at the same time. Several subtle differences belie this notion, however. For example:

S384

hair combed back, flat on head
left side moustache trimmed low
right shoulder board flat on tunic
left shoulder board flat
Pour le Mérite low on collar
no Hanseatic Cross ribbon
tarnished Pilot's Badge
no belt

S420

hair combed back, has wave in it
left side moustache trimmed high
right shoulder board pulled up from tunic
left shoulder board arched
Pour le Mérite at middle of collar
Hanseatic Cross ribbon in 2nd buttonhole
shiny Pilot's Badge
wide belt

Conversely, though S420 and S421 appear quite different from each other, subtle similarities indicate that they came from the same timeframe. For example, all the following factors are identical in both: the hair, combed straight back, has a wave in it before reaching the crown; the left side of the moustache is trimmed high and not in a straight line; the right side of the white shirt collar curves down and disappears where the tunic collar closes; the white collar's left side does not close with the right and disappears under the tunic collar about half an inch back from where the tunic collar closes; the tunic collar bulges open slightly above where the *Pour le Mérite* emerges; the *Pour le Mérite* is positioned at the middle of the tunic collar opening with the points of its low cross arm dipping over and just below the top tunic button. Unfortunately, Frankl's overcoat prevents us from comparing the rest of his outfit.

The covered spinner of what appears to be an Albatros scout looms in S421's background. We know that the Albatros fighter made its debut with *Jasta 2* on the Western Front in September 1916, so *Jasta 4* probably received its first examples soon thereafter. We also have a copy of S421's original picture that was sent to the *Vaterländische Frauenverein* (German National Women's Association) on the occasion of their 50th anniversary by Frankl himself (FRANKL2). His handwritten salutation at the bottom is signed "*Frankl, Schloss Vaux 5.11.16 Frankreich*" ("Frankl, Chateau Vaux, 5 November 1916, France"). The discrepancy between where Frankl said he was located (Vaux) and where modern historians have said he should have been (Roupy) is not easily explained. Whatever the explanation, we can assume that he knew best where he actually was. The combination of the Albatros in the background and Frankl's 5 November signature date points to a September to early November period for S421's photo; and the foliage forming S420's backdrop conforms to a fall setting. The fallen leaves on the ground are plainly visible in FRANKL3, a copy of the original photograph behind S420's image.[1]

Our guideline assigns S420 and S421's initial publication to January 1917. Why did Sanke publish these cards then? We know of nothing that occurred in Frankl's career that was particularly noteworthy at this time and we do not see his name or picture in major publications from this period.[2] Perhaps the answer lies in the nature of the other cards that followed in early 1917. Six of the first eleven *Pour le Mérite* airmen had been killed by the close of 1916 – Boelcke, Immelmann, Wintgens, Mulzer, Parschau, and Leffers.

Sanke revisited all but one of the survivors in the opening months of 1917: Frankl's S420-21 after his prior S384, Berthold's S423 after S402, Althaus' S430-31 after S382-83, and Buddecke's S433-34 following S371. Sanke also returned to some of his other previous subjects (e.g., Hirth's S422 following his prewar cards; Cossel's S424 after S401; Baldamus' S432 after S390). It is as though Sanke was trying to remind and reassure the public that other talented German airmen still lived to carry on the fight.

Notes

[1] FRANKL3 is A. Grohs Illustrations Verlag's print No.3619, which states on the reverse: "*Leutnant der Reserve Frankl, der bis zum 5. April 1917 siebenzehn Flugzeuge herunter geschossen hat.*" (2nd Lieutenant of the Reserves Frankl, who up to 5 April 1917 had shot down 17 aircraft). Though slightly inaccurate (officially, Frankl had a total of 15 as of 5 April), the notation nevertheless indicates that Grohs had not received the print until well after Sanke's S421 had been published. So it is unlikely that A. Grohs was Sanke's source in this particular instance.

[2] Frankl became the commanding officer of *Jasta 4* on 1 January 1917, but our guideline appears to indicate that this would have been too late to have spurred the cards' publication in early January.

The German National Women's Association received this autographed version of S421's image for their 50th anniversary.

FRANKL2

189

FRANKL3

Left: A print from the original photograph behind S420, kept in the files of Berlin's A. Grohs Illustrations Verlag during the war.

Opposite: For his sixth confirmed victory, *Lt.* Wilhelm Frankl shot down this RFC No.20 Squadron FE.2b No.5206 on 21 May 1916. Its occupants, 2nd Lt. H.L.C. Aked and Capt. C.E.H. James, were taken prisoner and later photographed in front of their plane with Frankl (see O'Connor, *Aviation Awards II*, p.71).

Below: Frankl was flying Albatros D.III 2158/16 when he lost a battle with several Bristol fighters on 8 April 1917. This picture shows the tragic aftermath.

Bottom: The reverse of this photograph states that it is a picture of *Lt.* Frankl's fighter plane after the end of a dogfight on 29 November 1916. The airplane is a Halberstadt D.II that was fitted with two Spandau machine guns. Unfortunately, the serial number is not visible from this angle.

Engl. Kampfflugzeug abgeschossen durch Ltn. Frankl am 21. Mai 1916 bei Tenbrielen.

S422
HIRTH
Hellmuth
Leutnant

Taken: September to October 1914
Publ: January 1917
Reason: prewar aviator

Decorations:
WR: Iron Cross, 2nd Class; Pilot's Badge
MB: None
RB: None
BH: None

Other Cards:
Unnumbered Sanke
(L7824; N6012)

Key Dates:
c.25 Oct 1914   S422 photo published in *Illustrierte Kriegs-Zeitung* 12, p.6

Like Alfred Friedrich (see S394-95), Hellmuth Hirth was a famous prewar aviator, who as an *Ingenieur* (engineer) received German Pilot License No.79 on 27 March 1911. Hirth was born on 24 April 1886 in Heilbronn, and as an 18-year-old traveled to the United States where he was employed by the Singer Sewing Machine Company, then by Thomas Edison's laboratory. He returned to Germany in 1909 and worked with August Euler on some of Germany's earliest powered aircraft. It is also related that at one point he served on the team of technical designers for Zeppelin airships. In 1911, he helped develop the Rumpler *Taube*, a single-wing design that became one of the most celebrated airplanes in Germany before the war. He taught other aviation pioneers to fly, including Amelie "Melli" Beese, the first woman in Germany to earn a pilot's license.[1] He set records in altitude and distance competitions and won several cross-country contests as well, including one in late June 1911 that required a "purely German airplane" to fly from Munich to Berlin within 36 hours. Hirth won handily, taking a passenger (his mechanic, Alfred Dierlamm) along with him and covering the 535 kilometer distance from Munich to Nuremberg to Leipzig to Berlin in only 5 hours and 41 mintues – a remarkable achievement at the time. In 1912 he carried a military passenger, *Lt.* Schöller, with him from Berlin to Vienna in 6 hours and 35 minutes. These and similar feats won him considerable notoriety throughout Germany. As a result, he authored a book in 1913 entitled "*20000 Kilometer im Luftmeer*" ("20,000 Kilometers in the Sea of Air"), which was expanded and republished under the new title "*Meine Flugerlebnisse*" ("My Flying Experiences") in 1915.

Not much is known about Hirth's wartime career, though it is clear that he was with the Air Service at the beginning of the war. Sanke featured him in HIRTH1, an unnumbered card that celebrated his award of the Iron Cross 2nd Class for outstanding reconnaissance work. One extant example is dated 13 December 1914. The same photo appears in the c. 25 October 1914 edition of *Illustrierte Kriegs-Zeitung* above a caption stating that Hirth had been promoted to *Leutnant* and decorated with the Iron Cross after barely six weeks of military service (i.e., six weeks after the start of the war). Combined, both point to a late September or early October 1914 occurrence for these events, demonstrating that Hirth was one of the Air Service's earliest recipients of this decoration. The September 1914 awards of the Iron Cross 2nd Class to *Leutnante* Mertens (observer) and Canter (pilot) of *Feldflieger-Abteilung 14*, and *Lt.* Rudolf Berthold (observer) of *Feldflieger-Abteilung 23*, are thought to have been among the first.[2]

Hirth survived the war and in 1920 founded a company that supplied pistons, brake wheels, oil filters, and other parts to the aircraft industry. He then started another firm in 1927 that developed air-cooled, inverted inline engines for aircraft. Their performance and reliability brought his company considerable success in the 1931 Air Races. On 1 July 1938, Hirth was killed in an airplane crash near Karlsbad. The Civil Aviation Reichsministry oversaw his company until 1941 when its operations were turned over to the Heinkel company.

Like HIRTH1, S422's photograph shows his Iron Cross 2nd Class being displayed from his tunic's buttonhole. This usually meant that the decoration had recently been awarded. In addition, his *Leutnant* shoulder boards appear to be fairly new (i.e., straight and stiff) and are of the slip-on type often used to replace NCO insignia (as opposed to the sewn-in variety issued to commissioned officers). Both are indications that the picture was probably taken soon after his decoration and promotion in either late September or early October 1914.[3] It is not known why such an early portrait would have been issued by Sanke as late as January 1917.

Notes
[1] Beese was given her license on her birthday, 13 September, in 1911. She too was featured in several pre-war Sanke cards.

[2] *Illustrierte Kriegs-Zeitung* 10 (p.8) refers to a *Flieger-Unteroffizier* Zanettel as being the first non-commissioned flying officer to receive the Iron Cross. The presumed date for this edition, c. 11 October 1914, indicates that he probably received his award, like Hirth, in late September or early October.

[3] The same photograph was used to adorn the cover of his 1915 book, *Meine Flugerlebnisse*.

Three early postcards that were issued when Helmuth Hirth was decorated with the Iron Cross 2nd Class. The first is an unnumbered Sanke card that attributed the award to his "outstanding reconnaissance flights." The second proclaimed that he won it "for bravery and heroic deed," whereas the third, which used a pre-war picture of Hirth in a Rumpler *Taube*, linked his award and promotion to his "bold flights."

HIRTH

Illustrierte Kriegs-Zeitung No.10, published c.11 October 1914, announced that a certain *Uffz*. Zanettel was the first NCO airman to be decorated with the Iron Cross 2nd Class.

A pleasant portrait of Helmuth Hirth.

S423
BERTHOLD
Rudolf
Oberleutnant

Taken: 17 December 1916
Publ: January 1917
Reason: post-*Pour le Mérite*

Decorations:
WR: *Pour le Mérite*, Iron Cross, 1st Class; Pilot's Badge
MB: None
RB: Royal Hohenzollern House Order, Knight's Cross/ Sw; Iron Cross, 2nd Class; Military Merit Order, 4th Class/ Sw (Bav); Military St. Henry Order, Knight's Cross (Sax)
BH: None

Other Cards:
S402, S408, S629
(L7793)

Key Dates:
| 12 Oct 1916 | awarded *Pour le Mérite* |
| 16 Oct 1916 | CO of *Jasta 14* |

When we last encountered *Oblt*. Rudolf Berthold in S402, a drawing of a *Pour le Mérite* had been added to his photo to celebrate his receipt of the award on 12 October 1916. In S423, the decoration is real. Shortly after its bestowal, Berthold was additionally rewarded with the command of *Jasta 14* at Marchais, just east of Laon. BERTHOLD4 shows the ace during a visit to his former observation unit, *Feldflieger-Abteilung 23*, and we are told that the duty roster board in the background identifies the date as 17 December 1916 (see O'Connor, *Aviation Awards III*, p.88). Berthold's appearance in this photo is identical to that in S423. Apart from the same decorations, all these factors are shared in both pictures: dark tunic with lighter grey riding breeches, slight protrusion of white neck collar above tunic collar, distinct bend upward in middle of right shoulder board, shallow curve of left shoulder board, center bulge in the vertical line where the tunic collar joins, slight protrusion of shirt cuffs from tunic (with the bottom of the right shirt cuff folding under its top half), and thin chain bracelet on left wrist. Even the uneven trim of his moustache – the right side is wider and more angled than the left – is precisely identical. There seems little doubt then that S423's photograph was taken at or quite near the same time. Evidently, it soon found its way into Sanke's hands and was published, according to our predictive timeline, about four weeks later as S423.

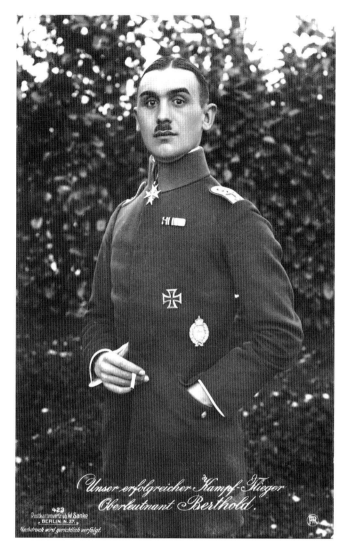

Above: A snapshot of *Oblt.* Rudolf Berthold when he was CO of *Jasta 14*. (photo courtesy of UTD)

Below: *Oblt.* Rudolf Berthold, *Staffelführer* of *Jasta 14*, visits his former unit, *FFA 23*, on 17 December 1916. *FFA 23*'s commanding officer, *Hptm.* Hermann Palmer, is on Berthold's left.

BERTHOLD4

S424
COSSEL
Maximilian von
Oberleutnant

Taken: 7 October to 16 November 1916
Publ: January 1917
Reason: post-sabotage mission

Decorations:
WR: Iron Cross, 1st Class; Observer's Badge
MB: None
RB: Iron Cross, 2nd Class; Royal Hohenzollern House Order, Knight's Cross/ Sw; Merit Cross, 3rd Class/ Sw (Wald); Hanseatic Cross (Lüb)
BH: None

Other Cards:
S373, S401, S408
(L7720, L7756, L7783, L7793; N6003)
Note: Cossel only airman to be awarded Merit Cross 3rd Class/ Sw

Key Dates:

2-3 Oct 1916	conducts sabotage mission behind Russian lines
5 Oct 1916	awarded Merit Cross 3rd Class/ Sw (Wald)
7 Oct 1916	receives Royal Hohenzollern House Order, 3rd Class/ Sw from *Kaiser*
16 Nov 1916	awarded Military Merit Cross, 3rd Class/ war decoration (AH)
17 Nov 1916	given command of *Kampfstaffel 12*

The daring sabotage mission behind Russian lines that first brought national attention to Cossel is described in S401. As a result of that successful adventure, he received two of the awards seen in S424: the Royal Hohenzollern House Order (from the hands of the *Kaiser* himself) and Waldeck's Merit Cross. The Military Merit Cross that Austria-Hungary bestowed on him on 16 November 1916 is not visible, even though we have proof that it was eventually represented on his ribbon bar (see O'Connor, *Aviation Awards VII*, p.371 for a picture of Cossel's actual medal and ribbon bars).[1] This indicates that S424's photo was taken at some point during a 7 October to 16 November timeframe.

Cossel returned to the Western Front as the commander of *Kampfstaffel 12* (attached to *Kampfgeschwader 2*) on 17 November 1916. He took command of *Kampfstaffel 8* (another *Kampfgeschwader 2* unit) the following 5 June 1917. On 25 June, in the company of pilot *Vzfw.* Grabow, he shot down two balloons to give him a total of three of these most dangerous targets. As far as we know, this record remained unsurpassed by any other observer during the war. Cossel's luck finally ran out just three days later on 28 June, when he was shot down and taken prisoner. He would not come home again until 8 February 1920.

Our guideline projects that S424 was issued in late January 1917. His previous exploits had evoked considerable public interest, so S424 was probably offered by Sanke as an updated image and follow-up to S401.

Note
[1] Evidently, when the Austro-Hungarian medal was added to his ribbon bar, the ribbon for his Lübeck Hanseatic Cross was reversed.

Oberleutnant von Cossel

S425
BERR
Hans
Oberleutnant

Taken: early January 1917
Braunschweig, by Josef Raab
Publ: January 1917
Reason: *Pour le Mérite* award

Decorations:
WR: *Pour le Mérite*; Iron Cross, 1st Class; Pilot's Badge
MB: None
RB: None
BH: Royal Hohenzollern House Order, Knight's Cross/ Sw; unknown

Other Cards:
S426
Note: Taken same time as S426
Pour le Mérite has "pie-slice" attachment

Unser erfolgreicher Kampf-Flieger Oberleutnant Berr.

Unser erfolgreicher Kampf-Flieger Oberleutnant Berr.

S426
BERR
Hans
Oberleutnant

Taken: early January 1917
Braunschweig, by Josef Raab
Publ: January 1917
Reason: *Pour le Mérite* award

Decorations:
WR: *Pour le Mérite*; Iron Cross, 1st Class; Pilot's Badge
MB: None
RB: None
BH: Royal Hohenzollern House Order, Knight's Cross/ Sw; unknown

Other Cards:
S425
Note: Taken same time as S425
Pour le Mérite has "pie-slice" attachment

Key Dates:
22 Oct 1916	victory #6
26 Oct 1916	victories #7 and #8
1 Nov 1916	victory #9
3 Nov 1916	victory #10
10 Nov 1916	awarded Royal Hohenzollern House Order, Knight's Cross/ Sw
4 Dec 1916	awarded *Pour le Mérite*
2 Jan 1917	on leave
14 Jan 1917	S425-26 similar photo published in *Berliner Illustrirte Zeitung* 2, p.23

Hans Berr was a *Leutnant* with *Magdeburgisches Jäger-Bataillon Nr.4* when the war started.[1] After being severely wounded, he was promoted to *Oberleutnant* on 15 January 1915. He then entered the Air Service as an observer, but later retrained as a pilot in late 1915. He gained two victories flying a Fokker *Eindecker* with *KEK Ost* at Avillers in March 1916. When a portion of the unit became reorganized as *Jasta 5* on 21 August 1916, he became its first commander. By 3 November, Berr had compiled a total of ten victories, with the last five coming so quickly that the Royal Hohenzollern House Order (normally awarded for six) and the *Pour le Mérite* (eight) did not catch up with him until 10 November and 4 December 1916, respectively. This last award, cited in recognition of his tenth victory, has long confounded historians because three other pilots who equaled or surpassed that count in November – Manfred von Richthofen (11), Stefan Kirmaier (11) and Hans von

Keudell (10) – were not recognized in like manner. In fact, Kirmaier and Keudell never did receive Prussia's premier combat decoration. The next pilot after Berr to receive the *Pour le Mérite* was Richthofen on 12 January 1917, and his was specifically attributed to his 16th victory (shot down 4 January). Thus it appears that a key qualification for receiving the *Pour le Mérite* had been changed. Some authors, probably because of Berr's citation, have theorized that the bar had been raised from eight to ten, but this seems unlikely given that Kirmaier, Richthofen, and Keudell all achieved that total in November as well. There may be another explanation, and that is that the victory total required for an airman to be automatically entitled to the *Pour le Mérite* was increased to 16 as of 1 November 1916. Gustav Leffers had brought down his eighth on 17 October while Albert Dossenbach had done the same on 23 October – and they were the last two airmen before Berr to win the *Pour le Mérite*. The same decoration did not follow, however, for those who scored number eight in November: Stefan Kirmaier (1 November), Hans Schilling (3 November), Manfred von Richthofen (9 November), and Hans von Keudell (16 November). How did Berr fit into this equation? Neal O'Connor reported that the second of Berr's two victories on 26 October 1916 was not confirmed until sometime after 3 November (*Aviation Awards II*, p.221). Consequently, Berr's chronological ninth (1 November) was officially recorded as his eighth, his chronological tenth (3 November) was written as his ninth, and his earlier victory of 26 October became his tenth. It was this belated recognition that probably led to the eventual realization that Berr had actually qualified for the *Pour le Mérite* under the old rule – that is, that he had brought down eight aircraft before the 1 November cutoff. This would explain why his award came in early December and also why his tenth official victory, which actually was his chronological eighth, was cited in his award document.

So it may well be that as of 1 November 1916, 16 downed airplanes were needed by German airmen to automatically qualify for the *Pour le Mérite*. Eight had been a remarkable tally when Boelcke and Immelmann had first achieved it; yet as the war progressed, improved technology and greater opportunity made that mark increasingly attainable. It has therefore been offered that a new level may have been established to preserve the elite status of Prussia's highest award. But was the 28 October 1916 death of Oswald Boelcke, Germany's greatest air hero, the catalyst that forced the change? Perhaps it is only coincidence that both events occurred almost simultaneously and that the new limit was set at twice what Boelcke's had been. Then again, it may have been perceived as an appropriate tribute that in order to be placed in his company, an airman would have to achieve something as truly extraordinary as Boelcke had in his day.

Once again, we have the *Berliner Illustrirte Zeitung* to thank for giving us the origin of S425-26's images. Its 14 January edition printed a picture (BERR1) attributed to a certain "Phot.Raab" that appears to have come from the same sitting. Other postcards (e.g., L7003-06) demonstrate that Josef Raab was a photographer based in Braunschweig who also served the Duke and Duchess of Brunswick. Berr hailed from Braunschweig, and it is highly likely that he went there during his leave that began on 2 January 1917. Indeed, BERR2 appeared in a local publication, *Die Braunschweiger im Weltkriege* (No.13, p.483), sometime after Berr's death and it almost certainly is another Raab portrait taken the same time as S425-26.[2] We have already seen that a photograph often took about two weeks to make its way into a newspaper (see p.36) and about three weeks to come out as a postcard. The early January timing of Berr's proposed visit to a photographic studio in Braunschweig may well have led to a mid-January appearance in a newspaper and the later January publication of S425-26.

BERR1

Oblt. Hans Berr's portrait, taken by Josef Raab and later published in *Berliner Illustrirte Zeitung*.

Opposite

Top left: Another portrait of *Oblt.* Hans Berr, taken the same time as S425-26, that appeared in a hometown publication, *Die Braunschweiger im Weltkriege*.

Top right: Hans Berr early in his military career and before he grew his moustache.

Bottom left: *Oblt.* Hans Berr became a fighter pilot with *Fokkerstaffel Avillers* (later *KEK Ost*), which was located in the Verdun region under command of the German 5th Army and its leader, Crown Prince Wilhelm. Here we see Berr (left) in conversation with his commander and Crown Prince. Several of the unit's *Eindeckers* can be spotted in the background. (photo courtesy of UTD)

Bottom right: After Oswald Boelcke left *FFA 62* in late January 1916, he was sent to Jametz to help protect the artillery spotters of *Artillerie-Flieger-Abteilung 203*. There he met Hans Berr, who Boelcke himself identified on the back of this picture from his personal collection as "*Oblt.* Berr, *Art. Flieger 203*, Jametz." Berr had previously served with *Feldflieger-Abteilung 60* (whose arm patch is still visible on his sleeve). Unfortunately, we do not know if Boelcke's notation signified that Berr was still flying two-seaters in February 1916 (and not a Fokker *Eindecker* as others have speculated) or if the Fokker pilots at Jametz considered themselves a part of *AFA 203*. If the former is true, one wonders if Boelcke was the one who inspired or even recruited Berr to switch to single-seat duties around this time. In any event, Berr was later assigned to *Fokkerstaffel Avillers*, where he achieved his first victory on 8 March 1916.

BERR2

Notes

[1] The numeral '4', apparently a remnant of his former service with this unit, can be seen on Berr's shoulder boards.

[2] As J. Müller apparently did for Boelcke's N5579, N5580, N6005, and BOELCKE6 series (see p.17), and another photographer did for Buddecke's S433-34, Raab had Berr pose in different chairs during one sitting.

Hans Berr's coffin and *Ordenskissen* before his burial in Potsdam on 14 April 1917. Neal O'Connor (*Aviation Awards V*, p.220) has already discussed the curious nature of some of the decorations on display, so this writer will only comment further on the missing *Pour le Mérite* badge. The badge was required to be worn "at all times" and we have evidence that several pilots even did so in combat (e.g., Allmenröder, Immelmann, Loewenhardt, Voss, Wintgens). Perhaps Berr's was destroyed or even lost after his mid-air collision with *Vzfw.* Paul Hoppe. Its devastating results can be seen in O'Connor, *Aviation Awards V*, p.226. (photo courtesy of UTD)

S427
HOEPPNER
Ernst von
Generalleutnant

Taken: late 1915 to late 1916
Publ: January 1917
Reason: recent appointment

Decorations:

WR: Red Eagle Order, 2nd Class/ Sw and Oakleaves; Iron Cross, 1st Class
MB: None
RB: Iron Cross, 2nd Class; unknown; unknown; unknown; Albert Order, Knight 1st Class/ Crown (Sax); remainder unknown
BH: None

Other Cards:

S505, S509, S519, S568, S600
(L7847, L7894; N6049, N6061)
Note: Taken same time as S505

Key Dates:

14 Dec 1915   announcement of award of Red Eagle Order 2nd Class/ Sw and Oakleaves
12 Nov 1916   appointed Commanding General of the Air Force

Erich Ludendorff replaced Erich von Falkenhayn as Chief of Staff of the German Army in late August 1916. A few months later, Ludendorff decided that most of the military's various air organizations and responsibilities needed to be regrouped under one command (the only exceptions being the Naval Air Service and the Bavarian Inspectorate of Aviation). His man for the job, *Generalleutnant* Ernst von Hoeppner, described how the new order of things came about:

> "Influenced by the serious situation in which our air forces had been placed during the Battle of the Somme, the new Chief of the General Staff of the German Army decided in favor of the views which the Chief of Aviation had advanced as early as the Spring of 1915. On October 6, 1916, a decree from H.M. The Emperor ordained that 'owing to the increasing importance of aerial warfare all the aerial activities throughout the army whether offensive or defensive, at the front or in the interior, were to be grouped in one branch of the service.' Therefore, anti-aircraft, aerial defense, and all activities which had been hitherto under the Chief of Aeronautics – i.e., balloons, dirigibles, and the meteorological services, were to be put under the orders of a 'General in Command of the air forces' charged with 'securing unity and method in the construction, concentration and use of all aerial means of waging war.' I was given this new title and took up the duties of the commanding general and the officer who had been Chief of Aviation became my Chief of Staff." (*Germany's War in the Air*, p.78)

Generalleutnant von Hoeppner
Kommandierender General der Luftstreitkräfte.

Effective 12 November 1916 (after the initial reorganization in October), Hoeppner became the new *Kommandierender General der Luftstreitkräfte* (or *Kogenluft* for short) with former *Feldflugchef Obstlt.* Hermann Thomsen as his Chief of Staff.

Hoeppner's new responsibilities were announced by *Berliner Illustrirte Zeitung* in its 3 December 1916 edition, accompanied by a different, much earlier photograph. Nevertheless, S427 was probably intended to note the same event, as seen by the title under Hoeppner's name. The likely date of S427's portrait is difficult to pinpoint, though we might guess that it was taken shortly after his receipt of the Prussian Red Eagle Order, 2nd Class that is displayed at his neck.[1] It is just as possible, however, that it was taken any time after the award up to about three weeks before S427's predicted publication in the middle of January 1917, giving us a broad, one year timeframe of late 1915 to late 1916. A companion portrait, snapped during the same sitting, was presented later in S505 in recognition of Hoeppner's receipt of the *Pour le Mérite*.

Note

[1] His decoration was announced in the 14 December 1915 issue of the *Militär-Wochenblatt*. Such announcements usually postdated the actual time of award by several weeks.

Above and below: Two photos of *Generalleutnant* Ernst von Hoeppner sometime between his promotion to that rank (18 June 1915) and his receipt of the Red Eagle Order, 2nd Class with Swords and Oakleaves (late November or early December 1915). During this period, Hoeppner was Chief of the General Staff of the 2nd Army.

Above and below: *Generalleutnant* Ernst von Hoeppner on visits to frontline *Fliegertruppe* units. (second photo courtesy of UTD)

S428
PFEIFER
Hermann
Leutnant

Taken: 14-31 December 1916
Leffincourt
Publ: January 1917
Reason: victory score

Decorations:
WR: Iron Cross, 1st Class
MB: None
RB: None
BH: None

Other Cards:
S451
(N6205)
Note: Not wearing Pilot's Badge

Key Dates:
21 Nov 1916	promoted to *Leutnant*
24 Nov 1916	victory #7
2 Dec 1916	victory #8

Like so many other future fighter pilots, Hermann Pfeifer began the war in the army. He obtained a transfer to aviation in July 1915 and in March 1916 arrived at *Feldflieger-Abteilung 10* as a two-seater pilot. *Feldflieger-Abteilung 10* was part of *Armee Oberkommando 3* which also had its own Fokker fighter unit. Pfeifer switched over to that group on 30 July, and was still flying with it as a *Vizefeldwebel* when it was converted into *Jasta 9* on 5 October 1916 under the command of *Oblt.* Kurt Student.

The key to S428 occurs in PFEIFER1, a picture taken of the men of *Jasta 9* near their airfield at Leffincourt. *Lt.* Hartmut Baldamus and *Lt.* Hermann Pfeifer are in the middle of the back row framed by a structure made from birch branches. The right side of the same structure appears again behind Pfeifer in S428. This and the fact that he seems to be dressed identically in PFEIFER1 and S428 indicates that they were taken at the same occasion, whose approximate time can be determined by three factors. First, Pfeifer is dressed as a *Leutnant* and had been promoted to that rank on 21 November 1916. Second, Messrs. Franks, Bailey, and Duivan inform us that two of PFEIFER1's *Jasta 9* contingent, *Lt. Graf* von der Recke and *Lt. Prinz* von Thurn und Taxis, left the squadron in December 1916 (*Jasta Pilots*, pp.237 and 280).[1] Thus the pictures must have been snapped at some point after 21 November but before January 1917. Third, *Lt.* Willy Rosenstein (also present in PFEIFER1) was away from *Jasta 9* as a flight instructor at Fâmars (near Valenciennes) from 9 November to 13 December, so PFEIFER1 must have been taken during the last half of December after Rosenstein's return but before Recke and Thurn und Taxis had left.[2] By this point, Pfeifer and Baldamus had become the squadron's scoring stars, running up respective totals of eight and nine downed aircraft by 2 December (neither would score again until after the new year). This not only probably explains why the pair were so neatly framed in the center of PFEIFER1, but also why Sanke featured Pfeifer in S428.[3] Eight victories, which as recently as October had automatically brought a pilot the *Pour le Mérite*, was a highly respectable score. By the end of December 1916, only 21 airmen had achieved that mark. Of those 21, 14 had already appeared on a Sanke card with 12 of them wearing the *Pour le Mérite*.

Notes
[1] Prince von Thurn und Taxis is wearing a black armband that probably honored *Kaiser* Franz Josef of Austria who died on 21 November 1916.

[2] See Rosenstein's biography in C&C 25:4.

[3] Baldamus, first seen in S390, would appear again soon after Pfeifer in S432. In addition, images of Baldamus and Pfeifer in their Albatros D.II fighter planes were published consecutively by NPG as N6204 and N6205. Another shot of Pfeifer in his airplane from the same time, a similar portrait of *Oblt.* Kurt Student (their commanding officer) in his Albatros fighter (also seen in Franks, Bailey, Duivan, *Jasta Pilots*), and Baldamus' S390 picture were presented on the same page of the 31 March 1917 edition of *Berliner Illustrirte Zeitung*. Were these all, with the exception of S390, taken close to S428 and PFEIFER1? The timing would be right because Pfeifer, Baldamus, and Student are seated in early D.II models that bore fuselage-mounted Windhoff radiators that were abandoned in favor of wing-mounted Teves and Braun radiators in late 1916.

S429
REIMANN
Leopold
Offizier-Stellvertreter

Taken: November 1916 to January 1917
Publ: January 1917
Reason: unknown

Decorations:
WR: Iron Cross, 1st Class; Pilot's Badge
MB: None
RB: Iron Cross, 2nd Class; Silver St. Henry Medal (Sax); Silver Friedrich August Medal (Sax); unknown; unknown
BH: None

Other Cards:
None

Key Dates:

Sep 1916	promoted to *Offizier-Stellvertreter*
10 Sep 1916	awarded Iron Cross 1st Class
22 Oct 1916	wounded in action
31 Dec 1916	married
24 Jan 1917	killed in accident

PFEIFER I

Members of *Jasta* 9 at Leffincourt in the last half of December 1916. Seated, left to right: *Oblt.* Walter Zietlow, *Oblt.* Kurt Student (CO), *Lt. Prinz* von Thurn und Taxis. Back row, left to right: *Lt.* Willy Rosenstein, *Lt.* Werner Marwitz, *Lt.* Hartmut Baldamus, *Lt.* Hermann Pfeifer, *Lt.* Friedrich Dinkel, *Lt.* Heinrich Kroll, *Lt. Graf* von der Recke.

Leopold Reimann was wounded in the spring of 1915 while serving with *1. Pioniere-Bataillon Nr.12*, and by the end of the summer had transferred to the *Fliegertruppe*. One year later, on 24 June 1916, Reimann began his fighter service with *Kampfeinsitzer-Kommando Bertincourt (KEK B)*, later known as *Abwehr-Kommando Nord (AKN)* and then *Kampfeinsitzerstaffel Bertincourt (Kest B)*. There he was destined to "rub elbows" with such talented airmen as Gustav Leffers and Max Müller (already there), Otto Parschau (a July arrival), Hans von Keudell, and Hans Bethge (who both came in August). The unit was converted into *Jasta 1* on 22 August 1916 under the command of *Hptm.* Martin Zander, but it was Reimann who brought down the squadron's first victim two days later, which also qualified as the first official victory by a *Jagdstaffel*. Reimann fell in among even more illustrious company when he and Max Müller were assigned to Oswald Boelcke's *Jasta 2* on 1 September. Reimann continued to give a good account of himself, keeping pace with then beginner Manfred von Richthofen, until he was wounded on 22 October:

Date	Reimann	Richthofen
17 Sep		#1
22 Sep	#2	
23 Sep		#2
27 Sep	unconfirmed	
30 Sep		#3
7 Oct		#4
16 Oct	#3	#5
21 Oct	#4	
22 Oct	#5	

After his recovery, Reimann was married on New Years' Eve. His former *Jasta 1* CO, Martin Zander, who was now running the fighter pilot school at Fâmars near Valenciennes, invited Reimann to join him there as an instructor. Reimann reported to the school and was killed in a plane crash on 24 January 1917.

Reimann is wearing the Iron Cross 1st Class he was awarded on 10 September 1916, so we know S429's picture was taken after that point. It also has the look of a formal studio portrait taken back in the German homeland. Reimann's record demonstrates that he

Unser erfolgreicher Kampf-Flieger
Offz.-Stellv. Reimann

429
Postkartenvertrieb W. Sanke
BERLIN N. 37
Nachdruck wird gerichtlich verfolgt.

was busy at the Front until he was wounded in combat, so it is unlikely that S429's photo originated before 22 October. Reimann appears fit and shows no obvious signs of having been wounded, so it is possible that he had already recovered. As we shall see later on, Pfiefer's S451 was taken on or about his wedding day, and it is tempting to speculate that the same might have been true for S429. Unfortunately, unlike Pfeifer, Reimann's right hand has been obscured and we cannot discern if he wore a wedding ring. Therefore, we can only project that Reimann's portrait originated from some point late in his recovery period (November 1916) up to his departure for the *Jastaschule* near Valenciennes (January 1917).

It is difficult to decide on exactly what spurred the publication of S429. Guideline 2 places its debut in late January around the time Reimann was killed in a flying accident, but too early for that to have been the impetus behind its origin. Nevertheless, as we have noted before, the guidelines are only approximations of publication dates; so we cannot rule out the possibility that the card was a commemorative issue that came out shortly after Reimann's death. In fact, the reverse of an original S429 photograph owned by A. Grohs Illustrations Verlag noted the following: *"Kampfflieger Offiziers Stellvertreter Reimann, der 5 Flugzeuge herunter geschossen hatte und kürzlich tötlich verunglückte."* ("Combat flier Warrant Officer Reimann, who shot down five airplanes and was recently killed in an accident"). This plainly demonstrates that A. Grohs – a major source of pictures during the war – did not have this particular image of Reimann until after his death. The same was probably true for Sanke as well. Reimann's portrait, however, numbered "3615" in the A. Grohs series, is preceded by Böhme's 3614, which the firm obtained in March 1917 (see Müller S447); so A. Grohs could not have been Sanke's source in this instance.

Above: A. Grohs Illustrations Verlag image No.3615.

Below: *Vzfw.* Rudolf Reimann stands before an Albatros D.I, possibly 426/16, that was brought to *Jasta 2.*

S430
ALTHAUS
Ernst *Freiherr* von
Oberleutnant

Taken: August to December 1916
Berlin, by Rudolf Dührkoop
Publ: January 1917
Reason: post-*Pour le Mérite*

Decorations:

WR: *Pour le Mérite*; Iron Cross, 1st Class; Pilot's Badge
MB: None
RB: Miltary St. Henry Order, Knight's Cross (Sax); Iron Cross, 2nd Class; Royal Hohenzollern House Order, Knight's Cross/ Sw; Saxe-Ernestine House Order, Knight 2nd Class/ Sw (SD); War Merit Cross, 2nd Class (Brun); General Honor Decoration for Bravery (Hes)
BH: None

Other Cards:

S382, S383, S408, S431
(L7751, L7793)
Note: Taken same time as S431
Cipher for former unit, *Husaren-Regiment (1. sächsisches) Nr.18*, on shoulder boards

Unser erfolgreicher
Kampfflieger
Oberleutnant
Freiherr von Althaus.

Unser erfolgreicher Kampf-Flieger
Oberleutnant
Freiherr von Althaus.

S431
ALTHAUS
Ernst *Freiherr* von
Oberleutnant

Taken: August to December 1916
Berlin, by Rudolf Dührkoop
Publ: January 1917
Reason: post-*Pour le Mérite*

Decorations:
WR: *Pour le Mérite*; Iron Cross, 1st Class, Pilot's Badge
MB: None
RB: Miltary St. Henry Order, Knight's Cross (Sax); Iron Cross, 2nd Class; Royal Hohenzollern House Order, Knight's Cross/ Sw; Saxe-Ernestine House Order, Knight 2nd Class/ Sw (SD); War Merit Cross, 2nd Class (Brun); General Honor Decoration for Bravery (Hes)
BH: None

Other Cards:
S382, S383, S408, S430
(L7751, L7793)
Note: Taken same time as S430

Key Dates:
21 Jul 1916   awarded *Pour le Mérite*

S430 and S431 exhibit noticeable differences between them. Althaus, wearing an overcoat and cap, rests against a draped table with gloves in hand in S431, while in S430 the coat is gone, the gloves have been replaced with a cigarette, and the cap rests on a table. Nevertheless, they both come from the same sitting. His casual posture, the high white collar under his Hussar tunic, the angles of his tunic buttons, and even the bracelet's position on his wrist are identical in S430-31; and despite someone having brushed out S430's leafy wallpaper in S431, he is leaning against the same draped table in both. The ubiquitous table and S430's leafy wallpaper appear again in Müller's S447 and Höhne's S524. Müller's S446-47 series is much the same as S430-31 in that Müller's pose leaning against the table without his overcoat in S447 is identical to Althaus' in S430. Moreover, both airmen are depicted in their overcoats against a brushed out background in the other half of their series (i.e., S446 and S431). The leafy wallpaper similarly appears and disappears in Höhne's S524-25 series. It is therefore obvious that these three series all came from the same studio. We might never have known where that studio was if it were not for an obscure booklet entitled *Deutsche Heldenflieger*, published around May 1917. It reprinted the top of S431 and assigned the photo's origin to "R. Dührkoop, Berlin."[1] Althaus (born in Bavaria), Müller (a Saxon), and Höhne (from

Wiowitz near Breslau) came from different parts of Germany and did not serve together in any of the same military units. Berlin was the center of the German Air Service and its aircraft industry, so it rings true that a trip there – and by chance to the same photography studio – was the common factor.

Unfortunately, we know little about Althaus' activities between July 1916 and January 1917 – the month in which our guideline predicts that S430-31 made their first appearance. We currently have no way of determining when Althaus visited Berlin, so we are left with an August to December 1916 timeframe for the pictures' origin. In addition, the reason behind why Sanke issued S430-31 in January 1917 is not readily apparent. Following the death of six of the first eleven *Pour le Mérite* airmen by the close of 1916, Sanke issued new pictures of all but one of the survivors in the beginning of 1917: Frankl S420-21, Berthold S423, Althaus S430-31, and Buddecke S433-34. He also revisited other previous subjects like Hirth S422, Cossel S424, and Baldamus S432. Perhaps Sanke was trying to remind and reassure the public that other talented German airmen still lived to carry on the fight.

Note

[1] Though the portrait is marked with a death cross (Althaus in fact survived the war), the data otherwise presented in the booklet are quite accurate, including the victory counts of various pilots by the end of April 1917. In particular, the author appears to have been meticulous in listing the sources of dozens of photographs. Many were attributed to "W. Sanke," while others like Richthofen's S503 (C.J. von Dühren), Baldamus' N6204 (Bild und Film-Amts) and Müller's N6229 (A.L. Müller) correctly identified their different origins. Rudolf Dührkoop had studios in Berlin and Hamburg, and his photographs were used by Liersch and NPG. He was the apparent favorite of Prince and Princess August Wilhelm of Prussia, who visited him often for personal and family portraits.

Right: Another formal portrait of *Oblt.* Ernst von Althaus in his Hussar uniform.
Below: *Oblt.* Ernst von Althaus, his dog Mousse, and other comrades in front of a *Jasta 4* Halberstadt D.II around the time of the unit's formation on 25 August

1916. From left to right: Weisser (mechanic), Neumann (orderly), Althaus, and Reiche (mechanic). Judging from his uniform, Neumann apparently accompanied Althaus from their former Hussar Regiment.

S432
BALDAMUS
Hartmut
Leutnant

Taken: March to early September 1916
Dresden, by Hugo Erfurth
Publ: January 1917
Reason: victory score

Decorations:
WR: Iron Cross, 1st Class; Pilot's Badge
MB: None
RB: None
BH: Iron Cross, 2nd Class; Albert Order, Knight 2nd Class/ Sw (Sax)

Other Cards:
S390
(L7754; N6204)
Note: Taken same time as S390

Key Dates:

c.24 Sep 1916	S390 similar photo published in *Illustrierte Kriegs-Zeitung (Das Weltbild)* 112, p.8
18 Feb 1917	S390 similar photo published in *Berliner Illustrirte Zeitung (Das Weltbild)* 7, p.90
31 Mar 1917	S390 photo published in *Berliner Illustrirte Zeitung* 13, p.174

The many similarities that exist between the pictures of *Lt*. Hartmut Baldamus in S390 and S432 make it clear that they came from the same sitting, despite having been published as postcards almost five months apart. If one examines Baldamus' left arm in S432, a slight irregularity where S390's armpatch was erased becomes apparent. See Baldamus' S390 for a discussion of how it was determined that his S390 and S432 photographs were taken together sometime between March and early September 1916, and how they and Curt Wüsthoff's S560, S563-64, S566, and S586-88 all came from Hugo Erfurth's studio in Dresden.

Our guideline's prediction that S432 was first sold in late February 1917 is in step with *Berliner Illustrirte Zeitung*'s 18 February 1917 publication of BALDAMUS1 (see S390), yet another portrait of the airman taken the same time as S390 and S432.[1] The newspaper specified that Baldamus was being recognized for his 11th victory (shot down on 2 February). That he had actually brought down two more (on 15 and 16 February) before its publication date again illustrates the time lag that was experienced between when an event occurred and when it was reported in pictorial newspapers. Our three-week rule dictates that it may have been his 10th on 23 January that inspired S432's creation. In any event, such a score (10 or 11) was indeed noteworthy and would have earned him the *Pour le Mérite* had the requirement for that award not been raised from eight to sixteen the prior November. As it was, his number 10 tied him at the end of January 1917 with Berr, Buddecke, and Mulzer – all holders of the coveted decoration – for ninth place among Germany's highest scoring airmen. There is little doubt that the eyes of the German press were upon him because the 31 March 1917 edition of *Berliner Illustrirte Zeitung* included his portrait once more on the occasion of his 15th victim (brought down on 17 March), when he was only one score away from becoming eligible for Prussia's highest decoration. This time the photo was the one that Sanke had used for S390, though it was credited not to him but to a "Hugo Erfurt." Baldamus went on to bag his 16th on 6 April and two

more on 12 and 14 April. The last, however, resulted from a collision that led to his death. *Nachrichtenblatt der Luftstreitkräfte Nr. 8* made special mention of his end:

> "Ltn. d. Res. Baldamus was killed in air combat on 14 April 1917, when he collided with an enemy airplane and suffered a fatal crash. Leutnant Baldamus joined Fl.-Abt. 20 on 11 March 1915. After shooting down five enemy airplanes as a two-seater pilot, he transferred to Jasta 9. His career as a fighter pilot was distinguished by a string of splendid victories. Now he has joined his 17 opponents in death. His name will live on in the history of the Fliegertruppe." (OTF 14:3, p.273)

The *Pour le Mérite* was not given posthumously, so if a recommendation for the award was been placed in process, it came to an end when his life did.

Note
[1] This is the same photo that had appeared earlier in *Illustrierte Kriegs-Zeitung*'s c. 24 September 1916 edition, presumably in honor of Baldamus' fifth victory.

S433
BUDDECKE
Hans-Joachim
Hauptmann

Taken: August to November 1916
Publ: February 1917
Reason: post-*Pour le Mérite*

Decorations:
WR: *Pour le Mérite*; Iron Cross, 1st Class; Pilot's Badge; War Medal (Ott)
MB: None
RB: Iron Cross, 2nd Class; Royal Hohenzollern House Order, Knight's Cross/ Sw; Miltary Merit Order, 4th Class/ Sw (Bav); Military St. Henry Order, Knight's Cross/ Sw (Sax); War Merit Cross, 2nd Class (Brun); Golden Imtiaz Medal/ Sw (Ott); Golden Liakat Medal/ Sw (Ott); Silver Imtiaz Medal/ Sw (Ott); Silver Liakat Medal/ Sw (Ott); War Medal (Ott)
BH: None

Other Cards:
S371, S408, S434
(L7793, L7825; N5600)

Note: Taken same time as S434
Cipher for former unit, *Leibgarde-Infanterie-Regiment (1. gross-hessisches) Nr. 115*, on shoulder boards

S434
BUDDECKE
Hans-Joachim
Hauptmann

Taken: August to November 1916
Publ: February 1917
Reason: post-*Pour le Mérite*

Decorations:
WR: *Pour le Mérite*; Iron Cross, 1st Class; Pilot's Badge; War Medal (Ott)
MB: None
RB: Iron Cross, 2nd Class; Royal Hohenzollern House Order, Knight's Cross/ Sw; Miltary Merit Order, 4th Class/ Sw (Bav); Military St. Henry Order, Knight's Cross/ Sw (Sax); War Merit Cross, 2nd Class (Brun); Golden Imtiaz Medal/ Sw (Ott); Golden Liakat Medal/ Sw (Ott); Silver Imtiaz Medal/ Sw (Ott); Silver Liakat Medal/ Sw (Ott); War Medal (Ott)
BH: None

Other Cards:
S371, S408, S433
(L7793, L7825; N5600)
Note: Taken same time as S433
Cipher for former unit, *Leibgarde-Infanterie-Regiment (1. grosshessisches) Nr. 115*, on shoulder boards

Key Dates:

14 Apr 1916	awarded *Pour le Mérite*
7 May 1916	visits *FFA 23* Vaux airfield
Jul 1916	hosts Boelcke in Turkey
25 Aug 1916	CO of *Jasta 4* at Vaux airfield
1 Dec 1916	to Turkey in *FFA 5*
Feb 1918	to France in *Jasta 18*

Unlike his first Sanke card, Buddecke is wearing a German uniform with the single "pip" of an *Oberleutnant* in S433 and S434. Nevertheless, Sanke continued to refer to him in his temporary Turkish service rank of *Hauptmann* (see S371).

There is no question that S433 and S434 were taken at the same time, despite the fact that each contains a different chair. The curtain backdrop, Buddecke's uniform accoutrements, white shirt collar, and even the folds of his visor cap are identical in both. BUDDECKE5, published in *Deutsche Heldenflieger* (p.24), may have been taken around the same time period. The manner in which his white shirt collar folds in on itself and the subtle bends in his shoulder boards are matched by S433-34. He is, however, wearing the Golden Imtiaz Medal (note the difference in size compared with S371's Golden Liakat Medal) in BUDDECKE5 in place of the ribbon bar seen in S433-34. Such a discrepancy would normally disqualify it as belonging with the others except for two facts. First, BUDDECKE5 was credited to "W. Sanke, Berlin." Though it never appeared on a Sanke postcard (at least that we know of today), it is plausible that it belonged to a group of photos that Sanke had acquired the rights to. Second, we have at least one other instance where a different arrangement of decorations can be seen between Sanke postcards and a contemporaneous picture not published by Sanke (i.e., Gontermann's S558-59 and N6252). We also have Bernert's S442-43 series where the first included his ribbon bar and the second did not (see p.212).

Because Buddecke is wearing a German uniform, we can surmise that he was no longer in the Turkish service. This would place the origin of these pictures sometime between his return to the Western Front as the commanding officer of *Jasta 4* on 25 August 1916 and his reassignment to Turkey's *Feldflieger-Abteilung 5* the following 1 December. This is supported by two photos taken at the funeral held for *Lt.* Kurt Wintgens in St. Quentin on 29 September 1916 (see Nowarra, *Jew with the Blue* Max, p.18). Of all the surviving pictures of Buddecke, these are the only two where his appearance is the same as it is in S433-34: German tunic with cuff and collar *Litzen*, high white shirt collar, ribbon bar on the left breast, Iron Cross 1st Class slightly above and almost touching the Prussian Pilot's Badge, dress belt, and straight-legged trousers. Buddecke's appearance in all four photos is so similar that it is tempting to speculate that they came from the same occasion. In the absence of any other information, however, we must settle for an August-November 1916 timeframe.

Our Sanke publication guideline predicts an early February 1917 debut for S433-34. See Frankl's S420-21 for a possible explanation of why they were issued at this time.[1] By this time, Buddecke had returned to Turkey, which may explain why Sanke referred to him as a *Hauptmann* on the cards.

Right: A drawing of *Oblt.* Hans-Joachim Buddecke that was recorded by Berliner Illustrations Gesellschaft as image No.22190 and touted as his *"neueste Aufnahme"* ("latest picture").

Note
[1] BUDDECKE6, from A. Grohs Illustrations Verlag, is a copy of the original image behind S434. This particular print was not Sanke's source, however, because the reverse refers to Buddecke's death (on 10 March 1918) and bears the advanced serial number "5038" – two things that place it much later than S434's debut in early 1917.

The early 1917 book, *Deutsche Heldenflieger*, attributed this image to W. Sanke of Berlin. We have no further evidence, however, that it ever appeared on a Sanke postcard.

BUDDECKE5

BUDDECKE6

Top left: A. Grohs Illustrations Verlag image No.5038. Top right and below: Hans-Joachim Buddecke's brother, a *Kapitänleutnant* in the navy, visited him in the fall of 1916 when these two pictures were taken. While the first includes just the two brothers, many of the officers of *Jasta 4* turned out for the second. From left to right: *Lt.* Eberhardt Fügner, *Lt.* Leo Strauch, *Lt.* Trentepohl, *Oblt.* Ernst von Althaus, *Kptlt.* Buddecke, *Lt.* Hans Malchow, Hans-Joachim Buddecke, *Lt.* Wilhelm Frankl, *Lt.* Joachim von Ziegesar, unknown navy officer, unknown, unknown, *Lt.* Fritz Otto Bernert, *Lt.* Karl Stehle, and *Lt.* Kurt Veltjens. If Franks, Bailey, and Duivan are correct, Ziegesar was only with the unit 1-16 October 1916 before he moved on to *Jasta 14* (see *Jasta Pilots*, p.305). Trentepohl is listed as having joined the squadron on 1 October, and Veltjens is said to have left it in November, so all in all it seems that these photographs originated from Roupy during the first half of October 1916. (first photo courtesy of UTD)

S442
BERNERT
Fritz Otto
Leutnant

Taken: 25 to 31 January 1917
Publ: February 1917
Reason: victory score

Decorations:
WR: Iron Cross, 1st Class; Pilot's Badge
MB: Iron Cross, 2nd Class; Royal Hohenzollern House Order, Knight's Cross/ Sw; Albert Order, Knight 2nd Class/ Sw (Sax)
RB: None
BH: None

Other Cards:
S443, S521
(L7826)
Note: Taken same time as S443

S443
BERNERT
Fritz Otto
Leutnant

Taken: 25 to 31 January 1917
Publ: February 1917
Reason: victory score

Decorations:
WR: Iron Cross, 1st Class; Pilot's Badge
MB: None
RB: None
BH: Royal Hohenzollern House Order, Knight's Cross/ Sw; Iron Cross, 2nd Class; Albert Order, Knight 2nd Class/ Sw (Sax)

Other Cards:
S442, S521
(L7826)
Note: Taken same time as S442

Key Dates:
9 Nov 1916	victories #5, #6, #7
25 Jan 1917	awarded Royal Hohenzollern House Order, Knight's Cross/ Sw

25 Feb 1917   S443 photo published in *Berliner Illustrirte Zeitung* 8, p.104

Otto Bernert would never have become a military pilot under today's standards. First, he wore glasses (see S521). The successes achieved by Wintgens, Berthold, Tutschek, Kissenberth, and other less famous, bespectacled pilots demonstrate that this could be successfully overcome. The second obstacle he faced, however, was far more serious. While serving in the trenches with *Infanterie-Regiment Nr. 173*, Bernert was wounded four times. The last was a bayonet thrust to his left arm that severed the main nerve. Several authors have claimed that the arm, as a result, became virtually useless, but photographic evidence indicates this is probably an exaggeration.[1] Nevertheless, such an injury surely would have made life much more complicated during the rigors and maneuvers of air combat.

Bernert began his flying career as an observer with *Feldflieger-Abteilungen 27* and *71* before he trained as a fighter pilot and joined *Kek Vaux* in 1916. He scored his first victory on 17 April with this famous unit that counted Berthold, Frankl, Höhndorf, Althaus, and Buddecke among its members. Following its conversion into *Jasta 4* on 25 August, Bernert's second, brought down on 6 September, was logged as the new squadron's first official victory. He then achieved a "hat trick" by bringing down three aircraft on 9 November 1916 – an unparalled feat at the time that none of the *Pour le Mérite* aces, including the great Boelcke, had ever accomplished. His 1916 tally ended on this high note, and he would not score again until after he had been transferred to *Jasta 2* in March 1917. In the meantime, he was awarded Saxony's Albert Order, Knight 2nd Class on 5 January and Prussia's Royal Hohenzollern House Order, Knight's Cross on 25 January. He can be seen wearing both of these decorations in S442.

Despite some notable differences between them, there is no doubt that S442's and S443's pictures were taken at the same sitting. Both display the same wicker chair, uniform accoutrements, and tunic and cap creases and folds. S442's background is white while S443's is dark, but it is difficult to tell if one was artificially created or if both existed as separate areas in the same studio. Another interesting feature is that Bernert is wearing his *Grossordensschnalle* (medals bar) in S442 but not in S443, though the small loops that held it are still visible. His decorations are instead represented in S443 by three ribbons attached to his buttonhole. We have other examples of different types of award displays between contemporaneous photos (see the discussions of Mulzer's S385, S396-98; Gontermann's S527-29, S558-59, and N6252; and possibly Buddecke's S433-34 and BUDDECKE5). But what makes S443 more curious is that his buttonhole ribbons were in fact drawn in. Under magnification, they appear rather crude and one button actually peeks through a spot where the ribbon's dark band would otherwise have overlapped it.[2] The same picture used in S443 was also published in the 25 February 1917 edition of *Berliner Illustrirte Zeitung* (see BERNERT3). It too includes artificially created ribbons – but they are not identical to those seen in S443! A close comparison shows that the sword devices representing his Royal Hohenzollern House Order are lower down on the ribbon and the ribbon widths are of slightly different proportions. Exactly why this artwork was added in on two separate occasions remains a mystery, but it would appear that independent sources deemed it important to depict Bernert with at least some sign of his recently awarded Royal Hohenzollern Order.

BERNERT3, the photo printed in *Berliner Illustrirte Zeitung*, is credited to "B.I.G.," the acronym for Berliner Illustrations Gesellschaft (Berlin Illustration Company). It is almost certain, however, that the photo originated from a now unknown private studio and that the Berlin Illustration Company subsequently obtained the rights to it. Interestingly, the newspaper caption also credits Bernert with eight total victories; yet his eighth, at least officially, did not come until the following 19 March.

The fact that Bernert received his Hohenzollern award on 25 January 1917 and that S443's picture of him with it was published on 25 February relegates the date of S442-43's images to late January or early February 1917. Our guideline assigns their publication as Sanke cards to late February, about four weeks after his Hohenzollern award.

Notes

[1] Bernert is gripping his gloves in his left hand in S442, while S443 has his left arm positioned behind his back. BERNERT1-2 capture him holding his pilot's headgear in his left hand while another photo opposite depicts him resting both arms on a cane. These, along with other photographs like the one seen in O'Connor's *Aviation Awards VII* (p.412), where Bernert is casually resting his left arm on the back of the bench he is sitting on, indicate that he retained at least some control and flexibility in his injured limb.

[2] Liersch's L7826 is a duplicate of S442, but a close comparison of the two shows that Bernert's medals and wristwatch were slightly touched up in S442, presumably to depict them more clearly than the original had.

Opposite and above: These photographs and others demonstrate that Otto Bernert had more mobility in his left arm than several authors have claimed. The first two were taken at *Jasta 12*'s airfield at Epinoy upon the occasion of a visit by Bernert and two *Jasta Boelcke* pilots. In the first, from left to right: *Hptm.* Adolf *Ritter* von Tutschek, *Lt.* Friedrich Hochstetter, *Hptm.* Eberhard von Seel (*Jasta Boelcke*), *Vzfw.* Arthur Schorisch, and Bernert. The second, left to right: Seel (*Jasta Boelcke*), Tutschek, Schorisch, Bernert, *Vzfw.* Grigo, *Lt.* Hans Eggers (*Jasta Boelcke*), *Vzfw.* Robert Riessinger, and *Lt.* Friedrich Roth. According to several sources, Tutschek left *Jasta Boelcke* and arrived at *Jasta 12* as its CO on 30 April 1917, Bernert was ordered from *Jasta Boelcke* to lead *Jasta 6* on 1 May, and Seel left *Jasta Boelcke* to command *Jasta 17* on 10 May. Therefore, these images were probably recorded close to the time that Tutschek and Bernert were transferred. The third picture catches Bernert enjoying a cigar and a beer during "*Geburtstagsfeier Feldw. Hoch in Premont*" ("Sgt. Hoch's birthday party in Premont"), according to an inscription on the reverse. The air unit and date are unknown.

Below: A closeup of the slightly different drawn-in ribbons seen in the 25 February 1917 *Berliner Illustrirte Zeitung* version of S443. Right: Otto Bernert when he was an observer in 1915 with either *FFA* 27 or 71. (photo courtesy of UTD)

BERNERT3

213

Two above: *Lt.* Bernert, prior to his receipt of the *Pour le Mérite*, in front of a *Jagdstaffel* airplane shed. Note that the Albatros fighter behind him in the first picture is no longer there in the second. (photos courtesy of UTD)

Unser erfolgreicher Kampfflieger
Leutnant Max Müller.

S444
MÜLLER
Max (*Ritter* von)
Leutnant

Taken: April 1916 to June 1917
Munich, by Ostermayr Brothers
Publ: September 1917
Reason: victory score and promotion

Decorations:
WR: Iron Cross, 1st Class; Pilot's Badge (Bav)
MB: Bravery Medal in Silver (Bav); Military Merit Cross, 3rd Class/ Crown and Swords (Bav); Iron Cross, 2nd Class; *Prinzregent* Luitpold Medal in Bronze (Bav); Long Service Distinction, 3rd Class (Bav)
RB: None
BH: None

Other Cards:
S552, S553, S583, S584
(N6271)

Key Dates:

18 Feb 1916	awarded Silver Bravery Medal (Bav)
28 Jun 1917	awarded Gold Military Merit Medal (Würt)
14 Jul 1917	awarded Member's Cross/ Sw of the Royal Hohenzollern House Order
10 Aug 1917	victory #21
17 Aug 1917	victory #22
19 Aug 1917	victories #23 and #24

21 Aug 1917	victories #25 and #26
25 Aug 1917	promoted to *Leutnant*
26 Aug 1917	S444 original photo published in *Berliner Illustrirte Zeitung* 34, p.445
3 Sep 1917	awarded *Pour le Mérite*
c.23 Sep 1917	S444 original photo published in *Illustrierte Kriegs-Zeitung (Das Weltbild)* 164, p.1

Max Müller's S444 presents one of the more puzzling Sanke card mysteries. Normally, we would have assigned its first appearance to sometime in February, given its numerical place in Sanke's series. Yet S444 identifies Müller as a *Leutnant,* a rank he did not hold until five months later on 25 August 1917. In addition, someone altered S444's original photograph, MÜLLER1, to ensure that it conformed to his new rank. The *Offizier-Stellvertreter* insignia on his collar were erased to create an officer's standing collar, and his shoulder boards were altered to look like those of a *Leutnant.* There is no question then that S444 was issued after Müller's promotion and therefore out of sequence with the cards surrounding it. One explanation would be that like some of Immelmann's or Boelcke's cards, it was an updated version of an earlier S444 that originally displayed Müller as an *Offizier-Stellvertreter.* The problem with this is that apart from the "great ones," we have only seen this done one other time for Göttsch's S518; in addition, no example of an "*Offizier-Stellvertreter* Müller" S444 has yet come to light. Though we might never know the reason why S444 was published out of sequence, we can at least predict when it occurred.

Our first indication of S444's actual debut rests in the fact that Müller's S444, S552, and S553 originated from one sitting: S444 and S553 share a common background, the very same decorations hang identically in S444 and S552 and only slightly differently in S553, Müller's tunic is puckered in like manner above and below his medals bar in S444 and S553, and his haircut is an exact match in them all. That his collar and shoulder boards were updated in the same manner in all three photos suggests that they were altered simultaneously. Our guideline predicts that S552-53 first came out in mid-September 1917 – about three weeks after MÜLLER1 appeared in the 26 August edition of *Berliner Illustrirte Zeitung* (celebrating Müller's 21st victory) and around the time it reappeared in the c.23 September edition of *Illustrierte Kriegs-Zeitung* (announcing both his promotion and his receipt of the *Pour le Mérite*). Thus S444, S552, and S553 may have been issued together in September 1917 in recognition of Müller's 26 victories and his field promotion, at least. Whether they also recognized the *Pour le Mérite* that ensued shortly thereafter is a matter of debate. Curiously, that decoration does not appear in any of the cards even though it would have been a relatively simple matter to add an artist's rendering of it to images that had already been substantially altered. Does this reflect that the card was already in the works by the time the news of Müller's award had become widespread? Whatever the answer, we can be sure that Müller's *Pour le Mérite* inspired N6271, yet another version of MÜLLER1. In this instance, his rank was also updated to *Leutnant,* though in a different manner. The *Offizier-Stellvertreter* insignia on his collar were erased and replaced with an officer's collar *Litzen,* lace trim was added to his left sleeve (but not his right), and his original NCO shoulder boards were redrawn to resemble wire ones. Unlike Sanke's cards, someone placed a drawing of a *Pour le Mérite* at Müller's neck.

MÜLLER2-5 are earlier pictures of Müller that were taken in the same studio as S444's original shot. MÜLLER2-4 are a set, with MÜLLER3 depicting the same landscape in its background that appears in S444. MÜLLER3 also contains the base of the painted pillar seen in S444 and MÜLLER5. Fortunately for us, the studio's identity is stamped on the face of MÜLLER4 and on the back of the rest: "*Gebr. Ostermayr*" ("Ostermayr Bros.") of Munich.[1]

Having said that, we have reason to believe that Sanke did not obtain S444's photo directly from the Ostermayr brothers. Rather, it appears to have come from a well-known intermediary. As mentioned earlier, S444's unedited image appeared in the 26 August edition of *Berliner Illustrirte Zeitung.* The caption underneath named its source as "B.I.G.," Berliner Illustrations Gesellschaft. MÜLLER1 is the original photo from the company's files, and on the back is a typewritten message translated as "Warrant Officer Müller, one of our successful combat fliers, knight of the Iron Cross 1st and 2nd class, as well as the holder of various awards for bravery in the face of the enemy," which someone later appended with the handwritten ending, "achieved his 20th and 21st air victories." The photo's number (stamped on the back) indicates that it had been in Berliner Illustrations Gesellschaft's possession since late 1916 or early 1917; the added note shows that it was brought out again in August 1917. This timing coincides with *Berliner Illustrirte Zeitung*'s publication of the photo with a caption that similarly noted that *Offz-Stv.* Müller had defeated 21 of the enemy by 11 August.[2] When *Illustrierte Kriegs-Zeitung* announced Müller's promotion with the same image in late September, it too credited B.I.G. as its source, so there is no doubt that the firm possessed the photo and distributed it to others before Sanke brought out his modified version reflecting Müller's rise in rank.

S444, S552, and S553 all display the medals that Müller had received up to his Bavarian Silver Bravery Medal (awarded 18 February 1916) but not his Golden Military Merit Medal from Württemberg (28 June 1917) or his subsequent awards. This therefore dates the images to the rather wide timeframe of March 1916 to June 1917.

Notes

[1] Franz and Peter Ostermayr started a film production company in 1907 that later became one of Germany's largest studios, Die Bavaria Film- und Fernsehstudios GmbH. The Ostermayr Brothers studio where Müller had his pictures taken was probably started by them or their father, who had taught them professional photography.

[2] This is yet another example of how the accounts related in pictorial newspapers were generally a week or two behind current events, because Müller had actually brought down five more aircraft by the time his 21st was announced in the 26 August publication.

Two passages from Müller's letters home indicate that he had received little publicity before this time. The first, dated 9 June 1917, states:

> "This is to inform you that I shot down a triplane yesterday. Again it fell in a thousand pieces. The day before, at 8:15 in the morning, and at 12:00 noon I shot down a Spad on each occasion so that I have brought down 17 aircraft without dispute. Let that be put in the newspaper sometime. I am not going to do it. I don't know why it doesn't appear in the Army Communiqué. I think they are chagrined that an *Offizier-Stellvertreter* can shoot down 17 Englishmen. Or they are waiting until I become an officer." (O'Connor, *Aviation Awards IV*, p.185)

Someone must have heard him because just two days later he wrote:

> "Yesterday, I was mentioned in the Army Communiqué for my 14 victories, the others will appear later." (O'Connor, *Aviation Awards IV*, p.185)

Though it does seem curious that Müller had not received much attention in official communiqués and the press before this time, it further supports the notion that his S444 was published later in September rather than in March 1917, when he had a total of five victories and was relatively unknown to the public.

MÜLLER I

Top left: The original photo that someone altered to create S444 after Max Müller's promotion to *Leutnant*.

Top right: N6271, yet another modified version of S444's original image.

Opposite
Top two, and bottom left: Three images from a photo session at the Ostermayr Brothers' studio in Munich. Then *Sergeant* Max Müller proudly displays his most recent decoration, Bavaria's Military Merit Cross, 3rd Class with Crown and Swords, that he won on 14 January 1915. His next award, the Iron Cross 1st Class, came the following March or April 1915, but he is not wearing it here (though it was later drawn into the last picture). The "*Gebr. Ostermayr*" stamp is plainly visible at the bottom of the final image. (photos courtesy of UTD)

Bottom right: This snapshot better displays the background also seen in Müller's S444. Müller is now wearing the Iron Cross 1st Class he won in March or April 1915 and his Bavarian Military Merit Cross, 3rd Class is represented by a buttonhole ribbon. His shoulder boards carry metal, rather than sewn-on, *Fliegertruppe* insignia, an indication of the *Offizier-Stellvertreter* rank he was raised to on 9 November 1915. There is no sign of the Bavarian Bravery Medal in Silver that he won on 18 February 1916, so this picture was taken some time in between. The identity of the other *Offizier-Stellvertreter* next to Müller is unknown. (photo courtesy of UTD)

MÜLLER2

MÜLLER3

MÜLLER4

MÜLLER5

S445
KIRMAIER
Stefan
Oberleutnant

Taken: July to November 1916
Publ: February 1917
Reason: victory score and memorial

Decorations:
WR: Iron Cross, 1st Class; Pilot's Badge (Bav)
MB: None
RB: None
BH: Military Merit Order, 4th Class/ Sw (Bav); Iron Cross, 2nd Class;
Order of the Zähringer Lion, Knight 2nd Class/ Sw (Bad)

Other Cards:
None

Key Dates:
11 Jul 1916	receives Pilot's Badge
9 Oct 1916	assigned to *Jasta 2*
30 Oct 1916	CO of *Jasta 2*
1 Nov 1916	victory #8
22 Nov 1916	killed in action

A very young *Uffz.* Max Müller before the war. (photo courtesy of UTD)

Unser erfolgreicher Kampf-Flieger
Oberleutnant Kirmaier

445
Postkartenvertrieb W.Sanke
, BERLIN N.37.,
Nachdruck wird gerichtlich verfolgt.

Lt. Stefan Kirmaier was serving with Bavaria's *Infanterie-Regiment 'Grossherzog Friedrich II. von Baden' Nr.8* at Verdun when he was seriously wounded on 28 October 1914. His surviving medical records describe in detail how a bullet traversed his face, entering the right cheek just below the upper jaw and exiting along the lower left jaw line.[1] Though he was able to leave a Metz hospital on 22 December 1914, his recovery continued at two Munich facilities until 18 August 1915, when it was judged that he would be "*garnisondienstfähig*" ("fit for garrison duty") in four weeks and "*felddienstfähig*" ("fit for field duty") two weeks after that. Kirmaier was indeed posted to a reserve infantry unit near Metz on 11 September 1915, but sometime thereafter was accepted by Bavaria's Schleissheim school for flight training. After being promoted to *Oberleutnant* on 14 January 1916, he went to *Kasta 33*, a unit attached to *Kampfgeschwader 6*, on 1 April 1916. Once there, he quickly distinguished himself on several combat missions.

Kirmaier's career as a fighter pilot began on 10 June 1916 when he was assigned to fly a Fokker *Eindecker* with the *Artillerie-Flieger-Abteilung 203* detachment that later became known as *KEK Jametz*. Within a week, Kirmaier met the great Oswald Boelcke, who had flown over from Sivry at the special request of *KEK Jametz*'s CO. Boelcke later wrote:

"But there was another quite decent show that day. Section 203 of the artillery fliers had orders to photograph all the French artillery positions at Belleville and west of Verdun. Captain Vogt wanted to cross the lines in squadron formation and asked two other Fokkers and myself to come along as escorts. I was only too happy to help him. I flew across with their squadron, and as I kept pretty close to them I was on the spot when two French scouts attacked the squadron. The first did not get to grips, but the second dived straight on to the biplane containing Captain Vogt. As the latter was scanning the ground below through his glasses, he did not notice the Frenchman coming down; moreover his pilot only caught sight of him at the last moment and went into such a steep turn in his fright that Vogt was nearly jolted out of the cockpit. Then I came to the rescue and engaged the Frenchman. My word, how suddenly he cleared off! I hardly got him in my sights – he zigzagged about, with me behind him. I gave him a good burst when we were down to eighteen hundred metres and then left him alone – he did not worry my squadron again." (Werner, *Knight of Germany*, pp.177-78)

KIRMAIER1 is a photograph taken of Boelcke, Kirmaier, and other *Artillerie-Flieger-Abteilung 203* members around the time of this mission.

Kirmaier shot down his first three planes the next month, formally earning his Pilot's Badge the same day as his second victory on 11 July 1916.[2] His success brought him a place in one of the earliest *Jagdstaffeln*, *Jasta 6*, when it was formed on 25 August. On 9 October, he was transferred to Oswald Boelcke's *Jasta 2*, where he bagged the remainder of his 11 total victories. After Boelcke's death on 28 October, Kirmaier was selected to replace him as the unit's *Staffelführer*. Victory number eight, which hitherto had brought the *Pour le Mérite* to other pilots with such a total, fell a few days later on 1 November. It appears, however, that Kirmaier just missed winning the illustrious order because the qualifying count – perhaps that very day – had been raised to 16 (see the discussion of Berr's S425-26). He also did not live to see the award that normally preceded it, for the announcement of his receipt of the Royal Hohenzollern House Order came on the day he was killed in combat on 22 November 1916. His victor, Capt. John O. Andrews of RFC No.24 Squadron, later recalled in an interview:

"In my log book I have an account of this fight so I am not entirely relying on my memory. I was coming back I think alone; why I should be alone I can't imagine, whether the other people had dropped out of the show, for we very rarely went out alone across the lines. Coming back from the Bapaume direction across towards Amiens, and suddenly looking up, between me and the lines were six Hun Albatri about 500 feet above me and I thought oh dear, oh dear, this does not look too good. Above me, what do they do now? While I was thinking this out, they still came on...But they just flew steadily on. I looked at them and thought oh dear, oh dear, these must be Huns following their flight commander who is taking them along just his side of the lines showing them the country, and giving them an afternoon's outing. So I'll nip in on this and as they went over, I climbed behind them and shot down the bloke at the rear, or towards the rear, and then before they could do anything about

it, I stuffed my old nose down for the ground, because I was up at their height, then and fled for home. I wasn't going to take on any more for one was enough, and that apparently was Kirmaier." (O'Connor, *Aviation Awards VI*, pp.169-70)

Kirmaier was killed by a single shot to the head.

Kirmaier received four of his five decorations seen in S445 before 1916 while serving in Bavaria's 8th Infantry Regiment. As noted earlier, however, his Pilot's Badge came later in July 1916, which means that the photograph was taken sometime afterward but obviously before his death in November.

The cards surrounding S445 make it fairly certain that it was issued after Kirmaier's death, yet it shows no overt sign of being a memorial card. We shall see that several other cards that came out after a pilot's death similarly bore no death cross or black border, so it appears that such devices were generally reserved for the "greats" such as Boelcke, Immelmann, and Richthofen.[3] Our guideline predicts that S445 first appeared around late February 1917, and we can only speculate why it was published three months after Kirmaier's fall. Perhaps it took this long to obtain the photo. Whatever the underlying explanation, it seems clear that he was featured because of his outstanding record. Kirmaier was tied for sixth place among Germany's leading scorers when he was killed, and by the time that S445 was published three months later, only three more pilots had surpassed him.

Notes

[1] The resulting scars, evident in several other photographs (e.g., see O'Connor, *Aviation Awards VI*, p.167), were erased from S445's portrait.

[2] Before and during the early days of the war, German military airmen had to pass a series of formal tests at flight school before being granted their Pilot's Badge. As the war progressed, it appears

Below: *Hptm.* Oswald Boelcke in the company of members of *Artillerie-Flieger-Abteilung 203*, presumably at their base near Jametz. He had been invited over from Sivry by their CO, *Hptm.* Vogt (possibly third from the right, front row), to provide them with fighter protection during a reconnaissance mission that, according to Boelcke's correspondence home, occurred at some point between 12 and 18 June 1916. This snapshot was probably taken around then. Note that *Oblt.* Stefan Kirmaier (second from the right, front row), who had joined the unit on 10 June shortly before the mission, is not wearing his Pilot's Badge – something he would not earn until 11 July 1916.

that combat experience also played an increasingly important role in the award. In some cases, the exigencies of war delayed final examination until after a pilot had already flown in combat. But in others, combat experience became a prerequisite, either as a substitute for one or more of these tests or as an added requirement. In fact, some fighter pilot's like Kirmaier did not officially win their Pilot's Badge until after they had shot down one or more airplanes.

[3] Fahlbusch's S418 and Rosencrantz's S419 seem to be the only exceptions. Otherwise, we have the following posthumous cards without death symbols: Nathanael S537, Schulte S547, Keudell S555-56, Wendelmuth S594, Tutschek S650, Schreiber S661, and Collin S665. Other possible candidates are Mulzer S396-98, Manschott S448-49, Festner S510, and Eisenmenger and Gund S636.

S446
MÜLLER
Hans Karl
Leutnant

Taken: February 1917
Berlin, by Rudolf Dührkoop
Publ: March 1917
Reason: victory score

Decorations:
WR: Iron Cross, 1st Class; Pilot's Badge
MB: None
RB: Iron Cross, 2nd Class; unknown
BH: None

Other Cards:
S447
(N6229)
Note: Taken same time as S447

S447
MÜLLER
Hans Karl
Leutnant

Taken: February 1917
Berlin, by Rudolf Dührkoop
Publ: March 1917
Reason: victory score

Decorations:
WR: Iron Cross, 1st Class; Pilot's Badge
MB: None
RB: Iron Cross, 2nd Class; unknown
BH: None

Other Cards:
S446
(N6229)
Note: Taken same time as S446

Key Dates:
26 Dec 1916   wounded in action
14 Jan 1917   promoted to *Leutnant*

While serving with *Kampstaffel 11* (part of *Kampfgeschwader 2*), Hans Müller may have been the victor in an air battle near Verdun on 26 March 1916. Though some sources cite this as his first victory,

On 31 October 1916, after Oswald Boelcke's funeral cortège had arrived at Cambrai's train station, "the coffin lay in state once more before the draped railway carriage, while General von Below delivered an oration in the name of the Emperor and Lieut. Kirmaier spoke on behalf of Jagdstaffel 2." (Werner, *Knight of Germany*, p.234) Among the photos accompanying S363†, one captured Kirmaier delivering his speech. In this one, Kirmaier (fourth from the left) watches while Prof. Max Bölcke receives condolences from Crown Prince Rupprecht of Bavaria. Standing behind the Professor are two of his sons, namesake Max (wearing a service cap) and either Heinrich or Martin (in the *Tschako* helmet).

Unser erfolgreicher Kampf-Flieger
Leutnant Hans Müller

it apparently was not officially recognized as such because Müller's *Ehrenbecher* (a metal goblet usually awarded to airmen after their first victory) was given to him on 14 July 1916 following his 9 July downing of a balloon while flying a Fokker *Eindecker* with *KEK Avillers*. This was only the second time in the war that a German single-seater had officially destroyed one of the "gasbags" (*Lt.* Otto Parschau had claimed the first just six days earlier on 3 July).[1] Müller scored again with *KEK Avillers* before it was reorganized as *Jasta 5* under the command of *Oblt.* Hans Berr on 21 August 1916. Müller became its "big gun" when he secured the unit's first two victories by the end of the month, bringing his official total to four – two more than Berr had at the time. Müller's record becomes confused at this point, though it appears that he maintained his lead over his CO until at least the end of October. Berr shot down an airplane and a balloon on 26 October, giving him the all-important total of eight that also brought him the last *Pour le Mérite* awarded before the qualifying total was raised to 16 (see the discussion of Berr's S425-26). Various sources list Müller with anywhere from seven to nine victories by this time. If he had been officially credited with eight or more, he probably would have become one of the war's earliest recipients of Prussia's Golden Military Merit Cross – the enlisted man's equivalent of the *Pour le Mérite*.[2] It was not to be, however, and after two (some say three) more successes his combat service came to a close when he suffered a severe abdominal wound during a 26 December 1916 dogfight. While recovering, he was promoted to *Leutnant* on 14 January 1917.[3] He eventually worked as a test pilot for the Siemens-Schuckert company until *Hptm.* Adolf *Ritter* von Tutschek had him assigned to *Jagdgeschwader Nr.2* as its Technical Officer in early February 1918. Müller was posted out in March 1918 after *Hptm.* Rudolf Berthold came on board as Tutschek's replacement. Müller reportedly went back to Siemens-Schuckert until the end of the war.

We have three contemporaneous photos of Müller: S446, S447, and HMÜLLER1. HMÜLLER1 comes from the files of A. Grohs Illustrations Verlag, as does HMÜLLER2, the image behind S447; and both are identified with the consecutive numbers "3613a" and "3613b." This and the fact that Müller's appearance is identical in them all confirms that they originated from the same sitting. Müller's *Leutnant* insignia date the images to some time after his promotion on 14 January 1917, and his apparently fit condition after his recovery from the stomach wound he received the day after Christmas most likely pushes the time out even further. If the March publication date predicted by our guideline is correct, then these three photos were most likely taken in February 1917.

The forest-patterned wallpaper behind Müller in S447 discloses where they were taken. It makes a separate appearance in Althaus' S430-31 series (as well as Höhne's S524-25). A little-known booklet entitled *Deutsche Heldenflieger* printed the top half of S431 and named "R. Dührkoop, Berlin" as the photographer (see the discussion of Althaus' S430-31). An autographed copy of S446 confirms Müller's presence in the area because it lists his address as Charlottenburg – a Berlin suburb.[4] It is possible that this is where he lived while working at the Siemens-Schuckert plant in Berlin.

The reverse of HMÜLLER2 bears the usual notice "*Alle Rechte vorbehalten*" ("all rights reserved"), but a separate stamped message also states: "*Bei Veröffentlichung dieses Bildes mache es zur Bedingung, dass meine Firma nicht genannt wird*" ("In case of publication of this picture, make it a condition that my firm is not named"). This curious stipulation also occurs on the back of BÖHME1 (see S502) – another photo known to have originated from an independent source. Was this the result of the kind of arrangement normally reached between A. Grohs and private sources, a reflection of the fact that the A. Grohs firm did not possess full copyright to such photos, or was it even an evasive tactic to avoid detection? Interestingly, HMÜLLER1-2 numerically precede Böhme's photo

(No.3614) in A. Grohs' system, whose reverse stated: "*der bereits bis zum 1. März sein 12. Flugz. Heruntergeschossen hatte*" ("who had already shot down his 12th airplane by 1 March"). This suggests that A. Grohs obtained all three images in March 1917, a little later than Sanke.

The identity of the second decoration seen on Müller's ribbon bar is unknown. Given that Müller hailed from the Saxon district of Loschwitz, just outside of Dresden, it is likely that it was a Saxon award; and if so, its dark gray and white striped appearance would match up with either the Albert Order (for officers) or the Albert Cross (for non-commissioned officers), both of which came on a grass green, white striped ribbon.

Notes

[1] Franks, Bailey, and Guest, *Above the Lines*, p.135 notes that Josef Jacobs reportedly claimed a balloon on 22 March 1916, whereas O'Connor, *Aviation Awards V*'s extensive biography of Jacobs (pp.23-60) based on several personal interviews never mentions the claim. Jacobs himself marked his *Ehrenbecher* (see O'Connor, p.36) with the details of his 12 May 1916 victory over a French Caudron G.IV, which clearly indicates that either the balloon incident never occurred or that it was never officially confirmed.

[2] The first award of Prussia's Golden Military Merit Cross went to *Vzfw.* Georg Dülz on October 15, 1916. The second did not occur until 14 June 1917.

[3] The reverse of A. Grohs' S447 photo relates: *"Flieger Hans Müller, der kürzlich infolge seiner Tapferkeit zum Leutnant befördert wurde, er hat 8 Flugzeuge und 7 Fesselballon heruntergeschossen."* ("Pilot Hans Müller, who was recently promoted to 2nd Lieutenant because of his bravery, shot down eight aircraft and seven balloons"). One wonders if Müller's unofficial total of 15 victories was conveyed to Sanke as well. If it had been a confirmed total, it would have placed Müller in a tie for fifth place with Frankl, Immelmann, and Baldamus, behind Boelcke (40), Manfred von Richthofen (32), Werner Voss (22), and Kurt Wintgens (19), making Müller an even more attractive candidate for one of Sanke's postcards.

[4] Müller kept a letter from one young admirer that perhaps typifies many of those sent to other German aviators during the war:

"Heidenau
28 January 1918

Dear Lieutenant:
The World War has shown us many brave heroes whom we highly revere. I read in the newspaper with great eagerness of our brave flying heroes, and I have started a collection of autographs and ask also you to grant the simple wish of a German youth who is completely filled with a deep love for the Fatherland, by inscribing your autograph on the picture side of the enclosed pictures. I would very much like something by which I can remember our heroes of the air and hope that you will grant my wish. With greatest appreciation and respect.

Rich. Wagner" (C&C 23:4, p. 372)

An autographed example of S446 that was sent to another Heidenau resident, a "Paul Büttner," has survived to this day. Heidenau is just on the outskirts of Dresden, so the word evidently got out that their local hero would sign pictures upon request.

HMÜLLER1

HMÜLLER2

Nos.3613a and 3613b from the files of A. Grohs Illustrations Verlag. The first was taken in sequence with S446 and S447, while the second is the original image behind S447.

S448
MANSCHOTT
Friedrich
Vizefeldwebel

Taken: January to February 1917
Publ: March 1917
Reason: victory score

Decorations:
WR: Iron Cross, 1st Class; Pilot's Badge
MB: None
RB: None
BH: None

Other Cards:
S449
(N6196)
Note: Taken same time as S449

Another stamp from the series issued to raise money for a pilots' charity fund (see Parschau's S380) that employed a portion of MÜLLER 1. Though identified here as copyrighted by Sanke, this particular image never appeared on any Sanke postcard known to us today.

S449
MANSCHOTT
Friedrich
Vizefeldwebel

Taken: January to February 1917
Procher?
Publ: March 1917
Reason: victory score

Decorations:
WR: Iron Cross, 1st Class; Pilot's Badge
MB: None
RB: None
BH: None

Other Cards:
S448
(N6196)
Note: Taken same time as S448

Key Dates:

Jan 1917	transferred to *Jasta* 7
16 Mar 1917	killed in action
18 Mar 1917	S449 photo published in *Berliner Illustrirte Zeitung* 11, p.146
21 March 1917	S448 photo published in *Flugsport* 6, p.177
c.25 Mar 1917	S449 photo published in *Illustrierte Kriegs-Zeitung* 138, p.5

c.8 Apr 1917   S449 photo published in *Illustrierte Kriegs-Zeitung* 140, p.8

Vzfw. Friedrich Manschott was serving with *Flieger-Abteilung (A) 203* when he had his first taste of victory on 15 December 1916. Soon thereafter he was transferred to *Jasta 7*, and from then on he scored at an ever increasing pace: two victories in January, four in February (one unconfirmed) to become *Jasta* 7's first ace, and six in March. Three of his final four successes were over balloons, giving him the distinction of becoming one of the most successful early "balloon busters" in the German Air Service.[1] His meteoric rise came to an abrupt end on 16 March, however, when immediately after his last balloon victory he tangled with four French Caudrons and was shot down and killed. His brief career nevertheless brought him considerable notoriety. Manschott's S448 image was printed in the 21 March 1917 edition of *Flugsport,* and his S449 photo was included in the 18 March and c.25 March editions of two illustrated newspapers. All three noted his eighth victory (which occurred on 2 March) in their captions but not his demise – another example of the delay often seen in reporting such events.[2] That announcement followed in the c.8 April 1917 edition of *Illustrierte Kriegs-Zeitung,* again accompanied by S449's image. His death also merited a special announcement in *Nachrichtenblatt der Luftsteitkräfte Nr.4*:

> "On 16 March, Vzfw. Manschott of Jasta 7 died a hero's death in air combat for his Fatherland, shortly after destroying an enemy captive balloon. He had eleven victories in all, having destroyed eight airplanes and three captive balloons. A glorious end for the young airman! Vfw. Manschott, who had just recently completed his 24th year of life, had been a pilot since 24 April 1915. He received his pilot's badge on 10 August 1916. Among Prussian decorations, he held the Iron Cross, First and Second Class. The entire Air Service mourns this young, successful comrade!" (OTF 14:2, p.169)

When Josef Jacobs took over the command of *Jasta 7* about five months after Manschott's death in August 1917, he still recalled that Manschott was "one of the most celebrated flyers of this *Jagdstaffel*" (C&C 6:4, p.309).

The pictures featured in S448-49 were taken at the same time at what seems to be an airfield. S448 depicts Manschott in front of an Albatros D.II with serial number D.1746/16, while S449 shows him standing in front of what appears to be a canvas structure of some sort – possibly a tent hangar. The scenes may be from Procher where *Jasta 7* was stationed between 2 November 1916 and 4 May 1917. Whatever their place of origin, we can deduce that they were taken in close sequence because Manschott's appearance is the same in both right down to the precisely identical folds in his service cap. Given the presence of the Albatros fighter in S448 and the absence of the "203" patch seen on his arm in N6196, we can also assume that they were snapped during Manschott's tenure with *Jasta 7*, which began in January 1917. For S449's image to have appeared in an early March Sanke card, it probably had to have been taken no later than February.

Notes
    [1] *Ltn.* Otto Parschau's last two victories were over balloons on 3 and 9 July 1916. *Vzfw.* Hans Karl Müller shot down two on 9 July and 31 August 1916. The following pilots had brought down a single balloon each before March 1917: *Oblt.* Stefan Kirmaier (11 July 1916); *Lt.* Renatus Theiller and *Oblt.* Otto Schmidt (11 July); *Uffz.* Alfred Ulmer (1 October); *Vzfw.* Weichel (21 October); *Oblt.* Hans Berr (26 October); *Vzfw.* Walter Göttsch (14 November); *Uffz.* Hans

Unser erfolgreicher Kampf-Flieger
Vfw. Manschott
449
Postkartenvertrieb W. Sanke
BERLIN N.37.
Nachdruck wird gerichtlich verfolgt.

Körner (10 January 1917); *Lt.* Lothar Rehm (14 February). A balloon-busting flurry then followed in March with 17 of the inflatables shot down: *Lt.* Renatus Theiller (1 March); Manschott (4, 9, 16 March); *Lt.* Werner Albert (9 March); *Lt.* Robert Dycke (10 March); *Lt.* Walter von Bülow-Bothkamp (11 March); *Vzfw.* Schendel (11 March); *Oberflugmeister* Kurt Schönfelder (11 March); *Lt.* Wilhelm Allmenröder (16 March); *Oblt.* Fritz von Bronsart und Schellendorf (16 March); *Feldwebelleutnant* Fritz Schubert (16 March); *Lt.* Erich Loewenhardt (24, 28 March); *Lt.* Rudolf Matthaei (24 March); *Vzfw.* Ulbrich (28 March); *Lt.* Otto Brauneck (31 March). Manschott and other *Jasta 7* pilots led the way, accounting for seven of these destroyed balloons, and getting special mention by *Oberstleutnant* Hermann Thomsen in *Nachrichtenblatt der Luftstreitkräfte Nr. 7* (see OTF 14:3, p.266).
    [2] The back of the S449 photo owned by Berliner Illustrations Gesellschaft (the probable source for the newspaper pictures) similarly noted: "*Vizefeldwebel Manschott, der kürzlich im Heeresbericht als Sieger mit 8 feindlichen Flugzeugen erwähnt wurde*" ("Vice-Sergeant Manschott, who was recently mentioned in the Army Report as the victor over eight enemy aircraft").

Berliner Illustrations Gesellschaft's photo No.16665, a print from the original image behind S449.

Another portrait of *Vzfw.* Friedrich Manschott, this time from Berlin's R. Sennecke Internationaler Illustrations Verlag, No.2961. Along with this identification, the reverse also carries the phrase, *"Mitglied des Verbandes Deutscher Illustrations Photographen"* ("Member of the Federation of German Illustration Photographers"). Many of the photos published in German illustrated newspapers of the day identified Sennecke as their source.

S450
RICHTHOFEN
Manfred *Freiherr* von

Taken: 2 to 3 February 1917
Berlin, by C. J. von Dühren
Publ: March 1917
Reason: *Pour le Mérite* award, victory score

Decorations:
WR: *Pour le Mérite*; Iron Cross, 1st Class; Pilot's Badge
MB: Iron Cross, 2nd Class; Royal Hohenzollern House Order, Knight's Cross/ Sw; Oval Silver Duke Carl Eduard Medal/date clasp and Sw (SCG); Military Merit Cross, 3rd Class/ war decoration (AH)
RB: None
BH: None

Other Cards:
S503, S509, S511, S519, S532-34, S554, S606, S619
(L7835, L7846, L7847, L7894, L7895, L7898, L7932, L7933; N6255, N6306)
Note: Taken same time as S503
Cipher for former unit, *Ulanen-Regiment 'Kaiser Alexander III. von Russland (westpreussisches)' Nr.1*, on shoulder boards

Key Dates:

12 Jan 1917	awarded *Pour le Mérite*
2 Feb 1917	arrives in Berlin for meeting
4 Feb 1917	arrives in Schweidnitz
23 Mar 1917	promoted to *Oberleutnant*
7 Apr 1917	S503 photo published in *Die Woche* 14, p.461
15 May 1917	next trip to Berlin

Thanks to his mother's diary, later published under the title *Mein Kriegstagebuch*, we are able to ascertain when *Lt.* Manfred von Richthofen posed for the photo presented in S450. Richthofen had been awarded the *Pour le Mérite* on 12 January 1917 – one year to the day after Boelcke and Immelmann had been granted theirs. His 16th kill on 4 January had doubled their qualifying count of eight and had made him Germany's most successful living ace.[1] He reported to his new command, *Jasta 11*, a few days later and compiled three more victories while showing them the ropes. The last of these fell on 1 February. On 4 February, Manfred's mother, *Freifrau* Kunigunde von Richthofen, wrote:

> "It is still early, the house sleeps, the bitter cold makes it good to be in bed. I believe I hear a sound. I turn on the light,

the clock shows seven in the morning. Then, the door quickly opens, and Manfred stands in front of my bed, fresh and happy, no trace of fatigue after the long night's journey. The blue star glitters at his throat – the *Pour le Mérite*. I hold his hand, speak, as if praising the boy: Bravo, you have done well, Manfred. And ask: How did you get in? Was the garden gate open? No, it wasn't, but it didn't matter. The Knight of the *Pour le Mérite* climbed over the fence…'Where have you been, Manfred?' A long-winded, less pleasant business. It has happened more frequently in recent times, that German fliers have had wings break off in the air. He wanted to call the attention of a competent authority in Berlin to these construction faults…Manfred has produced a *Berliner Zeitung* with yesterday's date and passes it to us. It is there written that he has shot down his 19th opponent." (Fischer, *Mother of Eagles*, pp.115-16)

Lower wing failures on the recently introduced Albatros D.III had led to the deaths of *Lt*. Hans Imelmann and *Vzfw*. Paul Ostrop – two of Richthofen's former squadron mates from *Jasta Boelcke* – on 23 January. The very next day, Richthofen (who had brought along his own D.III from *Jasta Boelcke*) also suffered a cracked lower wing but managed to land safely. Evidently, he took a trip to the Inspectorate of Miltary Aviation in Berlin to see what could be done about the problem.[2] He would not return again to the capital city until the following May.

S450 identifies C.J. von Dühren of Berlin as its photographer. Richthofen is wearing his *Pour le Mérite* in the picture, and we have an S450 example postmarked 10 March 1917; so the only occasion that Richthofen had to have this photo taken was during his 2-3 February visit to Berlin on his way home.[3] The discovery of another picture taken at the same sitting verifies this conclusion. A 1927 German calendar marked the anniversary of Richthofen's death with his portrait (MVR1) and a poem. The portrait depicts him in the same dark blue Uhlan dress outfit and decorations seen in S450. It is also signed and dated "22 February 1917" in what appears to be Richthofen's handwriting. We know that he was back at the Front by 14 February because he shot down his 20th and 21st victims that day; so clearly, the recorded date did not refer to when the image was taken. It more likely cataloged when it was presented or sent to someone. That someone may have been his mother, Baroness Kunigunde von Richthofen. The use of a person's first name in a photo dedication was normally reserved for only the closest family members; and this portrait has a more intimate feel than usual, capturing more of the young man than the warrior. We know that the Baroness possessed at least a copy of it because it was displayed in Manfred's room at Schweidnitz after the war.

The decorations displayed in S450 further point to a time preceding Richthofen's May visit to Berlin. The last to be received among them was his *Pour le Mérite*. Württemberg's Military Merit Order, Knight (13 April 1917), Saxony's Military St. Henry Order, Knight's Cross (16 April), and Bavaria's Military Merit Order (29 April) came next, but none of them is present in the photo. Lastly, Richthofen's shoulder boards are those of a *Leutnant* (only his regimental cipher is present on them), and Richthofen was promoted to *Oberleutnant* on 23 March 1917.

The discussion of S503 notes that it bears evidence of being another member of the S450 and MVR1 series. Its image appeared

in the 7 April 1917 edition of *Die Woche* – again, long before Richthofen's next visit to Berlin in mid-May. All signs therefore point to S450's photo being snapped during Richthofen's trip there on 2-3 February 1917. Three weeks later brings us to the end of Feburary, and we have a postmarked example of S450 dated 10 March 1917.

Notes

[1] Only two deceased pilots had better scores: Oswald Boelcke with 40 victories, and *Lt*. Kurt Wintgens with 19. Richthofen had surpassed *Lt*. Wilhelm Frankl (who would be shot down on 8 April 1917) and the late Max Immelmann, both of whom had 15.

[2] Richthofen's and other Albatros D.IIIs were later recalled from the Front to undergo certain modifications.

[3] Though it is also possible that he went through Berlin on his way back from Schweidnitz to the Front, we have no idea if he would have just passed through or indeed if he ever made such a trip.

MVR I

A more relaxed portrait of *Lt.* Manfred von Richthofen that was taken 2-3 February 1917 in Berlin, the same time as his more widely publicized S450 and S503 pictures. The accompanying picture and its magnified section demonstrate that the same portrait was hung in Richthofen's room at his home in Schweidnitz after it had been converted into a museum.

S450
(reissue)
RICHTHOFEN
Manfred *Freiherr* von
Rittmeister

Taken: 2 to 3 February 1917
Berlin, by C. J. von Dühren
Publ: late April or May 1917
Reason: promotion

Decorations:
WR: *Pour le Mérite*; Iron Cross, 1st Class; Pilot's Badge
MB: Iron Cross, 2nd Class; Royal Hohenzollern House Order, Knight's Cross/ Sw; Oval Silver Duke Carl Eduard Medal/date clasp and Sw (SCG); Military Merit Cross, 3rd Class/ war decoration (AH)
RB: None
BH: None

Other Cards:
S503, S509, S511, S519, S532-34, S554, S606, S619
(L7835, L7846, L7847, L7894, L7895, L7898, L7932, L7933; N6255, N6306)
Note: Taken same time as S503
Cipher for former unit, *Ulanen-Regiment 'Kaiser Alexander III. von Russland (westpreussisches)' Nr.1*, on shoulder boards

Key Dates:
6 Apr 1917	promoted to *Rittmeister*
21 Apr 1918	killed in action

Sanke released this updated version of S450 following Richthofen's promotion to *Rittmeister* on 6 April 1917. The image is identical to its predecessor's, so it appears that the purpose was to recognize Richthofen's new rank. It probably came out faster than the usual three weeks after an event because it was not dependent upon the attainment and preparation of a new photograph. Though it seems likely that it would have first appeared in May when Richthofen and his squadron were a "hot item," it theoretically could have been issued at any point after his promotion up to around the time of his death on 21 April 1918. Nevertheless, our postmarked example of Immelmann's S362-*Oblt.* indicates that such cards were issued soon after an airman's promotion. We would expect any post-death publication of a Richthofen card to have been marked with a "†" or a black border, as was the case with S503† and S532-34†.

S451
PFEIFER
Hermann
Leutnant

Taken: December 1916 to February 1917
Publ: March 1917
Reason: victory score

Decorations:
WR: Iron Cross, 1st Class; Pilot's Badge
MB: None
RB: None
BH: Iron Cross, 2nd Class

Other Cards:
S428
(N6205)

Rittmeister Manfred Frhr. von Richthofen

450
Postkartenvertrieb W. Sanke
BERLIN N. 37.
Nachdruck wird gerichtlich verfolgt.

Phot. C. J. von Dühren
BERLIN

Key Dates:
21 Nov 1916	promoted to *Leutnant*
2 Mar 1917	awarded Military Karl Friedrich Merit Order, Knight's Cross (Bad)
11 Mar 1917	victory #9
31 Mar 1917	photo of Pfeifer in Albatros fighter published in *Berliner Illustrirte Zeitung* 13, p.174
20 May 1917	killed in accident

Lt. Hermann Pfeifer appears in his off-duty dress *Litewka* in S451. He is wearing the identical outfit in PFEIFER2, a photo published in O'Connor, *Aviation Awards VI* (p.56) that originally came from the personal collection of Pfeifer's widow; and naturally so, because it was taken on their wedding day. A close comparison of S451 and PFEIFER2 indicates that they likely shared the same origin.[1] The dress sword that is plainly seen in S451 is just barely detectable in PFEIFER2: Pfeifer's right hand grasps the hilt and his left rests on its pommel. More significantly, his wedding band can be seen on the third finger of his right hand (in accordance with European custom) in both. Unfortunately, we do not know the day of their wedding ceremony, or we would have a precise date for S451's origin. Pfeifer is not wearing the Military Karl Friedrich Merit Order given to him by his native Baden on 2 March 1917. There also is no sign, however, of Baden's Silver Miltary Karl Friedrich Merit Medal that he received on 27 September 1916 before he became a *Leutnant*. As O'Connor pointed out, it appears that Pfeifer "chose to wear only a modest 'black and white' front for the occasion (meaning only his Prussian decorations)." Pfeifer's scoring record demonstrates that after his 21 November promotion to *Leutnant*, he was at the Front at least until 2 December (the date of his eighth victory) and again from at least 11 March (his ninth) until his death on 20 May when he crashed the captured Nieuport 17 he was test flying at *Jasta 9*'s Leffincourt airfield. Therefore, the best guess we can make is that S451 and PFEIFER2 were taken sometime during December 1916 to March 1917; but if our guideline is correct in placing S451's debut in March, the photos would have been taken no later than February 1917.

We cannot determine precisely why he was featured again in a Sanke card in early March after his prior appearance in S428. His tally had not increased since S428's January debut, and it would have been unusually fast work for Sanke to have been responding to the news of Pfeifer's Miltary Karl Friedrich Merit Order. Even the 31 March edition of *Berliner Illustrirte Zeitung* that featured a picture of Pfeifer in his Albatros fighter still only credited him with the same eight victories he had when S428 was issued. Perhaps it was the news of his marriage that brought him once again into the public eye. Whatever the reason, Hermann Pfeifer was honored by Sanke for the second and final time by S451.

Pfeifer's death was given special mention in *Nachrichtenblatt der Luftstreitkräfte Nr.14* by the army group to which his *Jasta 9* was attached:

Left: *Lt.* Hermann Pfeifer and his bride, Paula, on their wedding day. Above: Pfeifer in his Albatros, as presented in the 31 March 1917 edition of *Berliner Illustrirte Zeitung*.

PFEIFER2

"On the morning of 20 May, Ltn. Pfeifer of Jagdstaffel 9 crashed to his death in the vicinity of the Leffincourt Airfield, as a result of engine failure. In him, the 3. Armee loses one of its most successful fighter pilots, the day after he had brought down his 12th opponent. Unvanquished, like Ltn. Baldamus, he too has met his death. We honor the memory of the fallen air hero in grateful admiration at what he achieved for us, and in the proud conviction that the spirit which inspired him will forever live on in our airmen." (OTF 16:2, p.180)

Note

¹ There are some notable differences, however. The foliage in their backgrounds is similar, but not a match, and Pfeifer is seated in S451 in a different chair than the one occupied by his bride in PFEIFER2.

S452-501

THE GAP

This is another one of the mysteries presented by the Sanke series. No example of a Sanke card numbered S452 through S501 has ever been brought to light. Did Sanke reserve S452-501 for another series that never came about? If so, and if he wanted to set aside an even 50 spots, why did he choose such odd beginning and end points? We have evidence to suggest that Sanke's series was interrupted chronologically as well. One example of Richthofen's S450 (S451's immediate predecessor) displays a 10 March 1917 date, whereas Böhme's S502 – by virtue of its photograph being taken in late March – does not appear to have come out until late April. So a break as long as almost two months may have occurred in Sanke's publication timeline between S451 and S502. Interestingly, there are signs that a similar two-month break could have occurred one year later, except that in this instance the numbers carried on continuously (this will be discussed more fully in the next planned volume). Does this mean that Sanke closed shop around this time of year for a holiday or some other now unknown reason? If so, it still does not explain why numbers S452 through S501 were never used. Perhaps their absence was due to something as innocent as a clerical error or even a lapse in memory (following a two-month break?) where a confused printer vaguely remembered the last published card as 5-0-1 instead of 4-5-1 and mistakenly continued with 502. Unfortunately, we might never solve this gap's mystery because it appears that no additional information has survived to help explain it.

S502
BÖHME
Erwin
Leutnant

Taken: 18 to 31 March 1917
Düsseldorf, by Ella Kohlschein
Publ: April 1917
Reason: victory score

Decorations:
WR: Iron Cross, 1st Class; Pilot's Badge
MB: None
RB: Royal Hohenzollern House Order, Knight's Cross/ Sw; Iron Cross, 2nd Class; War Merit Cross, 2nd Class (Brun); Military Merit Cross, 3rd Class/ war decoration (AH)
BH: None

Unser erfolgreicher Kampf-Flieger Leutnant Böhme
502
Postkartenvertrieb W.Sanke
BERLIN N.37.
Nachdruck wird gerichtlich verfolgt.

Other Cards:
None

Key Dates:

11 Feb 1917	wounded in left arm
11 Mar 1917	awarded Royal Hohenzollern House Order, Knight's Cross/ Sw
18 Mar 1917	goes to Düsseldorf
6 Apr 1917	returns to the Front

In a 14 February 1917 letter to his fiancée, Annamarie Brüning, who worked as a nurse in Hamburg, *Lt.* Erwin Böhme furnished the details of how he had been wounded three days earlier:

"In school, in calligraphy, I usually received a 'III' or 'IV' – today you would grade me even worse. That's because I am writing to you in bed. My left hand is of no use in holding the sheet of paper still. The bed from which I am writing is in a field hospital in Cambrai. I find myself to be in a field hospital because of a malevolent Englishman, who, the day before yesterday and who by all rights should no longer be alive, treacherously shot me in the left arm. It was a two-seater Sopwith which I had already put out of action and who was headed downward. For that reason, I spared him in a burst of sportsmanlike grace – that's what I get for my noblesse!" (OTF 5:1, p.49)[1]

Another letter from Böhme to his fiancée, dated 17 March 1917, informs us that he was sent to Düsseldorf the next day to complete his recovery:

"Yesterday I finally escaped from the physicians with a jump for joy. I even flew a consolation honor lap over the field today, but it went only moderately well. My arm is still stiff and cannot be completely straightened. As a result, I still have to go for follow-up treatment (orthopedic exercises) in the interior, in fact to Düsseldorf. I suggested that they send me to Hamburg, but the right kind of orthopedic specialist (a beautiful German word!) supposedly is not there. Nevertheless, I will go to Düsseldorf gladly, because there I will find my dear brother in-law's folks, the Kohlscheins…Already tomorrow I will arrive at the Rhine [which flows through Düsseldorf]…Last Sunday, the General of the Air Force surprised me with a telegram reporting that the Kaiser had awarded me the Hohenzollern House Order with Swords. I have been walking around almost one week now with this decoration." (Werner, *Briefe eines Kampffliegers*, pp.97-98, trans. by this writer)

Böhme's brother, Gerhard, was married to the daughter of Hans and Ella Kohlschein; and Hans was a professor and professional artist. Böhme visited his brother's in-laws often during his stay in Düsseldorf, but then had to report back to the Front on 6 April. In a letter dated the day before his departure, he wrote:

"Dear Miss Annamarie,
I am sitting here at my desk with a very gloomy face. Instead of planning for the ongoing trip to Hamburg, I must plan for a return trip to the front tomorrow." (OTF 17:2, p.142)

In another letter written on 21 November 1917 – just one week before his death in combat – Böhme disclosed the origin of S502's photograph:

"Enclosed immediately is a reciprocal gift. Yesterday while rummaging I came across a whole pile of picture postcards of 'Our successful fighter pilot *Leutnant* Böhme' based upon a photograph taken by Ella Kohlschein. They are from a Berlin art store which publishes a whole series of 'Heroes' Postcards. I am sending a dozen to you presently, so that you do not need to rob the Hamburg shop windows of their decorations." (OTF 11:1, p.15)

BÖHME1 is a copy of Ella Kohlschein's photograph that was once owned by A. Grohs Illustrations Verlag. The caption "*Leutnant Böhme, der bereits bis zum 1. März sein 12. Flugzeug heruntergeschossen hatte*" ("2nd Lieutenant Böhme, who had already shot down his 12th airplane by 1 March") occurs on its reverse. This suggests that it had come into A. Grohs' possession sometime after early March but before Böhme's next score in July, possibly in time to serve as Sanke's source. Like HMÜLLER2 (see Hans Müller's S447), another A. Grohs image known to have originated from an independent photographer, BÖHME1 also bears the curious stamped

message: "*Bei Veröffentlichung dieses Bildes mache es zur Bedingung, dass meine Firma nicht genannt wird*" ("In case of publication of this picture, make it a condition that my firm is <u>not</u> named"). Once again, we are left to speculate on whether this phrase denoted some form of deference to Kohlschein's original ownership or possibly even an evasive technique to prevent Kohlschein from tracing any unauthorized publication back to A. Grohs.

Professor Hans Kohlschein painted several portraits of Böhme that still exist today.[2] BÖHME2 is the one that most closely resembles S502, and in the collection of Böhme's letters entitled *Briefe eines deutschen Kampffliegers an ein junges Mädchen*, it is identified as "Erwin Böhme in March 1917 in Düsseldorf" (see the caption in BÖHME2). Ella Kohlschein had taken S502's picture during Böhme's March visit so that her husband could refer\to it while painting his portrait.[3]

According to our three-week rule, a picture taken in the last half of March 1917 would not have appeared in a Sanke card until the last half of April. Our guideline complies with this timeframe and predicts a late April 1917 debut for S502.

Böhme, a faithful writer, sent his fiancée a scenic postcard of the land around Solling on 28 November 1917:

"In the spring we should look for primroses in this meadow, dearest! We can rove about the entire day without meeting any annoying people. How I look forward to it!
Now I am waiting for your new picture, but more so for the day I myself will see you again." (OTF 11:1, p.17)

The next morning, he dashed off a quick note:

"My love! Now just a quick affectionate morning greeting! The *Staffel* is already waiting for me. This evening I will write a proper letter to you." (OTF 11:1, p.17)

Böhme never strolled the fields of Solling with Annamarie, nor did he live to write the evening letter he had promised. During his second patrol of the afternoon and shortly after achieving his 24th victory, he was shot down in flames behind enemy lines and buried there in an unmarked grave.

Notes
[1] In the third installment of his series of articles on Böhme (OTF 17:2, pp.137-38), *Dr. Ing.* Niedermeyer notes that Werner's *Briefe eines deutschen Kampffliegers an ein junges Mädchen* misreported the date of this letter as 13 February 1917 when it was actually written on 14 February.
[2] Hans Kohlschein was a well-known artist during the war who also did illustrations for pictorial newspapers such as *Die Wochenschau* (e.g., see the center spread in the 10 June 1916 edition, pp.752-53).
[3] Evidently, Professor Kohlschein did not faithfully follow all the details, because the color version of the painting presented on the cover of OTF 11:1 shows that he not only replaced Böhme's Royal Hohenzollern House Order ribbon (with crown and swords device) with what appears to be Bavaria's Military Merit Order ribbon (also with crown and swords device), but that he also switched its position with the adjacent Iron Cross ribbon. No doubt he followed a certain degree of artistic license.

Erwin Böhme
im März 1917 in Düsseldorf
Ölbild von Prof. Hans Kohlschein

Above: Image No.3614 from A. Grohs Illustrations Verlag – a print from Ella Kohlschein's original photograph.

Top right: An oil painting of *Lt.* Erwin Böhme by Hans Kohlschein. It was based on a photograph taken by Kohlschein's wife, Ella, in the last half of March 1917 while Böhme was recuperating near their home in Düsseldorf.

Right: After Böhme's death in combat on 29 November 1917, Kohlschein added a *Pour le Mérite*, a brief dedication, and his signature to the painting.

Lt. Erwin Böhme achieved his sixth victory on 9 November 1916 when he wounded the pilot, Capt. T. Maplebeck, of FE.8 No.7624 (RFC No.40 Squadron) and forced him to land near Arleux. The same plane was later transported to *Jastaschule I* at Fâmars (see Zander's S407).

S503
RICHTHOFEN
Manfred *Freiherr* von
Rittmeister

Taken: 2 to 3 February 1917
Berlin, by C. J. von Dühren
Publ: April 1917
Reason: post-*Pour le Mérite*

Decorations:
WR: *Pour le Mérite*
MB: None
RB: None
BH: None

Other Cards:
S450, S509, S511, S519, S532-34, S554, S606, S619
(L7835, L7846, L7847, L7894, L7895, L7898, L7932, L7933;
N6255, N6306)
Note: Taken same time as S450

Key Dates:
12 Jan 1917	awarded *Pour le Mérite*
2 Feb 1917	arrives in Berlin for meeting
4 Feb 1917	arrives in Schweidnitz

A ceremony was held at Dessau's war cemetery on 28 October 1917 to commemorate the first anniversary of Oswald Boelcke's death. *GenLt.* Ernst von Hoeppner sent a delegation of 25 airmen to the ceremony that included *Jasta Boelcke*'s CO at the time, *Lt.* Erwin Böhme. Pictured here is the inscribed bow that was attached to the wreath that Böhme presented on behalf of the squadron. On his way back to the Front the next day, Böhme visited Annamarie Brüning in Hamburg and they became engaged to be married.

23 Mar 1917	promoted to *Oberleutnant*
6 Apr 1917	promoted to *Rittmeister*
7 Apr 1917	S503 photo published in *Die Woche* 14, p.461
15 May 1917	next trip to Berlin

On the surface, S450, MVR1, and S503 appear to have little to link them to one another except their subject, Manfred von Richthofen, and their photographer, C.J. von Dühren. In S450 and MVR1, Richthofen is bare-headed and attired in his dress blue uniform against a dark background, whereas in S503 he is wearing an overcoat and service cap in front of a lighter backdrop. Our discussion of S450 and MVR1 pointed out that following Richthofen's receipt of his *Pour le Mérite*, the only opportunity that he had to have his portrait taken in Berlin before his 15 May trip there was on 2-3 February when he visited the Inspectorate of Military Aviation. Two things conclusively prove that S503's image originated before 15 May. The first is the same picture's appearance in the 7 April 1917 edition of Berlin's *Die Woche*, where the caption recognized *Oblt. Freiherr* von Richthofen's 30th victory.[1] The second is a postmarked example of S503 dated 26 April 1917. So it is now clear that S503, like S450 and MVR1, originated from the same portrait sitting at the Berlin studio of C.J. von Dühren that was held on either 2 or 3 February 1917. If we observe them more closely, we can discern their common characteristics. Where we once might have assumed that Richthofen's tunic in S503 was dark because of the shadow play of his overcoat's upturned collar, we now recognize that he is wearing the same dark blue *Ulanka* he wore in S450 and MVR1. This is also disclosed by the fact that the button to the left of his *Pour le Mérite* is polished and shiny – a feature of such a dress tunic and not the *feldgrau* (field-gray) service tunic that sported more subdued, patterned buttons. That he is wearing an overcoat in one picture and not in another from the same sitting has already been observed in Althaus's S430-31 and Müller's S446-47 and will be again in Wüsthoff's S586-88, Kroll's S625-26, Rumey's S665-67, and Bolle's S685 and BOLLE1 (in the next volume). Alternate light and dark backgrounds occur in Bernert's S442-43, Schleiffer's S538 and N6244, Müller's S552-53, Wüsthoff's S563-64 and S586-88, and Rumey's S665-67; and the light, variegated background seen in S503 and MVR1 may be a match. WOLFF1, a rare photo of Kurt Wolff (see S542), offers us a peek at S503's full portrait. Under magnification, it shows evidence of what may be the bulge of Richthofen's dress tunic's epaulettes under his overcoat. Lastly, we should also keep in mind that where Richthofen's S450 and S503 appear to have been separated by 52 cards, they were most likely only two cards apart because numbers S452 through S501 appear to have never existed.

Our guideline predicts that S503 first appeared in late April, a time possibly confirmed by the 26 April 1917 date encountered for one example. It is also supported by the fact that S503 refers to Richthofen as *Rittmeister*, a rank he attained on 7 April 1917.

Note

[1] By this point in time, Richthofen had already added six more aircraft to his score and had been promoted to *Rittmeister*.

Despite what the caption states, these are the remains of Richthofen's 26th victim (his 25th burned and fell into no-man's-land). Richthofen brought down BE.2d No.6232 of RFC No.2 Squadron and its occupants, 2nd Lt. James Smyth and 2nd Lt. Edward Byrne, on 11 March 1917.

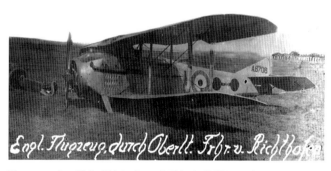

Victory number 30 for Richthofen on 24 March 1917. It was Spad 7 No.A6706 of RFC No.19 Squadron, flown by Lt. R.P. Baker, who was taken prisoner.

S503 (†)
(memorial)
RICHTHOFEN
Manfred *Freiherr* von
Rittmeister

Taken: 2 to 3 February 1917
Berlin, by C. J. von Dühren
Publ: May 1918
Reason: memorial

Decorations:
WR: *Pour le Mérite*
MB: None
RB: None
BH: None

Other Cards:
S450, S509, S511, S519, S532-34, S554, S606, S619
(L7835, L7846, L7847, L7894, L7895, L7898, L7932, L7933;
N6255, N6306)
Note: Taken same time as S450

Key Dates:
21 Apr 1918   killed in action

Many articles and several entire books have been devoted to the controversy surrounding the great ace's death in action on 21 April 1918. This work will studiously avoid adding anything further to the subject, except to offer a factually flawed but nevertheless interesting newspaper report of his death that appeared in the 23 April 1918 edition of *The New York World*:

"BARON RICHTHOFEN, GERMAN AIR STAR, KILLED IN PICARDY

Famous War Flyer Is Brought Down in Somme Valley – Body Buried Yesterday by Allies With Full Military Honors.

LONDON, Aprill 22 – Perry Robinson sends the following despatch to the Daily News from the British headquarters in France:

Yesterday, the official German communiqué announced 'Rittmeister Freiherr von Richthofen at the head of his trusty eleventh pursuit flight has gained his seventy-ninth and eightieth victories in the air.'

Before that had been published Richthofen was dead. He was brought down behind our lines not far from the Somme, and is to be buried this afternoon in a village in the neighborhood where he fell. I am just leaving to attend the funeral.

Foes Concede His Greatness

While probably not as brilliant as Capt. Ball, all our airmen concede that Richthofen was a great pilot and a fine fighting man. Richthofen was the head of the famous German circus squadron, so called at first because of the extraordinary acrobatics of its pilots. The circus, however, has now become a recognized part of present day air fighting. It was organized to be able to move quickly to threatened parts of the line, and particular attention was directed to prevent enemy reconnaissance and observation machines operating.

Boelke, the famous Fokker pilot, formed the first circus and Richthofen was a member of his squadron. When Boelke was killed in October, 1916, Richthofen took command.

The general plan of operations of the German circus was to climb fairly high over the infantry firing line and from a superior height to dive upon the enemy machines and develop a regular air battle. An early British squadron, organized to meet the German circus, was commanded by Major Hawker, V.C., who was killed in a fight with Richthofen himself.

In September last Richthofen was said to have been seriously wounded, having received two bullets in his head during a fight with British airmen over the German lines. After his marriage in the following month to Fraeulein von Minkwitz, heiress of the Duke of Saxe-Coburg's master of horse, he was appointed equerry airman to the Kaiser, and it was understood he was to devote himself to the training of fighter squadrons.

Somme His Happy Hunting Ground

In his recent book, 'The Red Battle Flyer,' Richthofen described many of his fights, and declared during his whole life he had not found a happier hunting ground than the Somme battlefield. 'In the morning as soon as I had got up,' he wrote, 'the first Englishman arrived, and the last disappeared only long after sunset. Boelke once said this was the Eldorado of flying men.' He was regarded by our flying men as a true sportsman.

Counseled Calmness

'One feels such superiority over the enemy that one does not doubt for a moment of success,' he wrote in his book. 'The aggressive spirit of the offensive is the chief thing everywhere in war, and the air is no exception. Altogether the fight itself is the least exciting part of the business as a rule. He who gets excited in fighting is sure to make mistakes. He will never get his enemy down. Besides, calmness is, after all, a matter of habit.

'When one's benzine tank has been holed and when the infernal liquid is squirted around one's legs the danger of fire is very great. One has in front an explosion engine of more than 150 horse power which is red hot. If a single drop of benzine should fall on it the whole machine would be in flames.

'Capt. Ball was most certainly commander of the anti-Richthofen squadron. I believe the Englishmen will give up their attempt to catch me (since Capt. Ball was lost). I should regret it, for in that case I should miss many nice opportunities to make myself beloved by them.'

The best British record to date is that of Capt. McCudden, who, when awarded the V.C. at the beginning of April, had brought down fifty-four enemy machines. The late Capt. Ball, V.C., had also more than forty enemy machines to his credit."

The next day, the same newspaper printed:

RICHTHOFEN DIED IN DASH TO BREAK THROUGH BRITISH

Rittmeister
Manfred Frhr. von Richthofen ✝ 503
Phot. C. J. von Dühren.
Berlin

Captured Document Shows He Had Been Ordered to Run Blockade of Foe Airmen for Reconnaissance of Amiens

CONFUSION DURING FIGHT IN WHICH HE MET DEATH

Just How Flyer Was Killed Not Known – British Officer Ties Rope Around Body to Pull It to Trenches Under Fire

WITH THE BRITISH ARMY IN FRANCE, April 23 (Associated Press) Capt. Baron von Richthofen apparently was killed while trying to break through the British aerial defenses in the Ancre region in order that enemy reconnaissance machines might cross the lines to make observations on the defenses. A document captured on Sunday reveals the reason for his presence there. It was a communication from the 'group commander of aviation' to the 1st Pursuit Squadron of which von Richthofen's 11th Pursuit Flight was a part, saying:

Ordered to Break Aerial Barrier

'It is not possible to fly over the Ancre in a westerly direction on account of strong enemy opposition. I request that this aerial barrage be forced to break in order that a reconnaissance up to the line of Marieux-Puchevillers (10 miles from the front) may be carried out.' (The Ancre River runs southward through Albert, flowing into the Somme east of Amiens, the region where the next German attack is expected to be made. Sailly-le-Sec, where von Richthofen was buried, is about 25 miles east of Amiens.)

Full Honors at Grave of Aviator Richthofen

LONDON, April 23 – Perry Robinson writing to-day to the Daily News from British Headquarters in France, says:

Richthofen's funeral yesterday afternoon was a simple but impressive ceremony. The coffin, which was borne by six officers of the air force, was deposited in a corner of a French cemetery in a little village, from the ground near which, before the ceremony, one could look at the Amiens Cathedral standing clear and beautiful in the afternoon sun.

The Germans were not shelling Amiens at the time, but shells were bursting freely along the high ground to the south of the city. The coffin bore an aluminum plate with an inscription in English and German setting forth the name and rank of the dead man, 'Rittmeister' being translated 'Cavalry Captain,' and that he had been killed in an air fight.

Army Code of Respect

The English service was read and the last salute fired over the grave. The German aviator was buried with as much respect and solemnity as if he had been a British soldier of rank. I know many people at home will dislike this honoring of the memory of an enemy who has killed so many of our own brave men, but the sense of the army is, I believe, overwhelmingly in favor of our maintaining self-respect and playing the game with decency, no matter how the enemy behaves. And Richthofen was unquestionably a very gallant man.

There is some uncertainty about the precise method of his death. He commanded what is called a circus, which is a squadron of picked airmen with machines of different types, but all painted red or red in combination with some other gaudy colors, which traveled about the enemy lines from airdrome to airdrome with the object of setting an example of spectacular fighting for the assistance and encouragement of local flying men. On this occasion three machines from one of our squadrons fell in with one of these flights at a height of 8,000 feet, and a fight followed in which two of the enemy machines were driven down.

Confusion About Fight

The fight took place exactly over the spot where Richthofen fell. Meanwhile, however, others of our machines had met at a lower altitude other enemy machines, and a great mixed fight took place, in which, when it reached a low altitude, machine guns from the ground were also able to take a hand.

Whether Richthofen's was one of the machines driven down in this fight or was one of those which crashed from the higher level seems uncertain, and in the absence of an official decision on the subject must remain so. The direction of the wound, which passed through the chest from the back to the front, shows that Richthofen was shot in the air from approximately his own level and not from the ground. Another slight wound on the chin might have been made upon landing.

The spot at which the machine came down was very close to the lines, and as soon as the airplane landed the Germans started shelling it, presumably wishing to break it up. One of our officers crawled out and, finding the pilot dead, fastened a rope around the body under fire and then crawled back again, and from the shelter of the trench the body was dragged out of the machine to our lines.

From the papers on the body the dead man was identified. Later, the wreckage of the machine was recovered. I saw the wreckage, which had once been Fokker Triplane No.2009 with Le Rhone engines made in Frankfort March, 1918. "

Given the "†" death cross next to Richthofen's name and the card's black border, it is obvious that S503† was issued as a memorial card sometime after 21 April 1918. It was probably published fairly soon thereafter, not only because it would have been in high demand, but also because its base photo was identical to S503's and would have been relatively easy to convert to a memorial form. Indeed, we have dated proof that Immelmann's L7705, Boelcke's S363†, and Richthofen's S533† and S619 were all issued within a few weeks of their deaths.

S504
THOMSEN
Hermann
Oberstleutnant

Taken: April 1916 to March 1917
Publ: May 1917
Reason: *Pour le Mérite* award

Decorations:
WR: Iron Cross, 1st Class
MB: None
RB: None
BH: None

Other Cards:
S519, S600
(L7894; N6099)
Note: Name expanded to von der Lieth-Thomsen after postwar marriage

Key Dates:

22 Mar 1916	promoted to *Oberstleutnant*
8 Oct 1916	appointed Chief of Staff of the German Army Air Force
8 Apr 1917	awarded *Pour le Mérite*
18 Apr 1917	S504 similar photo published in *Flugsport* 8, cover
21 Apr 1917	S504 similar photo published in *Die Woche* 16
22 Apr 1917	S504 similar photo published in *Berliner Illustrirte Zeitung* 16, p.223

Hermann Thomsen was born on 10 March 1867 in Flensburg. After several years of service in the military, he was appointed to the General Staff in 1901 and later became its Inspector of Air and Motor Vehicles in the spring of 1914. On 11 March 1915, *Major* Hermann Thomsen was named *Chef des Feldflugwesens* (Chief of Field Aviation), or *Feldflugchef*. The new post, which consolidated all the logistical aspects of most of the army air services under one command, had been the idea of *Major* Wilhelm Siegert, who then became Thomsen's righthand man. Together, the two men transformed the German Army Air Force into a much more coordinated and efficient weapon. It was also their work with men like Boelcke that eventually led to the formation of the *Jagdstaffeln,* or hunting groups, whose primary purpose was to go on the offensive and seek out and destroy enemy aircraft. They even suggested that the Air Force become a third branch of the military, independent from both the army and navy. Though this concept was rejected at the time, it undoubtedly had considerable influence on Ludendorff's subsequent decision to create the office of the Commanding General of the Air Force (or *Kogenluft* for short), whose expanded responsibilities encompassed all of Germany's air warfare activities except those of the Naval Air Service and the Bavarian Inspectorate of Aviation. Thomsen was named Chief of Staff of *Kogenluft* on 8 October 1916, which was soon followed by *Generalleutnant* Ernst von Hoeppner's appointment as its top officer on 12 November. Siegert continued to work for Thomsen, having already assumed the command of the *Inspektion der Fliegertruppe* (Inspectorate of Aviation), or *Idflieg*.

Five months later on 8 April 1917, Thomsen and Hoeppner were both given the order *Pour le Mérite* as a result of their "outstanding leadership in the development, planning, and operations" of the *Luftstreitkräfte* (see Hamelman, *History Pour le Merite*, pp.484-85). *Lt.* Werner Voss received his *Pour le Mérite* the same day, and all three men were honored in the series S504-06. Though neither Thomsen's nor Hoeppner's photo displays the award, Voss' does, which tells us that S504-06 celebrated their common achievement. This is also supported by our publication guideline, which predicts their initial appearance in early May 1917.

THOMSEN1 is a picture of Thomsen taken within minutes of S504's photograph. Everything matches between the two, right down to the pen in his hand. Cropped versions of THOMSEN1 were published in one periodical and two newspapers on 18, 21 and 22 April 1917.[1] This and the fact, as mentioned earlier, that they do not include his *Pour le Mérite* provide us with an outer limit of the end of March for their origin. Unfortunately, Thomsen is not wearing any of his many other decorations except the Iron Cross 1st Class that he won in 1914. His shoulder boards have the single "pip" designation of an *Oberstleutnant*, which he became on 22 March 1916. So we know that the pictures were not taken before then, giving us a one-year timeframe of April 1916 through March 1917.

Shortly after assuming his new role as *Chef des Generalstabes der Luftstreitkräfte*, Thomsen had the sad duty of delivering a eulogy for Oswald Boelcke at the airman's funeral service in Dessau. His speech and some additional remarks were printed on a notice sheet and distributed among members of the *Fliegertruppe*:

"Am Tage der Beisetzung unseres unvergesslichen Hauptmanns Boelcke in Dessau am 2. November 1916 habe ich im Namen der Fliegertruppe folgende Worte am Grabe unseres heimgegangenen Kameraden gesprochen:

'Boelcke ist gefallen! Als diese Trauerkunde uns, seine Kameraden, traf, ward unser Herz gelähmt. Boelcke ist gefallen! Nach einer Kriegerlaufbahn voll unerhörter Erfolge, nach 40 ruhmreichen Luftsiegen ist er als unbezwungener Held von uns gegangen, er, unser Freund und unser Meister.

Fürwahr, die deutschen Luftstreitkräfte haben unendlich viel verloren durch seinen frühen Tod, aber sie haben auch unendlich viel gewonnen durch sein Leben und sein Wirken.

Heut' ist kein frischer deutscher Junge in der Heimat, dem nicht Heimlich im Herzen der Wunsch brennt: "Ich möchte ein Boelcke werden!" Und es ist keener unter unseren jungen Fliegern draussen an der Front, in dem nicht die heisse Sehnsucht glüht: "Ich möchte ein Boelcke werden!"

Das ist ein stolzer Trost, den wir alle, Eltern und Geschwister, Freunde und Kameraden, heute von der letzten Ruhestätte unseres teueren und unvergesslichen Kameraden mit heimnehmen.

Und so lege ich denn als letzte Scheidegruss an dem Grabe unseres treuen Freundes diese Worter nieder, die ein feierliches Gelöbnis sein sollen jedes einzelnen unserer deutschen Flieger: "Ich möchte ein Boelcke werden!"

So lange dieses Wort unser Leitstern bleibt, so lange Boelckes Geist und Boelckes Können in unserer Fliegertruppe lebendig bleibt, so lange: "Lieb' Vaterland magst ruhig sein!"''

Ich spreche die zuversichtliche Hoffnung und Erwartung aus, dass alle Angehörigen der Fliegerwaffe bestrebt sein werden, wann und wo immer es sei, dieses Gelöbnis zu halten, und nie nachlassen werden, dem grossen Vorbilde unseres Boelcke mit aller Kraft des Geistes und des Körpers nachzueifern. Um auch äusserlich unsere nie schwindende Dankbarkeit für alles das, was Boelcke uns gab, zu kennzeichnen und sein Andenken hochzuhalten, habe ich Vorsorge getroffen, dass für alle Zeiten von der jeweils höchsten Fliegerkommandostelle die Ruhestätte des Hauptmann Boelcke an seinem Geburts- und an seinem Todestage mit frischem Lorbeer geschmückt wird, und dass das gleiche auch an hohen vaterländischen Gedenktagen geschieht.

Gross Hauptquartier   THOMSEN
Den 2. November 1916. Chef des Generalstabes der Luftstreitkräfte."

"On 2 November 1916, the day of our unforgettable Captain Boelcke's funeral in Dessau, I spoke the following words at the grave of our departed comrade on behalf of the German Air Service:

'Boelcke has fallen! When this sad news reached us, his comrades, our hearts were stilled. Boelcke has fallen! After a military career of incredible successes, after 40 glorious air victories, he has left us as an unconquered hero – he, our friend and master.

Indeed, the German Air Force has suffered an interminable loss through his early death, but it has also gained infinitely from his life and deeds.

Today, there is no spirited German lad in the homeland whose heart does not burn with the secret desire: "I want to be a Boelcke!" And away at the Front, there is not one among our young airman who does not burn with the fervent aspiration: "I want to be a Boelcke!"

This is a proud consolation that we all, parents and siblings, friends and comradres, here at the final resting place of our dear and unforgettable comrade can take away with us this day.

And so as a final farewell I lay upon the grave of our faithful friend these words that shall be the solemn vow of each one of our German airmen: "I want to be a Boelcke!"

As long as these words remain our guiding star, as long as Boelcke's spirit and Boelcke's prowess remain alive in our Air Service, then "may our dear fatherland be at peace!"'

I express the confident hope and expectation that all members of the Air Force will, whenever and wherever they can, always strive to maintain this vow to emulate Boelcke's great model with all their spiritual and physical strength. Also, in order to mark our never-ending gratitude for all that Boelcke gave us and to uphold his memory, I have arranged from this day forward that each of the highest Air Service command posts will decorate Boelcke's resting place with fresh laurel on the anniversaries of his birth, his death, and also on high, national days of remembrance.

Supreme Headquarters   THOMSEN
2 November 1916   Chief of Staff of the Air Force"

(trans. by this writer)

Thomsen was promoted to *Oberst* in 1918 and remained active in the military's air efforts after the war, sometimes working covertly because of the limitations imposed by the Versailles Treaty. He also changed his name to Hermann von der Lieth-Thomsen around this time. A deteriorating eye condition reportedly caused him to retire in 1928, but he was called back to service as events began to head toward World War II. He rose to the rank of *General der Flieger* and acted as a special consultant to the Commander in Chief of the Air Forces and Ministry of Aviation. He died in Sylt on 5 August 1942 and was buried in Berlin's Invalidenfriedhof cemetery.

Note

[1] All three announced his receipt of the *Pour le Mérite*. A portion of THOMSEN1 was also published as N6099.

THOMSEN1

Another picture of *Oberstlt.* Hermann Thomsen at his desk at the time that S504's photo was snapped.

Right: *Oberstlt.* Hermann Thomsen sent this portrait to a friend along with the notation that it had been taken at Supreme Headquarters at Münster-am-Stein in 1917/18. (photo courtesy of UTD)

S505
HOEPPNER
Ernst von
Generalleutnant

Taken: late 1915 to late 1916
Publ: May 1917
Reason: *Pour le Mérite* award

Decorations:
WR: Red Eagle Order, 2nd Class/ Sw and Oakleaves; Iron Cross, 1st Class
MB: None
RB: Iron Cross, 2nd Class; unknown; unknown; unknown; Albert Order, Knight 1st Class/ Crown (Sax); remainder unknown
BH: None

Other Cards:
S427, S509, S519, S568, S600
(L7847, L7894; N6049, N6061)
Note: Taken same time as S427

Key Dates:

14 Dec 1915	announcement of award of Red Eagle Order 2nd Class/ Sw and Oakleaves
12 Nov 1916	appointed Commanding General of the Air Force
8 April 1917	awarded *Pour le Mérite*

Oberstlt. Hermann Thomsen and staff before he was awarded the *Pour le Mérite.* Starting second from the left, we have *Maj.* Wilhelm Siegert (head of *Idflieg,* the Inspectorate of Aviation), Thomsen, and *Oblt.* Fritz von Falkenhayn (*Idflieg*). (photo courtesy of UTD)

The *Feldschnalle*, or ribbon bar, that is displayed in S505 (and also appears in S427) is difficult to decipher. First of all, the monochrome film used at the time, which frequently translated red and yellow to black/dark gray or blue to white/light gray, complicates the precise identification of each ribbon. Second, the decorations we know that Hoeppner held up to this point in the war do not match up well against what is seen on his *Feldschnalle*. Neal O'Connor, in his sixth volume on German aviation awards (pp.161-62), said Hoeppner held the following:

> Red Eagle Order, 3rd Class with Bow (Prussia)
> Crown Order 3rd Class (Prussia)
> Officer's Long Service Decoration (Imperial Germany)
> Order of the Zähringer Lion, Knight 1st Class (Baden)
> House Order Honor Cross 2nd Class with Oakleaves (Lippe)
> Griffin Order Honor Cross (Mecklenburg)
> Albert Order, Knight 1st Class with Crown (Saxony)
> House Order Honor Cross, 2nd Class with Oakleaves (Schaumburg-Lippe)
> The Royal Victorian Order Commander's Cross (Great Britain)
> Order of St. Maurice and Lazarus Commander's Cross (Italy)
> Military St. Henry Order, Knight's Cross (Saxony)
> Military Merit Order 2nd Class with Swords and Star (Bavaria)
> Red Eagle Order 2nd Class with Swords and Oakleaves (Prussia)
> The Iron Cross, 1st and 2nd Class, must also be added to this list.

Hoeppner is wearing the Red Eagle Order 2nd Class at his neck and it would not have appeared on his ribbon bar. The Iron Cross 1st Class and Griffin Order Honor Cross can also be eliminated because they were ribbonless badges pinned to the tunic. It is also unlikely that Hoeppner would have worn decorations awarded by Germany's enemies on his wartime ribbon bar. Indeed, the ribbons for his Royal Victorian Order (Great Britain) and Order of St. Maurice and Lazarus (Italy) seem to be absent. This leaves us with 10 remaining awards; yet his *Feldschnalle* carries at least 12 ribbons. So the inevitable conclusion is that he received other decorations of which we are not aware.

Generalleutnant von Hoeppner
Kommandierender General der Luftstreitkräfte

505
Postkartenvertrieb W.Sanke
BERLIN N.37.
Nachdruck wird gerichtlich verfolgt

To add to the confusion, even where some of Hoeppner's known decorations seem to match a spot on his ribbon bar, their positions do not always conform to the military's conventional order of precedence. Though this is sometimes encountered among airmen of lower rank, one would think that Hoepnner, as a *Generalleutnant*, would not have violated the accepted practice. Thus the only two decorations that can be confirmed with any confidence are the Iron Cross 2nd Class in the first position (black ribbon with white side stripes) and Saxony's Albert Order, Knight 1st Class with Crown in the fifth position (grass green ribbon with white side stripes, crown insignia). The ribbon immediately preceding the Albert Order's seems to have some kind of device attached to its upper portion that may represent the star of his Bavarian Military Merit Order, 2nd Class with Swords and Star. Moreover, the ribbon displays a thin black side stripe against a light background. This Bavarian decoration came on a white ribbon with black and blue side stripes, and many period photos show that the blue stripes often disappeared against the white background because of the film used at the time.[1] This identification, however, is by no means certain.

The pictures for S505 and the earlier S427 were taken together within a late 1915 to late 1916 timeframe. The Red Eagle Order at Hoeppner's neck, however, figures quite prominently in them both, so they may have been inspired by its award. If so, the photo session probably occurred soon after he received the decoration, i.e., late 1915 to early 1916.

As noted in Thomsen's S504, the S504-06 series commemorated their subjects' simultaneous receipt of the *Pour le Mérite* on 8 April 1917. Evidently, unlike Werner Voss in S506, portraits of Hoeppner and Thomsen with their new orders were not available to Sanke.

Note

[1] E.g., see Immelmann's S361. For examples not printed in this volume, see Tutschek's S572 and Müller's S553, S583-84. The same phenomenon can be observed in many period photos with the *Pour le Mérite*, where its blue enamel often appears bright white.

Two above: *GenLt.* Ernst von Hoeppner, wearing the *Pour le Mérite* he was awarded on 8 April 1917, visits *Jasta 18* at Halluin. *Jasta 18*, under the command of *Rittm.* Karl von Grieffenhagen, was based there until 12 August 1917. Grieffenhagen may be the man with his back to the camera in both pictures. (photos courtesy of UTD)

Right: Another photograph of Hoeppner visiting a flying unit in the field.

S506
VOSS
Werner
Leutnant

Taken: 9 to 30 April 1917
Krefeld, family photo
Publ: May 1917
Reason: *Pour le Mérite* award

Decorations:
WR: *Pour le Mérite*; Iron Cross, 1st Class; Pilot's Badge
MB: None
RB: None
BH: Royal Hohenzollern House Order, Knight's Cross/ Sw

Other Cards:
S520, S554
(L7848)

Key Dates:

17 Mar 1917	awarded Royal Hohenzollern House Order, Knight's Cross/ Sw
8 Apr 1917	awarded *Pour le Mérite*
7 May 1917	victory #25

Before *Lt.* Werner Voss departed *Jasta Boelcke* to serve with *Jasta 5* on 20 May 1917, he gave a portrait of himself to the *Staffel*'s chief administrative officer, *Oblt.* Karl Bodenschatz. Signed "Werner Voss, May 1917," it is the same picture that we see on S506 (see Musciano, *Lt. Werner Voss*, p.24). Voss is sitting on a brightly-patterned quilt that crops up again in VOSS1, a photo taken during Manfred von Richthofen's June 1917 visit to the Voss family home in Krefeld. Together, these two images tell us that S506's photo was taken shortly after his receipt of the *Pour le Mérite* on 8 April 1917 while he was home on leave.[1] This explains why he is wearing his Royal Hohenzollern House Order on his button flap. He had received it only three weeks before his *Pour le Mérite* and apparently had not had or taken the time to have it formally mounted. It also explains why Voss experienced a gap in his otherwise consistent scoring streak at a time when other German pilots were so successful that the month later gained the sobriquet of "Bloody April."[2] We know Voss was back at the Front on 7 May (Franks and Giblin, *Under the Guns*, p.102 reports that he returned from leave on 5 May) because that was the day he brought down Second Lt. R.M. Chaworth-Musters of RFC No.56 Squadron's "B" flight.[3] S506's image was snapped at the Voss family home in Krefeld sometime during the last three weeks of April 1917, and was published as a Sanke postcard the following May. VOSS2-4 are three other photos taken the same time as S506.

Notes
[1] See the discussion on pp.38. In addition, we have Erwin Böhme's letter dated 25 April 1917 that states: "Voss, who already has 24 victories and the *Pour le Mérite*, is himself on leave…" (Werner, *Briefes eines Kampffliegers*, p.106, trans. by this writer).

[2] Voss destroyed eight planes in February, eleven in March, but only two in April (on 1 and 6 April). He brought down seven in May, three in June (before being sent on another leave, probably to recuperate from a slight wound received on 6 June), then four in August and ten more in September before being killed on the 23rd in his epic battle with nine members of RFC No.56 Squadron.

[3] No.56 Squadron's A, B, and C flights had begun the evening patrol together, but cloudy weather separated them before Chaworth-Musters' fatal encounter with Voss. A little over an hour later, Capt. Albert Ball, leader of A flight, crashed to his death – the alleged victim of Lothar von Richthofen. One can only imagine what the action might have been like if Ball had encountered Voss and Richthofen together.

VOSS I

Opposite
Top left: A companion portrait to S506. This one was dated 27 June 1917 by Voss and dedicated to "Ilseken," the affectionate form of "Ilse."

Right: An early portrait of Werner Voss when he was a private serving with *Husaren-Regiment (2. westfälisches) Nr.11*. It comes from before 27 January 1915, when Voss was promoted to *Gefreiter*.

Bottom left: Werner Voss when he was a Hussar soldier in the trenches.

Right: *Uffz.* Werner Voss in his dress Hussar uniform. He was raised to this rank on 18 May 1915.

Uffz. Werner Voss was acccpted into the *Hiegertruppe* on 1 August 1915 and was later posted at *Flieger-Ersatz-Abteilung 7*. This appears to be a photo of him (back row, center) among FFA 7 comrades before his promotion to *Vizefeldwebel* and transfer to *Kasta 20* on 2 March and 10 March 1916, respectively.

Below: *Vzfw.* Werner Voss, third from the right, poses with some of his comrades from *Kasta 20* (attached to *Kampfgeschwader 4*) near their base at Etreillers. To Voss' right is then *Offz.-Stv.* Hermann Frommherz. Voss was assigned to *Kasta 20* on 10 March 1916 and Frommherz was promoted to *Leutnant* on 1 August 1916, so this picture originated sometime between those dates. (photo courtesy of UTD)

S507
SCHAEFER
Karl-Emil
Leutnant

Taken: 19 June to July 1916
Publ: May 1917
Reason: victory score

Decorations:
WR: None
MB: None
RB: None
BH: Iron Cross, 2nd Class; Cross for Faithful Service (Sch-L)

Other Cards:
S511, S512
(L7844, L7846)
Note: Numeral "7" for former unit, *Reserve Jäger-Battalion Nr.7*, on shoulder board

Key Dates:
19 Jun 1916	awarded Cross for Faithful Service (Sch-L)
22 Jun 1916	first air combat assignment

Vzfw. Werner Voss won his Pilot's Badge on 28 May 1916 while serving with Kasta 20. This is a snapshot of him after that date but before he was promoted to Leutnant on 9 September 1916. .

22 Jan 1917	victory #1
early Mar 1917	awarded Iron Cross 1st Class

Lt. Karl-Emil Schaefer, like so many other German pilots, started the war in the infantry.[1] Awarded the Iron Cross 2nd Class while serving with *Reserve Jäger-Battalion Nr.7*, he was wounded in the thigh in late September 1914. After several months of recuperation, he applied for a transfer to the Air Service that was granted on 16 January 1916. He attended the flying school at Köslin and then reported to *Flieger-Ersatz-Abteilung 8*. He was posted to *Kampfstaffel 8* (part of *Kampfgeschwader 2*) near Verdun on 22 June 1916, and then traveled with the unit to Kovel in July. There, he must have become acquainted with *Lt.* Manfred von Richthofen of *Flieger-Abteilung 69*, also based at Kovel, because later in February 1917 they had the following terse exchange by telegram:

> Schaefer: *Können Sie mich brauchen?* (Can you use me?)
> Richthofen: *Sie sind bereits angefordert.* (You've already been requested.)

> (see Schäfer, *Vom Jäger zum Flieger*, p.80)

His first taste of victory had come one month earlier when he had shot down a Caudron on 22 January after his unit had returned to the Western Front and formed its own fighter detachment, *Kampfstaffel 11*. Schaefer apparently decided that he could do better in an independent fighter squadron, and upon learning that his friend Richthofen had recently been placed in charge of one (*Jasta 11* on 14 January), he appealed to Richthofen for a transfer. As is now well known, Schaefer turned out to become one of Richthofen's star pupils. After his arrival on 21 February at *Jasta 11*'s La Brayelle airfield

Leutnant Schaefer.

Postkartenvertrieb W.Sanke
„BERLIN N.37.„
Nachdruck wird gerichtlich verfolgt.
507

near Douai, Schaefer wasted little time in shooting down his next airplane on 4 March. He reported the event in a letter home, clearly believing that he had made a spectacular debut with his new unit. After noting that Richthofen had once accounted for three out of five squadron victories, he continued with:

> "*Gestern am ersten Flugtag seitdem hat's 4 Abschüsse gegeben, davon 3 von ihm selbst, denkt Ihr wohl? Verkehrt! Einer von Richthofen und 3 von mir! Ja, ja, der Schäfer!*" (Schäfer, *Vom Jäger zum Flieger*, pp.106-7)

> "Yesterday, on the first flying day since then, four aircraft were brought down. You are probably thinking that three again were by Richthofen, right? Wrong! One by Richthofen and three by me! Yes, me, Schaefer!" (trans. by this writer)

Unfortunately for him, the authorities did not quite see it that way. The official record credited Richthofen with two victories that day, and Schaefer with only one. Whether he really did get a "hat trick," or in the heat of battle just thought he had, he was taught the lesson that not everything claimed would be counted. Undaunted, Schaefer racked up six more official kills that month, giving him a total of eight that was the highest among *Jasta 11*'s other rising stars: Allmenröder (5), Wolff (5), Festner (2), and Lothar von Richthofen (1). By mid-April, or about the time that Sanke might have begun the pursuit of his picture, Schaefer was still in the lead with 19 victories compared with Wolff's 16, Festner's 12, Lothar von Richthofen's 8, and Allmenröder's 7.

Three things help us bracket when S507's photograph was taken. They are the just barely detectable numeral "7" on his left shoulder board, the absence of his Iron Cross 1st Class and Pilot's Badge, and the ribbon he is wearing for Schaumberg-Lippe's Cross for Faithful Service. The "7" signified his former unit, *Reserve Jäger-Bataillon Nr.7*, which points to an early date, but his Cross for Faithful Service was apparently awarded to him on 19 June 1916 right before he was posted to his first air combat assignment with *Kampfstaffel 8*.[2] Schaefer did not receive the Iron Cross 1st Class until early March 1917, as divulged in a letter home dated 6 March. In his typically self-deprecating style, he informed his parents:

> "*Seit ich das E.K.I. besitze, habe ich eine hochmütige, überlegene Äusserlichkeit angenommen und fühle mich mindergeschmückten Mitmenschen riesig überlegen.*" (Schäfer, *Vom Jäger zum Flieger*, p.106)

> "Now that I possess the Iron Cross 1st Class, I have adopted an arrogant, lofty appearance and feel terribly superior to my less bemedaled fellow man." (trans. by this writer)

So the picture was snapped sometime between late June 1916 and February 1917. SCHAEFER1 is another portrait taken at the same time. The absence of his Pilot's Badge and the presence of the "7" instead of the Air Service's winged propeller insignia suggest that both photos came from early on in this period. It was not atypical for a German pilot to receive his Pilot's Badge a month or two after already having been in combat (e.g., see Mulzer and Windisch in the discussion of S401, or Kirmaier in S445), so this may have been the case for Schaefer as well. When Schaefer arrived at *Kampfstaffel 8*,

it was based on the Western Front near Verdun. A few weeks later the unit moved to Kovel in Ukraine and did not return until winter. Schaefer's formal pose in S507 suggests that the photo was taken at his home or in a professional studio, and one doubts that Kovel had such a studio nearby. All in all, the evidence seems to point to a late June to July 1916 timeframe right after Schaefer was awarded the Cross for Faithful Service but before he left for the Eastern Front.

Notes

[1] Schaefer's signature shows that he, like Oswald Boelcke, preferred to use the Latin spelling of his name and did not follow his family's practice of spelling it with an umlaut (i.e., "ae" vs. "ä"). His letters home also demonstrate that he referred to himself, at least among family, as "Emil" – his middle name and the name of his father.

[2] The evidence for this possible date is presented in O'Connor, *Aviation Awards VII*, p.301.

SCHAEFER1

S507's photographer also took this picture of Schaefer at the same sitting.

Right: A relaxed *Lt.* Karl-Emil Schaefer in a less formal pose.

Below: On 9 March 1917, *Jasta 11* tore into the FE.8s of RFC No.40 Squadron and shot down four of them. Two fell to the guns of *Lt.* Karl-Emil Schaefer within minutes of each other, and this photo is of the one that came down last near Pont-à-Vendin. Franks, Bailey, and Duivan (*Jasta War Chronology*, p.35) have identified it as No.4874 flown by 2nd Lt. G.F. Heseler, who was taken prisoner.

S507
(reissue)
SCHAEFER
Karl-Emil
Leutnant

Taken: 19 June to July 1916
Publ: 18 June 1917 to December 1918
Reason: memorial

Decorations:
WR: *Pour le Mérite*; Iron Cross, 1st Class; Pilot's Badge
MB: Iron Cross, 2nd Class; Cross for Faithful Service (Sch-L); Military Merit Order, 4th Class/ Sw (Bav)
RB: None
BH: Royal Hohenzollern House Order, Knight's Cross/ Sw

Other Cards:
S511, S512
(L7844, L7846)
Note: Photo has been resized when compared with original S507

Key Dates:

3 Jun 1917	awarded Military Merit Order, 4th Class/ Sw (Bav)
5 Jun 1917	killed in action

Leutnant Schaefer

507
Postkartenvertrieb W.Sanke
BERLIN N.37.
Nachdruck wird gerichtlich verfolgt.

This is the only known example of where an airman's initial Sanke card was later reissued with a significantly altered appearance. Someone drew in all of Schaefer's decorations, covering over his original Iron Cross 2nd Class and Cross for Faithful Service ribbons with a representation of a buttonholed Royal Hohenzollern House Order. In addition, his overall portrait was slightly downsized. Schaefer was awarded the last of his decorations, Bavaria's Military Merit Order, on the day before he died, so this postcard obviously was issued posthumously. Although one might suspect that it was done relatively soon after the news of his fall, we currently have no postmark evidence to attest to this. The only dated copy we can turn to at present comes from Schaefer's father and is signed "Krefeld 1918, Emil Schäfer" on the back.

Altering S507's appearance certainly was not without precedent. The cover of the c.24 June 1917 edition of *Illustrierte Kriegs-Zeitung Nr. 151* featured SCHAEFER2 in announcing the flier's death. In this instance, someone added an Iron Cross 1st Class and a Pilot's Badge; and there is reason to believe that the image's named source, Berliner Illustrations Gesellschaft, was responsible. The original photo from B.I.G.'s files has faded with time, but not the altered portion (see SCHAEFER3), giving us a rare glimpse at precisely how such changes were blended in. Later, in the August Scherl Company's 1918 publication of some of Schaefer's letters and diary entries entitled *Vom Jäger zum Flieger*, yet another amended version of S507's photo made an appearance as its frontispiece (SCHAEFER4). This time, a *Pour le Mérite*, Royal Hohenzollern House Order, Iron Cross 1st Class, and nondescript ribbon bar were rather crudely sketched in. Were these changes just innocent attempts to upgrade an old picture or were they made to try to circumvent existing copyright laws? The back of SCHAEFER3 notes B.I.G.'s copyright, but to which version: untouched or retouched? If B.I.G. held the rights to the untouched version as seen on S507, then they probably were Sanke's source. If not, Sanke's cards carried the strict warning, "*Nachdruck wird gerichtlich verfolgt*" ("Reproduction will be legally prosecuted"), and one has to wonder if alterations like those seen here technically avoided such threats of prosecution. Like so many other Sanke card mysteries, we might never know the answer.

Above: The cover of *Illustrierte Kriegs-Zeitung Nr. 151*, published in late June 1917, presented this altered version of S507.

Top right: Berliner Illustrations Gesellschaft's image No.17584. The portion of the picture that was touched up to add Schaefer's Iron Cross and Pilot's Badge did not fade along with the rest of the image. B.I.G. reissued the same amended image under the number 18244 upon the occasion of Schaefer's death.

Right: The frontispiece of Schaefer's 1918 biography, *Vom Jäger zum Flieger*.

Karl-Emil Schaefer's coffin is borne from Lille's St. Etienne's Church to an awaiting gun carriage on 8 June 1917.

This page and next: Schaefer's funeral procession turns a corner, heads into Lille's central plaza, La Grand Place, and files past La Colonne de la Déesse (The Goddess Column) on its way to the train station. Under magnification, the man carrying Schaefer's *Ordenskissen* in the second (foreground) and third (far left) photos resembles *Oblt.* Erwin Wenig, who joined *Jasta 28* on 20 April 1917. Wenig was shot down the same day as Schaefer, but escaped unharmed.

S508
BRAUNECK
Otto
Leutnant

Taken: 20 to 26 April 1917
Roucourt
Publ: May 1917
Reason: *Jasta 11* success

Decorations:
WR: None
MB: None
RB: None
BH: None

Other Cards:
None
Note: Albatros D.III has white bullet hole patch in fuselage; panels on ground show engine being worked on

Key Dates:
20 Apr 1917   joins *Jasta 11*

Lt. Otto Brauneck arrived at *Feldflieger-Abteilung 69* in Macedonia on 10 July 1916. Conditions in this theater of the war were primitive, and during heavy rains Brauneck had to travel on horseback to go between his quarters in the town of Monastir and the airfield. Nevertheless, he and his observer made frequent flights because as Brauneck himself put it in a 2 August 1916 letter home:

"We are the eyes of the Commanding Officer and the officers of the General Staff. Every day we are watching the enemy's activities and his movements." (C&C 24:2, p.154)

Brauneck received his Pilot's Badge on 10 September 1916, and it was around this time that he shot down his first victim.[1] On 14 December, he and his observer brought down a balloon, which earned them the Iron Cross 1st Class. Perhaps because of the scarcity of other air targets at the Macedonian Front, Brauneck made balloon hunting his specialty and eventually counted five of them among his official total (a sixth went unconfirmed). With three balloons and one airplane to his credit, he was transferred on 14 January 1917 without any further training to *Jasta 25*, a nearby fighter unit that sometimes worked in unison with *Feldflieger-Abteilung 69*.[2] Brauneck's first solo kill occurred just five days later, giving him an impressive tally of five in a theater of operations where encounters with enemy aircraft, much less victories, were difficult to come by. As a result, he was awarded the Royal Hohenzollern House Order, Knight's Cross with Swords. One of Brauneck's squadron mates, *Oblt.* Bodo von Lyncker, had undergone pilot training with Manfred von Richthofen in 1915, and with a victory of his own under his belt, wrote Richthofen to see if he and Brauneck might be welcome in *Jasta 11*. Before Richthofen could respond, Lyncker was killed in a collision with an enemy plane on 18 February. After collecting two more victories, Brauneck pursued the matter again and received Richthofen's answer on 31 March 1917:

"I just received your letter and wish to respond to it immediately.
I remember that Lynker (sic) had already written to me about you, and a recommendation from this wonderful man is sufficient. Therefore I am willing to request you at once. Today a telegram will be sent to your Kofl., and it will be followed by a telegram to Kogen. It is up to you to pressure your superior so

508
Postkartenvertrieb W.Sanke
BERLIN N. 37.
Nachdruck wird gerichtlich verfolgt.

Leutnant Brauneck.

that he will let you go from there, because without his willingness there is nothing one can do vis-a-vis the Kogen.
Much is going on here. We are downing at least one a day when the weather is good for flying.
You will also find a very nice group of comrades here. I am looking forward to your earliest possible answer." (C&C 24:2, p.163)

Brauneck must have been both confused and disappointed when his subsequent orders sent him to *Jasta Boelcke* at Pronville instead. On his way there, he stopped at his home in Salzbach and was surprised by a telegram from Richthofen stating that it had all been a mistake and that he was in fact ordered to report to *Jasta 11* after all. This Brauneck did on 20 April 1917.

Brauneck obtained his first kill with his new unit on 1 June while his commander was still away on a well-earned leave. He scored again with *Lt.* Carl Allmenröder and *Lt.* Alfred Niederhoff on 5 June, but any celebration must have been muted by the news later that day of the death of their comrade and former squadron mate, *Lt.* Karl-Emil Schaefer. Richthofen returned from his leave in mid-June, and when he was wounded on 6 July, the *Jagdgeschwader Nr.1* war diary notes that it was Brauneck and Niederhoff who followed him down and possibly kept him from being finished off (see Bodenschatz, *Hunting with Richthofen*, p.19). They landed near their fallen leader and flagged down a car that took him off to hospital. Five days later, *Lt.* Kurt Wolff was also wounded, and Brauneck took over as *Jasta 11*'s acting CO. On 22 July 1917, he proudly wrote:

> "This morning I got my 10th. It was part of a squadron from which my *Jasta* under my leadership shot down three of the enemy." (OTF 1:3, p.198)

On 25 July, Richthofen returned to command his fighter wing, *Jagdgeschwader Nr.1*, that had been formed from *Jagdstaffeln 4, 6, 10,* and *11* one month earlier. The next day, 94 airplanes took part in one of the largest air battles joined to date. Brauneck suffered hits to his head and upper thigh, but managed to limp back over the German lines before crashing to his death. His body was recovered later that night by his mechanic and another man. On 29 July, a memorial service was performed for Brauneck at St. Joseph's Church, Courtrai, after which his coffin was sent home to Sulzbach for burial there the next day.

S508's background confirms that its picture was taken at *Jasta 11*'s Roucourt airfield. The other photographs associated with it that are discussed in Appendix I appear to have originated during the week leading up to *Lt.* Karl-Emil Schaefer's departure for *Jasta 28* on 27 April 1917. Therefore, S508's portrait was taken shortly after Brauneck's arrival during the period 20-26 April 1917.

Notes
[1] Here we have yet another example of a pilot gaining his Pilot's Badge after already having been in combat.

[2] There he met *Vzfw.* Otto Könnecke, who also "cut his teeth" with *Jasta 25*, gaining an unconfirmed victory on 9 January 1917 and two confirmed ones in February before being reassigned to *Jasta 5* on the Western Front in April.

S509
RICHTHOFEN
Manfred *Freiherr* von
Rittmeister

HOEPPNER
Ernst von
Der kommandierende General der Luftstreitkräfte

Taken: 23 April 1917
Roucourt
Publ: May 1917
Reason: *Jasta 11* success

Decorations:
WR: None
MB: None
RB: None
BH: None

Other Cards:
S450, S503, S509, S511, S519, S532-34, S554, S606, S619 (L7835, L7846, L7847, L7894, L7895, L7898, L7932, L7933; N6255, N6306)

Key Dates:

20 Apr 1917	Brauneck joins *Jasta 11*
22 Apr 1917	Wolff shoots down *Jasta 11*'s 100th victory
23 Apr 1917	Hoeppner visits *Jasta 11*
25 Apr 1917	Festner killed in action
27 Apr 1917	Schaefer leaves for *Jasta 28*

Lt. Carl Allmenröder's biography identified this picture as *Jasta 11* with him as their acting CO in May 1917. From left to right: Allmenröder, his brother Wilhelm, *Lt.* von Hartmann, *Lt.* Otto Brauneck, unknown, *Lt.* Karl Esser, *Lt.* Matthof, *Lt.* Hans Hintsch, and *Lt.* Eberhard Mohnicke. Carl Allmenröder became acting CO on 13 May 1917 and 11 days later his brother was wounded and Hintsch was killed, so we can narrow the photo's timeframe down to 13-23 May 1917.

This time we see *Jasta 11* behind Chateau de Béthune near Marckebeke on 22 July 1917. From left to right: *Oblt.* Kurt Scheffer, *Oblt.* Karl Bodenschatz, *Lt.* Alfred Niederhoff, *Lt.* Eberhard Mohnicke, Prof. Arnold Busch, *Lt.* Otto Brauneck, *Lt.* Karl Meyer, *Lt.* Kurt Wolff, *Oblt.* Wilhelm Reinhard, *Lt.* Hans-Joachim Wolff (on Reinhard's shoulders), *Lt.* Wilhelm Bockelmann, unknown, *Lt.* Konstantin Krefft. The occasion was a visit by Manfred von Richthofen (wounded 6 July) and Kurt Wolff (wounded 11 July) from their hospital beds in Courtrai. Brauneck wrote home that the visit occurred on 22 July (see OTF 24:2, p.198). A better-known photo of most of the same men in this gathering has been published in several sources (e.g., Ferko, *Richthofen*, p.46 or Kilduff, *Illustrated Red Baron*, p.77). Evidently, Hans-Joachim Wolff had time to change clothes between them, because there he is dressed in a civilian suit whereas here he is in uniform. Otto Brauneck was shot down and killed only four days later on 26 July. (photo courtesy of UTD)

13 May 1917	S509 photo published in *Berliner Illustrirte Zeitung* 19, p.1

In *Nachrichtenblatt der Luftstreitkräfte Nr.10*, a weekly report issued by the German Air Force, *Generalleutnant* Ernst von Hoeppner inserted the following special recognition:

"In the time from 23 January to 22 April 1917, Jasta 11 has shot down 100 enemy airplanes. I am pleased to be able to announce this singular success to the Fliegertruppe. Here a small band of brave pilots, trained and led in combat by an outstanding leader, Rittmeister Freiherr von Richthofen, who took on these 100 airplanes with just 29, has performed deeds for the benefit of the hard-fighting troops on the ground, which deeds resound to the highest glory of the German Fliegertruppe." (OTF 15:1, p.65)

Hoeppner again made note of this special feat in his 1921 book on the air war:

"During the first week in April the conflicts between pursuit units took on the size of aerial battles. The enemy attacked with great ardor and with the conviction that he had a considerable numerical superiority. But he paid dearly for his zeal in attacking, for on April 6th, 44 enemy planes were seen to be shot down in flames by our better-armed and better-handled pursuit units. Of course, we, too, suffered dire losses among our experienced pilots. The pursuit squadron commanded by Baron von Richthofen distinguished itself conspicuously. In the period between January 23rd and April 22nd, 1917, it attained a hundred verified victories. Boelcke's spirit lived on in it." (Hoeppner, *Germany's War in the Air*, p.99)

Evidently, Hoeppner chose to visit *Jasta 11* to offer his personal congratulations, as witnessed by two existing photographs. S509 shows Hoeppner congratulating Richthofen personally, while MVR2 depicts Richthofen introducing the commanding general to various members of the squadron. One of the pilots in MVR2 is *Lt.* Otto Brauneck, who had just joined *Jasta 11* on 20 April. Standing next to him is *Lt.* Karl-Emil Schaefer, who had to leave for his new command at *Jasta 28* on 27 April. If Hoeppner's visit marked the unit's 100th victory scored by *Lt.* Kurt Wolff on 22 April, which seems likely, then he probably would not have arrived until the next day at the earliest. This leaves us with a 23-26 April timeframe. We can draw several links between MVR2 and MVR5 (see S511), a well-known image of most of *Jasta 11*'s flying personnel (see MVR5's caption); and if they indeed provide a direct connection, then we can narrow S509's timeframe down even further. This is because of *Vzfw.* Sebastian Festner's presence in MVR5. Festner (the subject of the very next card, S510) was killed in combat on the morning of 25 April, so MVR5 – and therefore MVR2 and S509 by association – must have been taken before then. This would restrict Hoeppner's visit to either the 23rd or 24th of April. Lastly, we have independent evidence that the visit occurred on 23 April in the form of a letter written to *Lt.* Hans Hintsch of *Jasta 11* by his mother on 25 April 1917:

"*Heute morgen brachte mir die Post Deinen lieben Brief vom 23. Herzlichen Dank dafür. Was hat der General zu Dir gesagt? Er stellt wohl an jeden so irgendeine Frage nach früherer Tätigkeit, nicht wahr?*" (Pietsch, p.272)[1]

"This morning the post office brought me your dear letter of the 23rd [April]. Thank you so much for it. What did the general say to you? He probably asked each of you some question about your recent activities, right?" (trans. by this writer)

Der kommandierende General der Luftstreitkräfte Exz. von Hoeppner beglückwünscht Rittmeister Frhr. von Richthofen.

Though she does not mention him by name, it seems virtually certain that "the general" was Hoeppner. This reference indicates that Hoeppner visited *Jasta 11* the very next day after their record achievement.

S509's image graced the cover page of the 13 May 1917 edition of *Berliner Illustrirte Zeitung*, which, according to what we know about the usual delay in news and photographs transmitted by illustrated newspapers, suits a late-April timeframe for the photo's origin as well. Our three-week publication rule places S509's earliest appearance in mid-May, which complies with Brauneck's dated S508 (30 May 1917) and Schaefer's autographed S512 (before his death on 5 June 1917).

Note

[1] Hintsch's mother's wartime letters were assembled in a private publication entitled "*'Mein lieber Hans...' Feldbriefe eine Mutter 1914-1917*" by Thorsten Pietsch (May 2004). My thanks to *Herr* Pietsch for providing me with a copy of his very interesting (and touching) work.

MVR2

Rittm. Manfred von Richthofen presents *Jasta 11* personnel to *GenLt.* Ernst von Hoeppner at Roucourt airfield on 23 April 1917. From left to right: *Hptm.* Maximilian Sorg (*6. Armee* officer in charge of aviation), Richthofen, Hoeppner, *Lt.* von Hartmann, *Lt.* Konstantin Krefft, *Lt.* Karl-Emil Schaefer, *Lt.* Otto Brauneck, *Lt.* Lothar von Richthofen, *Lt.* Karl Esser.

One of Manfred von Richthofen's Albatros D.IIIs, with aileron cables and elevator unattached, time and place unknown. Its fuselage and wheel covers have been painted over entirely in red, sparing only the manufacturer's symbol on the tail, but the wings appear to have retained their factory finish. The plane looks quite new and may have just been delivered. On the other hand, it is also possible that it had for some reason become unairworthy and was being disassembled for recovery. The attending soldiers' dress indicates that the weather was relatively warm.

S510
FESTNER
Sebastian
Vizefeldwebel

Taken: 17 to 21 April 1917
Roucourt
Publ: May 1917
Reason: *Jasta 11* success

Decorations:
WR: None
MB: None
RB: None
BH: None

Other Cards:
S511
(L7846)

Key Dates:

15 Apr 1917	*Jasta 11* moves to Roucourt airfield
25 Apr 1917	killed in action
5 May 1917	S510 photo published in *Die Woche* 18, p.607

510
Postkartenvertrieb W.Sanke
BERLIN N 37

Der erfolgreiche Kampfflieger
Vizefeldwebel Festner vor dem Start.

Vzfw. Sebastian Festner spent the early years of the war performing ground duty services with *Flieger-Ersatz-Abteilung 1* and *Feldflieger-Abteilung 7b*.[1] He must have caught the "flying bug" while doing so, because it has been said that he managed to convince his old friend, *Uffz.* Max Holtzem, an instructor with *Feldflieger-Abteilung 7b*, to give him unauthorized flying lessons. Festner was in good company, because Holtzem also claimed that he taught Eduard Dostler, Stefan Kirmaier, and Ludwig Hanstein when they were beginners.[2] After Holtzem was reassigned to test pilot duties with the Pfalz Factory on 21 July 1916, Festner went to *Feldflieger-Abteilung 2* (or *2b*) on 5 August. He then went back and forth among several two-seater units, and somewhere along the line passed flight tests that formally qualified him as a pilot. He was given a chance at single-seat fighters when he was posted to *Jasta 11* on 11 November 1916, one month after it had become operational. There he joined *Fw.* Hans Howe, *Lt.* Konstantin Krefft, *Lt.* Georg Simon, *Lt.* Carl Allmenröder, and *Lt.* Kurt Wolff. The unit did not exactly flourish under the command of fellow Bavarian, *Oblt.* Rudolf Lang, and not a single score was registered on his watch. It took the arrival of *Lt.* Manfred von Richthofen and his considerable skills on 15 January 1917 to light the spark that would make *Jasta 11* the German Air Service's most successful fighter squadron of the war. After Richthofen had demonstrated "how it was done" by shooting down three aircraft within a span of ten days, Festner was the first of his pupils to respond when he brought down a BE.2c near Neuville on 5 February. He scored again on 16 February, but this time was joined by Allmenröder (his first). March brought four more for Allmenröder, five for Wolff, seven for Schaefer, and even one for Krefft, who later became the unit's Technical Officer. Festner's guns were curiously silent that month, and one wonders if he was away from the Front or just experiencing a run of bad luck. No matter, for the floodgates opened in "Bloody April." Festner compiled 10 kills in 15 days.[3] Festner's accomplishments were rewarded with the Member's Cross with Swords of the Royal Hohenzollern House Order on 23 April. This was the NCO equivalent of the Knight's Cross for officers, and his was only the second such award to be given out during the war. He did not live to see it, however, because he crashed to his death just two days later. The British believed he was brought down by flak, but the Germans stated that his propeller broke in half during one of his attacks and caused his aircraft to go out of control. Perhaps the former caused the latter. On the other hand, return fire from the aircraft he was attacking also may have severed his blade. Another possibility is suggested by a picture taken of the nose of Karl-Emil Schaefer's plane after he had returned from a fight on 3 March 1917 (see Kilduff, *Illustrated Red Baron*, p.35). He had put at least six shots through his own propeller when the synchronization gear on his Albatros had failed. It would indeed be tragic if a similar malfunction (possibly another early problem with the new D.III model?) had led to Festner's demise.

FESTNER1, a more encompassing view of the airman in front of his Albatros, served as the basis for S510. FESTNER2, a discovery first published by Neal O'Connor in the fourth volume of his invaluable series on German decorations and the aviators who received them, was taken in sequence with FESTNER1. Obviously, both must have been recorded before his death on 25 April. Their location appears to be the Roucourt airfield that *Jasta 11* occupied on 15 April, so they must have originated during a 15-24 April timeframe. This period can be narrowed down further if we accept the theory put forth in Appendix I that certain associated photographs were taken sometime during 17-21 April 1917 when *Jasta 11* was visited by a journalist named Alfred Meyer. The 5 May 1917 edition of *Die Woche* featured several of these in addition to S510, Schaefer's S512, and Wolff's S513. Their appearance a few weeks later in the form of Sanke cards fits a pattern we have observed before.

Notes

[1] The "b" denoted a Bavarian unit; Festner was born in Holzkirchen, Bavaria.

[2] See C&C 12:2, p.174. Festner is reported there to have been Holtzem's personal mechanic at Schleissheim.

[3] The caption under Festner's S510 portrait in the 5 May 1917 edition of *Die Woche* mentions that he had forced *"den berühmten englischen Flieger Robinson"* ("the famous English flyer, Robinson") down behind German lines. Leefe Robinson, taken prisoner on 5 April, was not actually one of Festner's victims.

S511
JAGDSTAFFEL RICHTHOFEN

Vzfw. **Sebastian Festner**
Lt. **Karl-Emil Schaefer**
Rittm. **Manfred von Richthofen**
Lt. **Lothar von Richthofen**
Lt. **Kurt Wolff**

Taken: 23 April 1917
Roucourt
Publ: May 1917
Reason: *Jasta 11* success

Decorations:
WR: None
MB: None
RB: None
BH: None

Other Cards:
See Festner S510; Schaefer S507; Richthofen S450; Richthofen S526; Wolff S513
Note: card printed with two different captions

Key Dates:
20 Apr 1917	Brauneck joins *Jasta 11*
25 Apr 1917	Festner killed in action
13 May 1917	S511 photo published in *Berliner Illustrirte Zeitung* 19, p.1

This famous portrait of Richthofen and four of his squadron members can be dated because of its close association with MVR5, a more complete squadron grouping. *Lt.* Otto Brauneck and *Vzfw.* Sebastian Festner are both present in MVR5, and the dates of Brauneck's arrival (20 April) and Festner's death (the morning of 25 April) therefore bracket MVR5's origin to 20-24 April. The five pilots featured in S511 are also seen in MVR5, and they are dressed identically in both (except for Wolff, who has removed his leather coat in MVR5). The most convincing evidence of their connection comes in the form of a pronounced stain on the cloth wrapping around Festner's right leg – its pattern and location are exactly the same in S511 and MVR5. This would be virtually impossible if the cloth had been unwound and rewound on different or even consecutive days.[1] Appendix I discusses the many similarities that exist between this S511/MVR5 pair and the S509/MVR2 pair that recorded *Generalleutnant* Hoeppner's visit on 23 April (see S509). If the arguments presented there are accepted, then we can pinpoint S511 and MVR5 to 23 April 1917 as well.

MVR3 is how S511's photograph originally appeared before someone touched it up. Apparently, Festner's open mouth and partially visible tongue were deemed undesirable and were replaced by a somewhat wooden and truly artificial grin. MVR4 is a photo

Above: The original photograph that was cropped to create S510. As *Vzfw.* Sebastian Festner suits up for his flight, someone "off-camera" hands him his head gear. Below: Festner is ready to go now and sits on the fuselage for one more picture before settling into the cockpit.

5 unserer erfolgreichsten
Kampfflieger.

Vizefeldwebel Festner   Leutnant Schäfer
        Leutnant Frhr. von Richthofen
    Rittmeister Frhr. von Richthofen   Leutnant Wolff

S11
Postkartenvertrieb W. Sanke
BERLIN N. 37.
Nachdruck wird gerichtlich verfolgt.

Die fünf erfolgreichsten Flieger
der Jagdstaffel Richthofen.

Vizefeldwebel Festner   Leutnant Schäfer
        Leutnant Frhr. von Richthofen
    Rittmeister Frhr. von Richthofen   Leutnant Wolff

S11
Postkartenvertrieb W. Sanke
BERLIN N. 37.
Nachdruck wird gerichtlich verfolgt.

that was taken sequentially with S511 that had the added attraction of Richthofen's dog, Moritz.

The 13 May 1917 edition of *Berliner Illustrirte Zeitung* printed S511 in conjunction with S509, and our guideline predicts that Sanke's "Bloody April" series that incorporated them followed soon thereafter.

Curiously, S511 was printed with two different captions: either *"5 unserer erfolgreichsten Kampfflieger"* ("5 of our most successful combat fliers") or *"Die fünf erfolgreichsten Flieger der Jagdstaffel Richthofen"* ("The five most successful fliers of the Richthofen squadron"). Otherwise, everything else on the cards remained the same. Hopefully, reliable postmark evidence will someday tell us which was the first to be issued.

Note

[1] For example, we believe S510, S511, and MVR5 were all taken within days if not one day of one another. Nevertheless, the stains that appear on Festner's cloth legging in S510 do not exhibit the pattern seen in S511 and MVR5.

MVR4

MVR3

MVR5

Opposite

Top left: The original version of the picture used in S511 before someone touched up and covered over Festner's open mouth with a smile. Taken at Roucourt airfield, 20-24 April 1917. From left to right: *Vzfw.* Sebastian Festner, *Lt.* Karl-Emil Schaefer, *Rittm.* Manfred von Richthofen, *Lt.* Lothar von Richthofen, *Lt.* Kurt Wolff.

Top right: The same group seen in MVR3 at a slightly different time and with the addition of Richthofen's dog, Moritz.

Bottom: One of the most famous pictures of *Jasta 11*, taken during 20-24 April 1917 at Roucourt airfield. Sitting on the ground: *Lt.* Lothar von Richthofen. Kneeling behind him, left to right: *Lt.* Karl Esser, *Lt.* Konstantin Krefft. Standing, left to right: *Lt.* Carl Allmenröder, *Lt.* Hans Hintsch, *Vzfw.* Sebastian Festner, *Lt.* Karl-Emil Schaefer, *Lt.* Kurt Wolff, *Lt.* Georg Simon, *Lt.* Otto Brauneck. Sitting in plane: *Rittm.* Manfred von Richthofen.

S512
SCHAEFER
Karl-Emil
Leutnant

Taken: 15 to 26 April 1917
Roucourt
Publ: May 1917
Reason: *Jasta 11* success

Decorations:
WR: Iron Cross, 1st Class
MB: None
RB: None
BH: None

Other Cards:
S507, S511
(L7844, L7846)
Note: Albatros behind him has wing repair

Key Dates:

15 Apr 1917	*Jasta 11* moves to Roucourt airfield
27 Apr 1917	leaves for *Jasta 28*
5 May 1917	S512 photo published in *Die Woche* 18, p.607
5 Jun 1917	killed in action
9 Jun 1917	article published in *Die Woche* 23, pp.767-72

The upper wing of the Albatros fighter behind *Lt.* Karl-Emil Schaefer in S512 is of particular interest. An unpainted piece of fabric marks its recent repair and serves as a glaring reminder that success did not come easily or without considerable risk to these airmen. In marked contrast, Schaefer's attire includes a rather jaunty silk "dickey" around his neck, presumably to prevent his tunic collar from chafing his neck while on flight patrol. An examination of S511 under magnification discloses that he is sporting the same "dickey" there as well. This is also true for MVR2 (see below). Though a similar look at S511's companion picture, MVR5, is less conclusive, the open collar hook that is visible in S511 and the top of some kind of neckwear are both still evident.[1] This may be an indication that S511 and S512 were taken on the same day, i.e. 23 April (see Appendix I). In any event, S512's photograph appears to have captured Schaefer shortly before the three major events that occurred in his life on 26 April: the news of his transfer to *Jasta 28* as its Commanding Officer, his physical receipt of the Royal Hohenzollern House Order, and his award of the *Pour le Mérite*. The same *Oblt.* Rudolf Lang who had unsuccessfully led *Jasta 11* had moved on to *Jasta 28*. Unfortunately, his tenure there produced similar, lackluster results, and one of Richthofen's star protégés, Schaefer, was picked to replace him.

Schaefer performed brilliantly and by the end of his first month as its leader, *Jasta 28* had posted 16 kills – 13 more than it had scored in April, and six by Schaefer himself. As a result, he became the focus of a lengthy article that was published in the 9 June 1917 edition of *Die Woche*. Schaefer never had the opportunity to see the article in print though, because his luck had run out four days earlier on 5 June. The Royal Air Force's official historian provided this report of Schaefer's final flight:

"In the afternoon of the 5th a formation of seven F.E.2d's of No.20 Squadron had a running fight with about fifteen Albatros Scouts over the Ypres-Menin road. The German leader, in a red Albatros, early attacked one of the F.E.'s and mortally wounded its pilot, Lieutenant W.W. Sawden, who dived for home closely pursued by the Albatros. Another of the F.E.2d's (pilot, Lieutenant H.L. Satchell, observer, Second Lieutenant T.A.M.S. Lewis) went to the assistance of Lieutenant Sawden and engaged the red Albatros in a combat lasting fifteen minutes. The German pilot showed exceptional skill and tenacity, but, eventually, a burst of bullets from the F.E.2d at very close range shattered a part of the Albatros, which broke up in the air and crashed near Zandvoorde. The pilot proved to be Lieutenant Karl Schaefer, one of the foremost German fighting pilots who had, at the time of his death, thirty Allied aeroplanes to his credit." (Jones, *The War in the Air IV*, p.121)

The day before, Schaefer had written what turned out to be his final letter to his family:

> *"Es geht mir gut. Der Betrieb ist zwar seitens des Gegners sehr stark, wir haben aber so viel Jagdstaffeln hier und werden so planmässig eingesetz, dass wir nur zwei-, höchstens dreimal zu fliegen brauchen. Mit den Anstrengungen der Arras-Offensive ist kein Vergleich. Vetter Otto Remkes ist gerade hier und wird ein paar Tage in unserem Park faulenzen und dabei gut verpflegt. Er sieht besser aus als neulich in Brüssel.*
>
> *Heute schoss ich Nummer 30 ab.*
>
> *Herzliche Grüsse, Emil"* (Schäfer, *Vom Jäger zum Flieger*, p.115)

"All is well with me. Enemy activity is admittedly quite strong, but we really have so many squadrons that are so systematically deployed that we only have to go up twice, or at most, three times a day. It doesn't compare to the efforts made during the Arras offensive. Cousin Otto Remkes has just arrived and will be staying at our airfield a couple of days to eat well and be lazy. He looks better than he did a while ago in Brussels.

Today, I shot down number 30.

Kind regards, Emil" (trans. by this writer)

SCHAEFER5 purportedly is a snapshot of the aftermath of his last battle. This finds support in SCHAEFER6, a recently published picture of a *Jasta 28* celebration. The style, proportion, and heel details of the sole of the dead pilot's footwear in SCHAEFER5 (split open by the force of impact) are matched in SCHAEFER6 and therefore probably substantiate SCHAEFER5 as being the grim, final picture of the young ace.

Note
[1] Although we cannot see the dickey itself, the tips of the collar that protrude from the shadowy area under his neck are spread apart by something in a similar fashion.

Lt. Karl-Emil Schaefer's neckwear in MVR2 (see S509) under magnification. It is the same "dickey" also seen in S512.

Lt. Karl-Emil Schaefer's body lies among the wreckage of his downed Albatros fighter. (photo courtesy of UTD)

SCHAEFER5

SCHAEFER6

Jasta 28 entertains ladies from Wasquehal's theater troop. Its CO, *Lt.* Karl-Emil Schaefer, sits on the floor (right) next to *Lt.* Karl Bolle. The bottom of Schaefer's shoe (photos indicate he usually wore shoes topped with leather "gators" or puttees, not boots) in this image matches the style and size of that seen on the dead airman in SCHAEFER5.

Opposite
Top: *Lt.* Karl-Emil Schaefer, new knight of the *Orden Pour le Mérite*, poses in front of his Albatros D.III at *Jasta 28*'s airfield at either Wasquehal or Marcke. He had officially been granted the medal on 27 April 1917 but did not hear of it until three days later when he had already taken command of *Jasta 28*. The D.III behind him was probably flown over from *Jasta 11* (see OTF 15:1, p.13). When describing the red-bodied airplanes of *Jasta 11* around this time, Lothar von Richthofen recalled that Schaefer had his elevator, rudder and most of the back part of the fuselage painted black (Richthofen, *Ein Heldenleben*, p.205). The film of the day often translated red into black or dark gray, but we can still see a subtle tonal difference on the tail of this D.III. There is a discernible line approximately halfway between Schaefer's left arm and the fuselage's Maltese Cross that marks the start of a deeper shade on the tail. Note the suitcase or valise that rests on the ground beside the plane.

Bottom: A rather poor quality image of the airmen of *Jasta 28* under the command of *Lt.* Karl-Emil Schaefer (far left). *Lt.* Karl Bolle, wearing a white-topped service cap, stands in the center of the back row and *Offz.-Stv.* Max Müller is at the far right.

Lt. Karl-Emil Schaefer gives the camera a wary look, time and place unknown. (photo courtesy of UTD)

This artwork, done by Düsseldorf artist Fritz Reusing in 1919, borrowed from Schaefer's pose in S512. It was eventually donated to the Krefeld school that Schaefer had attended in his youth.

S513
WOLFF
Kurt
Leutnant

Taken: 15 to 26 April 1917
Roucourt
Publ: May 1917
Reason: *Jasta 11* success

Decorations:
WR: None
MB: None
RB: None
BH: None

Other Cards:
S511, S522-23, S542
(L7845, L7846)
Note: Wearing RFC leather flight coat

Key Dates:

15 Apr 1917	*Jasta 11* moves to Roucourt airfield
5 May 1917	S513 photo published in *Die Woche* 18, p.607

Lt. Kurt Wolff was transferred from *Eisenbahn-Regiment Nr.4* to the Air Service in July 1915. His first training flight ended in disaster when the LVG he was riding in crashed, dislocating his shoulder and killing his instructor. Most men might have reconsidered a flying career after experiencing such an ordeal, but Wolff, exhibiting the same fierce determination that he would later be known for in combat, continued on to earn his Pilot's Badge in December. After serving with various two-seater units, he was assigned to fly fighters with *Jasta 11* on 5 November 1916, where he joined such talented prospects as *Vzfw.* Sebastian Festner and *Lt.* Carl Allmenröder. None of them had much success, however, until *Lt.* Manfred von Richthofen, latest recipient of the *Pour le Mérite*, arrived as their new Commanding Officer on 15 January 1917. Of Richthofen's pupils, Festner and Allmenröder responded first in February. Newcomer *Lt.* Karl-Emil Schaefer and Wolff joined them on 4 and 6 March, respectively. By month's end, Wolff had caught up with Allmenröder (5 victories) and had surpassed Festner (2). Only Schaefer, with eight kills, had a higher tally. In "Bloody April," Wolff outshone them all by bringing down 22 more aircraft – one more than his esteemed commander, and a record for any single month's total by a German airman that remained standing for the rest of the war. He also recorded the Staffel's 100th victory, an event that earned special mention in the *Nachrichtenblatt der Luftstreitkräfte* and apparently prompted a visit by *Generalleutnant* Ernst von Hoeppner that was recorded in S509 and MVR2.[1] Wolff's performance in "Bloody April" also brought him the *Pour le Mérite* on 4 May 1917.

S513 is yet another of the series of photographs taken at *Jasta 11*'s Roucourt airfield in late April. Our discussion of S511 noted that it almost certainly originated the same day as MVR5, but at a different time because Wolff is wearing his captured British flight coat in one and not in the other. Contrastingly, though Wolff's pose in S511 is strikingly similar to the one adopted in S513, there are enough subtle differences between them to indicate that they were taken on separate days. His coat's belt and collar flaps are adjusted differently (see below) and the white shirt collar he is wearing in S511 and MVR5 is absent in S513. Combined, these factors indicate that S511 and S513 came from different days. Nevertheless, by virtue of S513's Roucourt location, its publication along with Festner's S510 and Schaefer's S512 in the 5 May edition of *Die Woche*, and the many similarities that it does share with other photos of the time, it seems virtually certain that S513's image was taken within at least a 15-26 April timeframe. Accordingly, it was published along with the rest of Sanke's "Bloody April" series about three weeks later.

Two other factors are particularly noteworthy in S513. The first is that Wolff is wearing a British-issue, leather flying coat that he evidently "liberated" from one of his victims. Photos of other similarly adorned German airmen (e.g., see Schleich's S644 or Carl-August von Schoenebeck and Joachim von Bertrab in O'Connor, *Aviation Awards VII*, pp.36 and 225) testify that it must have been a prized trophy. The second involves his service cap, whose crown material displays a peculiar sheen that is atypical of the traditional wool *Schirmmütze*. This characteristic is more clearly evident in Wolff's S522 and is exhibited again in many other Sanke cards.[2] It is known that all-leather caps were issued to motorcycle riders in the German Army. Yet the service cap worn by Wolff and the other airmen cited in footnote 2 possesses a cloth headband, and the crown appears to be made of a thinner and more pliable material than leather. The explanation may be found in the following exchange:

> "'Did the cavalry officers go on wearing their old uniforms in your time?' asked the new man. 'It looked really funny to see a lot of Uhlans, cuirassiers and dragoons as pilots!'
>
> 'Of course they did,' replied Rom, 'and we poor infantry privates spent our extra pay on togging ourselves out in the maddest sets of uniforms. Breeches that wide!' he indicated a most incredible width with his two hands, 'and tunics that fitted you like a glove…'
>
> '…And silk caps that perched on one side of your head, that made such a lovely crinkle,' Hamann exclaimed in the midst of the joyous laughter. 'It was one of those caps that was my undoing!'" (Kähnert, *Jagdstaffel 356*, pp.16-17)

Reference to the airman's "beautiful, expensive silk cap" is made again a few paragraphs later (*Jagdstaffel 356*, p.18). These passages come from a book originally published in Germany sometime after the war that was then translated and printed in England in the early 1930s. The action took place in 1918 and related what life was like in a German fighter squadron as the war drew to a close. Although the squadron was given a fictitious number and roll call of pilots, the book's contents nevertheless appear to have been based on actual wartime experiences. It would seem, then, that the shiny, pliable crown of the service cap worn by Wolff in S513 was made of silk or a silk blend. Ironically, Wolff's portrait – though not his name – was included in the book as one of the fictional squadron's pilots (see Kähnert, *Jagdstaffel 356*, opposite p.32).

Leutnant Wolff

Notes

[1] Although it seems almost certain that this was why Hoeppner visited *Jasta 11* at Roucourt, Wolff is nowhere to be seen in MVR5. The same goes for two of its other stars, *Vzfw.* Sebastian Festner and *Lt.* Carl Allmenröder, even though they all crop up in the apparently contemporaneous MVR5. When Hoeppner arrived, were they away on patrol?

[2] The most striking example can be found in Klein's N6339; but also see Zorer's S539 and N6243, Wüsthoff's S563-64 and S566, Tutschek's S572, Klein's S592-93, Göttsch's S613, Kroll's S625, Francke's S648, Mai's S660, Heldmann's S664, and Rumey's S665-67. Other possible candidates are Klein's S514-15, Dostler's S548, Adam's S557, Bongartz's S571, Kissenberth's S595, Loerzer's S616 and S651, Kirschstein's S623, Bäumer's S630, Donhauser's S677, and Wüsthoff's N6304. Many other pictures of German airmen display similarly shiny service cap crowns.

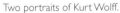
Two portraits of Kurt Wolff.

S514
KLEIN
Hans
Leutnant

Taken: April to early May 1917
Publ: May 1917
Reason: victory score

Decorations:
WR: Iron Cross, 1st Class; Pilot's Badge
MB: None
RB: None
BH: None

Other Cards:
S515, S592-93
(N6399)
Note: Taken same time as S515

S515
KLEIN
Hans
Leutnant

Taken: April to early May 1917
Publ: May 1917
Reason: victory score

Decorations:
WR: Iron Cross, 1st Class; Pilot's Badge ·
MB: None
RB: None
BH: None

Other Cards:
S514, S592-93
(N6399)
Note: Taken same time as S514

Key Dates:

Apr 1917	scores 8 victories
6 May 1917	victory #9

Lt. Hans Klein transferred to the Air Service in April 1916. He must have been a fast learner because by the following August he was already flying an *Eindecker* with *KEK Vaux*. On 20 August, Klein attacked a BE.2c during its bombing run that also came under the fire of a flak battery. Both claimed the victory, but following arbitration it was credited only to the ground gunners. After *KEK Vaux* had been reformed into *Jasta 4* under the command of *Oblt.* Hans-Joachim Buddecke and then reassigned to *Rittm.* Kurt von Döring, Klein finally gained his first offical score on 4 April 1917. He followed it with seven more that month, including double victories on 11 and 13 April. In fact, Klein's eight accounted for half of *Jasta 4*'s April tally, with *Pour le Mérite* ace *Lt.* Wilhelm Frankl coming in second with five.[1] This undoubtedly attracted the attention of High Command, the press, and Willi Sanke, who featured Klein in two cards apparently issued in May.

The photos themselves contain very few clues to help us pinpoint when they might have been taken. The Pilot's Badge that Klein is wearing could have been awarded as early as July or August 1916. But we have also seen other examples where a Pilot's Badge was earned after several months in combat (e.g., see Mulzer and Windisch in S401's discussion, Kirmaier S445, or Brauneck S508), so it may have come to him as late as October 1916. His Iron Cross 1st Class might have been earned during his pre-aviation service with the army. On the other hand, it might have been granted in recognition of his first victory on 4 April 1917. The June 1917 edition of *Die Luftflotte* announced that, "*Leutnant d.R. Kampfflieger Hans Klein, Stettin*"

had been awarded the Iron Cross 1st Class.[2] This publication was routinely many weeks late in reporting Iron Cross awards, so the implication is that he could well have received it in April. The background has the feel of a professional studio, which would indicate that Klein was away from the Front either at home in Stettin or visiting another place such as Berlin. His record suggests that he may have left *Jasta 4* for a brief time in April or shortly after his ninth victory. There is no other evidence, however, to support this suggestion. All we are really relying upon is *Die Luftflotte*'s uncertain reference when we estimate that the photos probably originated in April or early May 1917. Unfortunately, KLEIN1, a copy of the original portrait behind S515, is mute with regard to both its timing and source.

Notes

[1] Frankl had downed four airplanes in one day on 6 April, followed by a fifth on 7 April. His streak ended along with his life on 8 April when he was shot down during a battle with Bristol fighters.

[2] See *Die Luftflotte* 6, p.134.

A print from S515's original photograph, maintained as No.17956 by Berliner Illustrations Gesellschaft.

S516
BERTRAB
Joachim von
Leutnant

Taken: mid- to late April 1917
Publ: May 1917
Reason: victory score

Decorations:
WR: Iron Cross, 1st Class; Pilot's Badge
MB: None
RB: None
BH: Iron Cross, 2nd Class; Order of Henry the Lion, Knight 2nd Class/ Sw (Brun); War Merit Cross, 2nd Class (Brun)

Other Cards:
S530-31
Note: Bertrab only airman to be awarded Order of Henry the Lion, Knight 2nd Class/ Sw (Brun)

Key Dates:
6 Apr 1917	scores 4 victories
15 May 1917	victory #5

After flying an *Eindecker* with *Fokkerstaffel Metz* in 1916, *Lt.* Joachim von Bertrab joined *Jasta 30* on 3 March 1917. On 28 March, Bertrab's CO, *Oblt.* Hans Bethge, scored the squadron's first success since its formation on 25 January 1917. *Lt.* Gustav Nernst followed next with two victories on 3 and 5 April.[1] Then Bertrab really put *Jasta 30* on the map when he opened his personal tally by bringing down no fewer than four aircraft in two separate actions on 6 April. This unparalleled achievement brought him special notice in *Nachrichtenblatt der Luftstreitkräfte Nr.7* and quite possibly one of his native Brunswick's rarest decorations, the Order of Henry the Lion (see O'Connor, *Aviation Awards VII*, p.40).[2] Only five other German pilots ever equalled this mark: Wilhelm Frankl on the same day, Kurt Wolff (13 April 1917), Manfred von Richthofen (29 April 1917), Fritz Röth (1 April 1918), and Hans Müller (14 September 1918).[3] Only three would surpass it: Otto Bernert (24 April 1917), Heinrich Gontermann (19 August 1917), and Fritz Röth (29 May 1918), all with five. We now know that Frankl technically beat Bertrab to the record, having downed his fourth roughly an hour before Bertrab's. The same *Nachrichtenblatt* report, however, that cited Bertrab credited Frankl with three that day, so it must have been only sometime later that Frankl's fourth became official. In any event, Bertrab had made a spectacular debut. His next, and as it turned out, his last score came on 15 May. Whether it was this victory or more likely the remarkable four that preceded it, we can be sure that Bertrab's record caught Sanke's attention and led to the airman's appearance in what appears to have been the May publication of S516.

BERTRAB1 is the original image behind S516. Both show Bertrab wearing the ribbon for his Order of Henry the Lion in his buttonhole, thereby dating its origin to sometime after he had received the decoration as a consequence of his 6 April event. Our three-week rule and S516's predicted May appearance would restrict the photo's origin to not much later than the end of the month, giving us a mid- to late April timeframe.

Notes
[1] Nernst was killed in action later that month on the 21st.
[2] It also earned him several newspaper features, as in the special notice that appeared in *Illustrierte Geschichte des Weltkrieges* 149, p.379.
[3] This Hans Müller served with *Jasta 18* and is not the Hans Karl Müller featured in S446-47.

Opposite
Top left: This newspaper publication shows the original background in S516's photograph before it was brushed out. Note that S516's artist, however, failed to touch up the small gaps between Bertrab's arms and torso.

Right and bottom: These three photographs come from the Staudinger Collection housed in Munich's Bayerisches Hauptstaadtsarchiv and were identified as the two RFC No.45 Squadron Sopwith 1 1/2 Strutters that Joachim von Bertrab brought down within minutes of each other near Becq on 6 April 1917. The wreckage of one of them can be seen in the first picture, and two views of the other's remains are presented next. The planes appear to have crashed quite close to one another on either side of the line of tall trees visible in the background of the first two pictures. One of them was No.A2381, manned by 2nd Lt. C.St.G. Campbell and Capt. D.W. Edwards; the other was A1093 with 2nd Lts. J.A. Marshall and F.G. Truscott aboard.

BERTRAB I

S517
GONTERMANN
Heinrich
Leutnant

Taken: March to April 1917
Gonnelieu or Boistrancourt
Publ: May 1917
Reason: victory score

Decorations:
WR: Iron Cross, 1st Class; Pilot's Badge
MB: None
RB: Iron Cross, 2nd Class
BH: None

Other Cards:
S527-29; S558-59
(N6252)

Key Dates:
30 Apr 1917	CO of *Jasta 15*
6 May 1917	awarded Royal Hohenzollern House Order, Knight's Cross/ Sw
14 May 1917	awarded *Pour le Mérite*

Unser erfolgreicher Kampfflieger
Leutnant Gontermann.

Lt. Heinrich Gontermann made his debut as a fighter pilot with *Jasta 5* on 9 November 1916 and quickly notched his first victory just five days later. He added nothing more to his count until the following spring, when he burst back onto the scene with a scoring streak that would not end until he had earned the *Pour le Mérite*. With five confirmed victories in March, eleven in April, and four more in May bringing his tally to 21, he was sent home on leave with Prussia's premier decoration in mid-May 1917. Seven of these victims had been balloons – a target that he continued to menace throughout his career. After bringing down his 17th victim, he was given command of *Jasta 15*, and it was with this unit that he served until his death the following October.

GONTER1, the original photo from which S517 was derived, captures him and two mechanics alongside his Albatros D.III fighter. Most likely it is Albatros D.III 2249/16 that we knew he flew on 1 April 1917.[1] Gontermann evidently favored the special stippled finish that appears on its fuselage, because two sources show that it was repeated on an Albatros D.V that he flew later with *Jasta 15*.[2] Alex Imrie (*German Air Aces*, p.27) ascribed S517's photo to March 1917 when Gontermann was serving with *Jasta 5*. Though he did not cite the source of this information, several factors support his date. First, the new Albatros D.III did not begin arriving at *Jasta 5* until March. Second, Gontermann's airplane bears the number "2" on its fuselage that, like Edmund Nathanael's "3," served as his personal identification in *Jasta 5* (see Nathanael's S537). Third, though Gontermann could have taken his Albatros with him when he left to take command of *Jasta 15* on 30 April, the photo still seems to be from before May because there is no sign of either the Royal Hohenzollern House Order or the *Pour le Mérite* that he won the first half of that month.[3] If the March timeframe is correct, S517 is a picture of Gontermann when he had started his rise to fame and is perhaps from around the time he had become an ace with five victories (24 March). If not, April remains as the only other viable candidate.

Guideline 3's prediction of a late May debut for S517 indicates that it was Gontermann's noteworthy performance in April (he downed 11 aircraft that month and brought his total to 17) and not his *Pour le Mérite* award that inspired its origin.

Notes

[1] See O'Connor, *Aviation Awards V*, p.86.

[2] See Franks, *Albatros Aces*, p.39 and Rimell, *Albatros Fighters*, p.36. The Windsock publication notes that the "closely-stippled camouflage finish may have been dark green applied directly over the glossy clear-varnished or aluminum-doped fuselage in an attempt to reduce its brightness." Examples have been seen among several early Albatros D.V photos (*Jasta 15, 37,* and several Marine *Jagstaffeln*), but Gontermann's Albatros D.III in S517 preceded them all.

[3] Under magnification, we can see that the ribbon on Gontermann's chest does not display the swords device indicative of the Royal Hohenzollern House Order. It therefore represents the Iron Cross 2nd class.

GONTER I

S517's original photograph of *Jasta 5's Lt.* Heinrich Gontermann in the spring of 1917.

A picture of Gontermann sitting in the same plane seen in S517. Several factors including matched stippling patterns and a cut-out windscreen (that once accommodated a telescopic sight?) confirm the identification. This photo may have been taken around the same time because the trees in the background also match (see GONTER1).

Lt. Heinrich Gontermann, as a member of *Kampfstaffel Tergnier* (note the "T" on the plane's fuselage), sitting on top of one of the unit's Roland C.II *Walfisch* aircraft. *Kasta T* was Gontermann's first assignment following his flight training in early 1916. (photo courtesy of UTD)

A pre-*Pour le Mérite* photograph of *Lt.* Heinrich Gontermann in his quarters.

S518
GÖTTSCH
Walter
Offizier-Stellvertreter

Taken: October 1916 to 2 February 1917
Publ: May 1917
Reason: victory score

Decorations:
WR: None
MB: None
RB: None
BH: None

Other Cards:
S612-13
Note: Portion of fuselage forward of cockpit has been touched up

Key Dates:
3 Feb 1917   wounded in action
5 May 1917   victory #12

Vzfw. Walter Göttsch was one of the original members of *Jasta 8* when it was formed on 10 September 1916 and established its base at Rumbeke. After bringing down two FE.2d aircraft from RFC No.20 Squadron on 1 February 1917, he became the unit's first ace with a

total score of six. No.20 Squadron exacted their revenge two days later when another of their FE's shot Göttsch down near Wervicq. Franks, Bailey, and Guest (*Above the Lines*, p.118) states that after recovering from his wounds, Göttsch returned in April with the rank of *Leutnant*. *Nachrichtenblatt der Luftstreitkräfte Nr. 11, 12,* and *15*, however, refer to him as either a *Vizefeldwebel* or *Offizier-Stellvertreter* when listing his April and May victories. Göttsch was wounded again in June; but by the time of his next score, which came on 17 July, all sources agree that he had been promoted to *Leutnant*. The independent records therefore indicate that Göttsch returned in April as an *Offizier-Stellvertreter*, not a *Leutnant*, and that he only became a commissioned officer in June or July. S518 identifies Göttsch as an *Offizier-Stellvertreter* and its predicted May 1917 publication date is in keeping with this conclusion. In any event, at the end of April 1917, Göttsch was tied for 16th place among Germany's aces with a total of 9 victories – and only five of the men ahead of him had not appeared in a Sanke card by this point.[1]

An oddly textured patch – usually a tell-tale sign of photographic tampering – can be observed above and in back of Göttsch's left shoulder on the Albatros D.II fighter in S518. GÖTTSCH1, the original photo behind S518, indeed verifies that someone altered the

Left: The original picture behind S518 before someone erased the fuselage-mounted Windhoff radiator. (photo courtesy of UTD)

GÖTTSCH1

aircraft's appearance before the postcard's publication. It shows us that some unknown artist completely eradicated the D.II's fuselage-mounted Windhoff radiator, then added back the center wing-strut attachment panel and retraced a bracing wire. Interestingly, the D.II also displays a large rectangular access panel in front of the radiator where a vent was normally located – an unusual modification. Whether it was because of this unique feature or just routine caution, the Albatros D.II's image was evidently altered for reasons of military censorship.[2]

S518 offers only circumstantial evidence for the date of its photo. The Albatros D.II model seen in the background made its debut in late September 1916, with its numbers swelling from 28 serving at the Front in November to 214 in January 1917.[3] Toward the end of the D.II's production run, the Windhoff radiator seen in GÖTTSCH1 was replaced by the wing-mounted Teves and Braun radiator, though the older type continued to remain in use. The Albatros D.III began supplanting the D.II in early 1917, with 137 in service by March and 327 by May.[4] If the D.II behind Göttsch was his combat aircraft, the

Right: *Vzfw.* Walter Göttsch in front of what appears to be the smashed nose of a BE.2e. If so, it may have been his third victory, No.7190 of RFC No.6 Squadron, shot down on 5 January 1917. Its occupants, 2nd Lt. H. Jameson and Lt. D.W. Thomsen, were killed. It is the only BE.2 that he claimed as a *Vizefeldwebel*. He was serving with *Jasta 8* at Rumbeke at the time. (photo courtesy of UTD)

Below: The men of *Jasta 8*. Front row, from left to right: two unknowns, *Uffz.* Hans Körner, *Offz.-Stv.* Walter Göttsch, unknown, *Hptm.* Gustav Stenzel (CO), *Vzfw.* Alfred Ulmer, *Vzfw.* Wilhelm Seitz, two unknowns. Back row, left to right: *Hptm.* Rudolf von Esebeck, *Hptm.* Hans von Hünerbein, unknown, *Oblt. z See* Konrad Mettlich, two unknowns. After being wounded on 3 February 1917, Göttsch returned to *Jasta 8* as an *Offizier-Stellvertreter* in March or early April. Hünerbein transferred out on 7 April 1917 to take command of *Jasta 5*. So this picture originated from either late March or early April 1917. (photo courtesy of UTD)

presence of the Windhoff radiator indicates that the photo was probably taken between October 1916 and January 1917. This would have been when he first began attracting attention as a fighter pilot, with two victories in November 1916 followed by another two in January 1917. It certainly was taken before 3 February 1917, the day he was wounded and sent to hospital. He did not return until April, and by then it is doubtful that an older D.II model would still have been present at *Jasta 8*'s Rumbeke airfield.

Our timeline predicts a late May 1917 publication date for S518. A postmarked example dated 24 June 1917 demonstrates that it was no later than June.

Notes

[1] They were Edmund Nathanael (subsequently featured in S537) with 14 victories, and Walter von Bülow-Bothkamp (S582), Hans von Keudell (S555), Kurt Schneider, and Renatus Theiller, all with 12.

[2] For a similar occurrence, see the changes made to Immelmann's Fokker *Eindecker* in S347. The identification tag that Berliner Illustrations Gesellschaft attached to the back of its photos usually carried this or a similar message: "*Vom kommandierenden General der Luftstreitkräfte Presse-Abteilung zum Veröffentlichung freigegeben. Belegabdrucke wurden eingereicht. Veröffentlichungen können ohne nochmalige Zensur erfolgen. Der mit dem Zensurstempel versehene Abdruck befindet sich in unserem Besitz.*" ("Publication approved by the press department of the Commanding General of the Air Forces. Reference-copies were submitted. Publication can take place without repeated censorship. The [reference-copy] provided with the censorship stamp is in our possession.")

[3] See Höfling, *Albatros D-II*, p.7.

[4] See Connors, *Albatros Fighters*, p.13.

S518
(reissue)
GÖTTSCH
Walter
Leutnant

Taken: October 1916 to 2 February 1917
Publ: June to December 1917
Reason: promotion

Decorations:
WR: None
WR: None
WR: None
WR: None

Other cards:
S612-13
Note: see S518 (*Offz-Stv.*)

Key Dates:
Jun or Jul 1917   promoted to *Leutnant*

Except for the likes of Boelcke, Immelmann, and Richthofen, Sanke did not normally reissue one of his postcards to reflect a pilot's subsequent promotion. Walter Göttsch, however, appears to have been the exception. Initially identified as an *Offizier-Stellvertreter* in S518's first appearance in May 1917, this later reprint of the same card updated Göttsch's rank to *Leutnant*. We are not sure of the exact date of his commission, but several sources point to June or early July 1917 (see prior S518 discussion). We have one example postmarked 17 December 1917, so we know it was issued sometime in between, i.e., June to December. During the beginning of this period, Göttsch was recovering from a wound he had received on 29 June. He returned the following September but was wounded a second time on the 25th of that month and put out of action until January 1918.

S519
RICHTHOFEN
Manfred *Freiherr* von
Rittmeister

HOEPPNER
Ernst von
kommandierende General der Luftstreitkräfte

THOMSEN
Hermann
*Chef des Generalstabes der
Luftstreitkräfte*

Taken: 1 or 2 May 1917
Bad Kreuznach
Publ: May 1917
Reason: victory score

Decorations:
WR: *Pour le Mérite*; Iron Cross, 1st Class; Pilot's Badge (Richthofen only)
MB: None
RB: None
BH: Iron Cross, 2nd Class (Richthofen only)

Other Cards:
See Richthofen S450; Hoeppner S427; Thomsen S504

Key Dates:
1 May 1917	Richthofen goes to Bad Kreuznach
2 May 1917	Hoeppner dinner for Richthofen
3 May 1917	Richthofen goes to Bad Homburg
4 May 1917	Richthofen goes on hunting trip
13 May 1917	S519 photo published in *Deutsche Kriegszeitung* 19, p.3
15 May 1917	Richthofen goes to Berlin
16 May 1917	similar S519 photo published in *Flugsport* 10, cover

Oberstleutnant Thomsen
*Chef des Generalstabes
der Luftstreitkräfte*

Rittmeister
Freiherr v. Richthofen
unser erfolgreichster Flieger

Generalleutnant von Hoeppner
*kommandierender General
der Luftstreitkräfte*

519
Postkartenvertrieb W.Sanke
- BERLIN N 37.,
Nachdruck wird gerichtlich verfolgt.

Rittm. Manfred von Richthofen was sent home on a well-deserved leave following his and his squadron's magnificent performance in April 1917. Yet he was still required at the start of his trip to visit with several of his highest superiors. On 1 May 1917, *Jasta 11*'s Technical Officer, *Lt.* Konstantin Krefft, flew Richthofen to the *Kaiser*'s Supreme Headquarters at Bad Kreuznach. They arrived in the early evening and shortly afterward Richthofen met with *Generalleutnant* Ernst von Hoeppner. The next day, which was Richthofen's 25th birthday, he reported to General Staff Headquarters at the Hotel Oranienhof to meet with *General* Erich Ludendorff. He then went to the nearby royal residence, the *Kurhaus*, where he sat down to lunch with the *Kaiser*. Later that evening, Hoeppner hosted a dinner in honor of Richthofen and *Generalfeldmarschall* Paul von Hindenburg. *Oblt.* Fritz von Falkenhayn flew Richthofen to Bad Homburg vor der Höhe the next day, where he was greeted by *Kaiserin* Auguste Victoria and some of her retinue. That evening, he was again invited to be with Hindenburg. Having fulfilled his official duties, he was at last allowed to journey to the Black Forest to hunt grouse for the next 10 days. The next time he met up with Hindenburg came when they both attended a state dinner hosted by the *Kaiser* in early June.

MVR18 and MVR19 capture Hindenburg, Hoeppner, Thomsen, and Richthofen shortly before or after one of the early May dinners. We are certain they are from this time period because MVR19 was published in the 30 May 1917 edition of *Flugsport* that came out before Richthofen's next meeting with Hindenburg in June. The occasion was a formal one because Hoeppner and Thomsen are wearing their swords and Richthofen has on dress gloves. Richthofen, Hoeppner, and Thomsen are similarly, but not identically, attired in S519, MVR12, and MVR13 – three pictures that were snapped in sequence.[1] They show Richthofen in an *Ulanka* tunic that has exterior pocket flaps (versus his other tunics which displayed no such flaps), a slightly curved right shoulder board, a flat left shoulder board, and an angled Iron Cross 1st Class and Pilot's Badge alignment. This particular tunic is rarely seen among his many extant photographs, yet it turns up again in MVR14, an image of Richthofen taken during his meeting with the Empress in Bad Homburg on 3 May.[2]

Hoeppner and Thomsen are wearing their *Pour le Mérite* orders in S519 and MVR12, so we know that those pictures originated sometime after their award date, 8 April 1917. Richthofen was at the Front during all of April, and after a few days of official visits in early May, went on a hunting trip until 15 May, when he traveled to Berlin on his way home to Schweidnitz. MVR13 appeared in the 13 May 1917 edition of *Deutsche Kriegszeitung* and MVR12 was published in the 16 May 1917 edition of *Flugsport*, so it would seem that early May was the only occasion when Hoeppner, Thomsen, and Richthofen could have posed for this series. All signs therefore point to their being taken either when Richthofen reported to Hoeppner on 1 May, or sometime the next day before they changed into more formal attire for their dinner with Hindenburg.[3] Our guideline postulates that S519 came out in late May, or about three weeks later.

Notes

[1] The swords and gloves are missing. Also, Hoeppner's trousers are straight-legged in MVR18 and MVR19 as opposed to the riding breeches and boots seen in S519, MVR12, and MVR13.

[2] He can be seen wearing it again during the *Kaiser*'s review of the troops on 19-20 August 1917 (see Kilduff, *Illustrated Red Baron*, pp.50-51), which suggests that he may have reserved it for special occasions.

[3] It is theoretically possible that the photos came from Richthofen's visit to Bad Homburg on 3 May. There is no record, however, of either Hoeppner or Thomsen being present there.

Above: This snapshot of *Oberstlt.* Hermann Thomsen (left), *Rittm.* Manfred von Richthofen (center), and *GenLt.* Ernst von Hoeppner (right) appeared on the cover of the 16 May 1917 edition of *Flugsport* magazine. It was probably taken at Bad Kreuznach on either 1 or 2 May 1917. (photo courtesy of Rainer Haufschild)

Top right: A slightly different pose (e.g., Richthofen's left hand is at his side instead of behind his back) from S519's picture, published in the 13 May 1917 edition of *Deutsche Kriegszeitung*.

Right: *Rittm.* Manfred von Richthofen (left) with *Oblt.* Fritz von Falkenhayn during their visit with the Empress at Bad Homburg on 3 May 1917.

MVR18

Two photographs taken before or after *Rittm*. Manfred von Richthofen's dinner with *Generalfeldmarschall* Paul von Hindenburg on 2 May 1917 in Bad Kreuznach. The first shows, from right to left: *GenLt.* Ernst von Hoeppner, *Oberstlt.* Hermann Thomsen, unknown, Hindenburg, Richthofen, unknown officers. The second, taken a few seconds later, has from right to left: unknown, Thomsen, unknown, Richthofen, unknown, Hoeppner, two unknowns, Hindenburg, unknown. (second photo courtesy of Rainer Haufschild)

MVR19

Rittm. Manfred von Richthofen, second from the right, bows slightly as his *Kaiser* passes by (center). The bare-headed Richthofen shows no signs of the head wound he received in July 1917, so the event occurred either before then or after his wound had healed. We know of only two occasions when he visited with *Kaiser* Wilhelm before July 1917: on 2 May at the *Kurhaus* in Bad Kreuznach and on 12 or 13 June at a state dinner there. The *Kaiser* is wearing an overcoat that seems rather heavy for mid-June; and Richthofen's tunic and boots do not match the attire seen in other early May 1917 photos. We know from a number of sources that Richthofen's head wound took a long time to heal. Photographic evidence shows him wearing some kind of small bandage held by a string as late as the winter of 1917. By mid-January, the time that S606's picture was taken (see p.31), it was gone. Richthofen went to Berlin and Schweidnitz in late January 1918 before returning to the Front in February to prepare for the Spring Offensive in March. He remained there until his death on 21 April. Therefore, this photo was perhaps taken in January when Richthofen was in Berlin.

S520
VOSS
Werner
Leutnant

Taken: 20 December 1916 to 15 March 1917
Publ: May 1917
Reason: post-*Pour le Mérite*

Decorations:
WR: *Pour le Mérite*; Iron Cross, 1st Class; Pilot's Badge
MB: None
RB: None
BH: None

Other Cards:
S506, S554
(L7848)

Key Dates:

19 Dec 1916	awarded Iron Cross 1st Class
16 Mar 1917	awarded Royal Hohenzollern House Order, Knight's Cross/ Sw
8 Apr 1917	awarded *Pour le Mérite*
8 Apr 1917	S520 similar photo published in *Berliner Illustrirte Zeitung* 14, p.195
14 Apr 1917	S520 similar photo published in *Die Woche* 15, p.495

Unser erfolgreicher Kampfflieger
Leutnant Voß.

Werner Voss' aviation career began when he was transferred from *Husaren-Regiment (2. westfälisches) Nr.11* to the Air Service on 1 August 1915. He must have displayed a natural talent for flying because he was sent to *Flieger-Ersatz-Abteilung 7* in Cologne as an instructor on 12 February 1916 even before he had earned his own Pilot's Badge. That occurred on 28 May, followed by his promotion to *Leutnant* on 9 September 1916. On 21 November, he was posted to *Jasta Boelcke* where he was placed in the company of such talented airmen as Manfred von Richthofen, Erwin Böhme, and Max Müller. Just six days later on 27 November, Voss brought down two airplanes in two separate patrols. His third victory came less than a month later on 21 December. Voss did not score in January 1917, but made up for it in February by shooting down eight aircraft. No other pilot came close that month, with the nearest competitor being Friedrich Manschott's four victories. This spectacular performance propelled Voss into a sixth place tie among Germany's highest scorers, and only five living aces had a better total at this point in the war.[1] Remarkably, Voss then doubled his score to 22 in March. This put him alone in third place among all German aces, behind the late Oswald Boelcke (40) and Manfred von Richthofen (31), who had scored 10 of his own the same month. Voss added two more to his total by the time his *Pour le Mérite* was awarded on 8 April. Shortly afterward, he was sent home on a well-deserved leave (where his S506 photo was taken). One can only speculate how much deadlier "Bloody April" would have been had Voss been at the Front to participate.

It has been claimed that shortly after his return in early May, Voss and *Lt.* Rolf von Lersner conspired to have *Jasta Boelcke*'s commanding officer, *Hptm.* Franz Walz, replaced by complaining to his superiors about his lackluster leadership. Despite the supporting evidence (Walz, given command of *Jasta 19* on 25 October 1916 and then *Jasta Boelcke* on 29 November, did not score during either tenure), their breach of military etiquette could not be overlooked and it was Voss and Lersner who were transferred out on 20 May. Lersner was returned to his old two-seater unit, *Kampfgeschwader 3*, while Voss – who apparently avoided harsher treatment because he was a knight of the Order *Pour le* Mérite – was named *Staffelführer* of *Jasta 5*. Our knowledge of precisely where he went after that, and when, is somewhat confused. Some sources state that he was shuffled off to *Jasta 29* in June to serve as acting commander until 3 July, when he was reassigned as the acting commander of *Jasta 14*. Other sources claim that he was with *Jasta 5* until 7 July, and then went to *Jasta 14*. A more recent work notes that Voss remained with *Jasta 5* until 10 June before reporting to *Jasta 14* as its acting CO.[2] Whatever the exact details, it appears that High Command was not quite sure how to use his obvious talents. All sources agree that Voss at last found a home as *Staffelführer* of *Jasta 10* on 30 July. Evidently, Manfred von Richthofen valued Voss' fighting skills above all else and lobbied to have him brought into a key position within his new *Jagdgeschwader*.

Someone added a crudely drawn *Pour le Mérite* to S520's portrait. The original picture, sans *Pour le Mérite*, appeared in the 14 April 1917 edition of *Die Woche* that related the news of his award. Its source was Berliner Illustrations Gesellschaft's photo No.17205 (VOSS5). On 8 April 1917, *Berliner Illustrirte Zeitung* published VOSS6, a photo taken the same time as S520 that was used to announce his 17th victory (gained on 17 March). Obviously then, S520's photo was actually taken before the earlier S506 that depicted him with his genuine order. We know that S520's image postdates his 19 December 1916 receipt of the Iron Cross 1st Class (the result of his first two victories on 27 November) because it is present on his tunic. We can similarly surmise that it preceded his 16 March 1917 award of the Royal Hohenzollern House Order since there is no sign of that medal in the photo. Curiously, even though S520's photo can be dated to the time he was serving with *Jasta 2* (renamed *Jasta Boelcke* in honor of its former commander), his shoulder board still displays the number "7" – presumably a hangover from his *Flieger-Ersatz-Abteilung 7* days.[3]

If our timeline's May 1917 publication date is correct, then Sanke came out with S520 around the time that Voss was transferred out of *Jasta Boelcke* and shuffled about by High Command.

Notes

[1] They were Manfred von Richthofen (21), Wilhelm Frankl (15), Hartmut Baldamus (12), Erwin Böhme (12), and Walter Höhndorf (12).

[2] A note penned by Manfred von Richthofen on 19 June 1917 to the Voss family, thanking them for their hospitality during his recent visit in Krefeld, stated: "I think that within eight to fourteen days Werner will also become leader of a *Jagdstaffel*." This appears to support the notion that he was no longer CO of *Jasta 5*.

[3] Some might interpret this "7" as an upside down "2." German regulations, however, required that shoulder board insignia face out toward the shoulder, so it is unlikely that Voss reversed this. In addition, the pressed metal "7" insignia, though superficially similar to an upside down "2," is sufficiently different to be positively identified on Voss' shoulder board.

Right: Though quite similar in appearance to S520, a careful examination of this newspaper portrait of *Lt.* Werner Voss proves that they are not the same. Voss was facing the camera more directly in S520 (e.g., more of his right ear is visible, and his left earlobe and the edge of his neck are aligned differently).

The image behind S520 before Voss' *Pour le Mérite* was added.

VOSS5

VOSS6

A pleasing portrait of Voss wearing his *Pour le Mérite*.

Above and below: Voss and the motorcycle his parents gave him on his 18th birthday. He had a natural aptitude for all things mechanical and was known to spend many off-duty hours tinkering with his aircraft.

Lt. Werner Voss during an obviously relaxed moment.

These two images, along with many of the Voss pictures presented here, come from what is believed to have been a Voss family album. The first shows an interesting array of *Jasta 10* aircraft that should be of particular interest to students of aircraft markings. Starting at the far left is an Albatros D.III, an OAW-built Albatros D.III (its rudder is like the D.V's) that several sources have linked to Erich Loewenhardt, two Albatros D.Vs, a Pfalz D.III, and two more Albatros D.IIIs. All but the Pfalz appear to carry *Jasta 10*'s yellow identification color on their noses. The second photo shows the same Pfalz D.III (note the broadened proportions of its Maltese cross) in flight. Its fairly unique presentation in the Voss album may be an indication that Voss usually, or at least upon this occasion, was its pilot. The first, and perhaps the second, photo was one of several taken during an early September 1917 visit to the squadron's Marcke airfield by Prince Otto of Hapsburg, Crown Prince of Austria-Hungary.

S521
BERNERT
Fritz Otto
Leutnant

Taken: late April to May 1917
Publ: June 1917
Reason: *Pour le Mérite* award

Decorations:
WR: *Pour le Mérite*
MB: None
RB: None
BH: Royal Hohenzollern House Order, Knight's Cross/ Sw; Iron Cross, 2nd Class; Albert Order, Knight 2nd Class/ Sw (Sax)

Other Cards:
S442, S443
(L7826)
Note: Pince-nez eyeglasses

Key Dates:

23 Apr 1917	awarded *Pour le Mérite*
24 Apr 1917	five victories in one day
1 May 1917	CO of *Jasta 6*
1 Jul 1917	S521 photo published in *Der Feldzug* 11-13, p.499

With seven enemy aircraft to his credit, *Lt.* Otto Bernert was transferred to *Jasta Boelcke* on 1 March 1917. Two months later, on 1 May, he was transferred once more to *Jasta 6*, only this time he had a command of his own and the *Pour le Mérite* dangling from his collar. Bernert, who had scored twice in March, had also capitalized on the carnage of "Bloody April" by bringing down 15 more aircraft for a total of 24. This streak culminated in a new German Air Service record on 24 April that not even the great Richthofen ever equaled: five victories in a single air action within the space of 20 minutes. At least, that is what has become accepted today, because various contemporaneous sources offer confusing testimony for the events of 23-24 April 1917. The date of his *Pour le Mérite* award is given as 23 April 1917, yet his record gives him only 19 victories by then, and we are fairly certain that the qualification count for Western Front pilots at that time was 20.[1] On the other hand, *Nachrichtenblatt der Luftstreitkräfte Nr. 15* states:

> "The often tried and tested Jagdstaffel Boelcke, fighting on in the spirit of its unforgettable leader, has added a glorious new chapter to its history. On 24 April, Leutnant Bernert shot down 4 airplanes of an enemy squadron and thereby dispatched his 22nd opponent in air combat. For this, His Majesty the Kaiser and King has awarded the courageous and successful fighter pilot the highest military decoration, the Order *Pour le mérite*." (OTF 15:1, p.68)

This source clearly attributes Bernert's decoration to the events of 24 April, though it mentions only four aircraft downed and a 22nd victory. Perhaps the best we can do to reconcile these discrepancies is to summarize that all sources agree that Bernert received his award in recognition of having gained 20 or more victories by 24 April.

Bernert added three victims to his total as CO of *Jasta 6* before he was posted back to *Jasta Boelcke* as its *Staffelführer* on 9 June. He led that unit until he was replaced by *Lt.* Erwin Böhme in late August. A letter written by Böhme, dated 26 August 1917, explained the circumstances:

> "*Mein Vorgänger Ltn. Bernert ist aus Gesundheitsgründen auf längere Zeit in der Heimat, er hatte vor einigen Wochen bei einer Notlandung einen dummen Sturz getan und überdies kürzlich auf einer Bergfahrt in der Heimat ein weiteres Pech gehabt.*"

> "My predecessor 2nd Lt. Bernert will be in the homeland for a longer time because of health reasons. He had a silly crash during a forced landing a few weeks ago, and furthermore, recently had another accident during a climbing expedition at home." (trans. by this writer)[2]

Upon recovery, Bernert did not return to the Front, but was instead assigned to work with the *Inspektion der Fliegertruppen* or Inspectorate of the Flying Service, also known as *Idlfieg*. After contracting the influenza that was ravaging the world in 1918, Bernert died in a hometown hospital in Ratibor on 18 October.

S521's photo shows Bernert wearing his *Pour le Mérite* in front of an Albatros fighter. If our timeline is correct in predicting an early June publication date for S521, then the image must have been taken during a late April to May 1917 timeframe. The fact that it was snapped at an airfield supports this conclusion, because Bernert's record indicates that unlike other *Pour le Mérite* recipients, he remained on active duty until at least 19 May when he claimed a victory over an FE.2b that went unconfirmed. Support for this timing is found in the 1 July 1917 edition of *Der Feldzug*, which included S521's portrait of Bernert and credited its origin to "W. Sanke," thereby establishing that S521 must have come out before 1 July 1917. A late April to May 1917 timeframe means that this photograph was taken either just before Bernert left *Jasta 4* on 1 May or after his arrival at his next assignment, *Jasta 6*.

Notes

[1] See Franks, Bailey, and Guest, *Above the Lines*, p.70 for a list of Bernert's victories. The 25 February 1917 edition of of *Berliner Illustrirte Zeitung* featured Bernert's S443 picture and the following caption: *"Leutnant Bernert, erfolgreicher Kampfflieger, der den achten Gegner besiegt"* ("Second Lieutenant Bernert, the successful combat flier, who has defeated his eighth opponent"). *Above the Lines*, however, states that he had only seven confirmed victories at this time and that his eighth did not come until 19 March. Is there a victory missing from this list? Rick Duiven, coauthor of the indispensable works, *The Jasta Pilots* and *The Jasta War Chronology*, agrees with the later Franks, *Sharks Among Minnows* (p.166) in giving Bernert an additional victory on 16 November 1915 that is not included in *Above the Lines*; but it should also be noted that Duiven considers Bernert's 17 April 1916 victory, listed in *Above the Lines*, to have been unconfirmed. Perhaps both of these early successes were counted in Bernert's tally, at least as far as officials in 1917 were concerned. If so, then Bernert would have had eight by the time of the newspaper's 25 February report, and would have downed his 20th on 11 April, qualifying him for the *Pour le Mérite* that the record states came a few weeks later on 23 April.

[2] This letter was addressed to Professor Max Bölcke, father of Oswald Boelcke (who preferred the latin "oe" spelling of the family name). It is in this writer's collection and has never been published before.

Three different snapshots of *Lt.* Otto Bernert, times and places unknown. (photos courtesy of UTD)

S522
WOLFF
Kurt
Leutnant

Taken: 14 to 31 May 1917
Berlin, by Rudolf Dührkoop
Publ: June 1917
Reason: *Pour le Mérite* award

Decorations:
WR: *Pour le Mérite*; Iron Cross, 1st Class; Pilot's Badge
MB: None
RB: Iron Cross, 2nd Class; Royal Hohenzollern House Order,
Knight's Cross/ Sw
BH: None

Other Cards:
S511, S513, S523, S542
(L7845, L7846)
Note: Taken same time as S523
Crown of service cap made with shiny material

Staf besonderer Anzeige!

Von langer Krankheit, der Folge eines Absturzes, fast genesen und glücklich, seine erfolgreichen Dienste als Flieger in allernächster Zeit wieder seinem Allerhöchsten Kriegsherrn und dem Vaterlande widmen zu können, wurde gestern abends nach kurzem Krankenlager von der heimtückischen Grippe dahingerafft unser innigst geliebter, einziger Sohn und Bruder

Oberleutnant
Otto Bernert

ehedem Führer der Jagdstaffel Boelcke, Ritter des hohen Ordens Pour le Mérite, des Eisernen Kreuzes 2. und 1. Klasse, des Königlichen Hausordens von Hohenzollern mit Schwertern, des Königlichen Sächsischen Kreuzes 2. Klasse und des Albrechtsordens mit Schwertern und des Hamburgischen Hanseatenkreuzes.

Ratibor, den 19. Oktober 1918.

In tiefstem Schmerz:

Oberbürgermeister Bernert.
Katharina Bernert, geb. Bresgen.
Hedwig Bernert.

Beerdigung: Dienstag, den 22. d. Mts., nachmittags 2½ Uhr, von der Leichenhalle des städtischen Krankenhauses.

Leutnant Wolff.

522
Postkartenvertrieb W.Sanke
BERLIN N.37.
Nachdruck wird gerichtlich verfolgt.

Bernert's family posted this death notice in the newspaper: "Nearly recovered from a long illness that was the consequence of a crash, and fortunate to be able to dedicate his successful service again to the Supreme Warlord and the Fatherland in the very near future, our most dearly beloved and only son and brother, *Oberleutnant* Otto Bernert, died yesterday evening after a brief illness with the insidious flu. Former leader of *Jasta Boelcke*, Knight of the Order *Pour le Mérite*, Iron Cross 2nd and 1st Class, the Royal Hohenzollern House Order with Swords, the Royal Saxon Albert Order 2nd Class with Swords, and the Hamburg Hanseatic Cross. Ratibor, 19 October 1918. In deepest grief: Mayor Bernert; Katherina Bernert née Bresgen, Hedwig Bernert. Funeral: Thursday, 22nd of the month, 2:30 pm, at the City Hospital Mortuary." Neal O'Connor, in his indispensable series on German airmen and their awards, did not include Bernert among the ranks of Hamburg Hanseatic Cross recipients. It is doubtful that Bernert's family would have been mistaken on this point, so his name should now be added to the list.

S523
WOLFF
Kurt
Leutnant

Taken: 14 to 31 May 1917
Berlin, by Rudolf Dührkoop
Publ: June 1917
Reason: *Pour le Mérite* award

Decorations:
WR: *Pour le Mérite*; Iron Cross, 1st Class; Pilot's Badge
MB: None
RB: Iron Cross, 2nd Class; Royal Hohenzollern Order, Knight's
Cross/ Sw
BH: None

Other Cards:
S511, S513, S522, S542
(L7845, L7846)
Note: Taken same time as S522

Key Dates:

4 May 1917	awarded *Pour le Mérite*
6 May 1917	CO of *Jasta 29*
13 May 1917	victory #30
27 Jun 1917	victory #31
1 Jul 1917	S522 photo published in *Der Feldzug* 11-13, p.498

The Order *Pour le Mérite* was bestowed on *Lt.* Kurt Wolff on 4 May 1917 following his spectacular 22-victory performance in "Bloody April." He was placed in charge of *Jasta 29* two days later on 6 May as an additional reward (his predecessor, *Lt.* Ludwig Dornheim, had been killed in action on 29 April, the probable victim of French ace René Dorme). One week later Wolff brought down a French Spad for his 30th victory and *Jasta 29*'s fifth since its inception on 28 December 1916. His next victim would not fall until 27 June – an uncharacteristically long scoring gap considering the consistency he otherwise displayed. During the same period, three other pilots from his *Jasta 29* scored on 15 May, 30 May, and 1 June before the squadron moved to another sector on 21 June. Three airmen who were based fewer than 15 miles away at Leffincourt with *Jasta 9* brought down five aircraft on 14, 19, 20, and 25 May. *Jasta 14*, located at nearby Marchais, reported six victories on 29, 31 May and 1, 2, 3, 15 June. This information indicates that Wolff's scoring gap was not attributable to either inclement weather or a lack of enemy activity in the region. As with Werner Voss, Heinrich Gontermann, Adolf *Ritter* von Tutschek, Ernst Udet, and others, it may have been the result of Wolff being sent home on the leave that customarily accompanied the *Pour le Mérite*.

Both S522 and S523 display Wolff and his *Pour le Mérite*, so their images were undoubtedly taken after its receipt. We also know that he remained at the Front until at least 13 May when he brought down his 30th victim. Our guideline predicts an early June distribution, and we can be almost certain that they came out no later than the 27 June 1917 postmark we have for the subsequent S543. Further confirmation comes from S522's appearance and identification of "W.Sanke" as its source in the 1 July 1917 edition of *Der Feldzug*. This all means that the images must have originated in May or early June – precisely the time when Wolff experienced his scoring gap and when we have speculated he was home on leave. The chair seen in S523 appears again in Otto Höhne's S525, and we know that S524-25 originated at Rudolf Dührkoop's studio in Berlin. Thus it seems almost certain that Wolff's S522 and S523, which have the look of a professional artist's series, were taken by Dührkoop too. Wolff probably passed through Berlin on his way to or from his hometown of Greifswald in northern Germany. The c.9 September 1917 edition of *Illustrierte Kriegs-Zeitung* credits S522's picture to "Gross," but this is most likely a misspelling of "Grohs" as in the A. Grohs Illustrations Verlag.

S522 gives us a close look at the crown of Wolff's service cap and the peculiar sheen it displays when compared with the traditional *Schirmmütze*'s wool material. Evidence was presented in the discussion of Wolff's S513 that this shiny material, also seen in several other Sanke cards, was comprised of silk or a silk blend.

Leutnant Wolff.

Decorations:
WR: Iron Cross, 1st Class; Pilot's Badge
MB: None
RB: None
BH: None

Other Cards:
S525
Note: Taken same time as S525

S525
HÖHNE
Otto
Leutnant

Taken: March to May 1917?
Berlin, by Rudolf Dührkoop
Publ: June 1917
Reason: unknown

Decorations:
WR: Iron Cross, 1st Class; Pilot's Badge
MB: None
RB: None
BH: None

S524
HÖHNE
Otto
Leutnant

Taken: March to May 1917
Berlin, by Rudolf Dührkoop
Publ: June 1917
Reason: unknown

Leutnant Höhne.

Leutnant Höhne.

Other Cards:
S524
Note: Taken same time as S524

Key Dates:
10 Jan 1917	wounded in action
Sep 1917	recalled to *Jasta 2*

Lt. Otto Walter Höhne started his fighter pilot career with *KEK Nord* and was there when it was reformed into *Jasta 1* on 22 August 1916. One week later he was transferred and placed under *Hptm.* Oswald Boelcke's command at *Jasta 2*. He was one of the founding member's of the unit along with *Lt.* Wolfgang Günther, *Lt.* Ernst Diener, and *Lt.* Winand Grafe. They were joined in the coming weeks by *Oblt.* Günther Viehweger, *Lt.* Manfred von Richthofen, *Offz-Stv.* Hans Reimann, *Lt.* Erwin Böhme, *Offz-Stv.* Max Müller, and *Offz-Stv.* Leopold Reimann. Under Boelcke's tutelage, Höhne was the first of his comrades to score a victory (16 September) and was able to compile six victories by the close of November – only one fewer than Böhme and five behind Richthofen's tally for the same period. On 10 January 1917, two days before Richthofen was awarded his *Pour le Mérite*, Höhne was wounded during a skirmish with Sopwith two-seaters. Existing biographical sources inform us that he returned to the Front almost a year later on 27 December, when he was placed

in command of *Jasta 59*. But three recent discoveries – a letter and two autographed postcards – tell us a little more about his activities during this period. We saw in the discussion of Bernert's S521 that Bernert had to relinquish command of *Jasta Boelcke* for health reasons in August 1917. *Lt.* Erwin Böhme, his replacement, was himself recovering from a slight wound to the hand that he had suffered earlier that month while leading *Jasta 29*. Shortly before reporting to *Jasta Boelcke*, Böhme wrote a typewritten letter to Oswald Boelcke's father, Professor Max Bölcke, on 26 August 1917. This previously unpublished letter states:

> *"Meinen alten Kampfgefährten Ltn. Höhne, der seit seiner Verwundung in der Heimat war, habe ich mit seiner Zustimmung wieder für die Staffel angefordert, vorläufig als Offizier zur besonderen Verwendung, er hat dann Gelegenheit sich allmählich wieder an das Fliegen unter den neuen Verhältnissen zu gewöhnen."*

"I have requested, with his consent, my old fighting comrade 2nd Lt. Höhne to return to the squadron to serve for the time being as Officer for Special Duty [Adjutant]. He has been in the homeland since he was wounded and in this way will have the opportunity to gradually grow accustomed to the new flying conditions." (trans. by this writer)

Now that Höhne had sufficiently recovered to return to active duty, it seemed fitting for Böhme to be reunited with his old comrade at their former unit, where he could count on Höhne's experience and support to help him with his new command. But Böhme also realized that his friend, whose last combat experience had been during the heady days when the Albatros fighter commanded the skies in late 1916, would need time to adjust to the many changes that had come during his recuperation, for the tide had reversed and the Allies now enjoyed the advantage of technical supremacy in the air. Yet something apparently prevented this reunion from occurring, because *Jasta Boelcke*'s roll call lists *Lt.* Anton Stephan as its *Offizier zur besondern Verwendung* for September to mid-October, followed by *Lt.* Eberhard von Gudenburg for the remainder of the war.

During his recovery period, Höhne also kept in contact with his former commander's father, for he sent an autographed S524 postcard to Professor Bölcke marked "23 July 1917, Breslau." Two autographed examples of S524 bearing a similar inscription, "5 July 1917, Breslau," have also survived. The Breslau references are explained by the fact that Höhne was born in Wiowitz, near Ratibor in Silesia. Breslau was the largest city in the region, so he may have been recuperating in Breslau or stationed there in some temporary military capacity (perhaps at the nearby flight school).[1] The patterned wallpaper and cloth-covered table seen in S524's background appear again in *Lt.* Hans Müller's S447 and Althaus' S430 (see S430 for a fuller discussion); and Koerber (*Deutsche Heldenflieger*, p.21) names "R. Dührkoop, Berlin" as the photographer of S430's companion, S431.

We cannot say for sure when Höhne's S524-25 pictures were taken in Berlin. He is wearing an Iron Cross 1st Class that may have come after his first victory on 16 September 1916, but this is by no means certain. He apparently served at the Front continuously until being shot down the following January, so the photos probably originated afterward. Hans Müller, who had been seriously wounded in the stomach shortly before Höhne on 26 December 1916, may offer an analogy. It is clear that Müller's S446-47's photographs were taken after his convalescence because he was promoted to *Leutnant* on 14 January 1917 and his new rank was reflected in them. Perhaps the same was true for Höhne, and the photos published in S524-25 were also taken after his recovery. If so, then our best guess would be a March to May 1917 origin.

Höhne was probably among the first to use his postcards, sending them to family members, friends, and acquaintances. Michael Stacey, author of "Postcard Heroes and Paperback Warriors," stated that "Sanke customarily presented the subject with a complimentary set of 100 postcards to help fill the inevitable requests from admirers and well-wishers." (C&C 23:4, p.371) Stacey did not cite his source directly, but then went on to discuss his access to Hans Müller's collection of over 100 fan letters. Müller had moved to Texas in 1931 and had been interviewed by Stacey there before his death in 1977. So it seems likely that Müller had passed the information along to Stacey. Independent support of Sanke's customary gift can be found in Erwin Böhme's letter quoted in S502, where he mentions sending his fiancée a dozen examples from his stash of S502 postcards. That Höhne would have been one of the first to receive copies of S524-25 and use them for family, friends, and admirers not only suits the courteous conventions of the times, but makes good business sense as well. Indeed, the 5 July examples mentioned above are their earliest known use, and are only a few weeks after our guideline's prediction of an early June debut

Exactly why Sanke brought out Höhne's S524-25 at this time is unknown. Höhne did eventually rejoin *Jasta Boelcke*, but not as its adjutant. After a brief stint with *Jasta 59,* he returned to his old unit as its *Staffelführer* on 26 January 1918. He soon became ill, however, and was transferred out four weeks later on 20 February, ending up at *Inspektion der Fliegertruppe (Idflieg).*[2] This ended his career as a World War I fighter pilot.

Notes

[1] In a letter to Ed Ferko, Hans-Georg von der Osten related that after becoming ill, he was temporarily assigned as a flight controller at Breslau-Gandau airfield.

[2] This information, different from the oft-repeated account that Höhne relinquished his command because he did not feel he was up to the task, came from Paul Bäumer's family and was related in C&C 23:4, p.319.

A picture of *Lt.* Otto Höhne during his brief tenure as *Jasta Boelcke*'s CO. Left to right: *Lt.* Fritz Kempf, Höhne, unknown, *Lt.* Eberhard von Gudenburg. The picture was snapped sometime after Kempf had rejoined the unit on 30 January 1918 and before Höhne's departure the following 20 February. (photo courtesy of UTD)

A rare snapshot of *Lt.* Otto Höhne during his brief tenure with *Jasta Boelcke* as its CO in early 1918. Höhne is farthest to the right and *Lt.* Otto Löffler is next to him. (photo courtesy of UTD)

S526
RICHTHOFEN
Lothar *Freiherr* von
Leutnant

Taken: March 1915 to February 1916
Berlin, by C.J. von Dühren
Publ: June 1917
Reason: *Pour le Mérite* award

Decorations:
WR: *Pour le Mérite*; Iron Cross, 1st Class; Pilot's Badge
MB: None
RB: None
BH: Iron Cross, 2nd Class

Other Cards:
S511, S656
(L7846)
Note: *Pour le Mérite*, Iron Cross 1st Class, and Pilot's Badge drawn in

Key Dates:

Sep 1914	promoted to *Leutnant*
Oct 1914	awarded Iron Cross 2nd Class
Mar 1915	in Berlin hospital
Dec 1915	Christmas at home
Early 1916	joins German Air Service
Dec 1916	awarded Iron Cross 1st Class
Apr 1917	awarded Pilot's Badge
13 May 1917	wounded in action
14 May 1917	awarded *Pour le Mérite*
1 Jul 1917	S526 photo published in *Der Feldzug* 11-13, p.500

Lothar von Richthofen served with *Dragoner-Regiment 'von Bredow (1. schlessisches)' Nr.4* in the beginning of the war. He was promoted to *Leutnant* by the end of September 1914, and received the Iron Cross 2nd Class in late October.[1] He fought first on the Western Front and then on the Eastern Front until his brother Manfred convinced him to transfer to the *Fliegertruppe* in early 1916. Lothar joined *Kampfstaffel 23* of *Kampfgeschwader 4* as an observer and earned the Iron Cross 1st Class with that unit in December before becoming a fighter pilot. His first assignment as such was with *Jasta 11*, under the command of his brother, which he joined on 10 March 1917. Within a span of nine weeks and a day, Lothar brought down an incredible total of 24 aircraft before being wounded in combat on 13 May 1917. This remarkable achievement, unequaled by any other pilot during the war, earned him the *Pour le Mérite* the next day.

S526 displays the coveted decoration though only in the form of a drawing. Close inspection also finds that the Iron Cross 1st Class and Pilot's Badge subtly represented in the image are fabrications as well. Only the Iron Cross 2nd Class ribbon attached to his tunic button appears to be authentic. We know that S526 did not come out any later than the 27 June postmark of Allmenröder's later S543. Like Bernert's S521 and Wolff's S522, this is confirmed by S526's appearance – complete with added *Pour le Mérite* – in the 1 July 1917 edition of *Der Feldzug*. Subtracting three weeks from this date takes us back to a point in early June when Lothar was unquestionably still in the hospital recovering from his serious hip wound. So it would seem that Sanke had been forced to modify an older photograph of Lothar because no contemporary picture of him and his *Pour le Mérite* would have been available at that time.

The date of Lothar's picture is more difficult to determine. The presence of the Iron Cross 2nd Class ribbon indicates a post-October 1914 origin. The number "4" on his right shoulder board could stand for either his Dragoon regiment or *Kampfgeschwader 4*, though the prominence of his cavalry sword seems to favor the former. The absence of an Observer's Badge probably assigns the picture to sometime before 8 May 1916, when Lothar wrote home that he already had a few aerial combats behind him (see Kilduff, *Richthofen: Beyond the Legend*, p.45).[2] Lothar had several opportunities to visit C.J. von Dühren's Berlin studios between November 1914 and May 1916. According to his mother's diary, the first came in March 1915 when, after having served in Poland and Hungary, Lothar was sent to a Berlin hospital to recuperate from an unidentified illness. He was back in Germany in July and again in December 1915 to celebrate Christmas with his family. He flew home with Manfred in February 1916 and did not return again until late September. The best we can offer then is that the picture was taken between March 1915 and February 1916. As a final note, journalist Alfred Meyer disclosed this little-known fact in the article he wrote on his visit to *Jasta 11*:

> *"Rittmeister Manfred Freiherr von Richthofen, sein jungerer Bruder Lothar, der damals noch nicht das Flugzeugführer-Abzeichen sein nannte, obgleich er schon acht Gegner heruntergekämpft hatte, in unglaublich kurzer Zeit..."*

> "Cavalry Captain Manfred von Richthofen, his younger brother Lothar, who at the time did not yet have his Pilot's Badge

even though he had already brought down eight opponents in an unbelievably short time…"

Meyer's visit occurred sometime during 17-21 April 1917 at Roucourt. This means that only a few weeks before he became the acting CO of the German Air Service's most famous fighter squadron (when Manfred went on leave), and less than a month before he won Prussia's highest decoration, Lothar von Richthofen had not yet officially earned his Pilot's Badge!

Notes

[1] On 22 October 1914, Lothar wrote his mother: "Today I can inform you that I have received my Iron Cross." (Fischer, *Mother of Eagles*, p.58)

[2] Someone might argue that Sanke's modifications could have obscured an already-existing Observer's Badge; but then we would have to question why anyone would have bothered because, given its oblique angle, it would have passed for a Pilot's Badge anyways.

Lt. Lothar von Richthofen and other members of *Kasta 23* at Le Chatelet in 1916. Note the Fokker *Eindecker* with wings tied back along the fuselage behind them. (photo courtesy of UTD)

S527
GONTERMANN
Heinrich
Leutnant

Taken: 15 to 31 May 1917
Berlin, by Nicola Perscheid
Publ: June 1917
Reason: *Pour le Mérite* award

Decorations:
WR: *Pour le Mérite*; Iron Cross, 1st Class; Pilot's Badge
MB: None
RB: Iron Cross, 2nd Class, Royal Hohenzollern House Order, Knight's Cross/ Sw
BH: None

Other Cards:
S517, S528-29; S558-59
(N6252)
Note: Taken same time period as S528-29, S558-59

S528
GONTERMANN
Heinrich
Leutnant

Taken: 15 to 31 May 1917
Berlin, by Nicola Perscheid
Publ: June 1917
Reason: *Pour le Mérite* award

Decorations:
WR: *Pour le Mérite*; Iron Cross, 1st Class
MB: None
RB: Iron Cross, 2nd Class; Royal Hohenzollern House Order, Knight's Cross/ Sw
BH: None

Other Cards:
S517, S527, S529; S558-59
(N6252)
Note: Taken same time period as S527, S529, S558-59

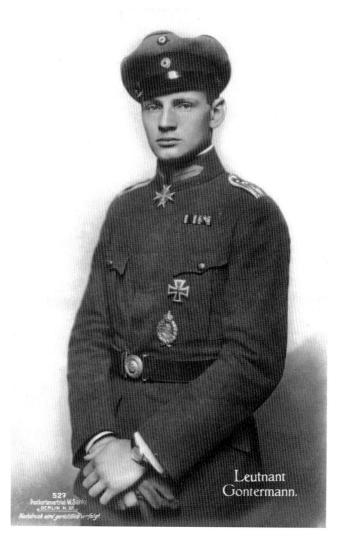

Leutnant
Gontermann.

527
Postkartenvertrieb W.Sanke
BERLIN N.37.
Nachdruck wird gerichtlich verfolgt.

S529
GONTERMANN
Heinrich
Leutnant

Taken: 15 to 31 May 1917
Berlin, by Nicola Perscheid
Publ: June 1917
Reason: *Pour le Mérite* award

Decorations:
WR: *Pour le Mérite*; Iron Cross, 1st Class; Pilot's Badge
MB: None
RB: Iron Cross, 2nd Class; Royal Hohenzollern House Order, Knight's Cross/ Sw
BH: None

Other Cards:
S517; S527-28; S558-59
(N6252)
Note: Taken same time period as S527-28, S558-59
S529 printed with and without N. Perscheid credit

Key Dates:
14 May 1917   awarded *Pour le Mérite*, goes on leave
19 Jun 1917   returns to *Jasta 15*

Lt. Heinrich Gontermann was awarded his *Pour le Mérite* on 14 May 1917 and according to Ernst Udet, was granted one month's leave, returning to the Front on 19 June (Udet, pp.38 and 44). The photographs in S527-29 were taken during this period because they include his new decoration, are attributed to Nicola Perscheid's Berlin studio, and must have occurred before the 27 June postmark of Allmenröder's S543. Adding three weeks to Gontermann's leave period gives us an earliest publication range of 4 June to 10 July; but Allmenröder S543 reduces this further to June alone. We can be sure that they were not much later than this because of a handwritten note on the back of one surviving copy of S529:

> *"Lt. Heinrich Gontermann schoss bisher (Juli 17) 23 feindl. Flugzeuge ab und wurde mit dem* Pour le Merite *ausgezeichnet."*

> "2nd Lieutenant Heinrich Gontermann up to now (July 1917) has shot down 23 enemy aircraft and has been awarded the *Pour le Merite*."

Gontermann downed his 23rd on 27 June and his 24th on 16 July, so the card appears to have been written in the first half of July.

There is little doubt that S527-29 were taken at one sitting. Gontermann's attire, his decorations, their positions, and the curve of his left shoulder board are identical throughout. In particular, the precise shape and indentations of his service cap in S527 are matched in S529. S528-29 give credit to Nicola Perscheid of Berlin as their photographer, and it follows that S527 was taken there as well. Gontermann's S558-59 and N6252 also appear to be a set. They share the same background, and the table displayed in S559 may be the same one that is covered by a map in S558 and N6252. N6252 bears the identification "H. Bensemann," a photographer from Metz also named in several pictorial newspaper publications, and it therefore seems reasonable to associate S558-59 with Bensemann as well.[1] This would normally conclude our discussion except that Gontermann's appearance is almost identical throughout all of these photographs, down to the same distinct bends in his shoulderboards and the precise hang of his *Pour le Mérite*. Intriguingly, the indentations in his service cap are identical in S527, S529 (Perscheid) and N6252 (Bensemann), yet different in S559 (probably Bensemann). Then we come across the most distinguishing characteristic: Gontermann's ribbon bar is different only in N6252. Where S527-29 and S558-59 share identical ribbons for both the Iron Cross 2nd Class and Royal Hohenzollern House Order, N6252 only has the House Order on a different ribbon with narrower white side stripes. It is also positioned lower down on Gontermann's chest.

Though we have observed elsewhere that photographers sometimes alternated various medal presentations during one photo shoot (Bernert's S442-43 and perhaps Buddecke's S433-34 and BUDDECKE5) and that different backgrounds were sometimes provided by the same studio during one sitting (Althaus' S430-31 and Müller's S446-47), there is no other reason to doubt the given studio identities: S527-29 from Nicola Perscheid in Berlin and S558-59, N6252 from H. Bensemann in Metz. What then might account for the similarities between them? Perhaps they all originated within a short time of each other, that is, during the first portion of Gontermann's leave back in Germany.

GONTER2 is an image of Gontermann that appeared in a 1918 newspaper publication. GONTER3, attributable to the last half of April 1917 – or shortly before Gontermann got his *Pour le Mérite* – captures the airman with various members of his *Jasta 5*. Both show him wearing a single Royal Hohenzollern House Order ribbon bar in the same spot on his tunic as where it occurs in N6252. Technically, he should have been wearing the Iron Cross 2nd Class ribbon alongside it, but it looks as though he simply attached the swords device to his pre-existing Iron Cross ribbon.[2] Was this what he was originally wearing when he first entered Bensemann's studio on his way back to Germany, only to have it replaced with the more technically correct ribbon display seen in the remainder of the Bensemann photos, the Perscheid images, and all his subsequent photographs? If so, GONTER2 might even belong to the Bensemann set. In any event, the implication is that Gontermann traveled from *Jasta 5*'s base at Boistrancourt to Metz first before continuing on to Berlin and his photo session at Nicola Perscheid's studio. Like Manfred von Richthofen and other pilots, Gontermann may have been required to report to Berlin first for some official functions before being allowed to finish his leave at home.[3]

Notes

[1] Though N6252 itself does not disclose the studio's location, *Illustrierte Geschichte des Weltkrieges* credits several pictures to "H. Bensemann, Metz" throughout various issues.

[2] The Iron Cross and Royal Hohenzollern decorations shared the same war ribbon (black with white side stripes).

[3] In fact, Richthofen was at Berlin's Johannisthal airfield to test various aircraft during this very time period, 15-18 May. Was Gontermann requested to do something similar?

Weltkrieg! Kriegs- und Ruhmesblätter published this portrait of *Lt.* Heinrich Gontermann in 1918.

Members of *Jasta 5*: (front row, left to right) *Hptm.* Hans von Hünerbein (CO), *Lt.* Heinrich Gontermann, *Lt.* Kurt Schneider, *Lt.* Kleeman, *Lt.* Vorländer, *Lt.* Rudolf Nebel. (back row, left to right) unknown, *Vzfw.* Josef Mai, *Offz-Stv.* Edmund Nathanael, *Vzfw.* Ernst Dahlmann, *Offz-Stv.* Alfred Sturm, *Offz-Stv.* Löwensen. Mai joined the unit on 17 April 1917 and Gontermann left it for *Jasta 15* on 30 April, so the picture originated sometime during that period. Hünerbein and Gontermann's clasped hands may be an indication that it was taken upon the occasion of Gontermann's departure.

NPG postcard No.6252.

This S529 version does not have Nikola Perscheid's name printed on the lower left corner.

S530
BERTRAB
Joachim von
Leutnant

Taken: mid-April to May 1917
Berlin, by Nicola Perscheid
Publ: June 1917
Reason: unknown

Decorations:
WR: Iron Cross, 1st Class, Pilot's Badge
MB: None
RB: Iron Cross, 2nd Class; Order of Henry the Lion, Knight 2nd Class/ Sw (Brun); War Merit Cross, 2nd Class (Brun)
BH: None

Other Cards:
S516, S531
Note: Taken same time as S531
Card printed with and without N. Perscheid credit

S531
BERTRAB
Joachim von
Leutnant

Taken: mid-April to May 1917
Berlin, by Nicola Perscheid
Publ: June 1917
Reason: unknown

Decorations:
WR: Iron Cross, 1st Class, Pilot's Badge
MB: None
RB: Iron Cross, 2nd Class; Order of Henry the Lion, Knight 2nd Class/ Sw (Brun); War Merit Cross, 2nd Class (Brun)
BH: None

Other Cards:
S516, S531
Note: Taken same time as S530
Card printed with and without N. Perscheid credit

Key Dates:
15 May 1917   victory #5
12 Aug 1917   shot down and POW

Lt. Joachim von Bertrab's S516 card was issued following his spectacular four victories in one day on 6 April 1917. His next (and final) score occurred on 15 May, making him an ace by modern standards. Little more is known about his wartime career other than that during a balloon attack on 12 August 1917 he had the misfortune of running into British ace Major Edward "Mick" Mannock of RFC Squadron No.40. Bertrab was subsequently shot down and interned as a prisoner for the remainder of the war.

Bertrab is wearing the ribbon for his Order of Henry the Lion, which he received soon after his 6 April event. Our guideline indicates a June publication for these cards, and going back three weeks

produces an outer time limit of around the end of May for their photos' origin. The portraits are identified as having been taken by Nicola Perscheid in Berlin, so Bertrab must have traveled there either between his fourth and fifth victories or shortly after his fifth. Why an airman with Bertrab's comparatively modest total of five aircraft would have been featured again on two postcards so soon after his S516 is somewhat of a mystery. Perhaps the cards that come immediately before and after, Gontermann's S527-29 and Richthofen's S532-34, provide us with a clue. They too came from Perscheid's studio, and it is just possible that they were all offered together as a group package to Sanke.

Once again, the bookends provided by the no-earlier-than-June publication of Wolff's prior S522-34 series and the 27 June postmark of the later Allmenröder S543 establish a June timeframe for S516's initial appearance.

Right: *Lt.* Joachim von Bertrab's fifth and final victim, brought down on 15 May 1917. It was FE.2d No.A6446 of RFC No.20 Squadron. Its occupants were taken prisoner.

Below: These examples of Bertrab's S530 and S531 do not have Nicola Perscheid's name printed at the bottom.

Leutnant v. Bertrab

530
Postkartenvertrieb W.Sanke
BERLIN N.37.
Nachdruck wird gerichtlich verfolgt

Leutnant v. Bertrab

531
Postkartenvertrieb W.Sanke
BERLIN N.37.

S532
RICHTHOFEN
Manfred *Freiherr* **von**
Rittmeister

Taken: 15-18 May 1917
Berlin, by Nicola Perscheid
Publ: June 1917
Reason: victory score

Decorations:
WR: *Pour le Mérite*; Iron Cross, 1st Class; Pilot's Badge
MB: None
RB: None
BH: Iron Cross, 2nd Class

Other Cards:
S450, S503, S509, S511, S519, S533-34, S554, S606, S619
(L7835, L7846, L7847, L7894, L7895, L7898, L7932, L7933;
N6255, N6306)
Note: Taken same time as S533-34
Cipher for former unit, *Ulanen-Regiment 'Kaiser Alexander III. von Russland (westpreussisches)' Nr.1*, on shoulder boards

S533
RICHTHOFEN
Manfred *Freiherr* **von**
Rittmeister

Taken: 15-18 May 1917
Berlin, by Nicola Perscheid
Publ: June 1917
Reason: victory score

Decorations:
WR: *Pour le Mérite*; Iron Cross, 1st Class; Pilot's Badge
MB: None
RB: None
BH: Iron Cross, 2nd Class

Other Cards:
S450, S503, S509, S511, S519, S532, S534, S554, S606, S619
(L7835, L7846, L7847, L7894, L7895, L7898, L7932, L7933;
N6255, N6306)

Note: Taken same time as S532 and S534
Cipher for former unit, *Ulanen-Regiment 'Kaiser Alexander III. von Russland (westpreussisches)' Nr.1*, on shoulder boards

S534
RICHTHOFEN
Manfred *Freiherr* von
Rittmeister

Taken: 15-18 May 1917
Berlin, by Nicola Perscheid
Publ: June 1917
Reason: victory score

Decorations:
WR: *Pour le Mérite*; Iron Cross, 1st Class; Pilot's Badge
MB: None
RB: None
BH: Iron Cross, 2nd Class

Other Cards:
S450, S503, S509, S511, S519, S532-33, S554, S606, S619
(L7835, L7846, L7847, L7894, L7895, L7898, L7932, L7933;
N6255, N6306)
Note: Taken same time as S532-33
Cipher for former unit, *Ulanen-Regiment 'Kaiser Alexander III. von Russland (westpreussisches)' Nr.1*, on shoulder boards

Key Dates:

15 May 1917	in Berlin for four days
19 May 1917	at home in Schweidnitz
12 Aug 1917	S532 photo published in *Berliner Illustrirte Zeitung* 32, p.425

Rittmeister Manfred Frhr. von Richthofen
534
phot. Nicola Perscheid

These postcards state that their photos were taken by Nicola Perscheid of Berlin. They include Richthofen's *Pour le Mérite*, won on 12 January 1917, but show no signs of the head wound he suffered on 7 July 1917. We know that Richthofen visited Berlin four times in between these events. He was there in early February and had his S450 portrait taken by C.J. von Dühren. It seems unlikely that he also would have visited Perscheid during the same trip. He passed through the city again on 31 May (on his way to to Vienna) and around 10 June (on his way to Karl-Emil Schaefer's funeral), but the short duration of these visits and their somewhat late occurrence to have been able to generate three mid-June postcards negates their suitability as well. This leaves Richthofen's 15-18 May trip when he visited with the Inspectorate of Military Aviation and test flew aircraft at Johannisthal airfield. Richthofen also met with the Verlag Ullstein publishing company during this period, which resulted in his autobiography, *Der rote Kampfflieger*, being dictated to an Ullstein company stenographer after he went home to Schweidnitz later that month. Notably, when the book was published a few months later, its frontispiece displayed Perscheid's S532 portrait. Shortly afterward, the front page of the 12 August 1917 edition of *Berliner Illustrirte Zeitung* announced Richthofen's book with the same picture and the caption:

> *"Unser erfolgreichster Flieger, Rittmeister Frhr. V. Richthofen, der die Schilderung seiner Lüftkampfe in einem soeben erschienenen Buch 'Der rote Kampfflieger' veröffentlicht hat. Zwei der eindrucksvollsten Kapitel sind in dieser Nummer enthalten."*

> "Our most successful flier, Captain Baron von Richthofen, who has given a description of his air battles in a just-published book, 'The Red Combat Flier'. Two of the most impressive chapters are contained in this edition." (trans. by this writer)[1]

This was no coincidence because the Ullstein firm also published *Berliner Illustrirte Zeitung*. Perhaps it was they who arranged for Richthofen's portraits at Perscheid's studio in anticipation of their book, though it is equally plausible that they merely licensed them from Perscheid. Whatever the actual circumstances, it was Sanke who brought them to the public first in June (the series falls between the early June appearance of Wolff's S522-23 and the 27 June postmark of Allmenröder's S543).

N6306 is another photo from this series. It looks very similar to S533, though Richthofen's other hand is on his hip and his expression is more serious. What is surprising is that "A. Müller" – not Nicola Perscheid – is named as its source. Among all the Sanke, Liersch, and NPG cards featuring airmen, Müller's name only appears on cards N6304-06. Both N6304, a picture of *Lt.* Curt Wüsthoff, and N6305, a snapshot of a *Lt.* von Ahlen who flew in the Balkan theater of operations, name Dresden-Loschwitz as the site of Müller's studio. Not much is known about Ahlen, but Wüsthoff certainly had connections with Dresden, so the name and location appear to be authentic.[2] Was Müller's name mistakenly carried over from the previous two cards, or did he somehow procure the photo from another source such as the Verlag Ullstein publishing house or even Perscheid himself?

The 15-18 May date for this Richthofen series finds support from another contemporaneous source. *Hptm.* Erich von Salzmann recalled what happened when Richthofen attended the races at Berlin's Grunewald track during that visit:

> "Once we were together at the races in Grunewald and for a while he remained unnoticed. That morning he had been at Johannisthal, had test flown some new aircraft and his 'dress' was not really very elegant racecourse attire. In general, Richthofen was little inclined toward superficial appearances, although he did not seek to neglect the way he looked. Suddenly people recognized him. Then the photographers came. I have seen other young celebrities in such moments, as they put on airs and posed. None of that for Richthofen. His complete self-confidence was obvious. The young girls rushed toward him. He was asked to sign their programs as souvenirs." (Kilduff, *Richthofen: Beyond the Legend*, p.156)

One of those candid photos, MVR15 (see page 30), was later published in newspapers and also served as the basis for N6255. It depicts Richthofen wearing the same tunic seen in S532-34. It has no pocket flaps, the left shoulder board has the identical wavy pattern, and his Iron Cross 1st Class and Pilot's Badge are vertically aligned in the same pattern. MVR15 therefore offers corroborative evidence that Richthofen was in Berlin during 15-18 May and that he wore the particular outfit captured in S532-34 and N6306.

Notes
[1] The two chapters were *"Boelcke's Tod"* ("Boelcke's Death") and *"Mein erfolgreichster Tag"* ("My Most Successful Day").
[2] See footnote 22, p.34.

Verlag Ullstein circulated this handbill to advertise Manfred von Richthofen's autobiographical *Der rote Kampfflieger*. Various newspapers also ran ads for the book in August 1917.

NPG postcard No.6306. Although its image undoubtedly originated from S532-34's sitting at Nicola Perscheid's Berlin studio, the card curiously credits "A. Müller," who was based in Dresden-Loschwitz.

An example of Richthofen's S532 that, similar to Bertrab's S530-31, does not have Nicola Perscheid's name printed at the bottom.

S532 (†)
(memorial)
RICHTHOFEN
Manfred *Freiherr* von
Rittmeister

Taken: 15-18 May 1917
Berlin, by Nicola Perscheid
Publ: May 1918
Reason: memorial

Decorations:
WR: *Pour le Mérite*; Iron Cross, 1st Class; Pilot's Badge
MB: None
RB: None
BH: Iron Cross, 2nd Class

Other Cards:
S450, S503, S509, S511, S519, S533-34, S554, S606, S619
(L7835, L7846, L7847, L7894, L7895, L7898, L7932, L7933;
N6255, N6306)
Note: Taken same time as S533-34

Cipher for former unit, *Ulanen-Regiment 'Kaiser Alexander III. von Russland (westpreussisches)' Nr.1*, on shoulder boards

S533 (†)
(memorial)
RICHTHOFEN
Manfred *Freiherr* von
Rittmeister

Taken: 15-18 May 1917
Berlin, by Nicola Perscheid
Publ: May 1918
Reason: memorial

Decorations:
WR: *Pour le Mérite*; Iron Cross, 1st Class; Pilot's Badge
MB: None
RB: None
BH: Iron Cross, 2nd Class

Other Cards:
S450, S503, S509, S511, S519, S532, S534, S554, S606, S619
(L7835, L7846, L7847, L7894, L7895, L7898, L7932, L7933;
N6255, N6306)

Note: Taken same time as S532 and S534
Cipher for former unit, *Ulanen-Regiment 'Kaiser Alexander III. von Russland (westpreussisches)' Nr.1*, on shoulder boards

S534 (†)
(memorial)
RICHTHOFEN
Manfred *Freiherr* von
Rittmeister

Taken: 15-18 May 1917
Berlin, by Nicola Perscheid
Publ: May 1918
Reason: memorial

Decorations:
WR: *Pour le Mérite*; Iron Cross, 1st Class; Pilot's Badge
MB: None
RB: None
BH: Iron Cross, 2nd Class

Other Cards:
S450, S503, S509, S511, S519, S532-33, S554, S606, S619
(L7835, L7846, L7847, L7894, L7895, L7898, L7932, L7933;
N6255, N6306)
Note: Taken same time as S532-33
Cipher for former unit, *Ulanen-Regiment 'Kaiser Alexander III. von Russland (westpreussisches)' Nr.1*, on shoulder boards

Key Dates:
21 Apr 1918   killed in action

Like Boelcke's two S363† examples, Immelmann's S361†, and Richthofen's S503†, Sanke took his previous S532-34 postcards, bordered them in black, and added the "†" death symbol next to Richthofen's name. They were probably brought out in early May 1918 following the great ace's death on 21 April.

Rittmeister
Manfred Frhr. von Richthofen ✝

THE END *of the* RED BARON

Wishes

for

A Merry Xmas

and

Happy New Year

from

209 Squadron,
Royal Air Force,
B. E. F.,
France.

Xmas, 1918.

Right: 209 Squadron, RAF was obviously proud of the role they played in bringing down Manfred von Richthofen when they issued this 1918 Christmas card. The cover took a black and white print of a painting by Joseph Simpson and bordered it in red.

S535
GÖRING
Hermann
Leutnant

Taken: 21 February to 16 May 1917
Publ: June 1917
Reason: victory score

Decorations:
WR: None
MB: None
RB: None
BH: None

Other Cards:
S573, S654-55
(N6272, N6443)

Key Dates:
15 Feb 1917	returns to active duty
10 May 1917	victory #7
17 May 1917	CO of *Jasta 27*
27 Jun 1917	S535 photo published in *Flugsport* 13, p.423

After recovering from a wound received in combat on 2 November 1916, *Lt.* Hermann Göring returned to active duty with *Jasta 26* on 15 February 1917. Six days later, *Lt.* Fritz Loerzer, the brother of Göring's friend and *Staffelführer*, Bruno Loerzer, joined them there. About three months after that, Göring left the Loerzer brothers to take command of his own squadron, *Jasta 27*.

GÖRING1 is a picture of Fritz Loerzer that is suspiciously similar to S535. Frank Olynyk, who studied the war diaries of various units that Göring served in, believed that S535 captured Göring in his Albatros D.III 2049/16 and that GÖRING1 probably showed Loerzer in his D.III 2024/16 when both men were at *Jasta 26*.[1] The implication is that the snapshots were taken contemporaneously, like the portraits of *Jasta 9*'s Hartmut Baldamus, Hermann Pfeifer, and Kurt Student in their Albatros fighters, which appear to have originated from the same time and place (see Pfeifer's S428, footnote 3). If so, then S535's picture and GÖRING1 must have originated between 21 February and 16 May 1917 when Göring and Loerzer served together in *Jasta 26*.[2]

Before his departure to *Jasta 27* (his war diaries note that he was transferred on 17 May 1917 but actually arrived there on 21 May), Göring had compiled a total of seven confirmed victories. Though this seems modest when compared with the records of the Sanke pilots who had come before him, it was good enough to qualify him as *Jasta 26*'s top scorer (CO Bruno Loerzer was next with five) and to earn him a command of his own. Evidently, it was also enough to catch the attention of Willi Sanke and the editors of *Flugsport*, who used the image of Göring and his Albatros for their June 1917 publications.

Notes
[1] See OTF 10:3, pp.195-235. The author notes that Göring's D.III 2049/16 accompanied him to his new command at *Jasta 27* in late May but had its fuselage painted black soon afterward.

[2] Fritz Loerzer stayed with *Jasta 26* when Göring left to take command of *Jasta 27*.

Leutnant Göring.

535
Postkartenvertrieb W.Sanke
BERLIN N.37
Nachdruck wird gerichtlich verfolgt.

Lt. Fritz Loerzer in the cockpit of an Albatros D.III, probably 2024/16. The picture is similar to S535. Göring and Loerzer were posted in February 1917 to *Jasta* 26, led by Fritz's brother and Göring's close friend, *Oblt.* Bruno Loerzer.

The reverse of this photograph identifies it as Göring, *Staffelführer* of *Jasta 27*. If true, and the plane behind him was his, then it probably is D.III 2049/16 that he brought with him from *Jasta 26*. It has its radiator inset in the center of the top wing, which was characteristic of D.IIIs up through serial number 2200/16, and the wing's leading edge on either side of the radiator also displays what appear to be the ends of inverted white chevrons that were known to adorn the same plane after its fuselage had been painted black with a white tail and nose. Accordingly, this image may have been snapped soon after Göring's arrival at his new command. (photo courtesy of UTD)

Above and below: Two pictures of *Lt.* Hermann Göring and *Lt.* Bruno Loerzer when they were with *FFA 25*. The first shows them standing side by side to the left of Crown Prince Wilhelm (second from right). The army units in *FFA 25*'s sector were commanded by the Crown Prince, who personally presented Loerzer and Göring with their Iron Crosses 1st Class on 22 March 1915. Perhaps this image came from that occasion. The second picture has Loerzer displaying the ribbon for his Baden Zähringer Lion Order, Knight 2nd Class with Swords that he won on 27 April 1915. Göring and Loerzer parted company on 29 June for different flight training courses at Freiburg and Schwerin, respectively. Göring reportedly won both his Pilot's Badge and his own Zähringer Lion Order before his return to *FFA 25* on 15 September. This picture includes his Pilot's Badge but there is no indication of the Baden award. (second photo courtesy of UTD)

S536
BRANDENBURG
Ernst
Hauptmann

Taken: 1915 to 24 May 1916
Frankfurt am Main, by Prof. A. Krauth
Publ: June 1917
Reason: *Pour le Mérite* award and London mission

Decorations:
WR: *Pour le Mérite*; Iron Cross, 1st Class
MB: None
RB: None
BH: Iron Cross, 2nd Class

Other Cards:
S541
(L7896)

Key Dates:
13 Jun 1917	conducts raid over London
14 Jun 1917	awarded *Pour le Mérite*
19 Jun 1917	injured in accident
22 Jul 1917	S536 photo published in *Berliner Illustrirte Zeitung* 29, p.405

This is the original picture behind S535, discovered in one of Hermann Göring's personal photo albums.

Ernst Brandenburg was born in Sophienfeld near what is now Znin, Poland on 4 June 1883. His military career began with *Infanterie-Regiment (6. westpreussisches) Nr.149*, quartered in Schneidemühl (now Pila, Poland). He was promoted to *Oberleutnant* on 18 August 1912, and then served as the regiment's adjutant. After the war broke out, he received the Iron Cross 2nd Class on 3 September, was raised to *Hauptmann* on 28 November, and was awarded the Iron Cross 1st Class on 24 December 1914. One source states that Brandenburg was wounded in ground fighting in 1914, and like so many other future airmen, applied for a transfer to the Air Service during his recovery. Perhaps his interest in this area had been sparked by a temporary assignment he had received in 1911 to attend the Institute and Laboratory of Aviation. By 1 November 1915, he had undergone training and become a member of the *Fliegertruppe*.[1] After earning his Observer's Badge on 25 May 1916, he was given command of a *Kampfstaffel* unit in the Somme region designated as *S 2*. By early 1917, he had become the CO of *Kampfgeschwader der Obersten Heeresleitung* (*Kagohl*) *3*. He had also earned the Knight's Cross of the Royal Hohenzollern House Order on 20 January. The first of *Kagohl 3*'s new Gotha G.IV large bombers (with a 77-foot wingspan and a length of 40 feet) reached the unit in March 1917, and in May and June they mounted two raids on the British mainland, the first at Folkestone and the second at Sheerness. Finally, on 13 June 1917, they were able to carry out the first *grosse "Wurf"* (great "drop") on London. The following account of this raid relies heavily upon the description given in Walter Zuerl's 1938 book, *Pour le mérite-Flieger*, which contains a wealth of information (though not always reliable) on the airmen who earned that decoration.

Early on the morning of 13 June, the squadron's meteorologist reported that very favorable conditions existed for a raid on London. A weak wind, which flowed toward the west at up to 4,000 meters altitude, reversed direction and blew to the east above 4,500 meters. It was therefore hoped that the squadron, laden with bombs, could ride the lower tailwind over the English Channel to their target, and after releasing their payload and gaining greater altitude, ride the higher tailwind back to base. Thunderstorms were expected to roll into the area around 3:00 in the afternoon, so take-off was slated for the morning so that the bombers could return in time to avoid the bad weather. At precisely 10:00 am, the flight leader's machine rose into the air, followed by three waves of aircraft for a total of 20, each containing a three-man crew, three machine guns, and 200 kg of bombs. They began assembling while simultaneously heading straight toward their target, pulling into a tight formation by the time they had reached Zeebrugge on the Belgian coast. A blanket of clouds obscured the view below them across the channel to Margate, but once past Margate, holes began to appear and they were able to recognize the south bank of the mouth of the Thames River. The cloud cover broke up further and then disappeared as they approached the English capital. Flak batteries opened up on the formation near Southend, but shot high. By the time they had reached London, six of the bombers had either turned back for mechanical reasons or become separated from the main body. The remaining 14 aircraft were afforded an unusually clear view of the target below and were able to identify all the landmark references for the city. Defensive fire from below was ineffective, and even though many fighters approached and buzzed around the formation, only one mounted a serious attack that was turned away. Relatively undisturbed, the squadron released their bombs with the majority falling on the docks and warehouses along the Thames. They quickly closed up their formation and then, considerably lighter without their payloads, gained enough altitude to leave their pursuers behind. All the Gothas that had left on the 4 1/2 hour mission returned successfully to base.[2]

BRANDEN I

Above: This is the original image behind S536 before Brandenburg's *Pour le Mérite* was drawn in. A portion of it was published in *Berliner Illustrirte Zeitung*'s 22 July 1917 edition.

Top right: *Hptm.* Ernst Brandenburg and an unknown airman while serving with either *Kasta S 2* or *Kagohl 3*.

Right: A portrait of *Hptm.* Ernst Brandenburg wearing his *Pour le Mérite*.

Brandenburg's 13 June raid, which various reports estimated left between 145 and 162 dead, 382 to 432 injured, and £126,000 to £130,000 in damage, caused considerable consternation among the English and great elation among the Germans. Brandenburg's *Pour le Mérite* award was announced the next day, and he was ordered to headquarters at Bad Kreuznach so that the *Kaiser* could bestow his highest decoration personally as well as hear about the mission firsthand. A few days later on 19 June, while being ferried back to base by one of his own men, Brandenburg's airplane crashed.[3] The pilot, *Oblt.* Hans-Ulrich von Trotha, was killed and Brandenburg suffered the loss of a leg.

A close inspection of S536 discloses that the *Pour le Mérite* at Brandenburg's neck, though skillfully crafted, was a later addition to an earlier portrait. The publication of the original picture, BRANDEN1, in the 22 July 1917 edition of *Berliner Illustrirte Zeitung* confirms this fact. He is wearing his Iron Cross 1st Class, so we know the photo postdates his award date of 24 December 1914. He is not wearing the Observer's Badge that he earned on 25 May 1916, so this is probably an indication that it predated that event. The photograph was most likely taken soon after his Iron Cross investiture or sometime during his training period with the Air Service. It is credited to the same Professor Krauth that took Dossenbach's S416 and N6149. It is known from other sources that Krauth's studio was located in Frankfurt am Main.

S536 leaves no doubt as to why it was published. Its caption reads:

> *"Hauptmann Brandenburg, welcher das Geschwader deutscher Grossflugzeuge beim Angriff auf die Festung London führte."*

> "Captain Brandenburg, who led the squadron of German large airplanes that attacked Fortress London."

Judging by the later Allmenröder S543's 27 June 1917 postmark, Sanke worked fast to bring this card out. This would account for the addition of the *Pour le Mérite* to an older picture, because Brandenburg himself would have been recovering in the hospital from his serious crash. S536 and S543 also lend support to the concept that, as opposed to publishing them in a staggered manner, Sanke probably brought them and the series of cards between them out together at the end of June.

Notes

[1] See Zuerl, *Pour le mérite-Flieger*, p.106.

[2] Zuerl actually wrote that 22 planes left for the target and that 17 eventually reached it. Neal O'Connor, a more careful scholar whose summary of this mission in his *Aviation Awards II*, p.108 states that 14 out of a total of 20 aircraft made it to London, appears to have had access to a more reliable source.

[3] Zuerl (p.111) gives the date as 17 June while O'Connor (p.108) says 19 June.

S537
NATHANAEL
Edmund
Offizier-Stellvertreter

Taken: March to early May 1917
Gonnelieu or Boistrancourt
Publ: June 1917
Reason: death /decoration

Unser erfolgreicher Kampf-Flieger
Offz. Stellvertreter Nathanael
537
Postkartenvertrieb W. Sanke
BERLIN N. 37.
Nachdruck wird gerichtlich verfolgt

Decorations:
WR: Iron Cross, 1st Class; Pilot's Badge; Wilhelm Ernst War Cross (Sax-Weim)
MB: None
RB: Iron Cross, 2nd Class; General Honor Decoration in Gold/ Sw clasp (Sax-Weim)
BH: None

Other Cards:
None

Key Dates:
5 Nov 1916	joins *Jasta 5*
11 May 1917	killed in action
5 Jun 1917	*Militär- Wochenblatt* announces award of Royal Hohenzollern House Order, Member's Cross/ Sw

Offz-Stv. Edmund Nathanael won all the decorations he is adorned with in S537 while he was a two-seater pilot with *Feldflieger-Abteilung 42*. The last of these, which came on 4 August 1916, was Saxe-Weimar's Wilhelm Ernst War Cross – a relatively rare award that only 22 other aviation personnel are known to have received. By the following November, Nathanael had become a fighter pilot in *Oblt.* Hans Berr's *Jasta 5*. His first score did not come until 6

March 1917 when he brought down a Morane Parasol, but the rest followed in rapid succession with four more falling in March, nine in April, and his 15th on 6 May. During this short interval, Nathanael was a witness to several key events in *Jasta 5*'s history: the mortal wounding of the unit's then highest scorer, *Lt.* Renatus Theiller (12 victories); the doubly fatal mid-air collision of Berr and fellow *Jasta 5* pilot, *Vzfw.* Paul Hoppe; the rapid ascent of *Lt.* Heinrich Gontermann, whose second victim fell the same day as Nathanael's first; and the emergence of *Lt.* Kurt Schneider, whose scoring streak left him only two behind Nathanael with 13. Nathanael's luck ran out on 11 May when a Spad 7, probably piloted by Capt. William J.C.K. Cochran-Patrick of RFC No.23 Squadron, turned the tables on him and sent his Albatros D.III down to crash near Bourlon Wood.

Albatros D.III 2247/16, in which Nathanael died, is probably the airplane that looms in S537's background. NATHAN1 is a copy of the original picture that was cropped for S537, and it shows the top of the numeral "3" on the airplane's fuselage that is also just barely visible under its lower right wing in S537. This was Nathanael's personal number in *Jasta 5*, just as Heinrich Gontermann's was number "2" (see S517). Alex Imrie identified Gontermann's S517 picture as having been taken in March 1917 after the first D.III's had been delivered to the unit. It certainly seems to have been no later than April because Gontermann left *Jasta 5* for another squadron on 30 April and there is no sign of the Royal Hohenzollern House Order that he won on 6 May. Was Nathanael's S537 snapped the same time as Gontermann's S517? If not, we must allow that it also could have originated in early May shortly before Nathanael's death on the 11th.

Brandenburg's S536 and Allmenröder's S543 make it clear that, like them, Nathanael's S537 first appeared in late June 1917 – more than four weeks after he had been killed. There is no black border or death "†" to confirm it as a memorial card, but Kirmaier's S445, Schulte's S547, Keudell's S555-56, and other indisputably posthumous cards demonstrate that Sanke generally reserved such devices for the likes of Boelcke, Immelmann, and Richthofen. At the end of May, even though he had been killed before it was half over, Nathanael remained tied for 12th place among Germany's highest scoring fighter pilots, with only 12 men having achieved a better tally.[1] Another contributor toward the publication of S537 may have been the *Militär-Wochenblatt*'s 5 June 1917 notice that Nathanael had been awarded the rare Member's Cross of the Royal

The original image used by Sanke to create S537. (photo courtesy of Greg VanWyngarden)

Edmund Nathanael in the cockpit of his Albatros fighter plane.

RFC No.43 Squadron lost this Sopwith Strutter No.A993 to *Offz-Stv.* Edmund Nathanael's guns on 28 April 1917. It was his 12th victory.

Hohenzollern House Order.[2] At this point in the war, it had been bestowed on only two other airmen, Fritz Kosmahl (9 January 1917) and Sebastian Festner (23 April 1917). The next man to receive it, *Vzfw.* Josef Schleiffer (30 May 1917), was featured in the very next Sanke card, S538. Curiously, despite the *Militär-Wochenblatt*'s announcement, Nathanael's name never did appear on the official roll of 16 recipients. Neal O'Connor suspected that Nathanael's death probably suspended the approval process that the *Militär-Wochenblatt* evidently believed was a certain thing (*Aviation Awards V*, p.94).

Notes

[1] They were Manfred von Richthofen (52), Boelcke (40), Wolff and Voss (30), Schaefer (29), Bernert (27), Lothar von Richthofen (24), Allmenröder (22), Gontermann (21), Frankl (20), Wintgens (19), and Baldamus (18).

[2] This announcement was repeated in *Flugsport*'s 27 June 1917 edition, although it incorrectly reported that he received the Knight's Cross (not Member's Cross) of the decoration.

S538
SCHLEIFFER
Josef
Vizefeldwebel

Taken: before 30 May 1917
Publ: June 1917
Reason: ground support mission

Decorations:
WR: Iron Cross, 1st Class; Pilot's Badge
MB: None
RB: None
BH: Iron Cross, 2nd Class

Other Cards:
(N6244)

See S539 for discussion

S539
ZORER
Eduard Wolfgang
Hauptmann

Taken: 18 April to early June 1917
Publ: June 1917
Reason: ground support mission

Decorations:
WR: Iron Cross, 1st Class; Pilot's Badge; Pilot's Badge (AH)
MB: None
RB: None
BH: Iron Cross, 2nd Class; Military Merit Order (Würt)

Other Cards:
(N6243)

Key Dates:

18 Apr 1917	Zorer promoted to *Hauptmann*
24 Apr 1917	Schleiffer & Zorer perform landmark ground support mission
30 May 1917	Schleiffer awarded Royal Hohenzollern House Order, Member's Cross/Sw
Jun 1917	Zorer named CO of *Kampfstaffel 1*

Vizefeldwebel Schleiffer

On 23 November 1916, *Hptm.* Hans Linke and his observer, *Lt.* Wilhelm Steinbrenner, met their deaths at the hands of Charles Nungesser (his 18th victory) while performing a strafing run against enemy positions. Linke had been in charge of overseeing *Kampfstaffel* 25's conversion into a *Schutzstaffel* (protection unit), whose explicit duties were to protect other two-seaters from enemy attack and to give support to ground troops. The dangers inherent in developing the tactics required for this new mission became manifest when Linke and Steinbrenner gave their lives in the process. *Hptm.* Eduard Wolfgang Zorer, who had expressed a similar interest in more aggressive two-seater tactics while serving with *Feldflieger-Abteilung 54* in the East, was called upon to replace Linke. He spent the beginning of 1917 drilling his unit, now designated as *Schutzstaffel 7*, in the close order attack of trenches, artillery emplacements, and other ground targets. On 23 April 1917, he received the following orders:

"The position of the infantry of the 17. Division in the railway sector north of Gavrelle as far as, but not including, Roeux has not been clarified. Do your utmost to make contact with the forwardmost infantry lines. Our side will attack in the direction of the above-mentioned line early tomorrow morning." (OTF 16:1, p.85)

He perceived this as a perfect opportunity to conduct an air attack in concert with, and in support, of the ground assault. But like many other great leaders, Zorer would not ask his men to do anything he himself would not do, so he planned a solo mission to test and hopefully validate his teachings. Zorer later wrote:

> "On the evening of 23 April, I had my best pilot, *Vizefeldwebel* (Sergeant-Major) Schleiffer, come to my room and said to him: 'First thing in the morning, my dear Schleiffer, we will make a low-level infantry-support flight. We will take off at the first sign of daybreak. We will attack from our side in the Gavrelle-Roeux sector. This is an important mission!'
>
> 'Everything will be in order, *Herr Hauptmann*. The airplane will be ready for take-off at 0545 hours,' Schleiffer answered and then departed.
>
> Once again and very carefully I looked at the map of the area where I would fly during the attack of our troops. Then I went to bed filled with uneasiness over carrying out this flight alone.
>
> Shortly after 0500 hours, my batman came and got me up. I got ready for the flight and by 0600 hours I was sitting in the airplane. Streamers were on the wings [for recognition by German troops]; inside the plane were flares for giving various signals from the air, an electrically-powered lamp and a machine gun. Everything was in order. Take-off had to be delayed for five minutes because it was still dark. From the Front came the sounds of the fiercest artillery barrages. " (OTF 2:4, p.295)

Zorer then described their departure, their harrowing approach to the front lines, and the terrifying experience of flying among shells being hurled through the air from both sides. Once oriented, Zorer and Schleiffer fired off colored flares that instructed the ground troops to lay down white panels that marked the general course of their advancing lines.

> "Close to 0650 hours, a wonderful sight presented itself: the barrage of this and the other side of the road between Gavrelle and Roeux – that headed toward Gavrelle itself – ceased, and now I could scarcely trust my eyes. Down below, which had been such a raging hell, there was life in the shellholes and dug-outs. We went ever lower to about 20 meters (60 feet) above the ground. There really were people, soldiers below us. They sprang up, individually and in groups and moved forward. I could clearly recognize individual infantrymen. Whenever Schleiffer dropped down close to them, I leaned out of the airplane and yelled as loud as I could: *'Feste Druff!'* (Give it to them!) and roared *'Hurra!'* at them. They waved back at me.
>
> At 0655 hours things were also active in the British trenches. Soon I saw the Tommies with their 'dish helmets.' Now Schleiffer with his fixed machine gun and I with my moveable machine gun alternately began to shoot at those fellows. He fired forward through the propeller arc and I fired over the side. The British went back, our troops went forward. After 500 rounds we let up on the enemy. But, gradually, the situation for us became ever less pleasant and ever more dangerous. Round after round from rifles and machine guns whistled by our ears. Then a machine-gun shot smashed into the fuselage behind my seat and ricocheted off the ammunition drum of my machine gun with a loud clank...I was watching the fighting in the ruins of houses in the northeast part of Gavrelle when a machine gun bullet hit our engine. Our oil line broke and covered us both with hot oil, thus requiring us to break away and make an emergency landing.
>
> Schleiffer cried out: 'Where should we land?'

Hauptmann Zorer

539
Postkartenvertrieb W.Sanke
„BERLIN N.37„
Nachdruck wird gerichtlich verfolgt.

> With hand motions I waved him away from the direction of the fighting. More and more it looked as though the engine would quit; oil poured out of it at a dreadful rate. It was a difficult piece of work for Schleiffer to get us back to the airfield at Douai with an engine malfunction, but he did it. The last drop of oil was used up when he set the airplane down.
>
> I turned to him and said: 'Schleiffer, that was magnificent! Thanks very much!'
>
> '*Herr Hauptmann*, that was a beautiful flight,' was his response." (OTF 2:4, p.295)

The success of their daring mission earned them prominent mention in the next day's *Heeresbericht* (the official Army communiqué), a special commendation by the Commanding General of the Air Force, Ernst von Hoeppner, in *Nachrichtenblatt Nr.10*, and instant notoriety.

What is not well known is that Zorer went ahead with the mission despite having injured his knee only two weeks before. This information comes to us from a 9 April 1917 letter written to *Lt.* Hans Hintsch, who had served under Zorer in *Schutzstaffel 7* until 1 April:

> "*Du, Hansel, der Unfall des Herrn Zorer tut uns sehr leid. Wenn die Kniescheibe schwerer verletzt ist, kann er am Ende ein steifes Bein behalten und das wäre doch sehr schmerzlich.*

Wenn Du ihn besuchen kannst, wünsche ihm bitte gute Genesung von uns. Wie ist denn das passiert?" (Pietsch, *"Mein lieber Hans…"*, p.265)[1]

"Hans, we are sorry about *Herr* Zorer's accident. If the kneecap is seriously injured, he could end up with a stiff leg that would still be quite painful. If you are able to visit him, please give him our wishes for a good recovery. How did it happen?" (trans. by this writer)

Zorer was placed in command of *Kampfstaffel 1* in June, and was accompanied by the diminutive Schleiffer. His request to retain control over *Schutzstaffel 7* was denied as too "experimental"; and as Zorer himself put it, "What I had so painstakingly put into practice was to be unlearned so that, months later, it could be re-created." (OTF 2:4, p.296)

The next time that *Schlachtflieger* (assault aviators) participated in a coordinated assault was on 15 August 1917 near Langemarck. Several *Kampfstaffel 1* pilots participated in multiple attacks and inflicted heavy losses on enemy positions. Zorer proudly wrote that *The Times* of London christened his aircraft "flying tanks." On 1 September, while flying another mission with Schleiffer, their aircraft was damaged by friendly fire and Zorer was wounded. Despite his injury, they escaped their captors for a day and a half until they were taken prisoner literally within earshot of their own lines. Prison was where they remained for the duration of the war.

The series of cards beforehand and Allmenröder's later S543 point to a late June publication of Schleiffer's S538 and Zorer's S539. Though there is little question that their subjects' landmark 24 April 1917 mission was the principal motivation, the 30 May 1917 award of the rare Member's Cross of the Royal Hohenzollern House Order to Schleiffer may have been another contributing factor. Schleiffer's card, which numerically precedes Zorer's, immediately follows Edmund Nathanael's, whose own Member's Cross was announced (albeit erroneously) by the *Militär-Wochenblatt* on 5 June 1917.[2]

Schleiffer's image in S538 shows no sign of the Member's Cross, so it was almost certainly snapped before 30 May. The number "3" on his shoulder board indicates that it may have been from a time before his service with *Kampfstaffel 25*, *Schutzstaffel 7* (both a part of *Kagohl 5*) or *Kampfstaffel 1* (part of *Kagohl 1*). Unfortunately, we have no record of when or even if he served with a unit numbered "3." Schleiffer's N6244 portrait, showing only a slightly different pose, was taken concurrently and listed "*Berl. Illustr. Ges.*" (Berlin Illustration Company) as its source.

Zorer's S539 offers less difficulty. His shoulder board bears two "pips," a certain symbol of the *Hauptmann* rank he was raised to on 18 April 1917. Working back three weeks from the postcard's late June issuance gives us an outside photo date of early June. S539's twin, published by NPG as 6243 and also attributed to "*Berl. Illustr. Ges.*," gives us a better glance at the badge hanging below his Iron Cross.[3] Interestingly, it is a Pilot's Badge and not an Observer's Badge, as we would have expected. Somewhere along the line, Zorer apparently qualified as a pilot as well. ZORER1, a photograph originally published with Peter Kilduff's translation of Zorer's reminiscences (quoted above), shows Zorer and the pilots of *Schutzstaffel 7* at a 10 April 1917 celebration of some sort. Zorer, the only one wearing a medals bar, is adorned with his full complement of decorations including something that is either a Pilot's or an Observer's Badge (the face is unrecognizable due to a bright glare). *Lt.* Pedell has his fingers behind the badge, pulling it forward as if to emphasize its significance. Was this a celebration of Zorer's attainment of the Pilot's Badge we see him wearing in S539/N6243?

Notes

[1] This is an excerpt from one of the many letters written to Hintsch by his mother, recently collected in a private publication (see footnote 1 to S509). From them, we now know that Hintsch was sent to *Kampfstaffel 25* in the middle of June 1916, and that he and his observer brought down their first plane on 3 November 1916. He remained with the unit when it was converted to *Schutzstaffel 7* the following January and was transferred to *Jasta 11* on 1 April 1917.

[2] Nathanael is not mentioned among the 16 men who are recorded as official recipients. Neal O'Connor speculated that this was because Nathanaels' death in combat on 11 May halted the final confirmation of the award, which was not given out posthumously (see S537's discussion).

[3] This is one of the few instances where NPG used the exact same photo as Sanke. Tutschek's S572/N6319 are another example.

ZORER I

A celebration by members of *Schutzstaffel 7* on 10 April 1917. From left to right: *Lt.* Berger, *Lt.* Borchard, *Lt.* Reuter, *Hptm.* Horn, *Oblt.* Eduard Wolfgang Zorer, *Lt.* Pedell, *Lt.* Heidenreich, *Lt.* Thum.

Hauptmann Wolfgang Zorer,
einer unserer erfolgreichsten Kampfflieger

6243

Phot. Berl. Jllustr. Ges.

Vizefeldwebel Schleiffer,
einer unserer bekanntesten Flugzeugführer

6244

Phot. Berl. Jllustr. Ges.

NPG's consecutive postcards of *Hptm.* Eduard Wolfgang Zorer and *Vzfw.* Josef Schleiffer, Nos. 6243 and 6244.

S540
TUTSCHEK
Adolf *Ritter* von
Oberleutnant

Taken: 26 May to early June 1917
München, by Erna M. Kollstede
Publ: June 1917
Reason: victory score

Decorations:
WR: Iron Cross, 1st Class; Pilot's Badge (Bav)
MB: None
RB: Military Max-Joseph Order, Knight's Cross (Bav); Military Merit Order, 4th Class/ Crown and Swords; Iron Cross, 2nd Class; Miltary Merit Cross, 3rd Class/war decoration (AH); *Prinzregent* Luitpold Medal in Bronze (Bav)
BH: None

Other Cards:
S572, S650
(L7899; N6319)

Key Dates:

17 Jan 1917	awarded Military Merit Order, 4th Class/ Crown and Swords (Bav)
3 Apr 1917	awarded Pilot's Badge (Bav)
28 Apr 1917	CO of *Jasta 12*
20 May 1917	victory #10
26 May 1917	goes home on leave
23 Jun 1917	returns from leave
3 Jul 1917	victory #11
11 Jul 1917	awarded Royal Hohenzollern House Order, Knight's Cross/ Sw

Oblt. Adolf *Ritter* von Tutschek received Bavaria's highest award, the Knight's Cross of the Military Max-Joseph Order, on 31 January 1916. The award, which entitled him to carry the non-hereditary title "*Ritter* von" ("Knight"), was backdated to 10 August 1915 in recognition of his outstanding achievements as a *Leutnant* with *Infanterie-Regiment Nr.40* on the Eastern Front. He was gassed the following March near Verdun, and during his recovery period – like so many other future German pilots – he applied for entry into the Air Service. He entered active duty as a two-seater pilot with *Feldflieger-Abteilung 6b* in late October 1916. In December, he wrote that he thought that he probably had to put in one to two months more with the unit until he could switch over to fighters with *Jasta Boelcke*. And so it was, for eight days after being awarded Bavaria's Military Merit Order, 4th Class with Crown and Swords on 17 January 1917, Tutschek was posted to *Jasta Boelcke*. By 20 May, he had downed 10 enemy aircraft. His 11th did not come until 3 July because he had gone home on leave on 26 May and did not return until 23 June.[1]

In S540's portrait, Tutschek is wearing all the decorations he had received up through 3 April 1917. Under very close scrutiny, the crown and swords device for his 17 January 1917 Bavarian Military Merit Order is just visible on his ribbon bar. Neal O'Connor reported that Tutschek did not formally earn the Pilot's Badge he can be seen wearing until 3 April 1917 – a very late date, considering that he had been flying in combat since October 1916 as a pilot with *Feldflieger-Abteilung 6b*.[2] There is no sign of the Royal Hohenzollern House Order he was granted on 11 July 1917, so the photograph must have originated between 3 April and 11 July. The identity of the photographer, given as "E.M. Kollstede, München," pinpoints the image to between 26 May and 23 June when Tutschek was back home on leave. If S540 was published in late June, as Guideline 3 and the cards surrounding it indicate, then its photograph was most likely taken during the earlier part of Tutschek's leave and no later than the beginning of June.

Notes

[1] We get this information from three of Tutschek's letters (dated 10 May 1917, 25 May 1917, and 24 June 1917) that were published in Tutschek's war diary, *In Trichtern und Wolken*, and later translated

Oberleutnant Ritter von Tutschek

540
Postkartenvertrieb W. Sanke
„BERLIN N. 37„
Nachdruck wird gerichtlich verfolgt
Phot.: E. M. Kollstede, München

in OTF 3:4. Here we have yet another example of an uncharacteristic gap in a pilot's scoring record being attributable to his being away on leave.

[2] Tutschek's service records show that he was recommended for the Pilot's Badge in a letter submitted by his CO on 28 December 1916. It noted that Tutschek, who had already fulfilled the "theoretical, practical and regulation final examinations" at Schleissheim as well as the "night flight requirement" at *FFA 6b*, merited the award because of his role in a particularly dangerous mission two days earlier. Once again (see Kirmaier's S445 or Lothar von Richthofen's S526), it seems that combat experience had become an additional prerequisite.

Oblt. Adolf Ritter von Tutschek while serving with *Infanterie-Regiment Nr.40*. He is wearing the Military Max-Joseph Order that he was awarded on 30 January 1916 for his actions in August 1915. Though it looks to be a part of his medals bar, the ribbon arrangement and its position at the center of his chest suggest that it was actually pinned on him separately (see next photo). (photo courtesy of UTD)

Opposite

Top left: *Oblt.* Adolf *Ritter* von Tutschek, either while in training at Schleissheim flight school (25 July to October 1916) or while serving with *FFA 6b* (October 1916 to 24 January 1917). He is wearing his dress belt and *Feldschnalle*, and his Military Max-Joseph Order is displayed prominently from his second tunic button. (photo courtesy of UTD)

Two at right: Two shots of Adolf *Ritter* von Tutschek (pilot) and *Lt.* Ferdinand-Wilhelm *Freiherr* von Stein-Liebenstein zu Barchfeld (observer) in an Albatros C.VII belonging to *FFA 6b*. Tutschek served with *FFA 6b* from late October 1916 to 24 January 1917, when he was transferred to *Jasta Boelcke*. These photos were taken in December 1916.

Bottom: Royal Prussian *Jagdstaffel 12* and their new Bavarian CO, *Oblt.* Adolf *Ritter* von Tutschek. From left to right: (seated) Tutschek, *Lt.* Bender, *Vzfw.* Grigo, *Vzfw.* Arthur Schorisch, *Lt.* Paul Billik; (standing) *Vzfw.* Otto Rosenfeld, *Lt.* Karl Schöck, *Lt.* Friedrich Hochstetter, *Lt.* Oskar Müller, *Vzfw.* Friedrich Gille, *Vzfw.* Robert Riessinger, *Vzfw.* Reinhold Jörke. Tutschek arrived on 30 April 1917: "I was welcomed nicely but somewhat suspiciously by the pilots. After all, I was a 'foreigner' among the Prussians." (OTF 3:4, p.299) Rosenfeld came later on 10 May and Schöck was killed on 19 May, so the photo was taken sometime in between at Epinoy. Jörke shows no evidence of the Silver Merit Medal with Swords of the Ducal Saxe-Ernestine House Order that he was awarded on 15 May (that we will see him wearing in S591), but it may have taken several days to reach him.

Hauptmann Brandenburg

S541
BRANDENBURG
Ernst
Hauptmann

Taken: 20 January to early June 1917
Publ: June 1917
Reason: *Pour le Mérite* award

Decorations:
WR: *Pour le Mérite*; Iron Cross, 1st Class; Observer's Badge
MB: None
RB: Royal Hohenzollern House Order, Knight's Cross/ Sw
BH: None

Other Cards:
S536
(L7896)

Key Dates:

20 Jan 1917	awarded Royal Hohenzollern House Order, Knight's Cross/ Sw
13 Jun 1917	conducts raid over London
14 Jun 1917	awarded *Pour le Mérite*
19 Jun 1917	injured in accident

When we last encountered *Hptm.* Ernst Brandenburg in S536, he had been badly injured in an airplane accident while returning from his *Pour le Mérite* investiture ceremony. *Hptm.* Rudolf Kleine was brought in to *Kagohl 3* as Brandenburg's successor and carried out 13 more raids on London until the unit was redirected to perform bombing runs in France. During one of those missions near Ypres on 12 December 1917, Kleine and his crew of three were shot down and killed by Capt. William W. Rogers of RFC No.1 Squadron. Brandenburg presided over their funeral and delivered a speech in their honor. He then resumed command of *Kagohl 3* (by then redesignated as *Bombengeschwader 3*) until the end of the war.

Like S536, a drawing of a *Pour le Mérite* was added to S541's portrait of Brandenburg. Unlike S536, we have a little more to go on regarding when S541's image was taken. Brandenburg's ribbon bar displays the Royal Hohenzollern House Order he was decorated with on 20 January 1917. The absence of an authentic *Pour le Mérite* tells us that the picture predated its award on 14 June of the same year. The 27 June 1917 postmark found on one example of Allmenröder's S543 assigns S541's debut to late June as well. At this time, Brandenburg was recovering in the hospital and would not have been available for a *Pour le Mérite* pose, so Sanke evidently obtained a relatively recent picture of Brandenburg and superimposed the decoration onto it.

Bombengeschwader 3
    O. H. L.
Abtlg. I Nr. *10507*

                                Stabsquartier, den 27. Ma i 1918.
                                Deutsche Feldpost Nr. 4.

       Herrn

          M a x   J u n g n i c k e l ,

              D r e s d e n - N. 12.

              Friedensstr. 16.

       Anliegend übersendet das Geschwader das Ihrem Sohne, dem

Flugzeugführer Gefreiten J u n g n i c k e l , im Namen S.M.

des Kaisers durch den kommandierenden General der Luftstreit-

kräfte verliehene

         E i s e r n e   K r e u z   II. K l a s s e .
      Besitzzeugnis ist beigefügt.
    1 E.K.I
    1 Anlage.
    Einschreiben.

                                 Hauptmann und Kommandeur.

Opposite
Top: *Hptm.* Ernst Brandenburg delivers a eulogy at Western Cemetery near Ghent for *Hptm.* Rudolf Kleine and his crew, *Lt.* Werner Bülowius, *Lt.* Günther von der Nahmer, and *Gefr.* Michael Weber, who fell together on 12 December 1917. Unlike many other airmen who sported a cane for fashionable reasons, Brandenburg used his to help him walk with an artificial leg – the result of a crash on 19 June 1917.

Bottom: Dated 27 May 1918 and signed by *Bombengeschwader 3's* CO, *Hptm.* Ernst Brandenburg, this document gave notice to Max Jungnickel that his son, *Gefr.* Walter Jungnickel, had been awarded the Iron Cross 2nd Class. The award was posthumous, however, because Jungnickel was one of the 17 *Bogohl 3* airmen killed one week earlier on the evening of 19/20 May during its final raid on England.

S542
WOLFF
Kurt
Leutnant

Taken: early June 1917
Juniville
Publ: June 1917
Reason: post-*Pour le Mérite*

Decorations:
WR: *Pour le Mérite*
MB: None
RB: None
BH: None

Other Cards:
S511, S513, S522-23
(L7845, L7846)

Key Dates:
4 May 1917	awarded *Pour le Mérite*
6 May 1917	CO of *Jasta 29*
13 May 1917	victory #30
27 Jun 1917	victory #31

S542 and WOLFF1, two photographs of *Lt.* Kurt Wolff that were taken at the same time, offer several noteworthy elements. First, he is wearing a summer lightweight tunic made from linen as opposed to wool. It is devoid of all decorations except his *Pour le Mérite*, which was officially directed to be worn "at all times." Second, the walls of his room are decorated with trophies from his victims. With regard to the visible serial numbers:

"3421" came from Wolff's sixth victory on 6 April 1917 over RE.8 No.A3421 from RFC No.59 Squadron. The observer, Lt. William L. Day, was killed during Wolff's first pass. Then the pilot, Lt. A. Clayton Pepper, was wounded, the controls were damaged, and the engine was hit. Pepper crash-landed near Bois Bernard inside the German lines.

"3469 Type 17," not a serial number, was cut from a Nieuport 17 fighter – either victory number 4 on 30 March 1917 or victory 14 on 14 April. His three other Nieuport 17 victims did not fall into German hands.

"A-333..." was from his ninth victory on 11 April 1917. Wolff attacked Bristol F.2a No. A3338 from RFC No.48 Squadron, wounded the observer, 2nd Lt. C.B. Holland, and damaged the engine. The pilot, Capt. David M. Tidmarsh, glided the plane down and landed intact on the German side of the lines.

"7...91" was his fifth victory on 31 March 1917. Lt. Leslie A.T. Strange was the pilot and 2nd Lt. William G.T. Clifton the observer

in FE.2b No.7691 from RFC No.11 Squadron. Wolff's initial pass killed Clifton and put holes in the plane's engine and fuel tank. Strange managed to bring the crippled plane down inside the German lines near Gavrelle.

The third noteworthy element is that WOLFF1 gives us a rare glimpse of C.J. von Dühren's original, full picture of Manfred von Richthofen before it was cropped for use in S503. The framed portrait, probably given to Wolff by Richthofen himself, rests in a prominent position on his desk. Was it a farewell gift from his leader and comrade when Wolff left *Jasta 11* to take command of *Jasta 29* two days after winning his *Pour le Mérite*?

The fourth concerns the question of location. Did S542 and WOLFF1 take place in Wolff's quarters in the field or at his room at home? We have pictures of a similar display at Manfred von Richthofen's home at Schweidnitz, though they certainly post-date his death.[1] We also know that Richthofen decorated his quarters at the Front in April 1917 in much the same way. An article in the 5 May 1917 edition of *Die Woche*, which reported on one day's visit to his squadron in April 1917, printed a contemporaneous photo of his room that was labeled: *"In Quartier des Rittmeisters Freiherrn von Richthofen. Eine Wand mit Nummern und Abzeichen von Flugzeugen, die er selbst abgeschossen hat."* ("In Capt. Baron von Richthofen's quarters. A wall with numbers and insignia from aircraft he has shot down.")[2] A slightly different view of the same scene accompanied another April interview conducted at Richthofen's airfield that was presented in Gustav Schwenn's *Fliegerbüchlein fürs deutsche Volk*. There, it is referred to as his *Wohnung* ("flat" or "accommodations").[3] Moreover, Richthofen himself referred to the chandelier seen in these images as hanging in his quarters.[4] Lastly, the biographical work, *Carl Allmenröder, der bergische Kampfflieger*, included a picture of *"Das Quartier Allmenröders mit den Jagdtrophäen"* ("Allmenröder's quarters with his battle-trophies").[5] With this in mind, it seems likely, though not certain, that S542 and WOLFF1 were snapshots of Wolff's billet in the field. If so, they would have originated either in early May, right after his *Pour le Mérite* award and transfer to *Jasta 29*, or in June after his return from his May leave. In either case, they would have come from *Jasta 29*'s base at Juniville. The June scenario is perhaps supported by the fact that S542 was published apart from and after Wolff's S522-23 series, which we determined was taken during his May leave.

Notes
[1] See Kilduff, *Illustrated Red Baron*, pp. 27, 53, and 60; and C&C 10:2, p.148.

[2] A reduced version of this same picture can be seen in Ferko, *Richthofen*, p.75. A slightly different version is printed in Kilduff, *Richthofen: Beyond the Legend*, opp. p. 96, whereas a larger view appears in Vigilant, *Richthofen: Red Knight*, opp. p.226. All these sources (perhaps because Kilduff and Ferko relied on Vigilant's identification?) incorrectly identify the site as the Richthofen home in Schweidnitz.

[3] The two contemporaneous interviews make it clear that their pictures of Richthofen's quarters were taken at the Front. We can verify this through other means. For example, the wallpaper is completely different from that seen in any authentic Schweidnitz museum pictures (see footnote 1). The Vigilant photo includes a doorway and the Schwenn photo displays a large mirror, telephone,

WOLFF1

Lt. Kurt Wolff, CO of *Jasta 29*, sitting in his quarters near Juniville. A portrait of his mentor and friend, Manfred von Richthofen, rests on his desk. (photo courtesy of Greg Van Wyngarden)

fireplace, and other furniture that do not appear in snapshots of the Richthofen museum. Lastly, where the interview pictures only include serial numbers from Richthofen's victims up through 14 April, Kilduff, *Illustrated Red Baron*, p.53 and C&C 10:2, p.148 depict "9299" from his 62nd victory on 23 November 1917.

[4] See Richthofen, *Der rote Kampfflieger*, p.203, where he wrote: *"In meinem Unterstand hängt an der Decke eine Lampe, die ich mir aus einem Flugzeugmotor habe basteln lassen. Erstammt aus einem Flugzeug, das ich abgeschossen habe. In die Zylinder hinein habe ich Lampen montiert, und wenn ich nachts wach liege und das Licht brennen lasse, so sieht dieser Kronleuchter an der Decke weiss Gott phantastisch und unheimlich genug aus."* ("A lamp that I had made from an aircraft engine hangs from the ceiling of my 'dug-out.' It came from an airplane that I had shot down. I mounted light bulbs in the cylinders and at night, when I lie awake and let the light burn, God knows that this chandelier on the ceiling looks fantastic and strange enough.")

[5] See Schnitzler, *Carl Allmenröder*, p.21. Neal O'Connor presented this photo in *Aviation Awards VI*, p.335, but incorrectly ascribed it to Allmenröder's room at his home. Many others have similarly mislabeled pictures of Richthofen's decorated quarters as those of his Schweidnitz museum, and vice versa.

Left: A closer look at the portrait of Manfred von Richthofen in Wolff's room. Richthofen's S503 image appears to have been cropped from it.

Oblt. Kurt Wolff's *Ordenskissen* is prominently displayed in front of his coffin, lying in state at St. Joseph's Church, Courtrai. (photo courtesy of UTD)

Oblt. Kurt Wolff's funeral procession through the streets of Memel.

S543
ALLMENRÖDER
Carl
Leutnant

Taken: 3 to 24 April 1917
Krefeld, family photo
Publ: June 1917
Reason: *Pour le Mérite* award

Decorations:
WR: *Pour le Mérite*; Iron Cross, 1st Class; Friedrich August Cross, 1st Class (Old); Pilot's Badge
MB: None
RB: None
BH: None

Other Cards:
None

Key Dates:

2 Apr 1917	victory #6
25 Apr 1917	victory #7
14 Jun 1917	awarded *Pour le Mérite*
27 Jun 1917	killed in action
11 Jul 1917	S543 photo (without *Pour le Mérite*) published in *Flugsport* 14, p.451

Leutnant Allmenröder

Lt. Carl Allmenröder and his older brother Wilhelm entered the German Air Service together on 29 March 1916. After completing their training they traveled to *Feldflieger-Abteilung 227* as observation pilots within a month of each other. The brothers harbored the same desire to fly single-seat fighters, but it was Carl who got the first crack at them when he was sent to *Jasta 11* on 20 November. There he joined *Lt.* Kurt Wolff, *Vzfw.* Sebastian Festner, *Lt.* Konstantin Krefft, and *Lt.* Hans Hintsch, among others. The squadron, which had been formed on 11 October under the command of *Oblt.* Rudolf Lang, achieved no combat successes until *Lt.* Manfred von Richthofen – new knight of the Order *Pour le Mérite* and victor over 16 enemy aircraft – took over its reins on 15 January 1917.[1] Richthofen set the example by bringing down two planes before the month was out and a third on 1 February. Festner was the first of his men to respond with a victory on 5 February. When his second fell on 16 February, it was joined by a BE.2c brought down near Roeux by Carl Allmenröder. After *Lt.* Karl-Emil Schaefer joined *Jasta 11* on 21 February, the group's victory tally soared. By the end of March, it was credited with 37 victories: Richthofen (15 out of his total 31), Schaefer (8), Allmenröder (5), Wolff (5), Festner (2), Krefft (1), and Lothar von Richthofen (1). "Bloody April" began with five more victories for the *Staffel* on 2 April. Manfred von Richthofen scored two of them while Allmenröder, Festner, and Krefft each bagged one. Though the rest of the squadron members continued to roll up their scores, Allmenröder's guns were strangely silent until 25 April. The explanation for his scoring gap is supplied by a brief postcard written by Allmenröder to his father:

"*2.IV.17*
Herzlichen Dank für Deine Zeilen. Vorgestern wurde mein ???
Kamerad abgeschossen. Ich warte die Beisetzung ab und komme
dann sogleich auf Urlaub. Ich erledigte meiner 5ter Engländer.
Gruss Dein Sohn."

"2 April 1917
Warm thanks for your lines. The day before yesterday my ??? comrade was shot down. I'll wait for the burial and come then immediately on leave. I finished my fifth Englishman. Greetings, your son." (trans. by this writer)[2]

A little-known commemorative work entitled *Carl Allmenröder, der bergische Kampfflieger*, published on the 10th anniversary of the airman's death, fills in the rest:

"*Carl Allmenröder unterbrach freiwillig seinen letzten*
Urlaub zu Ostern 1917, um seinen Kameraden in schweren
Kämpfen beizustehen." (Schnitzler, p.9)

"Carl Allmenröder voluntarily cut short his last leave at Easter 1917 in order to stand by his comrades during the heavy fighting." (trans. by this writer)[3]

The booklet also presented two photographs, ALLMEN1 and ALLMEN2, that were labeled *"Bilder vom letzten Urlaub, Wald, Ostern 1917"* ("Pictures from the last leave, Wald, Easter 1917"). Easter Sunday fell on 8 April in 1917, and it is now clear that Allmenröder was home on leave between his sixth and seventh victories (2 and 25 April).[4] It is also clear from ALLMEN1 that S543's image was taken at his home in Wald at that time. Besides Allmenröder's identical appearance, they share the same balcony railing and trees in the background. A drawing of a *Pour le Mérite* was added later to S543 in recognition of his receipt of that decoration on 14 June 1917. The fact that we have an example of S543 that was written on 27 June 1917 shows that Sanke was at times able to publish his postcards within two weeks of a known event. In this case, his task may have been made easier by the mere addition of a drawing to a photograph (Brandenburg's S536 provides a similar example) that may already have been in his possession.

Allmenröder had a lot of catching up to do when he returned from his leave, for the scores of his squadron mates had increased considerably during his absence. By 25 April they stood at: Manfred von Richthofen (47), Schaefer (21), Wolff (20), Festner (12), and Lothar von Richthofen (10). Allmenröder quickly joined in the killing spree, downing one plane a day from 25 to 27 April. May brought him 13 more victories (compared with the rest of the squadron's six), the companionship of brother Wilhelm who was posted to *Jasta 11* on the 6th, and temporary command of Germany's most illustrious fighter squadron. With Festner killed in action on 25 April, Schaefer and Wolff gone to their own commands, Manfred von Richthofen on

leave, and Lothar von Richthofen wounded on 13 May, the mantle of leadership fell on *Jasta 11*'s rising star:

"Just arrived home and found your letter and the telegram saying that you're leading the *Staffel*. Of course, I didn't even consider anyone else for it; I was just afraid that you wouldn't get it, but that someone more senior according to commission would be certain to. I'll be back at the front with you in five to six weeks. Regards to all the men.

Your Richthofen" (OTF 12:3, p.197)

Allmenröder's ascendancy was so rapid that it was not until 26 May that his name first appeared in the *Heeresbericht* (the official Army Report) with reference to his 20th victory the day before.[5] This milestone probably started the recommendation process for his *Pour le Mérite*, which was awarded on 14 June 1917. Richthofen resumed command of *Jasta 11* the next day, and by this time, Allmenröder had already increased his count to 26. Relieved of his command responsibilities and entitled to another leave by virtue of his *Pour le Mérite* decoration, he wrote his family:

"You keep emploring me to take leave but, at the moment, the situation at the front is just the same as it was around Arras this past spring. I wouldn't be able to rest there with you. Richthofen and I always fly together, we keep an eye on each other. Once again, new men have joined the *Staffel* and I am the only one of his old students that Richthofen still has with him. You can well imagine that he wouldn't like to let me go right now and that I myself wouldn't care to leave right at the moment, either. I intend to take a longer leave later on. Richthofen gave me the entire responsibility (for leading the *Staffel* during Richthofen's absence). Hopefully, I'll stay in his *Staffel* for a long time yet!" (OTF 12:3, pp. 198-99)[6]

Schnitzler reported that this letter arrived in Wald on 27 June 1917, the day that Allmenröder was killed. He had shot down an even 30 enemy aircraft.

Most accounts have attributed Allmenröder's death to the Canadian ace, Raymond Collishaw. Richthofen himself believed this, as told in his letter to Wilhelm Allmenröder, who was in the hospital recovering from a wound he had received on 24 May:

"*Schmerzlich ist es für mich, Ihnen diese Nachricht überbringen zu müssen. Um so schmerzlicher, da ich weiss, wie sehr Sie an Ihrem Bruder hingen. Gestern fiel Carlchen im Luftkampf. Ein Dreidecker schuss aus 800 Meter Entfernung. Man kann aber eigentlich nicht von einem Kampf reden, in den er verwickelt gewesen ist...800 Meter! Ich war selbst nicht mit. Mohnicke, der einige Flugzeuglängen neben ihm geflogen ist, sagte, er habe nicht einmal das Knallen gehört. Nur aus der Leuchtbahn konnte man erkennen, dass der Gegner schoss. Der Vogel machte eine Heimatkurve, Richtung Deutschland. Carlchen nahm noch das Gas weg, und die Maschine stürzte, immer steiler werdend, senkrecht herunter. Aus 2000 Meter Höhe in einem senkrechten Sturzfluge zur Erde. Es ist anzunehmen, dass ihn gleich die tödliche Kugel traf und er sofort die Besinnung verlor. Der Kampf war dicht hinter den Linien. Das Flugzeug schlug zwischen den Linien auf. Er flog eine D.III, eine gute, alte bewährte Maschine, die Sie ja noch kennen. Ich habe in den letzten 8 Tagen mit ihm noch manchen Engländer gejagt, und fast jedes Mal kamen wir nach Hause und konnten uns die Hände schütteln. Drei Tage vor seinem Tode schloss ich Brüderschaft mit ihm...Mir stehen jetzt noch die Tränen in den*

Augen, wenn ich daran denke, dass dieser Prachtmensch nicht mehr unter den Lebenden weilt. Ihnen, als seinem Bruder, von dem er gern und oft sprach, drücke ich in stiller Trauer herzlich die Hand. Mit bestem Grüss, Manfred von Richthofen."

"It is painful for me to have to bring you this news. All the more painful because I know how close you were to your brother. Yesterday, dear Carl fell in aerial combat. A triplane shot from 800 meters away. Actually, one can hardly say he was involved in a fight…800 meters! I was not with him. Mohnicke, who was flying only a few airplane lengths away, said he never heard the shots. One could only tell the opponent fired because of the tracer [ammunition] trails. The plane swung around in the direction of Germany. Carl throttled back quite a bit and the machine fell ever more steeply into a nosedive. It dove straight down to the earth from 2,000 meters. It is assumed that he was mortally wounded and lost consciousness immediately. The fight was close behind the lines and the airplane smashed into no-man's-land. He flew a D.III, a good, old, proven machine, which you well know, after all. I have hunted a good many Englishmen with him in the last eight days, and nearly each time we came home and could shake hands.[7] Three days before his death we formed a brotherhood together…[8] Tears still spring to my eyes whenever I remember that this fine example of a man is no longer among the living. I sincerely press your hand, as the brother of whom he spoke gladly and often, in silent mourning. Yours, Manfred von Richthofen." (trans. by this writer)

The late Neal O'Connor, however, published a Wuppertal (near Wald) newspaper article that related another eyewitness account of Carl Allmenröder's final moments:

"On 27 June 1917, from 8 to 10 hours, the infantryman Max Feuerstein of the 4th Company of the Bavarian 6th Reserve Infantry Regiment lay in a grenade shelter next to an alarm post. Nearby was an earth-covered concrete bunker in which his comrades slept and cleaned their weapons. Cloudy skies covered Flanders; heavy clouds rolled over the land from the sea.

Then, in a flock, the first English fliers arrived at the front. They go back and forth across the lines at low altitude like a swarm of hornets. Their keen eyes missed no movement. Then, rapidly, and violently out of the clouds, it broke loose like a storm. Blood-red single-seater fighters, well known by every soldier in Flanders, shot lightning-like below the English hornets. The first blue-white-red cockade pulled out towards its own lines, burning in a cloud of black smoke. Fleeing, the enemy sought its own territory. A red arrow shot out after it. Far behind the enemy lines the pursuer pressed on. Then the red arrow came back from the other side. Artillery and machine gun fire directed at it created a roar. It exploded and crashed around the plane. Gripping fear came over the field grays in the cratered field as the red machine veered and then spun. One wing broke off. A plume of smoke trailed behind. A tongue of fire shot out of the aircraft explosive like. It shuddered, fell, crashed out of control into the depths. The splintered machine with its doomed occupant fell into the mud near the bunker. Barely two hundred meters in front of the first English positions the red Albatros had bored itself into the ground enveloped in fire and smoke." (O'Connor VI, pp.336 and 339)

The two accounts of Allmenröder's death are actually quite similar: he pursued the enemy over no-man's-land, turned back toward home, then suddenly nosedived to earth. They only disagree on the source of the firing that brought him down.

Uffz. Reinhold Boxberger, who led the patrol assigned to retrieve Allmenröder's body, also told his story in the Wuppertal article. On 28 June, Boxberger received word from division headquarters that Allmenröder was the airman brought down near their position and that he was to recover the body at all costs. Experienced in such operations, Boxberger reasoned that he would need men who were armed (and good) with a pistol, since all the other gear they would have to carry – hand grenades, picks, shovels, tent, and carrying pole – would make rifles too cumbersome. They could not be timid men, either, so he chose three veterans who had already demonstrated their mettle: infantrymen Georg Hutzler, Georg Müller, and Max Feuerstein. They set out the evening of the 29th and arrived at the crash site quickly, whereupon Boxberger posted two men to the left and right as lookouts. He and the third man then surveyed what they were up against. The wrecked airplane's wings and tail section dotted the landscape in fragments, but the engine and cockpit were buried deep in the earth. To make matters worse, the plane had crashed in the middle of a war cemetery that contained corpses from the 1916 campaigns, and the smell and fumes threatened to overcome Boxberger and his team. They nevertheless began removing the soil on either side of the buried cockpit until they reached their goal over two hours later. They placed Allmenröder's remains in the tent they had brought and attached a pole to help them carry it. They had to crawl very slowly over the first 200 yards or so, two men dragging the body and the third covering their withdrawal with Boxberger. When they at last reached their own positions, they spent another day and night transporting the corpse first to battalion, then to regimental headquarters. There, they were finally allowed to transfer their burden to a medical car that carried the body back to division. With that, Boxberger ended with the simple statement:

"Die uns gestellte Aufgabe war erfüllt. Wir gingen wieder nach vorne."

"Our job was done. We returned to the Front."

Their efforts did not go unrewarded. *General* Friedrich Sixt von Armin saw to it himself that the Iron Cross 1st Class went to Boxberger and Müller, and the 2nd Class to Hutzler and Feuerstein.

After a brief ceremony in Courtrai on 1 July, Allmenröder was at last shipped home for burial. *Lt.* Otto Brauneck, who had joined *Jasta 11* on 20 April and for the most part had served under Allmenröder's temporary command, was at home on leave when he received a telegram from Manfred von Richthofen requesting that he represent the *Staffel* at the 5 July funeral in Wald. Allmenröder had been wearing his *Pour le Mérite* when he crashed, and Brauneck carried the *Ordenskissen* that displayed the damaged decoration in front of the procession. According to Brauneck's biographer, the way that Allmenröder's family conducted themselves throughout the funeral service so impressed him that he instructed his own parents that "in the event of his death they should also bear the loss proudly and carry through with his funeral in the same dignified manner." (OTF 1:3, p.197) Unfortunately, they had that opportunity less than a month later when they buried their son in Sulzbach on 30 July.

Allmenröder's official victory list is well known and has been published in several texts (e.g., Franks, Bailey, and Guest, *Above the Lines*, p.60 or O'Connor, *Aviation Awards VI*, p.337). None of these sources, however, has related the following information that was presented in the 12 July 1936 edition of the *Rheinische Landeszeitung* regarding eight unconfirmed kills that he also claimed:

Date	Type	Location
11 March 1917	BE	Lens-Vimy
19 March 1917	BE	La Bassee
24 March 1917	Spad	Lens
25 March 1917	Nieuport	Arras
28 March 1917	FE	Lievin
31 March 1917	FE	Arras
2 April 1917	FE	Douai-Arras
8 June 1917	FE	Ploegsteert-Kemmel

When checked against other victories on these dates, most of the above may have been disputed ones that were awarded to other *Jasta 11* members, including Festner, Krefft, and both Richthofen brothers.[9] As a final note, the same *Rheinische Landeszeitung* article provided a list of Allmenröder's decorations and their award dates. Rather intriguingly, the last of them was a posthumous *"Bayerische Militär-Kronen-Orden 4. Klasse"* ("Bavarian Military Crown Order, 4th Class") on 20 July 1917. This probably was an error for the *Bayerische Militär-Verdienst-Orden* (Bavarian Military Merit Order) that was given out to several illustrious airmen.

Notes

[1] The funeral program prepared for Allmenröder's burial at Wald on 5 July 1917 discloses that he had won his Pilot's Badge only one week earlier on 8 January.

[2] Allmenröder was referring to *Lt.* Hans-Georg Eduard Lübbert, who was killed on 30 March near Bailleul, apparently by Capt. R. Gregory of RFC No.40 Squadron.

[3] Perhaps Allmenröder, aware of his comrades' increasing successes, also felt like he was missing out on the action.

[4] Several local newspaper articles that were written after Allmenröder's death also reported that his last leave home was at Easter.

[5] The timing of S543's publication indicates that it was probably this Army Report that first attracted Sanke's attention and set him on the path of pursuing Allmenröder's photograph.

[6] OTF's translation faithfully followed what was inserted in Allmenröder's letter by Schnitzler as an interpretation of the sentence, *"Die ganze Verantwortung ist mir durch Richthofen genommen."* ("The entire responsibility is given to me by Richthofen"). Another possibility is that Allmenröder had meant that Richthofen had left it up to him to decide when to go home on leave.

[7] This presumably meant to celebrate a victory. Allmenröder scored on 18, 24, 25, and 26 June and Richthofen had victories on 18, 23, 24, and 25 June.

Trauerfeier
in der Evangelischen Kirche zu Wald-Rheinland für den
Flieger-Leutnant Karl Allmenröder
am 5. Juli 1917, nachmittags 3½ Uhr.

Ordnung der Feier:

1. Vorspiel der Orgel.
2. Gemeinsamer Gesang: Jesus, meine Zuversicht.
3. Chorlied (ges. vom M.-G.-V. Concordia u. der Nationalen Sängervereinigung): Sag', was zagest du?
4. Karl Allmenröders Lieblingslied (ges. von Schülern des Realgymnasiums): Kein Hälmlein —
5. Gedächtnisrede: Pfarrer Schöpwinkel.
6. Chorlied der Männervereine: Gebet von Theodor Körner.

Above and two below: Three photographs of *Lt.* Carl Allmenröder during his Easter leave, April 1917. The first is the original image used for S543, as presented on Allmenröder's funeral program. The second shows him on the same balcony. In the last photo, left to right: sister Luisa Hendrichs, brother Wilhelm, *Frau* Allmenröder, and Carl.

[8] This is where a close friendship was formally acknowledged by the friends agreeing to address each other by the more intimate *"du, dich, dir"* as opposed to *"Sie, Ihnen."*

[9] For other claims with the same dates, see Franks, Bailey, and Duivan, *Jasta War Chronology*. The *Rheinische Landeszeitung* article was written by Fritz Schmidt, an author from Allmenröder's hometown.

ALLMEN1

ALLMEN2

Carl and Wilhelm Allmenröder (seated in front row, second and third from the right) while attending grade school at the *Wald-Ohligser Realgymnasium.*

Lt. Carl Allmenröder, either while in training with *FEA 5* at Hanover (29 March to September 1916) or when he was a two-seater pilot with *FFA 227* (September to 19 November 1916).

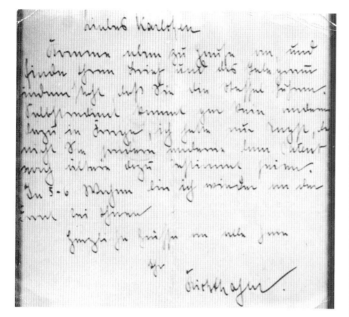

Manfred von Richthofen's letter to Carl Allmenröder, congratulating him on his assignment as Acting CO of *Jasta 11* on 13 May 1917 (see text above for translation).

Oberstlt. Hermann Thomsen's telegram, dated 16 June 1917, informing Allmenröder that he had been awarded the *Pour le Mérite*. The official date of the award was 14 June 1917.

Lt. Carl Allmenröder's body lies in state before the altar of St. Joseph's Church in Courtrai. The damage caused to Allmenröder's *Pour le Mérite* by his fatal crash is clearly evident in the second image. The last one captures *Lt.* Wilhelm Groos, *Jasta 11*'s representative, exiting the church and carrying Allmenröder's decorations behind the casket during the ceremony held on 1 July. (second photo courtesy of UTD)

Waiting among the mourners outside the church were Manfred von Richthofen and his father, Albrecht. *Maj.* Albrecht von Richthofen is second from the right (with slightly bowed head) in the foreground of the first image, and Manfred is fourth from the right (with gloved hands clasped behind his back). In the second picture, starting from the naval officer in dark overcoat and cap, they are third and fourth from the right. The officer standing just behind Albrecht von Richthofen may be *Lt.* Konstantin Krefft. Leading the procession of mourners (behind the wreath bearers with sword, overcoat, and *Pickelhaube*) is *Gen.* Sixt von Armin. (second photo courtesy of UTD)

Allmenröder's casket is carried into a special waiting area at Courtrai's train station and placed under an honor guard. Following this, his comrades gather in front of the mourning-draped site while *Gen.* Sixt von Armin (center) delivers a final tribute. Groos and Richthofen, standing side by side, are just visible below and to the left of the light pole near the bushy tree. (second photo courtesy of UTD)

Allmenröder's casket in Wald's Evangelist Church. The funeral service was held there on 5 July 1917 at 3:30 pm.

Above and two below: The funeral party exits Evangelist Church and proceeds through the streets of Wald to the *Ehrenfriedhof* (Honor Cemetery) south of town. *Lt.* Otto Brauneck carries Allmenröder's decorations and leads the casket to its hearse in the first photo. In the third, Brauneck, still holding the *Ordenskissen*, stands alone to the left of the protestant cleric as the pall bearers prepare to lower Allmenröder's remains into his grave.

An artist's rendering of *Lt.* Carl Allmenröder, produced in 1927, that was derived from S543's image.

A pleasing portrait of *Lt.* Carl Allmenröder.

2	victory total at end of month
�	PLM award month
☐	wounded
▭	died
■	postmark month
○	postmark date
●··········	postcard publication boundaries
★	same or similar photo in dated publication
●	anchor point
─(3)─ ━━	guidelines 1-3
─(A)─ ═══	guideline A
-F	Freiherr version
-H	Hauptmann version
-L	Leutnant version
-O	Oberleutnant version
-R	Rittmeister version

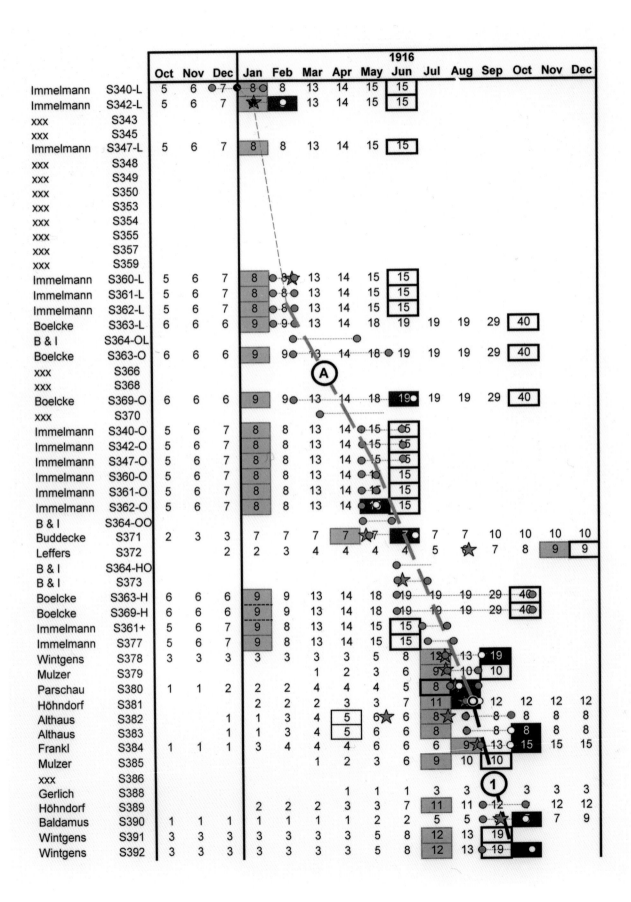

		Oct	Nov	Dec	Jan	Feb	Mar	Apr	May	Jun	Jul	Aug	Sep	Oct	Nov	Dec
										1916						
Immelmann	S340-L	5	6	7	8	8	13	14	15	15						
Immelmann	S342-L	5	6	7			13	14	15	15						
xxx	S343															
xxx	S345															
Immelmann	S347-L	5	6	7	8	8	13	14	15	15						
xxx	S348															
xxx	S349															
xxx	S350															
xxx	S353															
xxx	S354															
xxx	S355															
xxx	S357															
xxx	S359															
Immelmann	S360-L	5	6	7	8	8	13	14	15	15						
Immelmann	S361-L	5	6	7	8	8	13	14	15	15						
Immelmann	S362-L	5	6	7	8	8	13	14	15	15						
Boelcke	S363-L	6	6	6	9	9	13	14	18	19	19	19	29	40		
B & I	S364-OL															
Boelcke	S363-O	6	6	6	9	9	13	14	18	19	19	19	29	40		
xxx	S366															
xxx	S368															
Boelcke	S369-O	6	6	6	9	9	13	14	18	19	19	19	29	40		
xxx	S370															
Immelmann	S340-O	5	6	7	8	8	13	14	15	5						
Immelmann	S342-O	5	6	7	8	8	13	14	15	5						
Immelmann	S347-O	5	6	7	8	8	13	14	15	5						
Immelmann	S360-O	5	6	7	8	8	13	14	10	15						
Immelmann	S361-O	5	6	7	8	8	13	14	10	15						
Immelmann	S362-O	5	6	7	8	8	13	14	10	15						
B & I	S364-OO															
Buddecke	S371	2	3	3	7	7	7	7	7	7	7	7	10	10	10	10
Leffers	S372			2	2	3	4	4	4	4	5	6	7	8	9	9
B & I	S364-HO															
B & I	S373															
Boelcke	S363-H	6	6	6	9	9	13	14	18	19	19	19	29	40		
Boelcke	S369-H	6	6	6	9	9	13	14	18	19	19	19	29	40		
Immelmann	S361+	5	6	7	9	8	13	14	15	15						
Immelmann	S377	5	6	7	9	8	13	14	15	15						
Wintgens	S378	3	3	3	3	3	3	3	5	8	13	13	19			
Mulzer	S379						1	2	3	6	9	10	10			
Parschau	S380	1	1	2	2	2	4	4	4	7	11	12	12	12	12	
Höhndorf	S381				2	2	2	3	3	7	11	12	12	12	12	
Althaus	S382			1	1	3	4	5	6	6	8	8	8	8	8	8
Althaus	S383			1	1	3	4	5	6	6	8	8	8	8	8	8
Frankl	S384	1	1	1	3	4	4	4	6	6	6	9	13	15	15	15
Mulzer	S385						1	2	3	6	9	10	10			
xxx	S386															
Gerlich	S388							1	1	1	3	3	3	3	3	3
Höhndorf	S389				2	2	2	3	3	7	11	11	12		12	12
Baldamus	S390	1	1	1	1	1	1	1	2	2	5	5	6	7	7	9
Wintgens	S391	3	3	3	3	3	3	3	5	8	12	13	19			
Wintgens	S392	3	3	3	3	3	3	3	5	8	12	13	19			

		1916							1917							
		Jun	Jul	Aug	Sep	Oct	Nov	Dec	Jan	Feb	Mar	Apr	May	Jun	Jul	Aug
Boelcke	S393	19	19	19	29	40										
Friedrich	S394															
Friedrich	S395															
Mulzer	S396	6	9	10												
Mulzer	S397	6	9	10												
Mulzer	S398	6	9	10												
Mulzer	S399?	6	9	10	10											
Fokk/Wint	S400															
Coss/Wind	S401															
Berthold	S402	5	5	6	8	8	8	8	8	8	9	12	12	12	12	13
xxx	S403															
xxx	S405															
xxx	S406															
Zander	S407	2	2	3	4	5	5	5	5	5	5	5	5	5	5	5
12 heroes	S408															
Boelcke	S363+	19	19	19	29	40										
Boelcke	S409+	19	19	19	29	40										
Fokker	S410															
Meyer	S411		1	3	3+	5	5	5	5	6	6	7	7	8	8	8
Boenisch	S412	2	3	5	5	5	5	5	5	5	5	5	5	5	5	5
Leffers	S413	4	5	6	7	8	9									
Leffers	S414	4	5	6	7	8	9									
Leffers	S415	4	5	6	7	8	9									
Dossenbach	S416			5	8	8	9		9	9	9	14	14	15	15	
Leffers	S417	4	5	6	7	8	9									
Fahlbusch	S418		4	5	6											
Rosencrantz	S419		4	5	6											
Frankl	S420	6	6	9	13	15	15	15	15	15	15	20				
Frankl	S421	6	6	9	13	15	15	15	15	15	15	20				
Hirth	S422															
Berthold	S423	5	5	6	8	8	8	8	8	8	9	12	12	12	12	13
Cossel	S424															
Berr	S425	2	2	2	2	8	10	10		10	10	10				
Berr	S426	2	2	2	2	8	10	10		10	10	10				
Hoeppner	S427															
Pfeifer	S428			2	4	4	7	8	8	8	9	10	11			
Reimann	S429			1	3	5	5	5	5							
Althaus	S430	6	8	8	8	8	8	8	8	8	8	8	8	8	9	9
Althaus	S431	6	8	8	8	8	8	8	8	8	8	8	8	8	9	9
Baldamus	S432	2	5	5	5	5	7	9	10		15	18				
Buddecke	S433	7	7	7	10	10	10	10	10	10	12	12	12	12	12	12
Buddecke	S434	7	7	7	10	10	10	10	10	10	12	12	12	12	12	12
xxx	S435															
xxx	S436															
xxx	S437															
xxx	S438															
xxx	S439															
xxx	S440															
xxx	S441															
Bernert	S442	1	1	1	3	4	7	7	7	9	24	27	27	27	27	
Bernert	S443	1	1	1	3	4	7	7	7	9	24	27	27	27	27	

		1917												1918		
		Jan	Feb	Mar	Apr	May	Jun	Jul	Aug	Sep	Oct	Nov	Dec	Jan	Feb	Mar
Müller M	S444	5	5	5	7	13	18	19	26	7	29	32	36	36		
Kirmaier	S445															
Müller H	S446	9	9	9	9	9	9	9	9	9	9	9	9	9	9	9
Müller H	S447	9	9	9	9	9	9	9	9	9	9	9	9	9	9	9
Manschott	S448	3	7	2												
Manschott	S449	3	7	2												
MvR	S450-F	18	21	1	52	52	56	57	59	61	61	63	63	63	63	74
Pfeifer	S451	8	8	9	10	11										
Böhme	S502	9	12	12	12	12	12	13	13	15	21	24				
MvR	S503	18	21	31	52	52	56	57	59	61	61	63	63	63	63	74
MvR	S450-R	18	21	31	52	52	56	57	59	61	61	63	63	63	63	74
Thomsen	S504															
Hoeppner	S505															
Voss	S506	3	11	22	24	31	34	34	38	48						
Schaefer	S507	1	1	8	23	29	30									
Brauneck	S508	5+	6	7	7+		9	10								
MvR & Hoep	S509															
Festner	S510		2	2	12											
5 Aces	S511	18	21	31	52		56	57	59	61	61	63	63	63	63	74
Schaefer	S512	1	1	8	23		30									
Wolff	S513			5	27		31	33	33	33						
Klein	S514				8	9	12	16	16	16	20	22	22	22	22	22
Klein	S515				8	9	12	16	16	16	20	22	22	22	22	22
Bertrab	S516				4	5	5	5	5							
Gontermann	S517	1	1	6	17	21	23	25	35	38	39					
Göttsch	S518	4	6	6	9	12	1	14	14	17	17	17	17	17	17	18
MvR, H, T	S519															
Voss	S520	3	11	22	24	31	34	34	38	48						
Bernert	S521	7	7	9	24	27	27	27	27	27	27	27	27	27	27	27
Wolff	S522			5	27	30	31	33	33	33						
Wolff	S523			5	27	30	31	33	33	33						
Höhne	S524	6	6	6	6	6	6	6	6	6	6	6	6	6	6	6
Höhne	S525	6	6	6	6	6	6	6	6	6	6	6	6	6	6	6
LvR	S526			1	16	24	24	24	24	24	24	26	26	26	26	29
Gontermann	S527	1	1	6	17	21	23	25	35	38	39					
Gontermann	S528	1	1	6	17	21	23	25	35	38	39					
Gontermann	S529	1	1	6	17	21	23	25	35	38	39					
Bertrab	S530				4	5	3	5	5							
Bertrab	S531				4	5		5	5							
MvR	S532	18	21	31	52	52	56	57	59	61	61	63	63	63	63	74
MvR	S533	18	21	31	52	52	56	57	59	61	61	63	63	63	63	74
MvR	S534	18	21	31	52	52	56	57	59	61	61	63	63	63	63	74
Goering	S535	3	3	3	6	7	8	10	12	14	15	16	16	16	17	17
Brandenburg	S536															
Nathanael	S537			5	14	15										
Schleiffer	S538															
Zorer	S539															
Tutschek	S540			2	4	10	10	21	3	23	23	23	23	23	24	27
Brandenburg	S541															
Wolff	S542			5	27	30	31	33	33	33						
Allmenröder	S543		1	5	9	22	30									

JASTA 11 AT ROUCOURT

The outstanding success of *Rittm.* Manfred von Richthofen and his *Jasta 11* during April 1917 was the biggest military aviation event to hit the press since Immelmann, Boelcke, and the Fokker Scourge. Reporters and photographers flocked to the unit's airfields at La Brayelle, and then Roucourt, to witness such dramatic events as these: Richthofen's 41st victory that made him the greatest German ace ever (13 April), the destruction of an entire flight of RE.8 two-seaters from RFC No.59 Squadron (also 13 April), Karl-Emil Schaefer's 20th victory that would qualify him for the *Pour le Mérite* (21 April), Kurt Wolff's 20th that counted as the squadron's 100th victory and would bring him Prussia's highest honor as well (22 April), brother Lothar's rapid ascent with 15 victories in 19 days (11-30 April), and Richthofen's four kills in one day – a personal best and record for his squadron (29 April). *Prof. Dr.* Georg Wegener, a correspondent for *Die Kölnische Zeitung*, wrote about his visit to *Jasta 11* that began on 11 April. He reported on the youthful ebullience of the squadron members despite grim reminders of impending injury or death:

> "Scarcely half an hour had passed and they were all there again. The combatants climbed out of their seats and – laughing, proud, happy, recounting [events] animatedly – stood amidst their well-wishing comrades and enlisted men who shared the enthusiasm of their officers.
>
> No one was injured. It all looked like it could have been a successful sporting event. But Richthofen's machine showed how little it was really like that. An enemy machine-gun burst hit the lower left wing and the fabric for about a metre and a half looked like it had been slashed open by the swipe of a big knife. And on the outer wooden covering close to the pilot's seat ran a second scar showing that another shot came close to taking his life." (Kilduff, *Richthofen: Beyond the Legend*, p.94)

War correspondent Alfred Richard Meyer reported on what appears to have been a c.17-21 April visit to Roucourt in his article *"Ein Besuch bei Rittmeister von Richthofen und seiner Staffel"* ("A Visit with Cavalry Captain von Richthofen and his Squadron").[1] It incorporated three famous photographs: Richthofen's all-red Albatros in a *Jasta 11* lineup after the unit had moved to Roucourt on 15 April, Richthofen's quarters decorated with souvenirs from his victims, and Richthofen and four *Staffel* members as later seen in S511. A pictorial essay entitled *"Ein Tag bei der Jagdstaffel des Rittmeisters Frhrn. von Richthofen"* that appeared in the 5 May 1917

edition of *Die Woche* offered the same photos of Richthofen's all-red Albatros and decorated quarters, as well as scenes of Richthofen climbing into his Albatros from a ladder, brother Lothar being helped down from his plane, and individual portraits of Sebastian Festner, Karl-Emil Schaefer, and Kurt Wolff that were later published by Sanke as S510, S512, and S513. Lastly, the 13 May 1917 edition of *Berliner Illustrirte Zeitung* featured the two photos that would become Sanke cards S509 and S511.

The purpose of this discussion is to demonstrate how all these photographs originated during a 17-26 April timeframe when the press was reporting on *Jasta 11*'s incredible success. Page 25 of this work argues that Sanke capitalized on this popularity by issuing a *Jasta 11* photo series of his own, namely S508-13. Like many of the other photos taken that month, S508-13 captured the natural exuberance of an exceptional group of young men at the peak of their careers and lives – lives, however, that with only one exception would be tragically cut short by the war.

We begin with a comparison of S511's and MVR5's images (see S511). With a few minor exceptions, the overall appearance of each of the five men in S511 is matched in MVR5. The footwear, uniforms, overcoats, various folds and creases of their service caps, and even the degrees to which Festner's and Schaefer's coats are buttoned are all identical. Noteworthy differences between the two photos are: (i) Kurt Wolff, who is coatless and in a stocking cap in MVR5, is wearing his *Schirmmütze* and captured British flying coat in S511, (ii) Lothar von Richthofen's collar is up in MVR5 and down in S511, and (iii) Schaefer's collar is down in MVR5 and up in S511. Still, the cloth puttee on Festner's right leg provides a conclusive link between S511 and MVR5 – it is identically stained in each image (see below). Puttees like Festner's were wrapped and unwrapped each time they were used, so it would have been virtually impossible for the same distinct stain pattern to have recurred on different days. Consequently, the differences discerned between S511 and MVR5 may be attributable to Wolff having been caught before and after a flight (note that the neck of his tunic and its protruding white collar are the same) and Richthofen and Schaefer simply adjusting their collars in the meantime. Festner and Brauneck appear together in MVR5, which tells us that MVR5 and S511 originated between 20 April, the time Brauneck joined *Jasta 11*, and Festner's death in action on 25 April. This alone establishes the location as Roucourt, because *Jasta 11* moved there on 15 April. But if further proof is needed, one can visit the small French village where the line of trees and curved road seen in MVR5's background are still visible. In addition, the current Baron of Chateau Roucourt, who graciously accepted a visit by this writer in 2004, confirmed that wooden sheds like the one seen in S511 once stood among those trees, one of which remains in use on his Chateau grounds today.

Next come MVR2 (see S509) and S508. Once again, with only a few exceptions, the overall appearance of the men found in MVR2, MVR5, and S511 is the same. Manfred von Richthofen wears his leather flight coat, buttoned up to the silk scarf around his neck, and a well-worn pair of shoes topped with buckled leather "gators" or leggings. Krefft is dressed in flight gear. Under a fur-collared topcoat, Schaefer is in his M1915 style tunic (buttons covered with a flap) with open collar and "dickey" around the neck (see S512). He too wears shoes topped with leather gators, but his are buffed to a shine. Brauneck has on similar footwear and a plain-collared flight coat. Lothar von Richthofen sports a fur-collared coat, a high-peaked service cap, and cloth puttees above his scuffed shoes. Lastly, we see Esser in his long-bodied, fur-collared overcoat, shiny gator-topped shoes, and stiff *Schirmmütze*. The differences are (i) Krefft, dressed for flying with scarf, flight helmet, and goggles in MVR2, has opened his flight suit and is wearing a service cap in MVR5, and (ii) Brauneck, wearing a tunic under his coat in MVR2, is attired in a more comfortable turtleneck sweater in MVR5. Were both Brauneck and Krefft, like Wolff, getting ready for or returning from a mission when MVR5 was snapped? S508 captures Brauneck dressed in the same turtleneck and topcoat seen in MVR5, only in S508 he has on extra clothing to protect his legs – again as though he were just preparing for or returning from a flight. The wooden shed among the trees in the background identifies S508's location as Roucourt, and we know that Brauneck only joined *Jasta 11* there on 20 April. There is little doubt that MVR2 (and S509) originated from *Generalleutnant* Ernst von Hoeppner's visit to Roucourt following *Jasta 11*'s 100th victory (brought down by Wolff on 22 April). The presence of Roucourt's church steeple (see ROUCOURT1) to the right of Esser in MVR2 confirms the location. We also know that Schaefer (present in MVR2) left *Jasta 11* to take command of *Jasta 28* on 27 April. So at this point, MVR2's timeframe can be bracketed to 23-26 April. If we accept MVR2's direct association with MVR5 and S511, this period is reduced further to 23-24 April because of Festner's death on the 25th.[2] Finally, we have *Lt.* Hans Hintsch's letter to his mother that indicated that Hoeppner's visit came on 23 April (see S509). So all things considered, it is this writer's conclusion that S509, S511, MVR2, MVR4-5, and possibly S508 were all taken at *Jasta 11*'s Roucourt airfield on 23 April 1917. The strong evidence presented by their many close similarities outweighs the few otherwise explainable differences.

Alfred Meyer's article on his visit with Richthofen in late April 1917 incorporated S511's image along with pictures of *Jasta 11*'s lineup (MVR20) and Richthofen's quarters (MVR21). The implication is that like S511's image, the accompanying pictures originated from Roucourt as well. But can less circumstantial evidence be provided to support this? Roucourt's local inhabitants have confirmed that the brick building and smokestack in MVR20's background belonged to a brewery that eventually collapsed in a state of disrepair. Another building of similar shape was erected in its place, perhaps from some of the same materials. ROUCOURT2, taken from the same general location as MVR20, is a picture of that building as it stood in 2004, and ROUCOURT3 is a better shot of the tree-covered slope behind it that also formed MVR20's horizon. Several of the aircraft tents that are right of the brewery in MVR20 can also be seen in MVR2 and ROUCOURT4 – a photo of an Albatros D.III being rolled out of one of Roucourt's wooden sheds (the town's steeple is to the right). So there is no doubt that MVR20, like S511, orginated there. Nevertheless, it cannot be determined with any certainty if MVR20 was taken the same day as S511. As for Richthofen's quarters in MVR21, two "4997" serial number panels

Above and below: The cloth leggings on *Vzfw.* Sebastian Festner's right leg display an identical stain in both of these images. The first comes from the famous photo of *Jasta 11* in front of Manfred von Richthofen's Albatros (MVR5) and the second is from S511.

appear in the upper left and right corners. They came from his 43rd victory, which crashed into a house near Noyelle-Godault on 13 April at approximately 7:35 pm. Just above the one to the right is part of another serial number: "A67..." A post-war photograph of the Richthofen museum in Schweidnitz discloses its full identity as "A6796," which was cut from Richthofen's 44th after he had forced it down near Bois Bernard at 9:15 am on 14 April.[3] *Jasta 11* moved to Roucourt the next day. It is therefore just possible that MVR21 was taken at La Brayelle just before *Jasta 11*'s move, though the timing seems a little tight. Were these serial numbers available to Richthofen that quickly, and if so, would he have bothered to hang them up on the eve of his departure? If MVR21 did come from Roucourt, it probably would have taken a few days to move Richthofen into his new quarters, hang the rotary engine chandelier, and decorate the walls with his victims' serial numbers. Meyer's visit occurred sometime after 16 April (i.e., after Lothar von Richthofen's eighth victory), so a Roucourt location is at least equally possible if not more probable.

Die Woche featured a pictorial spread from "A day at Rittmeister *Freiherr* von Richthofen's *Jagdstaffel*" in its 5 May 1917 edition. It too included MVR20 and MVR21, but also presented an additional five photos: Manfred von Richthofen climbing into his Albatros (MVR22), Lothar von Richthofen being helped down from his (MVR23), and the images found in Festner's S510, Schaefer's S512, and Wolff's S513. Once again, does this signify that they all originated from Roucourt during the same period in late April 1917? MVR22 and a companion photo (see C&C10:2, p.104) show Richthofen getting suited up in his flight gear and climbing into an Albtaros

ROUCOURT1

A closeup view of Roucourt's church taken in 2004 from approximately the same angle as seen in MVR2 (see S509). The steeple, brick wall, and low building in between appear again at the right of ROUCOURT4 below.

Below and top page 334: Copies of these pictures, sometimes accompanied by other scenes from Roucourt field, appeared together in several German newspaper publications. The first displays a lineup of *Jasta 11* (and another unit's) Albatros fighters at Roucourt field, and the second shows Manfred von Richthofen's room, presumably at Chateau Roucourt, decorated with trophies from his victims.

MVR20

MVR21

ROUCOURT2

ROUCOURT3

Two pictures of Roucourt's former airfield, taken in 2004 from the same approximate vantage point as MVR20. The first shows a more modern building where the brick brewery once stood, and the second offers a closer look at the tree-covered slope that rose in the background.

D.III. One of Roucourt's wooden hangar sheds appears in the background of the companion photo, and the Albatros in MVR22 displays the same bullet hole patch just forward of the fuselage cross that is seen on the second Albatros in MVR20.[4] The aft portion (starting about halfway between the cockpit and the vertical stabilizer) of the Albatros that Lothar von Richthofen is exiting in MVR23 was painted with another color. The same airplane is fourth in line in MVR20.[5] Richthofen, however, is wearing an overcoat different from the one seen in the 23 April Hoeppner series (i.e., S511, MVR2, MVR4-5). Festner's S510 offers no conclusive link to Roucourt, and though his attire is similar to what he wore in the Hoeppner series, it is distinctly different.[6] Schaefer's S512 appearance is identical in the Hoeppner series right down to his neckwear and shiny footwear, except that he has removed his topcoat and service cap; and one of Roucourt's wooden sheds is in S512's background. Wolff's pose in S513 is reminiscent of S511's, but his *Schirmmütze* is crumpled differently, his topcoat's lined collar falls in a different manner, and the white shirt collar seen in S511 and MVR4-5 is missing. Nevertheless, he is obviously standing on the door to one of Roucourt's telltale sheds among the woods. So while MVR22-23 and S512-13 (and probably S510 by association) undoubtedly came from Roucourt, it looks like none of them (except possibly Schaefer's S512) originated the same day as the Hoeppner series. Their similar content, common location, and the fact that they were presented together under the title of "a day" at Richthofen's squadron (though not necessarily to be taken literally), strongly implies that they at least all originated within a few days of each other. We have already seen that it often took at least two to three weeks for a particular

event's photos to make its way into various publications. Perhaps significantly then, neither S511 nor S509 nor any of the other images definitely linked to Hoeppner's 23 April visit were included in *Die Woche*'s 5 May spread. Yet both S509 and S511 appeared in *Berliner Illustrirte Zeitung*'s later 13 May edition. The implication is that the photos that did appear in *Die Woche* came from a slightly earlier timeframe. It is believed that MVR20 includes airplanes from both *Jasta 11* and *Jasta 4*, which joined Richthofen's group at Roucourt on 20 April 1917. This was the same day that Otto Brauneck, seen in several of the photographs, came on board. Richthofen's quarters at Roucourt would have been set up, complete with chandelier and the serial numbers of his most recent victims, by this point.[7] Finally, 20 April falls within the period established for Meyer's visit to *Jasta 11*, i.e., 17-21 April.

In summary, all of the photos discussed here came from Roucourt after *Jasta 11* moved there on 15 April and before Manfred von Richthofen went home on leave on 1 May. S509 and MVR2 can be pinpointed to *Generalleutnant* Ernst von Hoeppner's visit on 23 April 1917 to celebrate *Jasta 11*'s 100th victory. S511, MVR4, and MVR5 share many similarities with the Hoeppner photos and were almost certainly taken the same day either before or after the visit. S508 is another possible candidate, though less certain than the others. Two of the 23 April series images, S509 and S511, were published together in a 13 May newspaper, which conforms to what we know about the two to three weeks it normally took for photos to appear in publications. S510, S512, and S513 originated around the same time as the Hoeppner visit, but not on the same day. By virtue of their publication together with MVR20-23 in an earlier 5 May newspaper

ROUCOURT4

Above and two on page 336: Three more shots from Roucourt airfield that were often published along with stories reporting on a visit there.

MVR22

MVR23

and the inclusion of some of them in an article centered on a 17-21 April timeframe, we can surmise that they most likely were taken before Hoeppner's visit.

Our purposes aside, the ability to assign a date to these images has other significance for students of aircraft markings, and in particular those who have debated when *Jasta 11* personnel other than Manfred von Richthofen began painting their aircraft red. After the war, Lothar von Richthofen wrote that when the squadron adopted the red color scheme, Manfred's was the only all-red one. The rest of them employed some other identifying color in addition to the red: "Schaefer, for example, had his elevator, rudder, and some of the back part of the fuselage in black, Allmenröder the same in white, Wolff green, and I yellow." (Richthofen, *Ein Heldenleben*, p.205, trans. by this writer). Lothar must have witnessed these changes before Schäfer left on 26 April, yet *Jasta 11*'s lineup in MVR20 – probably taken sometime during 17-21 April – does not show them. Though it displays two red-bodied aircraft, both, at least originally, belonged to Manfred. The Albatros seen second in line in MVR20 and again in MVR5 was his principal mount in April 1917. The red-banded one, third in line in MVR20, used to be his but had become a spare that he sometimes allowed his brother to fly.[8] *Lt.* Carl Bauer wrote in his diary on 30 April 1917 that an *Idflieg* officer had informed him that morning that "…the English had put a price on Richthofen's head with the stipulation that the red machine is shot down. As a consequence Richthofen has now had all machines of his *Staffel* painted red." (Ferko, *Richthofen*, p.23) This was news to Bauer, who had flown in a joint mission with *Jasta 11* as recently as 19 April.[9] We also have the previously unpublished photograph of Schaefer posing in front of his Albatros D.III at *Jasta 28* that is presented in our discussion of S512. The Albatros appears to have a black tail, just as Lothar described, that is distinct from the presumably red fuselage.[10] The paint job on the fuselage and wheels looks almost pristine when compared to the weather-worn appearance of the upper wing's leading edge. We know that other *Pour le Mérite* pilots (e.g., Manfred von Richthofen, Heinrich Gontermann) were permitted to take their airplanes with them to their new commands. Perhaps when Schaefer left *Jasta 11* for *Jasta 28* on 27 April, he brought his recently-painted Albatros with him (as indicated in OTF 15:1, p.13). Taken

together, all the evidence points to *Jasta 11* adopting a predominantly red color scheme during the period 20-26 April 1917.

Notes

[1] It was printed in the book entitled *Fliegerbüchlein furs deutsche Volk*, presumably published in late 1917 because of its reference to Richthofen having shot down over 60 planes. In the article, Meyer refers to Schaefer's 19 victories (as of 14 April) and Lothar von Richthofen's 8 (as of 16 April). They both added one more to their totals on the evening of 21 April, so it would appear that Meyer was no longer there at that point.

[2] The 3 July 1936 edition of *Rheinische Landeszeitung* placed the following caption under MVR5's photo:

> "*Eine Aufnahme der Jagdstaffel 11, Führung Rittmeister Manfred Frhr. v. Richthofen nach dem 100. Staffelsieg Ende April 1917.*"

> "A picture of *Jagdstaffel 11*, led by Cavalry Capt. Manfred *Frhr.* von Richthofen, after the squadron's 100th victory, end of April 1917."

Rheinische Landeszeitung served the region around Wald. Nine days later it featured a large story on local hero Carl Allmenröder, written by a Wald-based reporter. The Allmenröder family contributed much of the information and photographs used in the story, and perhaps an identified copy of MVR5's image, which included their son, was among them.

[3] See C&C 10:2, p.148 (top left). The color segmentation and numbers match precisely both in style and proportion, but the leftmost portion of the panel in the museum scene containing the "A" and part of the "6" seems darker than in MVR21. The viewer needs to remember that the orthographic film of MVR21's day often transposed blue shades into light gray or white (e.g. the *Pour le Mérite*'s blue enamel often appears white in period photographs). This of course was not true for later film such as that used for the museum shot.

[4] MVR20 shows only one Albatros with overpainted national insignia in *Jasta 11*'s lineup, so this plane and the one in MVR5 are probably the same. The various tones of the overpainted cross' white border seem to match, but Brauneck's position in front of where the patched bullet hole may have been makes a certain identification impossible.

[5] Lothar von Richthofen was also photographed in his brother's old machine that had a red band painted around the fuselage between the cockpit and fuselage cross. (see Ferko, *Richthofen,* p.15). Evidently, the entire fuselage (at least) had been repainted at some date, resulting in another coat over the band. Because such repainting was usually applied in more of a wash than a thick coat, this made the band redder and therefore slightly darker in period film images. This plane, displaying the same darker band behind the cockpit, is the third one in MVR20's lineup.

[6] In S511, MVR4, and MVR5, Festner's tunic has buttons on the front and a collar that only displays an NCO's lace trim trim around its edges. In S510, his tunic buttons are covered and he has *Litzen* tabs above the NCO collar trim. In addition, his cloth leggings do not show the characteristic stain observed in S511 and MVR4-5.

[7] Richthofen's 45th victim (16 April) fell inside British lines, so no souvenirs including its serial number were available to him.

[8] Lothar himself wrote that the red-banded one was a hand-me-down (Richthofen, *Ein Heldenleben*, p.222); and MVR23 demonstrates that Lothar flew other *Jasta 11* planes as well.

[9] The mission was mentioned in Bauer's diary entry of 20 April (see Ferko, *Richthofen*, p.23).

[10] On 6 June 1917, Max Müller wrote his father: "For a long time, the Englishman had been planning to destroy the red aircraft. *Leutnant* Schäfer was mistaken here for Richthofen." (O'Connor, *Aviation Awards IV*, p.185) Unfortunately, we do not know how long "a long time" really was to Müller, but Schäfer had only been with *Jasta 28* for a little over a month before this letter was written.

GLOSSARY OF ABBREVIATIONS AND TERMS

Abbreviations

a. D.	ausser Dienst
AFA	Artillerie-Flieger-Abteilung
AFP	Armee-Flug-Park
AH	Austria-Hungary
AKN	Abwehr-Kommando-Nord
Anh	Anhalt
Bad	Baden
Bav	Bavaria
BH	buttonhole
Brun	Brunswick
Capt.	Captain
CO	commanding officer
Cpl.	Caporal
FA	Flieger-Abteilung
FEA	Flieger-Ersatz-Abteilung
FFA	Feldflieger-Abteilung
Feldflugchef	Chef des Feldflugwesens
Fus.	Fusilier
Fw.	Feldwebel
Fwlt.	Feldwebelleutnant
Gefr.	Gefreiter
Gen.	General
GenLt.	Generalleutnant
Ham	Hamburg
Hes	Hesse
Hptm.	Hauptmann
Ing.	Ingenieur
Jasta	Jagdstaffel
JG	Jagdgeschwader
Kagohl	Kampfgeschwader
Kasta	Kampfstaffel
KEK	Kampfeinsitzer-Kommando
Kest	Kampfeinsitzerstaffel
KG	Kampfgeschwader

Kofl.	Kommandeur der Flieger
Kptlt.	Kapitänleutnant
Lt.	Leutnant
Lt.	Lieutenant
Lt. z. See	Leutnant zur See
Lüb	Lübeck
Maj.	Major
MB	medals bar (Grossordenschnalle)
MdL.	Maréchal-des-Logis
Meck-Sch	Mecklenburg-Schwerin
NCO	non-commissioned officer
Oblt.	Oberleutnant
Oblt. z. See	Oberleutnant zur See
Oberstlt.	Oberstleutnant
Offz.-Stv.	Offizierstellvertreter
Old	Oldenburg
Ott	Ottoman Empire
Publ	published
RB	ribbon bar (Feldschnalle)
Rittm.	Rittmeister
Sax	Saxony
Sax-Weim	Saxe-Weimar
SCG	Saxe-Coburg and Gotha
Sch-L	Schaumburg-Lippe
SD	Saxon Duchies
Sgt.	Sergeant
Sous-Lt.	Sous-Lieutenant
Uffz.	Unteroffizier
UTD	University of Texas at Dallas, McDermott Library History of Aviation Collection
Vzfw.	Vizefeldwebel
Wald	Waldeck
WR	wearing
Würt	Württemberg
/ Sw	with Swords

Formations and Organizations (German)

Abteilung	Detachment or unit (often translated as "squadron")
Armee-Flug-Park (AFP)	Army aviation supply depot
Armee Oberkommando	Army High Command
Artillerie-Flieger-Abteilung (AFA)	Artillery cooperation aviation detachment or unit
Bombengeschwader (Bogohl)	Bombardment squadron
Chef des Feldflugwesens (Feldflugchef)	Chief of Field Aviation or his staff
Chevauleger	Bavarian light cavalry
Eisenbahn	railway (troops)
Feldflieger-Abteilung (FFA)	Field aviation detachment or unit
Flieger-Abteilung (FA)	Aviation detachment/unit
Flieger-Ersatz-Abteilung (FEA)	Aviation replacement detachment or unit
Fliegerschule	Aviation training school
Fliegertruppe	Army Aviation troop or Air Service
Fokkerstaffel	Unit (a section or flight) equipped with *Eindecker* aircraft
Geschwader	Squadron
Inspektion der Fliegertruppe (Idflieg)	Inspectorate of Army Aviation or Air Service
Jäger	Light infantry "sharpshooters"
Jagdgeschwader (JG)	Permanent grouping of four *Jagdstaffeln*
Jagdstaffel (Jasta)	Fighter unit (section or flight)
Jastaschule	Fighter pilot training school
Kampfeinsitzer-Kommando (KEK)	Single-seat fighter command or establishment
Kampfeinsitzerstaffel (Kest)	Single-seater home defense unit (section or flight)
Kampfgeschwader (Kagohl)(KG)	Fighting squadron
Kampfstaffel (Kasta)	Fighting unit (section or flight)
Kommandeur der Flieger (Kofl)	Officer or staff attached to Army headquarters responsible for the deployment of aviation units assigned to an Army
Kommandierenden General der Luftstreitkräfte (Kogenluft)	Commanding General of the Army Air Force or his staff
Kommando	Command or establishment
Luftstreitkräfte	Army Air Force
Marine Feldjasta	Naval land-based fighter unit (section or flight)
Schutzstaffel	Protection unit (section or flight)
Seeflugstation	Naval air station

Formations and Organizations (French)

Escadrille	Squadron

Ranks and Titles (German)

Feldflugchef	Chief of Field Aviation
Feldwebel (Fw.)	Sergeant
Feldwebelleutnant (Fwlt.)	Sergeant Lieutenant (equivalent to U.S. Warrant Officer)
Flugmeister	Petty Officer in the Naval Air Service
Flugobermaat	Chief Petty Officer in the Naval Air Service
Frau	Mrs.
Fregattenkapitän	Frigate Captain (equivalent to U.S. Navy full Commander)
Freifrau	Baroness
Freiherr	Baron
Gefreiter (Gefr.)	Private 1st Class
General (Gen.)	General
General der Flieger	Air Marshal (equivalent to U.S. Lieutenant General in the Air Force)
Generalfeldmarschal	General Field Marshal (equivalent to U.S. General of the Army
Generalleutnant (GenLt.)	Lieutenant General (equivalent to U.S. Major General)
Geschwaderführer	leader or commanding officer of a squadron
Geschwaderkommandeur	commander of a squadron
Graf	Count
Grossherzog	Grand Duke
Hauptmann (Hptm.)	Captain
Ingenieur	Engineer
Kaiser	Emperor
Kaiserin	Empress
Kapitänleutnant (Kptlt.)	Captain Lieutenant (equivalent to U.S Navy full Lieutenant)
Leutnant (Lt.)	Lieutenant (equivalent to U.S. 2nd Lieutenant)
Leutnant zur See (Lt.z.See)	Naval lieutenant (equivalent to U.S. Navy Ensign)
Major (Maj.)	Major

Oberflugmeister	Chief Petty Officer in the Naval Air Service
Oberleutnant (Oblt.)	Senior Lieutenant (equivalent to U.S. 1st Lieutenant)
Oberleutnant zur See (Oblt.z.See)	Naval Senior Lieutenant (equivalent to U.S. Navy Lieutenant Junior Grade)
Oberstleutnant (Oberstlt.)	Lieutenant Colonel
Offizier-Stellvertreter (Offz-Stv.)	Warrant Officer
Prinz	Prince
Prinzregent	Prince Regent
Ritter von	Knight (non-hereditary title bestowed upon recipient of Bavaria's Military Max Joseph Order)
Rittmeister (Rittm.)	Cavalry Captain
Staffelführer	Commanding Officer of a section or flight
Unteroffizier (Uffz.)	Corporal (also a generic term for all non-commissioned officers)
Vizefeldwebel (Vzfw.)	Vice Sergeant or Vice Sergeant Major

Ranks and Titles (French)

Caporal (Cpl.)	Corporal
Maréchal-des-Logis (MdL.)	Sergeant of Artillery or Cavalry
Sous-Lieutenant (Sous-Lt.)	2nd Lieutenant

Other German Terms

ausser Dienst	retired
Bluse	universal military tunic
Ehrenbecher	honor goblet, usually awarded to airmen after their first victory
Eindecker	monoplane
Einsitzer	single-seat aircraft
feldgrau	field-gray (as in a uniform)
Feldschnalle	bar with ribbons representing awards
Grossordenschnalle	bar with ribbons and full-size awards
Litewka	double-breasted, off-duty jacket
Litze	braid or embroidered cloth bar
Ordenskissen	orders cushion for displaying awards at a funeral
Schirmmütze	*visored cap*
Ulanka	tunic worn by Uhlan cavalry units

SELECT BIBLIOGRAPHY

Books

Bodenschatz, Karl. *Jagd in Flanderns Himmel*. Munich: Verlag Knorr & Hirth, 1935.

Bodenschatz, Karl. *Hunting with Richthofen,* trans. by Jan Hayzlett. London: Grub Street, 1996.

Buddecke, Hans-Joachim. *El Schahin (Der Jagdfalke)*. Berlin: Verlag August Scherl, 1918.

Connors, John F. *Albatros Fighters in Action*. Carrollton: Squadron/Signal Publications Inc., 1981.

Eberhardt, Walter von. *Unsere Luftstreitkräfte 1914-18*. Berlin: Verlag C.A. Weller, 1930.

Ferko, A.E. *Richthofen*. Berkhamsted: Albatros Publications, 1995.

Fischer, Suzanne Hayes. *Mother of Eagles, The War Diary of Baroness von Richthofen*. Atglen: Schiffer Military Press, 2001.

Franks, Norman, Frank Bailey, and Russell Guest. *Above the Lines*. London: Grub Street, 1993.

Franks, Norman, Frank Bailey, and Rick Duiven. *The Jasta Pilots*. London: Grub Street, 1996.

Franks, Norman, and Hal Giblin. *Under the Guns of the German Aces*. London: Grub Street, 1997.

Franks, Norman, Frank Bailey, and Rick Duivan. *The Jasta War Chronology*. London: Grub Street, 1998.

Franks, Norman, Frank Bailey, and Rick Duiven. *Casulaties of the German Air Service 1914-1920*. London: Grub Street, 1999.

Franks, Norman. *Sharks Among Minnows*. London: Grub Street, 2001.

Franks, Norman, and Greg VanWyngarden. *Fokker Dr I Aces of World War I*. Botley: Osprey Publishing, 2001.

Franks, Norman, and Greg VanWyngarden. *Fokker D VII Aces of World War I*. Botley: Osprey Publishing, 2003.

Franks, Norman. *Albatros Aces of World War 1*. Botley: Osprey Publishing, 2004.

Funk, Hauptmann a.D. *Unsere Luftwaffe*. Leipzig: Kunstverlag Bild und Karte, (late 1916).

Hamelman, William E. *The History of the Prussian Pour le Mérite Order, Volume III – 1888-1918*. Dallas: Matthäus Publishers, 1986.

Höfling, Rudolf. *Albatros D-II*. Atglen: Schiffer Publishing, 2002.

Hoeppner, Ernst von. *Germany's War in the Air*, trans. by J. Hawley Larned. Nashville: The Battery Press, 1994.

Immelmann, Franz. *Immelmann "Der Adler von Lille"*. Leipzig: Hafe & Koehler, 1942.

Immelmann, Franz. *Immelmann 'The Eagle of Lille'*, trans. by Claude W. Sykes. London: John Hamilton Ltd., unknown.

Imrie, Alex. *German Air Aces of World War One*. Poole : Arms and Armour Press, 1987.

Jones, H.A. *The War in the Air – Volume IV*. Oxford: Oxford Press, 1934.

Kähnert, M.E. *Jagdstaffel 356*, trans. by Claude W. Sykes. London: Greenhill Books, 1985.

Kilduff, Peter. *Richthofen: Beyond the Legend of the Red Baron*. New York: John Wiley & Sons, 1993.

Kilduff, Peter. *The Red Baron Combat Wing*. London: Arms & Armour Press, 1997.

Kilduff, Peter. *The Illustrated Red Baron*. London: Cassell Group, 1999.

Koerber, Adolf-Victor von. *Deutsche Heldenflieger*. Bielefeld and Leipzig: Verlag Velhagen & Klasing, 1917.

Langsdorf, Werner von. *Flieger am Feind*. Gütersloh: Verlag C. Bertelsmann, 1934.

Leaman, Paul. *Fokker Aircraft of World War One*. Marlborough: The Crowood Press Ltd., 2001.

Musciano, Walter. *Lt. Werner Voss, Germany's Greatest Teenage Ace*. New York: Hobby Helpers Publications, 1962.

Neumann, Georg P. *In der Luft unbesiegt*. Munich: J.F. Lehmanns Verlag, 1923.

Nowarra, Heinz J. *The Jew with the Blue Max*. Sun Valley: John W. Caler, 1967.

O'Connor, Neal W. *Aviation Awards of Imperial Germany in World War I and the Men Who Earned Them*. Volumes I-VI. Princeton: Foundation for Aviation World War I, 1988-99.

O'Connor, Neal W. *Aviation Awards of Imperial Germany in World War I and the Men Who Earned Them*. Volume VII. Atglen: Schiffer Publishing, 2002.

Pietsch, Thorsten. *"Mein lieber Hans..." Feldbriefe eine Mutter 1914-1917*. Dresden: Sächsisches Digitaldruckzentrum, 2004.

Richthofen, Manfred von. *Ein Heldenleben*. Berlin: Verlag Ullstein, 1920.

Richthofen, Manfred von. *Der rote Kampfflieger*. Berlin: Verlag Ullstein, 1933.

Richthofen, Manfred von. *The Red Baron*. Trans. by Peter Kilduff. New York: Barnes & Noble, 1996.

Rimell, R.L., ed. *Albatros Fighters*. 3rd ed. Berkhamsted: Albatros Publications, 1998.

Schäfer, Leutnant [Karl-Emil]. *Vom Jäger zum Flieger, Tagebuchblätter und Briefe von Leutnant Schäfer*. Berlin: Verlag August Scherl, 1918.

Schnitzler, Emil. *Carl Allmenröder, der bergische Kampfflieger.* Wald: Bergische Verlags-Aktiengesellschaft, 1927.

Schröder, Hans. *An Airman Remembers*, trans. by Claud W. Sykes. London: John Hamilton Ltd., year unknown.

Schwenn, Dr. Gustav. *Fliegerbüchlein fürs deutsche Volk.* Chemnitz: Verlag Walther Berlinicke, 1918.

Swope, Herbert Bayard. *Inside the German Empire.* New York: The Century Co., 1917.

Swope, Herbert Bayard. "Boelke, Air Hero of Kaiser, Makes Light of Deeds" in *The New York World*, 14 September 1916.

Thies, Andreas. *Katalog: Auktion Nachlass Oswald Boelcke.* Nürtingen, 2001.

Thies, Andreas. *Katalog: Historische Sammlungsgegenstände des 20. Jahrhunderts.* Nürtingen, 2002.

Treadwell, Terry, and Alan Wood. *Richthofen's Flying Circus.* Stroud: Tempus Publishing, 1999.

Tutschek, Adolf Ritter von. *In Trichtern und Wolken*, ed. by Thor Goote. Berlin: Georg Westermann, 1934.

Udet, Ernst. *Ace of the Iron Cross,* ed. by Stanley M. Ulanoff, trans. by Richard K. Riehn. New York: Doubleday & Co., 1970.

VanWyngarden, Greg. *'Richthofen's Circus.'* Botley: Osprey Publishing, 2004.

VanWyngarden, Greg. *Jagdgeschwader Nr. II.* Botley: Osprey Publishing: 2005.

Vigilant (a.k.a. Claud W. Sykes). *Richthofen, The Red Knight of the Air.* London: John Hamilton Ltd., 1967.

Wentscher, Bruno. *Deutsche Luftfahrt.* Berlin: Verlag Deutscher Wille, 1925.

Werner, Prof. Dr. Johannes. *Briefe eines deutschen Kampffliegers an ein junges Mädchen.* Leipzig: Verlag von K.F. Koehler, 1930.

Werner, Prof. Dr. Johannes. *Boelcke: der Mensch, der Flieger, der Führer der deutschen Jagdfliegerei.* Leipzig: Hase & Koehler, 1932.

Werner, Prof. Johannes. *Knight of Germany: Oswald Boelcke German Ace*, trans. by Claud W. Sykes. Rev. ed. Novato: Presidio Press, 1991.

Zuerl, Walter. *Pour le mérite-Flieger.* Munich: Curt Pechstein Verlag, 1938.

Newspapers

Berliner Illustrirte Zeitung. Berlin: Verlag Ullstein & Co., 1914-18.

Das Illustrierte Blatt . Frankfurt: Verlag der Frankfurter Societäts-Druckerei, 9 July 16.

Die Braunschweiger im Weltkriege. Brunswick: E. Appelhans & Co., "Ein braunschweigischer Ritter des Ordens Pour le merite," No.13, pp.482-84 (no date).

Der Feldzug 1914/17. Berlin-Schöneberg: Baltic-Separator, 1 July 1917.

Die Woche. Berlin: Verlag August Scherl, 1916-18 (intermittent issues)

Die Wochenschau. Essen: Verlag W. Girardet, 1915-18 (intermittent issues)

Illustrierte Geschichte des Weltkrieges. Stuttgart: Union Deutsche Verlagsgesellschaft, 1914-18.

Illustrierte Kriegs-Zeitung (Das Weltbild). Berlin: Verlag Vass & Garleb, 1914-17.

[Note: the issues available to this writer did not display the day and month of publication. They did list the year, however, and based on the number of issues per year, an approximate date could be extrapolated for each issue. Accordingly, the dates are preceded by "c." when referenced herein, but should be accurate within a few days.]

Illustrirte Zeitung. Leipzig: Verlag J.J. Weber, 1916.

The New York World. New York: The Press Publishing Co., "Boelke, Air Hero of Kaiser, Makes Light of Deeds," by Herbert Bayard Swope, 14 September 1916.

Periodicals

Cross & Cockade Journal (U.S.). Volumes 1-26.
Articles specifically cited:
Vol: No

6:4 Puglisi, William. "Jacobs of Jasta 7," pp.307-34.

10:2 Wynne, Hugh. "Von Richthofen: A Photo Album Essay," pp.98-152.

12:2 Flanagan, Brian. "The Holtzem Story," pp.169-86.

18:3 Ferko, A.E. "MvR and Voss (A Photo Essay)," pp.208-10.

23:4 Schmäling, Bruno. "Ltn. Paul Bäumer and his Fokker Dr.I 204/17," pp.318-34.

Stacey, Michael. "Postcard Heroes and Paperback Warriors," pp.371-78.

24:2 Schmeelke, Michael. "Leutnant der Reserve Otto Brauneck," pp.152-65.

25:4 Gill, Robert. "The Albums of Willy Rosenstein. Aviation Pioneer – Jasta Ace," pp. 289-331.

26:2 Sands, Jeffrey. "The Forgotten Ace. Ltn. Kurt Wintgens and His War Letters," pp.83-105.

Over The Front. Volumes 1-20.
Articles specifically cited:
Vol: No

1:3 Schmeelke, Michael. "Leutnant der Reserve Otto Brauneck, Part II," pp.195-200.

2:4 Kilduff, Peter (trans.). "Reminiscences of a Schlachtflieger: Eduard Wolfgang Zorer," pp.291-97.

3:4 Wills, Kelly Jr. (trans.). "The War Letters of Hauptmann Adolf Ritter von Tutschek," pp.291-311.

5:1 Vant, Douglas. "Many Battles and Many a Bold Venture, Letters of Oberleutnant Erwin Böhme," pp.35-52.

9:4 Lawson, Stephen, "'Kobes' in Fokkerstaffel-West," pp.292-334.

10:3 Olynyk, Frank. "The Combat Records of Hermann Göring," pp.195-235.

11:1 Vant, Douglas and Dr.Ing. Niedermeyer. "The End of An Action-Filled Life: Leutnant Erwin Böhme's Final Letters," pp.3-23.

11:3 Ladek, Jürgen. "From Uhlan to Fighter Ace, From the Memorabilia of Major a. D. Joseph Mai," pp.231-48.

12:3 Hayzlett, Jan (trans.). "Karl Allmenröder Remembered," pp.196-212.

14:2 Hayzlett, Jan (trans.) and Peter Kilduff (ed.). "Nachrichtenblatt der Luftstreitkräfte," pp.168-79.

14:3 Hayzlett, Jan (trans.) and Peter Kilduff (ed.). "Nachrichtenblatt der Luftstreitkräfte," pp.265-78.

15:1 Kilduff, Peter. "Flying Swabians – The History of Royal Württemberg Jagdstaffel 28," pp.10-49.

Hayzlett, Jan (trans.) and Peter Kilduff (ed.). "Nachrichtenblatt der Luftstreitkräfte," pp.63-83.

16:1 Hayzlett, Jan (trans.). "Nachrichtenblatt der Luftstreitkräfte No.13," pp.82-86.

16:2 Hayzlett, Jan (trans.). "Nachrichtenblatt der Luftstreitkräfte No.14," pp.178-82.

16:3 Hayzlett, Jan (trans.). "Nachrichtenblatt der Luftstreitkräfte No.15," pp.270-77.

17:2 Niedermeyer, Dr.Ing. "A Retrospective View of Ltn. Erwin Böhme," pp.137-60.

17:3 Täger, Hans. "A Man for 'Sonderfilme': Rudolf Windisch," pp.196-232.

Bronnenkant, Lance. "A Snapshot of Boelcke," pp.261-73

INDEX

Aviation Units

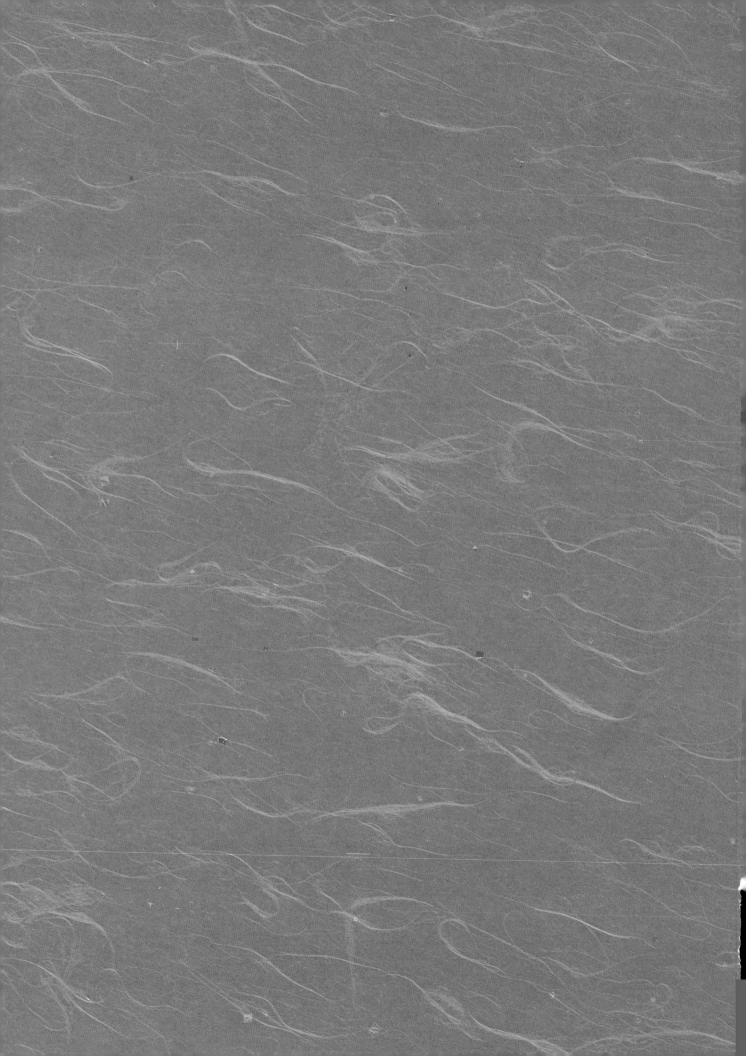